Ronald Dworkin
and
Contemporary Jurisprudence

PHILOSOPHY AND SOCIETY
General Editor: Marshall Cohen

ALSO IN THIS SERIES

RIGHTS
Theodore M. Benditt

ETHICS IN THE WORLD OF BUSINESS
David Braybrooke

MARX AND JUSTICE: The Radical Critique of Liberalism
Allen E. Buchanan

LUKÁCS, MARX AND THE SOURCES OF CRITICAL THEORY
Andrew Feenberg

THE REVERSE DISCRIMINATION CONTROVERSY: A Moral and Legal Analysis
Robert K. Fullinwider

THE MORAL FOUNDATIONS OF PROFESSIONAL ETHICS
Alan H. Goldman

FEMINIST POLITICS AND HUMAN NATURE
Alison M. Jaggar

A PHILOSOPHY OF FREE EXPRESSION: And Its Constitutional Applications
Robert F. Ladenson

ECOLOGICAL ETHICS AND POLITICS
H. J. McCloskey

THE LIBERTARIAN READER
Tibor R. Machan (ed.)

MORAL PROBLEMS IN NURSING: A Philosophical Investigation
James L. Muyskens

READING NOZICK
Jeffrey Paul (ed.)

AND JUSTICE FOR ALL: New Introductory Essays in Ethics and Public Policy
Tom Regan and Donald VanDeVeer (eds.)

SEX, DRUGS, DEATH, AND THE LAW: An Essay on Human Rights and Overcriminalization
David A. J. Richards

KANT'S POLITICAL PHILOSOPHY
Patrick Riley

EVOLUTIONARY EXPLANATION IN THE SOCIAL SCIENCES: An Emerging Paradigm
Philippe Van Parijs

WELFARE RIGHTS
Carl Wellman

Ronald Dworkin and Contemporary Jurisprudence

Edited and with a Preface by

MARSHALL COHEN

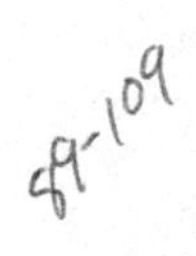

ROWMAN & ALLANHELD
Totowa, New Jersey

ROWMAN & ALLANHELD

Published in the United States of America in 1984
by Rowman & Allanheld
(A division of Littlefield, Adams & Company)
81 Adams Drive, Totowa, New Jersey 07512)

Library of Congress Cataloging in Publication Data
Main entry under title:

Ronald Dworkin and contemporary jurisprudence.

"Selected bibliography on Ronald Dworkin": p.
1. Law—Philosophy—Addresses, essays, lectures.
2. Jurisprudence—Addresses, essays, lectures.
3. Dworkin, R. M.—Addresses, essays, lectures.
4. Dworkin, R. M.—Bibliography. I. Cohen, Marshall.
K246.R66 1983 340'.1 83-11091
ISBN 0-8476-7124-0

83 84 85/ 10 9 8 7 6 5 4 3 2 1

Printed in the United States of America

For Betsy

Contents

Preface

In the opinion of the editor the jurisprudential writings of Ronald Dworkin constitute the finest contribution yet made by an American writer to the philosophy of law. In recent years Dworkin has expanded the range of his interests and he is now, in addition, one of the leading writers on moral and political philosophy as well. His contributions to the development of a liberal political theory are outstanding. These considerations alone would more than justify devoting a volume to a careful examination of his views and a reply to his critics. There is, however, a further justification for the present volume. Dworkin's views are highly controversial and they have elicited a response from writers on legal, moral, and political theory that is outstanding in its seriousness and in its exploratory nature. In addition to its value in locating and exploring Dworkin's own views, the literature on Dworkin can provide an unusually useful access to the interests and methods of many of the ablest writers on the topics Dworkin has investigated. This volume will, therefore, provide the reader with a penetrating introduction not only to the thought of Ronald Dworkin, but to contemporary jurisprudence in general.

Dworkin has cast much of his legal writing in the form of an attack on legal positivism, in particular on the form of legal positivism expounded in H. L. A. Hart's classic work, *The Concept of Law*. A key feature of traditional positivism is its insistence on a conceptual separation of law and morals. The classic forms of positivism suppose that there is a master test, which Hart calls a rule of recognition, that will identify those standards which are rules of the legal system. This ultimate rule is itself simply a social convention and its identification requires no appeal to moral or political rules or principles. Dworkin has argued aginst the existence of a rule of recognition and against the alleged separation of law and morals, and the essays in Part One of this collection, "Law and Morals," discuss these and related issues. E. Philip Soper appears to concede that Dworkin has moved us some distance from the view that there is a "master test" capable of actually identifying with some precision all of the standards relevant to legal decision. But he thinks the core of positivism is, in Hart's words, "the simple contention that there is in no sense a necessary truth that law reproduce or satisfy certain demands of morality." In Soper's view (and in Hart's) the master test might in fact incorporate moral criteria. But even if these criteria are too indeterminate to constitute a proof procedure, or are incapable of providing a test for the truth or falsity of the moral standards in question, Soper believes that this does not affect the central positivist contention that legal and moral standards are conceptually distinct.

Jules L. Coleman takes a view not unlike Soper's. For Coleman the authority of law depends on a fundamental convention of some sort, even if it is controversial what the rule requires in particular cases. To this Dworkin replies that if the rule is made abstract enough for Coleman's claim to be true, the positivist claim that a rule of recognition exists will be trivial. If the rule is made concrete enough for the thesis to be significant, the claim that there is always such a rule will be false. Against Dworkin's view that any theory of law, including positivism, is based in the end on some controversial normative theory David Lyons argues that for some positivists, at least, law is always simply "given," a matter of social fact. Against this Dworkin insists that law is a contested concept and that we must look for the deep sources of important theories of law in some assumptions of political morality—e.g, about how judges should in general or in principle decide cases, or about what social functions we should call upon our legal institutions to perform.

It is precisely these issues, which concern "The Judicial Decision," that are the subject of Part Two. On the positivist view, as Dworkin understands it, legal rules, identified by the master rule of recognition, dictate judicial decisions. In hard cases, however, no legal rule decides the case before him and in these circumstances the judge must appeal to extra-legal principles, perhaps to his own moral principles or to his conception of the best public policy. In hard cases, there is no right answer to the legal issue posed and neither the plaintiff nor the defendant has a right to win. Dworkin has challenged each of these positivist positions. He has argued that the law includes not only rules but principles, which dictate legal decisions just as rules do. There is "no right answer" in a hard case only if the arguments on both sides are equally good, and this will rarely be so. Lawyers and judges will disagree about which side has the better case, all things considered, but they will disagree about which answer is right rather than agreeing that none is. Judges may have to provide elaborate justifications of legal decisions, justifications that may appeal to legal and moral principles and, indeed, to the political morality that provides the most persuasive justification of the entire political system. Positivism, however, continues to have its defenders. Joseph Raz, for instance, denies that all the reasons for a judge's decision are necessarily legal reasons and he regards Dworkin's apparent victories over positivism as mainly verbal. Most contemporary defenders of positivism (like Soper) argue against Dworkin that a sophisticated version of the positivist's master rule can capture the legal principles Dworkin thinks elude it. But Raz allows that judges may appeal to nonlegal principles and therefore must exercize strong discretion. In his view Dworkin's rights thesis is simply a trivial consequence of his expansive redefinition of the idea of a legal reason and not, as Dworkin thinks, a substantive truth about the moral entitlements of litigants. Dworkin answers that the important question is not the verbal question of how lawyers use the word "legal," but the political question of what kinds of reasons provide good justifications for judicial decisions.

In order to honor the rights of litigants, judges must, in Dworkin's view, appeal to considerations of principle (here understood to mean considerations specifying their rights) and not to considerations of policy or appeals to the general welfare. To Kent Greenawalt's contention that Dworkin gives no persuasive arguments for judicial abstinence from policy considerations, Dworkin argues that he and other critics on this point fail to distinguish between policy arguments and arguments that appeal to consequences. To Donald H. Regan's contention that in an ordinary civil suit no one can have what Dworkin calls a "trump" right (but only a right in the sense of an individual claim), Dworkin replies that it is essential to distinguish between legislative rights, which are rights to or against certain legislation, and legal rights, which are rights to win in court. Both kinds of institutional rights are rights in the strong sense, but they hold against different institutions and, for that reason, have different content. It may be that, as Regan thinks, no one has a legislative right to a statute either denying or imposing civil liability for certain kinds of damage, but in the absense of such a statute someone may or may not have a legal right to compensation for such damage.

John Mackie objects to the determinacy Dworkin finds in the law and thinks the practical effect of Dworkin's views is to unsettle fixed points of law and to enlarge the scope of judicial legislation on the basis of necessarily subjective moral and political views. Dworkin responds that like the positivists, he only recommends that judges make controversial political decisions in hard cases. Of course, Dworkin contends that even in such cases judges are typically doing their best to find actual rights of the parties and are not disguising anything that positivists are frankly conceding. To the contrary, Dworkin's ideal judge Hercules makes plain, in his opinions, the influence of political morality on his decisions. Positivists who appeal to legislative intention or counterfactual judgments about what a legislature would have done if it had considered the situation in question often hide the influence of their convictions behind "a screen of decorated nonsense."

In Part Three, "The Objectivity of Law," A. D. Woozley claims to detect in Dworkin's confidence that for all practical purposes there will always be a right answer in the seamless web of our law the ghost of a natural law theory, which he thinks Dworkin tries to materialize into a logical theory of truth. Dworkin replies that Woozley operates with an inappropriate, transcendental concept of truth rather than with our actual concept of truth. This concept, like our others, takes its meaning from its complex functioning in our actual institutions and practices. Neil MacCormick argues that in adopting the "constructive" model of moral reasoning against the "natural" one, Dworkin has in effect capitulated to a skepticism about the objectivity of morality that he inconsistently refuses to concede. Dworkin replies that the constructive model does not have the relativistic implications MacCormick reads into it and rejects MacCormick's independent arguments for moral and legal skepticism about the possibility of developing a best moral or legal justification for the legal record.

Part Four is devoted to "Law and Politics." In Dworkin's view the right to equal concern and respect is the fundamental principle of our political morality and our constitutional law. As Dworkin sees it no utilitarian view can provide an adequate foundation for a theory that takes rights sufficiently seriously, and only a restricted utilitarianism that refuses to count external, as opposed to personal, preferences can hope to realize equalitarianism, which is one of the main sources of utilitarianism's appeal. Where no rights are violated, however, as in the case of affirmative action, Dworkin often endorses arguments of a utilitarian or majoritarian character. To Rolf Sartorius's argument that Dworkin comes too close to adopting a form of utilitarianism that does not take rights as seriously as they should be, Dworkin responds that he is far from thinking that even a restricted utilitarianism is the best general theory. When Sartorius argues that external preferences are sometimes legitimate and important, Dworkin responds that the political decisions they recommend must be supported by the reasons these legitimate preferences assume, not by the existence of the preferences themselves.

H. L. A. Hart, who also thinks that Dworkin works too much in the shadow of the very utilitarianism he professes to deplore, and who rejects Dworkin's view that counting external preferences is a form of double counting, is mainly concerned to deny that if someone's liberty is restricted this must be interpreted as showing that he is not being treated as an equal. Dworkin points out that his arguments do not assume that this is inevitably or even usually so, but only when the constraint is justified in some way that depends on the fact that others condemn a person's convictions and values. Michael Sandel distinguishes between a cooperative, and a constitutive, version of liberalism. He thinks that Dworkin's cooperative version cannot provide an adequate moral basis for liberalism's philosophy of sharing, of regarding each person as a rightful participant in the combined assets and endowments of his fellow citizens. Sandel thinks this is particularly clear in Dworkin's defense of affirmative action policies. Dworkin thinks Sandel is wrong to bring the question of who "owns" an individual's talents into the discussion at all. The important principle, that people are not entitled to any particular job or income just because of their abilities, does not depend on any answer to this question or on any philosophical picture of the "self" as either including or excluding these abilities. It depends on questions of political morality that do not intersect with these metaphysical issues.

Richard Posner is one of the leading figures in the movement to apply economic analysis to legal questions. These analyses are often founded on the utilitarian premises Dworkin rejects. Posner takes wealth maximization as a "proxy" (in Dworkin's view a very inadequate proxy) for utility maximization and argues that judges should decide civil cases, wherever possible, so as to maximize the aggregate wealth of society. Dworkin argues that no adequate foundation for this view can be found either in the idea that wealth is valuable in itself or even in the more plausible idea that it is valuable instrumentally. He suggests a very different account of why it often seems that judges should reach the decisions that the wealth maximization test would predict, which is that sound and familiar moral principles recommend these decisions in some, though not in all, cases. Utilitarianism and its proxies cannot provide an adequate political morality, and Dworkin's critique of its many manifestations is one of the most significant aspects of his account of the moral basis of law and politics.

PART ONE
Law and Morals

1

Legal Theory and the Obligation of a Judge: The Hart/Dworkin Dispute

E. Philip Soper

THE OBLIGATION OF A JUDGE

Confronted with standards beyond those obvious in purpose and rule, the positivist, says Dworkin, has two choices. He must either claim that such standards are only discretionary and hence not legally binding, or he may concede their binding status and argue that he identifies them as legal standards through reference, in some more complex way, to his theoretical master test.[1]

There is, however, a third possibility. The positivist might admit that some standards bind judges but explain that they play a role in the legal system sufficiently different from that of ordinary rules and principles to justify excluding them from the class of standards encompassed by the concept of "law." This position makes irrelevant the question whether such standards could be captured in advance by a master test: Even if "capture-proof," they would constitute no defect in a theoretical model designed to capture only legal standards. Dworkin insists that arguments of this sort can only beg the question in the present context because they assume the very distinction between legal and other kinds of standards that the positivist's rule of recognition is designed to establish.[2]

The aim of the present section is twofold: first, to develop the suggested distinction between two kinds of standards that bind judges, and, second, to consider whether all standards that bind judges must necessarily be deemed "legal" standards. In one sense, Dworkin is correct that the controversy at this point threatens to become merely verbal. But there is another, more important sense in which the difference between these kinds of standards appears sufficiently basic to justify (as more illuminating) a model of law that preserves, rather than dissolves, the distinction.

A. The Standards That Bind

At least some of Dworkin's principles exhibit one feature in particular that might seem to distinguish them from other legal standards. Principles appear to function in the first instance as guides to the judge in deciding what rules require and only secondarily as guides to a citizen's conduct. They seem to guide conduct, if at all, not by directly declaring what is and is not permitted, but only in the indirect sense of informing an individual that certain principles and policies will be considered by courts in determining what a rule requires.[3] This decision-guiding, rather than conduct-guiding, feature is most obvious in the case of principles of statutory construction. It also appears to be true, though perhaps less clearly, of such judicial maxims and principles as "no man shall profit from his own wrong." If principles are controversial, and if equally applicable principles may conflict with one another within the context of the same decision, it is somewhat strained to suggest that principles guide primary conduct in the same way that rules do.[4]

By itself, however, this decision-guiding characteristic will not justify a refusal to call all such standards "law." We have agreed, after all, that "purposes" must and can be admitted by the positivist to be among a system's legal standards, even though such purposes may also perform a similar decision-guiding function. If a statute prohibiting vehicles in the park is known to be aimed exclusively at promoting an energy conservation ethic, rather than at the preservation of peace and quiet, and if that difference in purpose leads to differences in interpretation and application, then the purpose guides conduct as well as decision for the same basic reason: It supplements the meaning of the term "vehicle" in borderline cases to indicate to judge and citizen alike just what it is that has been proscribed.

The decision-guiding function does suggest, however, a possible further refinement in the classification of standards that bind judges—one that the following rough analogy will serve to introduce. Scientists and philosophers of science devote considerable effort to the attempt to isolate acceptable "principles of induction" to serve as guides or tests for determining when one may properly claim to have discovered a "law" of science.[5] In this context it has become commonplace to distinguish the principles governing the accepted methodology from the substantive results of applying the method—that is, from the scientific "laws" that govern particular events. Would both the accepted methodological principles and the substantive rules in this case count as scientific "laws"? In one sense perhaps they would. Accepted principles of induction might be viewed as themselves stating true laws about, for example, the nature of knowledge and how it is acquired. The scientific community would expect its members to heed these principles as well as already established scientific laws in deciding whether a given hypothesis was, in fact, a "law." But more important than the fact that both types of standards are in this sense "binding" is the fact that the methodological and substantive standards apply to areas of human inquiry that in important respects are worth distinguishing.

In similar fashion, some standards in the legal context may be viewed as analogous to rules for proper scientific induction because they arise out of the investigation of a subject matter that is, in important ways, distinct from that with which typical legal standards are concerned. The subject matter of the former is not the regulation of human behavior in a particular society through the prescription of norms, but the regulation of any rational attempt to apply standards or to interpret human communications. If principles can be ascribed some such translegal status—in the sense that they are not peculiarly legal—then the claim that they are binding may be accepted, not because they are "law," but because they constitute minimally essential criteria for the proper conduct of certain types of rational activity. Such principles become clues, not to what "the law" requires, but to what the concept of "rationality" or "judging" requires. To the extent that legal systems require officials to be "judges," one discovers what that role entails, not only by inspecting particular provisions of the legal system (polling the system's officials to determine what they contingently happen to accept), but also by paying attention simply to what it means to apply standards rationally in a sense that transcends the particular context in which the role is assumed.

Which standards are candidates for such translegal status and what characteristics identify them? Our description of them as standards implicit in the concept of "judging" provides a starting point for answering the second half of the question: Standards binding on a judge are to be distinguished from legal standards if they are immune from deliberate change in the sense that an instruction to an official to ignore them makes the official no longer a "judge." While the task of defining the concept of judging may not be easier than the task of defining the concept of law, my only purpose at present is to suggest that some standards fall into this category, whether or not we can identify them all. They would include those principles referring to "characteristic judicial virtues" that Hart identifies as "impartiality and neutrality in surveying the alternatives, consideration for the interest of all who will be affected, and a concern that some acceptable general principle be deployed as a reasoned basis for decision."[6] They would also include, perhaps as a particular illustration of the last-named virtue, the principle of noncontradiction, reflected in the requirement that "like cases be treated alike." Dworkin insists that judges are subject to a strong requirement of "articulate consistency."[7] The source of the obligation even for Dworkin is not apparently the law, but a "doctrine of political responsibility."[8] It is not clear, however, that Dworkin means to suggest that the obligation is only "political," and thus subject to cultural variation or normative dispute, rather than, as the writings of Professor Lon Fuller suggest, an essential aspect of the concept of adjudication itself.[9] If to instruct judges to decide cases by flipping coins is to make them no longer judges, but agents of a legislative determination that any decision, right or wrong, is better than none,[10] it is hard to see that one does less violence to the concept of adjudication by instructing judges to ignore the demand for articulate consistency.

The process of distinguishing these standards (let us call them judicial technique principles) from other legal standards may be illustrated by considering one particular group of such standards: the maxims of statutory construction. Despite the tendency to debunk canons of construction as effectively cancelling each other, one may agree with H. M. Hart and Sacks that they at least perform the "useful function" of indicating "linguistically permissible" meanings, with final selection left to context.[11] In this respect, such maxims perform nicely the role Dworkin assigns to principles: They point, however weakly, in one direction while still leaving final results to await a complete stocktaking of all such pointers. Dworkin, in any event, appears explicitly to include such "techniques of statutory construction" among his putatively trouble-causing principles.[12] It is not necessary to canvass in depth elaborate textbook listings and discussions of these maxims in order to make the point that the source of many of them lies in "logic and common sense"[13] rather than in the contingently accepted norms of a particular society. This is particularly evident in the cases of the three most commonly cited canons: *noscitur a sociis, ejusdam generis,* and *expressio unius est exclusio alterius.*[14] The fact that standard treatises, themselves venerable, reach this conclusion about the common-sense origin of hoary Latin maxims[15] is a testament not so much to the early emergency of such principles in Anglo-American law, as to their fundamental link to the prerequisites of rational interpretation in any context and in any society. As such they are easily viewed, not as peculiarly legal principles, but as principles belonging to a "science of hermeneutics" that prescribes a methodology for interpretation in general, whether the subject be suicide notes, Dead Sea scrolls, wills, or statutes:

> [W]e shall find that the same rules which common sense teaches every one to use, in order to understand his neighbor in the most trivial intercourse, are necessary likewise, although not sufficient, for the interpretation of documents and texts of the highest importance, constitutions as well as treaties between the greatest nations.[16]

Not all such maxims, however, will appear to exhibit the suggested identifying feature of immunity from deliberate change. Maxims directing strict construction of criminal statutes or of statutes in derogation of the common law, for example, appear context-specific to particular legal systems in ways apparently open to cultural variation. To explain why some of these precepts might nevertheless be viewed as standards arising out of the role of judge *qua* judge rather than out of the peculiarly legal standards of the system in which one occupies that role requires a further distinction between the concrete shape a principle has assumed in a particular legal society and the abstract "principle of interpretation" it represents. The abstract principle that the common-law derogation maxim represents may be phrased in some such manner as the following: "Assume settled practices and expectations have not been radically and deliberately altered, unless . . . (the context, language, other principles so indicate)." The concrete form of the abstract principle is context-specific to a common-law jurisdiction, but the abstract principle is not. It is a common-sense guide to rational interpretation that would normally be accepted in any context. Its justification lies in assumptions about human behavior that are grounded in reason and experience and that transcend particular community norms. One who intends sharply to change known, accepted patterns of behavior will normally take care to make his instructions precise; where instructions are imprecise, he probably did not intend the radical interpretation.

Having made this distinction, one may still be unpersuaded that deliberate countermand of the common-law derogation maxim, however clear its origin in common sense, would essentially undermine the concept of judging in those cases where the maxim would otherwise apply. No less eminent an authority than Holmes, for example, urged that the maxim be eliminated from American jurisprudence,[17] and numerous state legislatures have in fact enacted statutes specifically purporting to abrogate it.[18] For the most part, however, these attacks appear to have been leveled at misuse of the canon—at judicial decisions that found the canon to be more than simply the abstract principle of interpretation described above. Such decisions implicitly viewed the canon as reflecting a substantive principle of power allocation between legislature and judiciary that gave the latter institution control over development of the common law in the face of superior, countervailing indicia of intended legislative change. But if one restricts the role of the maxim to the minimum function described by the abstract principle of interpretation, it then becomes difficult to reconcile legislative abrogation with a continued expectation that the court perform an exclusively judicial role in cases where the maxim would otherwise apply. One might even have difficulty knowing how to comply with an instruction that no presumption, however weak, should henceforth be made in favor of interpretations that more nearly accord with prior, accepted practice.[19] If the instruction is viewed as tantamount to a direction not to use common sense in interpreting communications—"do not assume the legislator in communicating directives acts as experience indicates most rational people do"—it becomes doubtful whether the "interpreting" official remains a "judge" any more than he would when acting on an instruction to resolve doubtful cases by flipping a coin.[20]

Contrast the second maxim mentioned above—that "criminal statutes should be strictly construed." Here it is difficult to see how our suggested identifying feature—immunity from deliberate change—would justify assigning the maxim binding but translegal status. If the abstract principle represented is thought to reflect solely a policy of providing fair notice concerning acts that will result in criminal sanctions, then it can be discovered only by inspecting community or legal norms concerning fairness, not judicial norms concerning techniques of rule interpretation and application. If a particular community decided no longer to value fair warning in issuing and enforcing criminal statutes, the maxim could be intelligibly and deliberately countermanded. One could establish a translegal status for such a maxim only to the extent one views it as reflecting an abstract principle of interpretation rather than substantive community goals—for example, "communicators who intend serious consequences to attach to actions will avoid ambiguity; where they did not avoid, they probably did not intend."

B. *Whether All That Binds Is Law*

Does a refusal to include among a society's "legal standards" those principles that are immune from deliberate change in the sense described amount simply to a verbal dispute, a definition of law "by fiat"?[21] Dworkin rejects out-of-hand any attempt to explain the obligation to take principles into account

> as a matter of judicial "craft," or something of that sort. The question will still remain why this type of obligation (whatever we call it) is different from the obligation that rules impose upon judges, and why it entitles us to say that principles and policies are not part of the law but are merely extra-legal standards "courts characteristically use."[22]

The above discussion essays an answer to this question based on differences in the source and character of judicial technique principles corresponding to the difference between standards that bind a judge *qua* judge and those that bind *qua* judge of a particular legal system.[23]

In one sense, of course, Dworkin is correct. Because the role of judge is itself assigned by the law, principles implicit in the concept of judging become incorporated in the legal system by reference. Furthermore, if judicial technique principles are too numerous to list and too unrelated to be generated from a formula, as we have assumed for purposes of argument,[24] then it must be false to claim that "some *social* rule or set of social rules exists within the community of [a nation's] judges and legal officials, which rules settle the limits of the judge's duty to recognize any other rules or principle as law."[25]

If all of this is conceded, in what sense could one continue to defend a model of law that ignored judicial technique principles in the account it gave of legal validity? The answer lies in part in the characteristics implied by the shared identifying feature of immunity from deliberate change. It is the peculiar characteristic of principles identified by this feature that they can be constructed in advance by an external observer, bent on determining "the laws" of a particular legal system, without regard for empirical questions concerning the existence or content of any legal standard in the society, including the rule of recognition. It is this claimed universality and independence of judicial technique principles that justifies excluding such standards in a model designed primarily to isolate a society's particular legal norms. Exclusion is justified for much the same reasons that one would not include the rules of grammar or language of the society in a model of "law," even though these too would be "binding" on a judge responsive to his obligation to understand and apply the signs used to convey legal standards.

Another way of making the point is to note that we are doing no more than separating a judge's obligation "to apply the law" into its constituent parts: the obligation (1) "to apply" (2) "the law." The second half is what the positivist's model is designed to reflect. The first half—the realm of standards that determine acceptable methods of interpreting and applying other standards and of deciding particular cases under such standards—is not the peculiar concern of the legal theorist. It is the concern as well of the theorist in any discipline, from philosophy to science, who must deal with the perplexing problems involved in the characterization and classification of fact situations and the justification of decisions under standards.[26] One need not deny that real differences may exist in the concept of rationality as it applies to these various disciplines in order to affirm that there is a common core that conscientious judges must heed for reasons quite different from those that explain why judges must also heed the standards identified by a contingently accepted rule of recognition.

The plea, in short, is for a distinction, also urged by others,[27] between the concept of legal reasoning and the concept of legal validity. Dworkin suggests that the question "What, in general is a good reason for decision by a court of law?" is in every respect simply another way of asking "What is Law?"[28] The view presented here declines as misleading this invitation to collapse all questions concerning how courts ought to decide cases into questions of what the law is. This viewpoint also explains why Hart might write an entire book on the concept of law and explicitly set aside, as a matter "that cannot be attempted here,'' the characterization of ''the varied types of reasoning which courts characteristically use . . . .''[29] It may be that of these two, the inquiry into legal reasoning is the more urgent and of more immediate, practical effect than the conceptual study of legal validity. It may even be that the perceived barrenness of conceptual theories of law in general justifies a view that finds more fertile possibilities in the American realist movement,[30] whatever the conceptual flaws of the legal theory produced by that movement.[31] But these normative evaluations are beside the point when the question concerns potential defects in the conceptual enterprise upon which Hart, after all, chose to embark.

The importance of distinguishing what are here called judicial technique principles does not, however, lie solely in the implications of the distinction for an adequate conceptual model of law. The distinction has implications as well for questions concerning the responsibility of individual judges to develop and correct such principles within an existing legal system. In the case of legal standards, individual judges who disagree with the justice or wisdom of the accepted rule of recognition do not breach—and indeed can only acquit—their duty *qua* judge by applying such standards. On the positivist's model, compliance with accepted standards *is* compliance with official duty. In contrast, official acceptance of particular judicial technique principles has no necessary connection to questions concerning the correctness of such standards and the obligation of a judge to employ them. An individual judge demonstrates compliance with official duty as respects these principles, not by pointing to the fact of convergent peer behavior, but only by pointing to the correctness in fact of the judicial technique principles he employs. And in establishing such correctness, the search for guidance must ultimately be directed well beyond the community of legal officials to the wider community of rational rule-appliers.

That much needs to be done in further characterizing and identifying such principles may be conceded.[32] The point of the present discussion is only to stress that, to the extent the judge's role is that of a rational rule-applier, the resulting implications for role theory should not be subsumed under legal theory in a way that obscures real differences in the nature and source of judicial obligation.[33] Llewellyn's elaborate exploration of ''rule, tool and technique''[34] in the process of judicial decision should not, under the rights thesis, be converted into an exploration of exclusively legal standards: rule and tool perhaps, but not technique.

C. The Limits of the Argument

Even if the above distinction is accepted, it will constitute a complete response to Dworkin's argument only if it can be applied to all of the principles Dworkin has in mind. Consider the principle that ''no man should profit from his own wrong.'' On its face, this at least appears to be a standard unrelated to any independently developed methodology of rule-discovery that might be thought to transcend the realm of the peculiarly legal. Dworkin suggests that we can imagine the standard being changed or eroded ''[i]f it no longer seemed unfair to allow people to profit by their wrongs.''[35] Can one justify a refusal to count this standard as law by a process similar to that applied to judicial technique principles?

The attempt to do so might take the following form. First, one might question whether in fact the "no-profit" principle could be disavowed as Dworkin suggests. If the principle is a concrete illustration of some more abstract principle, linking notions of right and wrong with notions of just desert ("good should be rewarded, evil punished"), the suggestion that the principle could have no weight at all in community judgments about "fairness" borders on a redefinition of the underlying normative concepts of "desert," "right," "wrong," and "profit." It will always be prima facie unfair to profit from one's own wrong, even though the prima facie case can sometimes, as in Dworkin's example of adverse possession, be overcome. Second, even if complete disavowal of the no-profit maxim is logically possible, it might be argued that the maxim (or the abstract principle it reflects) operates on such a level of generality that one could assume implicit acceptance of the principle as an empirical fact in any relevant social context. In this respect, such principles would resemble judicial technique principles: They are found not in the confines of a particular legal institution but in the essential preconditions of social intercourse in general.

If this hypothesis is correct, one should be able to discover the "no-profit" maxim and similar principles operating in nonlegal, rule-governed situations—in games, for example. Consider a referee at a basketball game played under rules that predate the introduction of specific provisions for intentional fouls. The generally applicable rule is that all bodily contact fouls "shall be called." A member of team *A*, which is losing in the closing minutes of the game, intentionally fouls the poorest shooter on team *B* with the hope that team *A* will get the rebound if the foul shot is missed. Team *B* urges that the rule be construed to allow the referee not to call the foul, thereby leaving team *B* with possession of the ball. No other relevant rules govern the situation, which has not previously arisen. One can imagine the referee deciding that, although the rules committee had not envisioned this particular situation, surely it had not intended for a team to "profit from its own wrong."[36] Whether or not that is the conclusion the referee reaches, the claim that he has a duty at least to consider the "no-profit" principle rests on assumptions about how critics and players would respond to a failure "to take the measure of these principles" that are similar to the assumptions Dworkin makes in arguing for the binding nature of the principle in *Riggs*.[37] In both cases a decisionmaker is urged to construe a rule, in the absence of express contrary indications, not to do violence to implicitly accepted general social principles. Although in that sense "binding," the context-neutral nature of such principles might be thought sufficient to explain why one does not include them specifically among the "rules of basketball" or the "laws" of society.[38]

I do not intend to explore this suggestion further because it seems clear that, however far one might push this process of distinguishing translegal from legal principles, one cannot in this manner account for all, or even most, of the principles that Dworkin has in mind. Some principles are surely not context-neutral. A principle that places "special burdens upon oligopolies that manufacture potentially dangerous machines''[39] derives its authority from standards accepted within the particular legal institution in much the same manner as other legal standards. A referee urged to apply the foul rule only to intentional fouls must consider the purpose and "spirit" of the particular game of basketball (it is not a kind of football or rugby) in order to reject the proposed interpretation. The fact that one would not include in the "rules of basketball" all the purposes and aims of the game that might become relevant to an interpretation of the rules provides no answer to Dworkin's argument that at least these principles operate functionally like other legal standards to determine results, and thus in that sense are institution-specific standards that must be included in an accurate theoretical account of the "laws" of the game or institution.

THE RIGHTS THESIS

What, then, should a judge do when the shared conventions of language and purpose alone do not point to a single result? Dworkin's answer is that the judge must expand his search beyond the legal standards implicit in any particular rule to those implicit in the entire legal system itself: "A principle is a principle of law if it figures in the soundest theory of law that can be provided as a justification for the explicit substantive and institutional rules of the jurisdiction in question."[40] Professor Sartorius provides a similar but not identical account: "The correct decision in a given case is that which achieves 'the best resolution' of existing standards in terms of systematic coherence . . . ."[41]

In his most recent article, Dworkin expands at length on this thesis by positing an ideal judge called Hercules.[42] Faced with a hard constitutional case, Hercules must first develop a "full political theory that justifies the constitution as a whole." If several political theories satisfy this test, he must refer to other constitutional rules and settled practices under the rules to select the theory that "provides a smoother fit with the constitutional scheme as a whole." By this process, he develops a theory of the Constitution "in the shape of a complex set of principles and policies that justify that scheme of government," and by reference to which he is now able to decide the hard constitutional issue in the case before him.[43] The same process is applicable to cases involving statutes and the common law. Hercules must "construct a scheme of abstract and concrete principles that provide a coherent justification for all common law precedents and, so far as these are to be justified on principle, constitutional and statutory provisions as well."[44]

Dworkin's dual claim that this search for the "soundest" solution to a hard case not only accurately describes the Anglo-American judicial function but will also yield a single correct decision in every case faces theoretical, empirical, and practical objections. In the remainder of this article, I briefly discuss these difficulties without attempting to resolve them, and then consider whether the rights thesis, even if valid, can be accommodated to the positivist's basic model.

A. Assessing the Thesis

1. THEORETICAL PROBLEMS

Any attempt to assess the above claims confronts at the outset the problem of understanding just what is meant, in the present context, by "coherence" or by "a soundest theory of law." Dworkin and Sartorius, however, have done much to try to clarify these notions, and I shall not expand on their efforts here.[45] Even if one understands what is required of a judge trying to apply the rights thesis, the plausibility of the thesis would still be difficult to test because of the clear separation of the claim that there is always a single right answer from the claim that any mere mortal could be expected to know that he had found it. Only Hercules can do that, as Dworkin illustrates.[46] Indeed, Sartorius goes so far as to admit "that it is unreasonable to expect that it would be possible, even in principle, to develop some form of judicial proof procedure which would permit one to demonstrate the correctness, let alone the unique correctness, of a putatively correct decision in all cases."[47]

These merely practical problems, however, prove the claim theoretically untenable only if one holds a theory of truth that makes the testability of a claim a precondition of its meaningfulness. Let us assume that claims can be true though they are unprovable "even in principle."[48] We can then also agree with Sartorius that uniquely correct decisions for legal cases exist if the following conditions are met: (1) there is a unique set of exclusively relevant legal standards that bear on the issue; (2) these standards have relative weights for use in cases of conflict; and (3) some method exists for resolving ties when conflicting standards are evenly balanced.[49]

Of these three conditions, Sartorius acknowledges a theoretical problem only in connection with the third: One has no guarantee that cases will not arise in which conflicting principles are evenly balanced. Sartorius' response is that this possibility is so unlikely that the theoretical model remains a viable hypothetical model for the judge and justifies his search for *the* correct answer in all cases.[50] The second condition—that unique, pre-established weights attach to the pluralistic and undoubtedly conflicting institutional standards one is likely to discover in any hard case—is more troublesome. Several commentators have argued that this aspect of the claim is unproved and implausible.[51] Sartorius, for example, simply asserts at this point in the argument that the same test of institutional support that isolates the relevant standards will also reveal their relative weights.[52] Again, the problem does not seem to lie with the theoretical claim that all institutional standards relevant to a decision *will* have fixed, relative weights at any point in time, but only with the likelihood that any procedure can be developed to reveal those weights. In this respect, the thesis is perhaps best viewed, as far as its theoretical validity is concerned, as a sketch of the hypothetical framework implied by judicial opinions that are written *as if* the decision in a hard case were uniquely required, much as Kelsen's theory may be viewed as an attempt to describe what must be hypothesized if one is to explain the normative aspect of law.

There remains, however, one problem that has been largely overlooked. In fact, the problem arises in connection with what has apparently been assumed to be the most plausible aspect of the thesis: the assumption that a unique set of pre-existing, decision-relevant legal standards exists in every case. Elaboration of the problem requires brief reference once again to Fuller's writings on the nature of adjudication, referred to earlier in this article, in a different context.[53] Fuller's view is that some kinds of disputes are inherently inappropriate for resolution through adjudicative methods. The explanation for and description of what constitutes these "limits of adjudication" is varied and sometimes obscure, with the "polycentric" nature of the issue usually serving as the predominant sign that the limits have been reached.[54] On one interpretation of this model, what makes some problems nonjusticiable is the absence of the pre-existing standards upon which rational, judicial decisionmaking depends.[55]

Now Sartorius explicitly draws on Fuller's theory of adjudication in developing the rights thesis as an apparent explication of the concept of adjudication.[56] Dworkin explicitly characterizes the thesis in its descriptive aspect as explaining "the present structure of the institution of adjudication."[57] If the rights thesis indeed amounts to an explication of the concept of judging, and if it is true that some problems can arise that are inherently nonjusticiable for lack of pre-existing decisional standards, then the validity of the claim that there is a single right answer in every case depends, even in theory, on a further empirical investigation into the kind and range of jobs we have, in fact, given to courts.[58] One may, of course, hope that courts have themselves properly applied doctrines of justiciability to limit the cases they accept to those with pre-existing decisional standards. But neither Dworkin nor Sartorius undertakes any such investigation. Courts may, after all, have made mistakes in applying justiciability doctrines. And although mistakes made by judges about the legally required result in normal cases leave untouched the claim that there *was* a right answer, mistakes in deciding what is justiciable leave the courts dealing with "polycentric" cases as to which the claim of single right answer is, by definition, false.[59] Furthermore, apart from the question of mistakes, not all state courts, let alone English courts, adhere to doctrines of justiciability similar to those that have been applied in federal courts. To the extent that the single-right-answer thesis is meant to apply to all cases heard by Anglo-American courts, its validity will again depend upon empirical investigations yet to be undertaken by proponents of the thesis.

The rights thesis advocate might, of course, reply that the single right answer claim applies only to those cases in which the deciding official *is* acting *qua* judge. But this response makes the thesis considerably less interesting. One may accept the rights thesis as an explication of the ideal embraced by the concept of adjudication and still be left with the problem of determining which of the cases that come before courts are compatible with that ideal. One cannot draw the line between these two kinds of cases on the basis of "those that do and those that do not have pre-existing standards and right answers," for that is precisely what is in question.

Clearly, much depends on how broad a claim is being made for the single-right-answer ("no discretion") thesis. Dworkin at one point appeared to exclude constitutional cases from the reach of the thesis[60] and at other times seems to have limited the common-law claim to the standard kinds of civil cases that courts customarily handle.[61] Depending on what counts as a "typical civil case," one might support the proposition that these at least fall into the class of the justiciable. But if legislative instructions to courts to decide matters that are not justiciable (or the voluntary acceptance by courts of such matters) are automatically disqualified as counterexamples to the thesis on the ground that they are not the sort of cases to which the claim applies, then the thesis again threatens to become as interesting as a tautology.

One can, perhaps, avoid these problems by looking for the limits of the thesis in the context of the dispute out of which it arose in the first place. Dworkin, after all, is talking about "hard cases"—those for which the positivist admits there are standards that can lead to only one result in some cases, but not in all. Dworkin's claim might be that if there are any admitted standards, then the solution to the case is always determined: once justiciable, then always and thoroughly justiciable. Whether this fully restores the theoretical base of the claim depends, perhaps, on whether one agrees that justiciability can only be an all-or-nothing matter, and that moving beyond what can be traced to a common or general consensus in applying standards entails a problem that is significantly different, as respects "justiciability," from problems raised by cases that are standardless from the beginning.[62]

2. EMPIRICAL PROBLEMS

Empirical problems arise when one looks for evidence that the rights thesis does, in fact, accurately describe the Anglo-American system of adjudication even in cases that are theoretically justiciable. Given the difficulty of the task demanded by the thesis and the present scarcity of Herculeses, it is, after all, entirely conceivable that a society would deliberately opt, in designing its legal system, for less than the ideal. A legal system might, that is, authorize judges (through the rule of recognition) to abandon the search for the right answer in hard cases despite its theoretical existence, and to exchange the role of "judge" in such cases for that of an informed, conscientious legislator.

In this respect, Dworkin's most recent article is puzzling, for it appears designed less to argue that the thesis holds than to provide an account, in the hypothetical sense described above, of how judges could in theory operate under such a thesis *assuming* that it holds. Consider the illustration from the game of chess that Dworkin employs.[63] We are to assume that the rules of chess include a rule directing the referee to forfeit a game if one of the players "unreasonably" annoys the other in the course of play. The referee must decide whether Tal's smile is sufficiently annoying to justify a forfeit by virtue of the rule. Like Hercules, the referee must construct from the institution of chess a sufficiently precise theory of the game to yield a single correct answer in every case of annoying conduct. But we know that this is what the referee must do only because Dworkin assumes that he has been instructed to treat the rule in this fashion, despite its vagueness. If chess really did include such a rule, a referee's proper response could normally be determined only after marshalling other evidence beyond the rule and the game of chess alone. If, for example, referees decided that they should first issue warnings before declaring forfeits (in reality, the most likely possibility) one would probably conclude that the referee believes he is authorized to exercise quasi-legislative power to declare rules prospectively. One would not have a "right" to a forfeit until conduct, now specifically described, occurred for a second time. The point is that whether a system of standards is to be viewed as a system of entitlements, like the question whether any particular standard is a rule or a principle, cannot be determined solely from a priori inspection of the standard or set of standards without considering the empirically determined attitudes toward such standards of those who must administer and live under them.

The evidence on which both Dworkin and Sartorius rest their empirical claim consists almost exclusively of what they discover in the attitudes of judges and ordinary litigants. They claim that this attitude, as reflected in judicial opinions and the arguments litigants make, reveals that the relevant judicial community believes it has been instructed to treat the legal system as a system of entitlements, however vague the standard that is being applied. But surely this is rather selective evidence. If one takes into account the views of the entire legal profession, as Dworkin seems prepared to do in deciding which principles are legal principles,[64] one would have to balance the cited empirical evidence against the contrary views of numerous scholars and judges who have claimed that judges are authorized to make fresh choices in hard cases.[65] One would also have to account for the increasing practice of prospective overruling in both common-law and constitutional cases.[66] Finally, even the cited evidence would normally have to be weighed against arguments designed to explain why judges and litigants might act as if their decisions were uniquely required, even though they knew in fact that they were not.[67]

3. PRACTICAL PROBLEMS

The practical objection to the rights thesis, ably presented in a recent article by Professor Greenawalt,[68] is a synthesis of both the theoretical and empirical problems. If one can transform vague standards into standards that embody entitlements simply by adding a directive to view them as such, it is not clear what practical difference the thesis makes to judges, litigants, or other participants in the system. Thus, Dworkin is prepared to accept sentencing decisions by judges as cases involving strong (legislative) discretion. Yet nothing in Dworkin's account explains why the standards to which a judge refers in determining a sentence could not, in theory, yield a single correct sentence via the Herculean route; these decisions should also become matters of right once the judges are instructed to include sentencing decisions within the ambit of the thesis.[69] Administrative agencies determining "fair rates" or "unfair trade practices" differ from judges determining "unreasonable restraints of trade" or standards of "due care" only because the latter are instructed to treat the standards as yielding institutionally correct answers, whereas the former are not. If we give the administrative agency's standard to the court, or, conversely, instruct the administrative agency to view the standard as incorporating institutionally correct solutions, then the distinction disappears—but only in theory. Even the legislator—the paradigmatic case of a decisionmaker with "legal discretion" to pass laws whether or not they conform to results thought to be required by moral or political theory—may lose his discretion if one incorporates in the constitution a directive to pass only legislation "in the public interest." Such a directive will presumably transform criticisms directed at the wisdom of the law into criticisms that the law is an incorrect measure of the public interest and thus a violation of pre-existing, system-incorporated rights.

Whenever the standard is vague, as in these cases, it is difficult to see what practical difference will result from these alternative methods of describing the system. By hypothesis, reasonable men will differ about what the standard requires, and more than one solution will fall within the range of reasonable difference. In the absence of a real Hercules to resolve the dispute, one is hard pressed to explain how behavior is affected by the fact that one is instructed to seek a system-determined "right" answer instead of being told that more than one solution (within the reasonable range) is system-acceptable, even though there may be in some theoretical sense an extra-systemic "right" answer.[70]

B. *Accommodating the Thesis to the Positivist's Model*

Despite the seriousness of the preceding objections, the rights thesis can at least be viewed as a plausible theoretical explication of the ideal embraced in the concept of adjudication. As such, Dworkin's writings provide a valuable check to the temptation to view controversial judicial decisions—simply because they are controversial—as nothing more than rationalizations of a judge's personal views. Even though the ideal has not been shown to be practically or empirically compatible with all the controversies that judges decide, Dworkin and Sartorius help draw attention to the unresolved questions that should be investigated before the thesis is rejected in any particular case as the model that should guide a conscientious judge. Let us assume that these questions can be resolved and that the rights thesis is correct. How might the positivist respond to the claim that the thesis provides a counterexample to his theory?

One possibility is simply to extend an argument that is often made in accommodating purpose to the positivist's model in the easy case. In such cases, the positivist can plausibly claim that the same master test that identifies the rule also identifies the commonly agreed purpose used to interpret the rule. The rights thesis asserts that legal standards beyond those implicit in language and purpose contribute to the resolution of the hard case. But the identification of these additional standards is not made through a process different in kind from that involved in the easy case. The only difference is that instead of confining one's attention to a particular rule and its purposes, the investigation now broadens to include the entire institution and all relevant rules and practices, together with their underlying purposes. In this manner, one extracts a complex set of standards for use in finding the soundest solution to the case in question. The ultimate test for whether a standard has the necessary "institutional support"[71] and hence counts as "law" will be exceedingly complex, but simplicity was never claimed as a feature of the positivist's theoretical model.

Professor Sartorius, who otherwise agrees with the essence of the rights thesis, argues along these lines that the thesis remains consistent with positivism:

> Although the actual filling out of such an ultimate criterion would be a complex and demanding task for any mature legal system, if it is indeed a practical possibility at all, the only claim that need be made is that it is in principle possible, and that it is just this possibility which in principle underlies the identification of something as an authoritative *legal* standard. Although perhaps it is a good way from Hart's version of positivism, it is in accord with the fundamental positivistic tenet as described by Dworkin: "The law of a community . . . can be identified and distinguished by specific criteria, by tests having to do not with . . . content but with . . . pedigree."[72]

Dworkin's response to this attempt to rescue positivism is found in the second article in his trilogy.[73] "Institutional support" cannot serve as an ultimate test for law in the positivist's sense, because the rights thesis does not require a judge, in attempting to construct the soundest theory of law, to accept as dispositive the fact that other judges accept any particular theory as the soundest. Each judge's task is to find the unique soundest theory, the content of which, however, is largely independent of what other judges think it to be. The distinction is between what Dworkin calls a "normative rule," which ascribes duties to individuals whether or not they accept or acknowledge them, and a "social rule," which only describes duties that are, in fact, accepted.[74] The positivist's test is a social rule. The rights thesis, in contrast, imports a test that makes relevant to the determination of legal validity normative arguments about what "ought" to be recognized as accepted practice, whether or not it is so recognized.

There are two paths one might take in evaluating this response, each corresponding to a different interpretation of what it means to say that "normative arguments" must occur in applying a test of "institutional support." The first interpretation views "normative arguments" as referring only to what is entailed by the need to provide a "consistent rationale" for accepted practices, with the latter still serving, in the positivist's sense, as the basic mark of a community's legal standards. This is the path Sartorius takes.[75] People can, after all, disagree about what consistency requires with respect to unanticipated or controversial issues, and in that sense disagree about what "ought" to be done, while still agreeing that maximum consistency with existing practices determines the correct answer. Normative arguments in this sense, although they may take into account the reasons for or the underlying purposes of existing practices, make no attempt to justify those underlying purposes or baseline practices. But Dworkin also uses "normative argument" in a sense that explicitly denies the conclusive relevance of any baseline reference to concordant practices. It is in this sense that a vegetarian might argue that it is a present duty of society to refrain from killing animals for food, even though existing practice does not conform to such a rule.[76]

Let us assume that normative arguments in this second sense are properly made whenever judges decide "hard cases." One might still be able to view the resulting legal system as compatible with positivism by distinguishing between two levels at which such normative arguments about the law may be advanced: At the basic level, determined by the rule of recognition, one may find a social rule setting forth instructions phrased in normative terms for the identification of legal standards; at a secondary level, one may discover normative arguments about whether those instructions have been followed. If normative arguments are limited to the secondary level, the master rule model remains theoretically intact and basically a social rule test for law, even though all of the crucial arguments about the legally required result in particular cases occur at this secondary, normative level.

The point can be illustrated by reference to an assumed Kingdom of Rex, with the social rule of recognition that "whatever Rex enacts is law" and a single enactment by Rex: "All disputes are to be settled as justice requires." In this simplified equity system, normative disputes (in the second sense) will arise over what is required by the system's explicit incorporation of moral standards. But what makes these disputes at all relevant as a means of determining the law is the fact that the appropriate officials accept, in Hart's sense, the basic rule of recognition. Hart is the first to concede that in this respect law and morality may well overlap, as evidenced in the United States, for example, by a variety of constitutional concepts that "explicitly incorporate principles of justice or substantive moral values."[77] Far from providing a counterexample to the positivist's conceptual model, such systems reenforce the theoretical validity of that model by making the legal relevance of the normative debate dependent on the instructions contained in the master test.[78]

Dworkin's description of the Anglo-American legal system differs from Rex's equity system only because the instruction given to judges is of the more complex form described by the rights thesis. Normative debates about the "soundest theory of law" occur and are legally relevant (assuming the empirical claims are established) only because the underlying social rule directs judges to engage in this method of resolving hard cases. That this is the case is revealed by the fact that at critical points throughout Dworkin's argument—in deciding whether standards are rules or principles and whether the legal system is a system of entitlements—resolution of the issue, as we have seen, turns on an inspection of the actual attitudes and practices of the relevant community. Indeed, the only empirical evidence for the rights thesis itself is based on claims about what is accepted in fact by judges and litigants as the proper way to decide cases. This inevitable recourse to empirically measured attitudes to resolve critical issues in Dworkin's account supports, rather than contradicts, the thesis that the ultimate test for law is a basic rule of recognition, determined by reference to the accepted practice of the officials of the system.

Viewed in this light, the dispute between Hart and Dworkin concerning judicial discretion in hard cases emerges as a dispute over the empirical question discussed in a preceding section: It is a disagreement over what are in fact the accepted "closure instructions"[79] for the system. Hart suggests that judges have accepted closure instructions directing them to decide the hard case through the exercise of quasi-legislative discretion.[80] Dworkin claims that the closure instructions in such cases require judges to perform the Herculean task described in *Hard Cases*. In either case, it remains true that how and whether a particular system is closed is an empirical question, to be determined by inspection of the directions that the judge finds in the positivist's master test—the accepted social rule of recognition.[81]

A determined nonpositivist might respond to this final attempt at reconciliation between positivism and the rights thesis in three ways. First, he may question whether it remains meaningful to talk of a "test" of "pedigree" in systems such as Rex's where the positivist's theoretical model is preserved, but only at the cost of rendering it of little practical use in resolving critical arguments about what "the law" requires. This objection highlights the ambiguity of the term "positivism" itself. It may be that we have moved some distance from the view that a "master test," capable of actually identifying with some precision all standards relevant to legal decision, forms the core of a positivist's theory. It may also be that those who believe there is a conceptual link between "legal standards" and some minimum degree of authoritative definiteness and clarity in such standards[82] will refuse to categorize the standards used to decide cases in Rex's system as "legal." But if the "core" of a positivist's theory is, instead, "the simple contention that it is in no sense a necessary truth that laws reproduce or satisfy certain demands of morality,"[83] then Rex's equity system and the rights thesis are both consistent with a positivist's perspective. Moral standards become relevant to legal decisions in both cases only because they are contingently, not necessarily, made relevant by social rules. Content is crucial in deciding which standards to use, but only because pedigree makes it so. The fact that one cannot provide a proof procedure either for checking the accuracy of decisions employing such legally adopted moral standards or for demonstrating which such standards are the correct ones, does not affect the core claim that legal and moral standards are conceptually distinct.[84]

A second response to the claim that the rights thesis represents a disagreement over closure instructions might try to capitalize on the very fact that such a claim concedes the existence of disagreement concerning this particular aspect of the rule of recognition. Even though the empirical evidence for the rights thesis may be inconclusive, it is, we have suggested, at least strong enough to indicate that a genuine and unresolved dispute exists over the question of how to decide hard cases. Thus, Dworkin has indeed provided a counterexample to the thesis that in every legal system there exists a social rule that settles the limits of a judge's duty *qua* judge. But this thesis is largely one of Dworkin's own making, rather than an essential aspect of positivism or a claim that Hart makes, "at least in his more careful moments."[85] Hart has never denied that the rule of recognition may itself be uncertain in some respects, and that authoritative resolution of some questions may thus depend on a court's success in getting a particular decision accepted by the rest of the relevant community. "Here all that succeeds is success."[86] One may agree with Dworkin that until such success is achieved, the positivist must admit that there simply is no social rule on the issue.[87] But that admission leaves the theoretical model intact, raising at most a question of the relationship between, on the one hand, the efficacy of a legal system, and, on the other, the degree of uncertainty that can be tolerated in the rule of recognition. When an unresolved question is fundamental, the existence of the legal system may be seriously threatened.[88] But when, as here, the question concerns how judges should decide hard cases, the riots occur in the academic journals, not in the streets, and are thus "system tolerable" in the extreme.[89]

A third possible response at once illustrates both the incompleteness of

Dworkin's argument and the potential threat that the rights thesis could pose for the positivist if the argument could be completed. The analogy to Rex's equity system, it might be suggested, misses the point or assumes what is in issue. The analogy assumes that the normative dispute turns into a sociological question of fact once one reaches the claim that "whatever Rex enacts is law." But it is this basic claim itself that the rights thesis subjects to legally relevant, normative debate. A judge in Rex's system does not acquit himself of his responsibility to apply "the law" by showing only that a particular decision is "just," and that Rex has decreed that cases be decided as justice requires. The judge must also be prepared to entertain, as legally relevant, arguments concerning the ultimate justification, if any, (not merely the stated or implicit reasons for acceptance) of the rule that "whatever Rex enacts is law." It is in this sense that the "process of justification must carry the lawyer very deep into political and moral theory, and well past the point where it would be accurate to say that any 'test' of 'pedigree' exists for deciding which of two different justifications of our political institutions is superior."[90]

Under this interpretation, the issue between Dworkin and the positivist is sharply joined in a way that admittedly does not permit reconciliation. But the interpretation raises two new problems. First, it now seems clear that one could no longer draw any distinction between legal standards, on the one hand, and extra-legal—moral or political—standards on the other;[91] as a result, the rights thesis collapses into the most traditional kind of classical natural law theory. Second, one is now left without any argument to support the newly interpreted thesis; for the thesis now appears to have left the confines of descriptive theory for the larger realm of conceptual inquiry into the meaning and nature of "law." Dworkin's analysis of "social" and "normative" rules may be both conceptual and accurate. One may concede, that is, that the language of obligation can be used either to describe acknowledged duties or to assert that duties exist, whether or not they are acknowledged. But what is missing from this account is an argument that demonstrates that "law" necessarily rests on an underlying normative rather than social rule. As an empirical matter, it is difficult to deny that social structures *can* be organized in ways that fit the positivist's model—that is, in such a way as to make the fact of acceptance the final court of appeal in determining the appropriateness of applying organized sanctions to specified conduct. Insistence upon the *necessary* legal relevance of normative appeals beyond what is, in fact, accepted requires one to explain what it is about the nature of "law" that makes this newly interpreted thesis a more accurate account of the concept of a legal system. In the conclusion to this paper, I shall briefly describe the kind of investigation that might be expected to provide such an explanation.

CONCLUSION

It may be helpful to place the preceding discussion into somewhat broader perspective by comparing Dworkin's attack on positivism with other nonpositivist theories.

Legal positivism's traditional target was the classical natural law theorist's claim that norms otherwise identifiable as "law" would not, in fact, qualify as law if they were sufficiently unjust. Dworkin's attack belongs to a more modern version of nonpositivism. The new nonpositivist does not deny that *if* one can determine a norm is law, further reference to content is unnecessary for determining the norm's legal status. Instead, the attack is directed at the antecedent of that hypothetical. In some cases, one cannot determine whether the norm is law at all without first inspecting content; in these cases, at least, the separation of fact and value becomes blurred and the conclusion that the norm is law may entail the conclusion that the norm is not unjust (at least not egregiously so).

The common feature of both the classical and modern approach (in addition to their rejection of the more extreme versions of legal realism) is a refusal to accept the positivist's insistence on the strict separation of the "is" and the "ought"; in this respect both might be thought to represent varieties of a natural law theory. But the obvious difference between the two approaches is important and should not be glossed over by the choice of a label designed to emphasize the common feature. Faced with an unambiguously evil statute, enacted by a supremely competent legislature, the new "natural law" theorist, unlike his classical predecessor, cannot deny the norm its legal status any more than does the positivist.[92] (Both may, of course, urge that its moral worth be considered in deciding whether it should be obeyed.) It is only when we move from the "unambiguous" to the "hard case" that the new theorist discerns an essential blurring of fact and value.

This difference in approach is sufficiently sharp that the classical theorist is not likely to view the modern nonpositivist as much of an ally. The impetus for the classical approach rested in part on the desire to construct a unified theory of obligation: With the bottom line for any actor—what one ought to do—as his ultimate goal, the classical theorist needed only to restrict legal norms to those that also passed moral muster in order to preserve a sense of unqualified fidelity to law while maintaining the primacy of moral reasons among the reasons for acting. In contrast, the new approach appears at times to be making a somewhat quibbling point about the inherent limits of language and human foresight. When language and purpose fail to guide unequivocally, one must fall back on something else, and that something else might just as well be (or "must be," depending on the particular variation of the theory) the judge's sense of what best "coheres" with the aim of the entire legal system. The new approach, in short, capitalizes on the problem of uncertainty to reintroduce value judgments into descriptions of the law, but in so doing gives away most of what the classical debate was about in the first place.

From another perspective, however, the modern approach represents a much more serious challenge to positivism precisely because it never was clear just what the classical debate *was* all about. The claim that "immoral law is not law" apparently assumes that there is a subject to which the predicate "immoral" can attach and thus seems to concede that there are *formal* tests for legal validity; the question whether one should also require substantive tests appears mainly as a problem of choice on pragmatic or theoretical grounds. The positivist's choice for the wider concept, for reasons of both conceptual clarity and practical merit in moral deliberation,[93] has never been easy to challenge. But when the claim that there are formal tests for validity itself is challenged, the positivist will never reach the question of choice until he reexamines his model of law to determine whether the alleged defects do in fact exist and, if so, whether the model can be repaired.

I have argued that the positivist's model remains intact in the face of Dworkin's argument, primarily because the rights thesis is cloaked in empirical claims and girded by arguments peculiar to a particular legal system. The conceptual theorist can discount the thesis—even if true—as an accidental, not an essential, aspect of law, explaining that the normative debates that the thesis entails occur only because social rules make such debates relevant to determining legal validity. The theory fails, in short, precisely because, and to the extent that, it is presented and viewed as a descriptive theory. If the arguments Dworkin makes for the need to refer beyond purpose and rule to the underlying justification of the entire institution could be connected to the concept of law itself, the blow of positivism would be more serious.

One possible direction that a further inquiry along these lines might take is the following. The fundamental premise of the inquiry would be that an adequate legal theory must preserve the distinction between legal and coercive systems—the basis, after all, for Hart's criticism of Austin. From that basic premise, the inquiry would explore the extent to which a model of law that roots legal validity in the fact of acceptance of a basic social rule by a group of officials accurately preserves this distinction between "obligation" and "being obliged." If one can show that the concept of obligation is accurately reflected only in a model of law that makes legal validity dependent, not on the fact of acceptance alone, but also on a good-faith claim that the system and standards thus described are "acceptable" to those governed by the system, to that extent the positivist's model will require modification. It is in this respect—in Dworkin's insights concerning the persistence with which claims of legal validity are linked with *claims* of normative validity—that one finds in the rights thesis valuable hints for the development of an improved, conceptual theory of law.

NOTES

1. Ronald Dworkin, "Social Rules and Legal Theory," *Yale Law Journal* 81 (1972): 874, note 3.
2. Ibid., pp. 871, 882–90.
3. See Note, "Understanding the Model of Rules," *Yale Law Journal* 81 (1972): 912, 921–34. See also note 36 below.
4. This conclusion receives some support from Dworkin's own description of principles. See Ronald Dworkin, "The Model of Rules," *University of Chicago Law Review* 35 (1967): 14, 26.
5. See generally, R. Carnap, *Logical Foundations of Probability,* 2nd ed. (1962); N. Goodman, *Fact, Fiction and Forecast* (1955); G. von Wright, *A Treatise on Induction and Probability* (1951).
6. H. L. A. Hart, *The Concept of Law* (1961), p. 200.
7. Ronald Dworkin, "Hard Cases," *Harvard Law Review* 88 (1975): 1064.
8. Ibid.
9. See L. Fuller, "The Forms and Limits of Adjudication" (unpublished paper prepared for the Roundtable on Jurisprudence, Association of American Law Schools, 1959); L. Fuller, "Collective Bargaining and the Arbitrator," *Wisconsin Law Review* (1963): 3.
10. See H. M. Hart and A. M. Sacks, *The Legal Process,* p. 666, (unpublished, 1958).
11. Ibid., p. 1221.
12. See Dworkin, "Model of Rules," p. 42.
13. *Broom's Legal Maxims,* 10th ed. (1939), p. 453.

14. See H. Read, J. MacDonald, J. Fordham, and W. J. Pierce, *Materials on Legislation* (1973), p. 903.
15. See J. Sutherland, *Statutory Construction,* 3rd ed. (Horack, 1943) § 4916.
16. F. Lieber, *Legal and Political Hermeneutics,* 3rd ed. (1880), pp. 17–18.
17. See O. W. Holmes, "Common Law and Legislation," *Harvard Law Review* 21 (1908): 383, 386–88.
18. For a survey of such states and resulting court reaction, see Jefferson B. Fordham and J. Russell Leach, "Interpretation of Statutes in Derogation of the Common Law," *Vanderbilt Law Review* 3 (1950): 438, 448–53.
19. Presumably, prior practice is maintained, despite the instruction, until it is overturned by statutes. Some statutes will intend "sharp" changes and some will not, with the line between the two, despite the instruction, still marked (in part) by language that avoids ambiguity. Cf. *Niblock* v. *Salt Lake City,* 100 Utah 573, 111 P.2d 800 (1941) (adhering to previous "strict" construction of statute in derogation of common law despite intervening legislative reversal of derogation canon). The only context in which repeal of presumptions of any kind in favor of established practices might be understandable is one in which it appears that the law-making institution thereby intends total disavowal of the relevance of existing practices as "background" against which to understand and interpret future directives, as in the case of a postrevolutionary committee. Even in that case, however, one can probably explain different interpretations of apparently identical pre- and post-revolutionary directives simply by noting, if true, that fundamental changes in societal goals have led to "other indicia" of intent or purpose that outweigh presumptions in favor of continuity. Only if one thinks it is possible "rationally" to declare irrelevant all respects in which background human behavior converges, can one strip the presumption of all weight, leaving judges to interpret on a totally clean slate.
20. Cf. Hart and Sacks, *The Legal Process*, p. 1240 (a "statute ought always to be presumed to be the work of reasonable men pursuing reasonable purposes reasonably").
21. See Dworkin, "Model of Rules," p. 37.
22. Ibid., p. 36.
23. By suggesting that standards can bind "*qua* judge," I mean to imply that judging occurs in nonlegal contexts and that, in all such contexts, observance of a core of common minimal standards makes it appropriate to speak of the official engaged in the activity as a judge, whether it be of beauty contests, Kent Greenawalt, "Discretion and Judicial Decision: The Elusive Quest for the Fetters That Bind Judges," *Columbia Law Review* 75 (1975): 368–69; of games, compare Hart, *The Concept of Law,* pp. 138–41, with Dworkin, "Judicial Discretion," *Journal of Philosophy* 60 (1963): 629; or of the law. I do not mean to deny that judges in legal systems may also be obliged to heed additional standards of judging technique that are peculiar to their role as legal judges. See Graham Hughes, "Rules, Policy and Decision Making," *Yale Law Journal* 77 (1968): 414–16.

In its broadest sense, "judging" need not be confined to acts of officials resolving disputes but may include any attempt of an individual to reach and justify decisions (make "judgments") under standards. See Dworkin, "Model of Rules," p. 33 (sergeant told to "pick the five most experienced men" for a patrol). In this sense, what the text refers to as standards implicit in the concept of judging might be characterized equally well as standards implicit in the concept of rationality. Compare Perry, "Judicial Method and the Concept of Reasoning," *Ethics* 80 (1969): 1, 3-6, and note 4.
24. If one thinks that judicial technique principles can be easily listed or otherwise captured, the positivist could, of course, save his model without recourse to the argument in this section. I ignore this possibility because Dworkin apparently treats these standards as among the principles that cannot be so captured and because the distinction urged in this section seems to me worth preserving even if other arguments for the positivist might also be made.
25. Dworkin, "Social Rules and Legal Theory," p. 869; see ibid., p. 874. That the social rule thesis quoted in the text may be a stronger claim than the positivist need make is noted below.
26. Cf. Wasserstrom, *Judicial Decision,* (1961), p. 32.
27. See Hughes, "Rules, Policy and Decision Making," p. 433.
28. Dworkin, "Wasserstrom, 'The Judicial Decision,' " *Ethics* 75 (1964): 47.
29. Hart, *The Concept of Law,* p. 144.
30. See Hughes, "Rules, Policy and Decision Making," pp. 437–39.
31. See Hart, *The Concept of Law,* p. 143.
32. See Hughes, "Rules, Policy and Decision Making," p. 439. It may be that there are

characteristics other than those suggested in this section that more appropriately identify the full class of judicially binding standards deserving of exclusion from the class of "legal standards." My primary concern is to describe the general nature of this class of standards and to justify its separation from inquiries into legal validity.

The leading reference point for studies characterizing what is peculiar and essential to the process of adjudication is still largely found in the writings of Professor Fuller. See sources cited at note 9; and Hart and Sacks, *The Legal Process,* pp. 662–69. For a thoughtful application of Fuller's model to questions of legal theory, see Paul Weiler, "Two Models of Judicial Decision-Making," *Canada Bar Review* 46 (1968): 406.

33. Philosophers and sociologists have long explored the extent to which obligations attach to, and define, roles, see, e.g., R. Dahrendorf, *Essays in the Theory of Society* (1968), pp. 19–87, and this literature is to some extent reflected in discussions of legal theory and legal reasoning, see Weiler, "Two Models of Judicial Decision-Making," p. 407, note 3. See also Robert B. Seidman, "The Judicial Process Reconsidered in the Light of Role-Theory," *Modern Law Review* 32 (1969): 516.

34. See K. Llewellyn, *The Common Law Tradition: Deciding Appeals* (1960), p. 402.

35. Dworkin, "Model of Rules," p. 41.

36. Professor Carrió discusses a similar example involving the "advantage rule" in soccer, which allows officials to avoid penalizing a team's infraction of a rule "if, as a consequence of the penalty, the offending side would gain an advantage and the non-offending side would be adversely affected" (G. Carrió, *Legal Principles and Legal Positivism* [1971], p. 6). Carrió uses the example to distinguish between second-order and first-order principles, the former characterized in part by their "topic neutrality" and in part by the fact that they are addressed to judges and indicate how other rules are to be understood and applied. But Carrió's second-order principles appear to include far more than what I have called judicial technique principles, and both sorts of principles appear for Carrió to be legal standards (see ibid., pp. 7, 16, 24). Thus the distinction is different both in content and purpose from the distinction developed in this article.

37. See Dworkin, "Model of Rules," p. 36.

38. This attempt to extend the argument used in the case of judicial technique principles can be placed in perspective by briefly comparing the thesis of this section with classical theories of natural law and with Hart's own theory concerning the "minimum content of natural law." For Hart, natural facts of human vulnerability, desire for survival, and the like, make minimal rules respecting persons, property, and promises necessary features of all social life. See Hart, *The Concept of Law,* pp. 189–95. Legal systems must include such minimal rules, not so they may count as "legal," but because it is unlikely that such systems could otherwise come into being or survive. The link here is an empirical one between universal but contingent truths about human beings on the one hand, and the *efficacy,* not the *concept,* of a legal system on the other. One would hardly be inclined to exclude these minimally necessary legal standards (which may take various concrete forms in particular legal systems) from a model of law simply because they appeared only in this sense in all legal systems. In this respect, the difference between such standards and judicial technique principles lies in part in the difference in subject matter with which they deal. Minimal rules concerning persons, property, and promises aim directly at the control of human conduct, rather than at control of the process of reasoning from standards to decisions in particular cases. It is the thesis of this section that the former enterprise, but not the latter, is what "law," even in its broadest, preanalytic sense, could possibly be said to be "about." Cf. Fuller, *The Morality of Law* (1964), p. 106. This thesis explains why a model of law that failed to reflect "the minimum content of natural law" *would* seem arbitrary in a way that a model that ignored judicial technique principles would not. For similar reasons, classical natural law theories, which assert conceptual links between "law" and substantive principles of justice or morality, would also require that such principles be included among the "legal standards" identified by legal theory.

The attempt in the text to provide a translegal account of principles such as the "no profit maxim" falls between the Hartian and the classical natural law theories. Like the latter, such principles are not limited to those based on the "natural necessity" reflected in a Hobbesian view of man's predicament, but embrace broader principles of fairness and justice generally in social contexts. Like Hart's theory, the claim that these principles would be universally accepted in any social context is only contingent, not conceptual. (Indeed the plausibility of even the contingent claim probably depends on interpreting the principles at a level so abstract that they threaten to become vacuous.) But like both theories, an attempt to exclude such substantive standards from a model of "legal standards" begins to appear arbitrary.

39. Dworkin, "Model of Rules," p. 41.
40. Dworkin, "Social Rules," p. 876.
41. Rolf Sartorius, *Individual Conduct and Social Norms,* (1975), p. 196; Rolf Sartorius, "Social Policy and Judicial Legislation," *American Philosophical Quarterly* 8 (1971): 158.
42. See Dworkin, "Hard Cases," p. 1083.
43. Ibid., pp. 1084–85.
44. Ibid., p. 1094.
45. For a further examination and critique of the notion of a "soundest theory of law," see Note, "Dworkin's Rights Thesis," *Michigan Law Review* 74 (1976): 1167.
46. See Dworkin, "Hard Cases," pp. 1083–101.
47. Sartorius, *Individual Conduct,* p. 201.
48. See ibid., p. 185: "[I]t is clear that, in mathematics, we have learned that truth cannot be equated with provability."
49. See ibid., pp. 189–99.
50. Compare Sartorius, "Social Policy," pp. 158–59, with Sartorius, *Individual Conduct,* pp. 199–204. This response, of course, concedes that the theoretical validity of the model cannot be established, however "rarely" one might suppose evenly balanced cases will occur. As one commentator notes, what may be "rare" in comparison to the totality of cases—easy and hard—may not be rare at all if "hard cases" alone are considered. See Note, "Dworkin's Rights Thesis," p. 1193.

At this point, the argument over whether judges should accept the model, despite the theoretical imperfections, shifts from the conceptual to the normative level. The proponent of the rights thesis anchors his normative claims primarily in considerations drawn from the role of a judge in a democracy and from the perceived unfairness of "retroactive" resolutions of social disputes. An opponent of the thesis might agree with Llewellyn that the "single right answer" view "tends, along with pressure of work and human avoidance of sweat, to encourage taking the first seemingly workable road which [appears], thus giving the more familiar an edge up on the more wise" Llewellyn, *The Common Law Tradition,* p. 25. Note that this normative dispute results from focusing on the impact of the rights thesis on judges at opposite ends of the spectrum from "easy" to "hard" cases. Judges who strike "new" ground in "hard cases" may find shelter in the thesis from accusations that judges are merely legislating their own personal views, but they do so arguably only at the cost of being too quick to decide in other cases that they are, in fact, dealing with an "easy" case.

51. See Gerald MacCallum, "Dworkin on Judicial Discretion," *Journal of Philosophy* 60 (1963): 638, 640; George Christie, "The Model of Principles," *Duke Law Journal* (1968): 656; Joseph Raz, "Legal Principles and the Limits of Law," *Yale Law Journal* 81 (1972): 846.
52. See Sartorius, *Individual Conduct,* p. 193.
53. See sources cited at note 9.
54. "A polycentric problem is one which has many centres of stress and direction of force, only some of which are likely to be the focus of attention when a decision in the area is made . . . ." Weiler, "Two Models of Judicial Decision-Making," p. 423.
55. Ibid., pp. 420–21. "Polycentricity" does not seem to mean the same thing as "lacking preexisting decisional standards." As Fuller uses the term, polycentricity seems to imply just the opposite—namely, that there are too many interrelated and decision-relevant standards to allow a court to manage them all in the adjudicative setting. Thus, it is not clear that polycentric issues would cause Dworkin's Hercules any problem, or, correspondingly, that Dworkin would concede that *any* issues are inherently nonjusticiable. See text at notes 68–70 and note 69.
56. Sartorius, *Individual Conduct,* p. 168 (emphasis original).
57. See Dworkin, "Hard Cases," p. 1101.
58. See generally MacCallum, "Dworkin on Judicial Discretion," p. 640.
59. By deciding a nonjusticiable case a court may, of course, by that very act (and the accompanying articulation of standards) make *future* such cases justiciable, although one is still left with an unavoidable instance of judicial legislation in the first decision.
60. See Dworkin, "Judicial Discretion," p. 634, note 6. But see Dworkin, "Hard Cases," pp. 1083–85; Greenawalt, "Discretion and Judicial Decision," p. 375, note 46.
61. See Dworkin, "Hard Cases," p. 1060.
62. Cf. ibid., p. 1080.
63. Dworkin, "Hard Cases," pp. 1078–82.
64. See Dworkin, "Model of Rules," p. 41.

65. Sartorius acknowledges that this is the "nearly universal view of academic lawyers and legal philosophers . . . [f]ound in journal articles too numerous to mention." Sartorius, *Individual Conduct,* p. 182, note 2. In addition to H. L. A. Hart, others whom either Sartorius or Dworkin have identified as holding views that, in varying degrees, are inconsistent with the rights thesis include Gerald MacCallum, Benjamin Cardozo, Felix Cohen, John Dickinson, William O. Douglas, Felix Frankfurter, Paul Freund, Gidon Gottleib, Henry M. Hart, Jr., Karl Llewellyn, Roscoe Pound, Albert M. Sacks, and A. W. B. Simpson. See Rolf Sartorius, "The Justification of the Judicial Decision," *Ethics* 78 (1968): 171, 172, 177, 178; Sartorius, *Individual Conduct,* p. 182, and pp. 190, 194, notes 2, 3, and 6; Dworkin, "Judicial Discretion," pp. 624–25, note 1. It must be admitted that attempts to characterize writers as belonging clearly to one side or the other of this dispute can be a risky business when one considers variations in context and in the way the issue is posed. Thus, it has been argued that none of Dworkin's representative antagonists, properly interpreted, can be said to support a view of strong judicial discretion—a claim that, if true, only lends weight to the empirical evidence for the rights thesis. See Noel B. Reynolds, "Dworkin as Quixote," *University of Pennsylvania Law Review* 123 (1975): 574.

66. See Greenawalt, "Discretion and Judicial Decision," p. 385, note 64.

67. See Llewellyn, *Common Law Tradition,* p. 24; cf. Voltaire, *Epitre a l'Auteur du Livre des Trois Imposteurs,* Nov. 10, 1770 ("If God did not exist, it would be necessary to invent him").

68. See Greenawalt, "Discretion and Judicial Decision," note 23.

69. Cf. ibid., pp. 372–74. One might resist this conclusion by suggesting that sentencing decisions are inherently nonjusticiable and thus not among the range of cases to which the rights thesis could apply. This response reintroduces the theoretical problem of explaining the scope of the thesis in a way that does not beg the question and that yields an independent test of justiciability. See text at notes 55–62.

70. On the basis of similar considerations, Sartorius now acknowledges that "[t]he issue about the existence of uniquely correct decisions is to some extent a red herring." Sartorius, *Individual Conduct,* pp. 201–2 (footnote omitted).

71. The term was employed by Dworkin in his original article and became the focus for his subsequent debate with Sartorius over the compatibility of positivism and the rights thesis. See Dworkin, "Model of Rules," p. 41; Sartorius, "Social Policy," p. 156; Dworkin, "Social Rules," pp. 874–78; Sartorius, *Individual Conduct,* pp. 204–10.

72. Sartorius, "Social Policy," p. 156.

73. Dworkin, "Social Rules," pp. 876–78.

74. See ibid., p. 860.

75. See Sartorius, *Individual Conduct,* p. 209.

76. See Dworkin, "Social Rules," pp. 861–62.

77. Hart, *Concept of Law,* p. 199.

78. The simplified equity system described in the text may strike many as too indeterminate to yield the kind of guidance normally associated with the existence of a "legal system." See Joseph Raz, *Practical Reason and Norms* (1975), pp. 137–39; L. Fuller, *The Morality of Law* (1963), pp. 34, 39. The force of this objection should diminish as courts begin to accumulate a body of case law and to recognize that "doing justice" includes taking account of settled expectations under such cases, even if it is thought that some of them had initially been decided erroneously. See Sartorius, "Social Policy," p. 152. Compare Sartorius, *Individual Conduct,* pp. 176–79, with Wasserstrom, *The Judicial Decision,* pp. 150–52. Indeed, it has never been clear that the common law, which includes judicial power to overrule past decisions, operates differently in any essential respect from a system that might have emerged from Rex's equity system. See Simpson, "The Common Law and Legal Theory" in *Oxford Essays in Jurisprudence* (2d series, edited by A. W. B. Simpson, 1973), pp. 77, 79, 85–88. But see Raz, *Practical Reason and Norms,* p. 140.

In any event, objections to counting such systems as "legal" do not affect the point made in the text: One who insists that such systems *are* "legal" will find that Hart's model can accommodate the system. Hart's version of positivism, in short, need not be seen as conceptually linking "law" with a requirement that legal standards be ascertainable with any specified degree of certainty. (Raz, in contrast, does insist on just such a conceptual link. See ibid., p. 146 [systems of "absolute discretion are not legal systems"]). Hart, it is true, claims that in cases of sufficient uncertainty the judge's decision is not determined by legal norms, but that claim can be explained as based not on what is logically entailed by Hart's definition of law or his account of social rules, but on empirical assumptions concerning what most legal systems could realistically expect and have, in fact, demanded of judges in hard cases. If Dworkin's Herculean instructions can intelligibly be given to judges and can be defended as yielding (in theory) externally determined solutions, as the rights thesis assumes, Hart's account of law can adjust to the different empirical assumption without altering the basic theoretical model. See text at notes 81–84.

79. Municipal legal systems are generally thought to have "closed" themselves by including "some kind of residual principle the effect of which is to occupy the space which would otherwise be devoid of law" (J. Stone, *Legal Systems and Lawyers' Reasonings* [1964], p. 189). The most common such principle, dubbed the "residual negative principle" by Professor Stone, provides "that everything which is not legally prohibited is deemed to be legally permitted" (ibid.).

80. See C.C. art. 1 (Swiss Civil Code 1972) (judge is to decide cases in which a rule is unclear as if he were a legislator); Stone, *Legal Systems,* p. 29, note 21, and p. 189, note 124.

81. See Stone, *Legal Systems,* pp. 188–89.

82. See note 78; John Dickinson, "The Problem of the Unprovided Case," *University of Pennsylvania Law Review* 81 (1932): 115, 126.

83. Hart, *Concept of Law,* p. 181.

84. Cf. Sartorius, *Individual Conduct,* pp. 208–9. See also note 78.

85. Sartorius, *Individual Conduct,* p. 210.

86. Hart, *Concept of Law,* p. 149.

87. See Dworkin, "Social Rules," pp. 871–72.

88. See Hart, *Concept of Law,* p. 149.

89. Thus, it is hard to agree with Dworkin that uncertainty in this respect is somehow more fatal to positivism than uncertainty concerning a rare issue such as Parliament's power to bind future parliaments. See Dworkin, "Social Rules," p. 872. It is true that "hard cases" arise more frequently than cases involving Parliament's power to pass entrenching clauses; in that sense the disagreement over closure instructions is an issue judges must continually face. But unlike the case of judges in disagreement about what to do if Parliament *did* pass an entrenching clause, disputes about how one is to decide "hard cases" will largely escape detection in the actual outcome of cases given the practical difficulty of distinguishing between the exercise of weak discretion on the one hand and strong, but wise, discretion on the other. See text at notes 69-71.

For similar reasons the fact that judicial decisions are written as if there is a "right answer" does not prove the judges have accepted the rights thesis. Because of the practical problems of distinguishing strong from weak discretion, decisions are not likely to distinguish explicitly between the claim that a decision is "correct" as measured by pre-existing legal standards (a judicial opinion) and the claim that the decision is "correct" as measured by political or moral philosophy (a legislative opinion). Of course, in applying closure instructions applicable only to "hard cases," judges can make mistakes in deciding when they are dealing with such a case.

90. See Dworkin, "Social Rules," p. 877.

91. Raz and Sartorius both conclude that Dworkin is driven to this position when he attempts to maintain his thesis as a counterexample to positivism. See Raz, "Legal Principles," p. 844; Sartorius, *Individual Conduct,* p. 208. Dworkin, on the other hand, appears steadfastly to resist the suggestion that his thesis entails the inability to distinguish legal from nonlegal standards. Compare ibid., p. 206, with Dworkin, "Hard Cases," pp. 1105–6.

92. The accuracy of this description of Dworkin's position in comparison to classical natural law theory depends on how one resolves the confusion concerning whether Dworkin thinks legal and nonlegal standards can ever be separated. See note 91.

93. See Hart, *Concept of Law,* pp. 205–7.

2
Negative and Positive Positivism

Jules L. Coleman

Every theory about the nature or essence of law purports to provide a standard, usually in the form of a statement of necessary and sufficient conditions, for determining which of a community's norms constitute its law. For example, the naive version of legal realism maintains that the law of a community is constituted by the official pronouncements of judges. For the early positivists like Austin, law consists in the commands of a sovereign, properly so-called. For substantive natural law theory, in every conceivable legal system, being a true principle of morality is a necessary condition of legality for at least some norms. Legal positivism of the sort associated with H. L. A. Hart maintains that, in every community where law exists, there exists a standard that determines which of the community's norms are legal ones. Following Hart, this standard is usually referred to as a rule of recognition. If all that positivism meant by a rule of recognition were "the standard in every community by which a community's legal norms were made determinate," every theory of law would be reducible to one or another version of positivism. Which form of positivism each would take would depend on the particular substantive conditions of legality that each theory set out. Legal positivism would be true analytically, since it would be impossible to conceive of a theory of law that did not satisfy the minimal conditions for a rule of recognition. Unfortunately, the sort of truth legal positivism would then reveal would be an uninteresting one.

In order to distinguish a rule of recognition in the positivist sense from other statements of the conditions of legality, and therefore to distinguish positivism from alternative jurisprudential theses, additional constraints must be placed on the rule of recognition. Candidates for these constraints fall into two categories: restrictions on the conditions of legality set out in a rule of recognition; and constraints on the possible sources of authority (or normativity) of the rule of recognition.

An example of the first sort of constraint is expressed by the requirement that in every community the conditions of legality must be ones of pedigree or form, not substance or content. Accordingly, for a rule specifying the conditions of legality in any society to constitute a rule of recognition in the

---

From *The Journal of Legal Studies* 11, no. 1 (January 1982), 139–64. Reprinted by permission of the author, *The Journal of Legal Studies,* and The University of Chicago Press.

positivist sense, legal normativity under it must be determined, for example, by a norm's being enacted in the requisite fashion by a proper authority.

The claim that the authority of the rule of recognition is a matter of its acceptance by officials, rather than its truth as a normative principle, and the related claim that judicial duty under a rule of recognition is one of conventional practice rather than critical morality, express constraints of the second sort.

Ronald Dworkin expresses this second constraint as the claim that a rule of recognition in the positivist sense must be a social, rather than a normative, rule. A social rule is one whose authority is a matter of convention; the nature and scope of the duty it imposes is specified or constituted by an existing, convergent social practice. In contrast, a normative rule may impose an obligation or confer a right in the absence of the relevant practice or in the face of a contrary one. If a normative rule imposes an obligation, it does so because it is a correct principle of morality, not, *ex hypothesi,* because it corresponds to an accepted practice.

Dworkin, for one, conceives of the rule of recognition as subject to constraints of both sorts. His view is that only pedigree standards of legality can constitute rules of recognition, and that a rule of recognition must be a social rule.[1] Is legal positivism committed to either or both of these constraints on the rule of recognition?

I. NEGATIVE POSITIVISM

Candidates for constraints on the rule of recognition are motivated by the need to distinguish legal positivism from other jurisprudential theses: in particular, natural law theory. Positivism denies what natural law theory asserts: namely, a necessary connection between law and morality. I refer to the denial of a necessary or constitutive relationship between law and morality as the separability thesis. One way of asking whether positivism is committed to any particular kind of constraint on the rule of recognition is simply to ask whether any constraints on the rule are required by commitment to the separability thesis.

To answer this question we have to make some preliminary remarks concerning how we are to understand both the rule of recognition and the separability thesis. The notion of a rule of recognition is ambiguous; it has both an epistemic and a semantic sense. In one sense, the rule of recognition is a standard which one can use to identify, validate, or discover a community's law. In another sense, the rule of recognition specifies the conditions a norm must satisfy to constitute part of a community's law. The same rule may or may not be a rule of recognition in both senses, since the rule one employs to determine the law need not be the same rule as the one that makes law determinate. This ambiguity between the epistemic and semantic interpretations of the rule of recognition pervades the literature and is responsible for a good deal of confusion about the essential claims of legal positivism. In my view, legal positivism is committed to the rule of recognition in the semantic sense at least; whether it is committed to the rule of recognition as a standard for identifying law (epistemic sense) is a question to which we shall return later.

In the language that is fashionable in formal semantics, to say that the rule of recognition is a semantic rule is to say that it specifies the truth conditions for singular propositions of law of the form, "it is the law in *C* that *P*," where *C* is a particular community and *P* a putative statement of law. The question whether the separability thesis imposes substantive constraints on the rule of recognition is just the question whether the separability thesis restricts the conditions of legality for norms or the truth conditions for propositions of law.

The separability thesis is the claim that there exists at least one conceivable rule of recognition (and therefore one possible legal system) that does not specify truth as a moral principle among the truth conditions for any proposition of law.[2] Consequently, a particular rule of recognition may specify truth as a moral principle as a truth condition for some or all propositions of law without violating the separability thesis, since it does not follow from the fact that, in one community in order to be law a norm must be a principle of morality, being a true principle of morality is a necessary condition of legality in all possible legal systems.

It is tempting to confuse the separability thesis with the very different claim that the law of a community is one thing and its morality another. This last claim is seriously ambiguous. In one sense, the claim that the law of a community is one thing and its morality another may amount to the very strong assertion that there exists no convergence between the norms that constitute a community's law and those that constitute its morality. Put this way, the thesis is an empirical one whose inadequacies are demonstrated by the shared legal and moral prohibitions against murder, theft, battery, and the like.

Instead, the claim may be that one can identify or discover a community's law without having recourse to discovering its morality. This is an epistemic claim about how, in a particular community, one might go about learning the law. It may well be that in some communities—even those in which every legal norm is a moral principle as well—one can learn which norms are law without regard to their status as principles of morality. Whether in every community this is the case depends on the available sources of legal knowledge, not on the existence of a conceptual relationship, if any, between law and morality.

A third interpretation of the thesis that a community's law is one thing and its morality another, the one Dworkin is anxious to ascribe to positivism, is that being a moral principle is not a truth condition for any proposition of law (in any community). Put this way the claim would be false, just in case "it is the law in *C* that *P*" (for any community, *C*, and any proposition of law, *P*) were true only if *P* stated a (true) principle of morality. Were the separability thesis understood this way, it would require particular substantive constraints on each rule of recognition, that is, no rule of recognition could specify truth as a moral principle among its conditions of legality. Were legal positivism committed to both the rule of recognition and to this interpretation of the claim that the law and morality of a community are distinct, Dworkin's arguments in Model of Rules I (MOR-I) would suffice to put it to rest.

However, were the claim that the law of a community is one thing and its morality another understood, not as the claim that in every community law and morality are distinct, but as the assertion that they are conceptually distinguishable, it would be reducible to the separability thesis, for it would assert no more than the denial of a constitutive relationship between law and morality.

In sum, "the law of a community is one thing and its morality another," makes either a false factual claim, an epistemic claim about the sources of legal knowledge, or else it is reducible to the separability thesis. In no case does it warrant substantive constraints on particular rules of recognition.

Properly understood and adequately distinguished from the claim that the law and morality of a community are distinct, the separability thesis does not warrant substantive constraints on any particular rule of recognition. It does not follow, however, that the separability thesis imposes no constraints at all on any rule of recognition. The separability thesis commits positivism to the proposition that there exists at least one conceivable legal system in which the rule of recognition does not specify being a principle of morality among the truth conditions for any proposition of law. Positivism is true, then, just in case we can imagine a legal system in which being a principle of morality is not a condition of legality for any norm: that is, just as long as the idea of a legal system in which moral truth is not a necessary condition of legal validity is not self-contradictory.

The form of positivism generated by commitment to the rule of recognition as constrained by the separability thesis I call negative positivism to draw attention both to the character and the weakness of the claim it makes.[3] Because negative positivism is essentially a negative thesis, it cannot be undermined by counterexamples, any one of which will show only that, in some community or other, morality is a condition of legality at least for some norms.

II. POSITIVE POSITIVISM: LAW AS HARD FACTS

In MOR-I, Dworkin persuasively argues that in some communities moral principles have the force of law, though what makes them law is their truth or their acceptance as appropriate to the resolution of controversial disputes rather than their having been enacted in the appropriate way by the relevant authorities. These arguments would suffice to undermine positivism were it committed to the claim that truth as a moral principle could never constitute a truth condition for a proposition of law under any rule of recognition. The arguments are inadequate to undermine the separability thesis, which makes no claim about the truth conditions of any particular proposition of law in any particular community. The arguments in MOR-I, therefore, are inadequate to undermine negative positivism.

However, Dworkin's target in MOR-I is not really negative positivism; it is that version of positivism one would get by conjoining the rule of recognition with the requirement that the truth conditions for any proposition of law could not include reference to the morality of a norm. Moreover, in fairness to Dworkin, one has to evaluate his arguments in a broader context. In MOR-I Dworkin is anxious to demonstrate, not only the inadequacy of the separability thesis, but that of other essential tenets of positivism—or at least what Dworkin takes to be essential features of positivism—as well.

The fact that moral principles have the force of law, because they are appropriate, true, or accepted even though they are not formally enacted, establishes for Dworkin that: (1) the positivist's conception of law as rules must be abandoned; as must (2) the claim that judges exercise discretion—the authority to extend beyond the law to appeal to moral principles—to resolve controversial cases; and (3) the view that the law of every community can be identified by use of a noncontroversial or pedigree test of legality.

The first claim of positivism must be abandoned because principles, as well as rules, constitute legal norms; the second because, while positivists conceive of judges as exercising discretion by appealing to moral principles, Dworkin rightly characterizes them as appealing to moral principles, which, though they are not rules, nevertheless may be binding legal standards. The third tenet of positivism must be abandoned because the rule of recognition in Dworkin's view must be one of pedigree, that is, it cannot make reference to the content or truth of a norm as a condition of its legality; and any legal system that includes moral principles among its legal standards cannot have as its standard of authority a pedigree criterion.[4]

The question, of course, is whether positivism is committed to either judicial discretion, the model of rules, or to a pedigree or uncontroversial standard of legality. We know at least that it is committed to the separability thesis from which only negative positivism appears to follow. Negative positivism is committed to none of these claims. Is there another form of positivism that is so committed?

Much of the debate between the positivists and Dworkin appears rather foolish, unless there is a version of positivism that makes Dworkin's criticisms, if not compelling, at least relevant. That version of positivism, whatever it is, cannot be motivated by the separability thesis alone. The question then is whether anything other than its denial of the central tenet of natural law theory motivates positivism?

One easy, but ultimately unsatisfying, response is to maintain that Dworkin's objections are to Hart's version of positivism. While this is no doubt true, such a remark gives no indication of what it is in Hart's version of positivism that is essential to positivism generally. Dworkin, after all, takes his criticisms of Hart to be criticisms of positivism generally, and the question remains whether positivism is committed to the essentials of Hart's version of it.

A more promising line of argument is the following. No doubt positivism is committed to the separability thesis. Still, one can ask whether commitment to the separability thesis is basic or derivative from some other, perhaps programmatic, commitments of legal positivism. That is, one can look at the separability thesis in isolation or as a component, perhaps even a derivative element, of a network of commitments of legal positivism.[5] We are led to negative positivism when we pursue the former route. Perhaps there is a more interesting form of positivism in the cards if we pursue the latter.

Certainly one reason some positivists have insisted upon the distinction between law and morality is the following: While both law and morality provide standards by which the affairs of people are to be regulated, morality is inherently controversial. People disagree about what morality prescribes, and uncertainty exists concerning the limits of permissible conduct and the nature and scope of one's moral obligations to others. In contrast, for these positivists at least, law is apparently concrete and uncontroversial. Moreover, when a dispute arises over whether or not something is law, there exists a decision procedure that, in the bulk of cases, settles the issue. Law is knowable and ascertainable, so that, while a person may not know the range of his moral obligations, he is aware of (or can find out) what the law expects of him. Commitment to the traditional legal values associated with the rule of law requires that law consist in knowable, largely uncontroversial fact; and it is this feature of law that positivism draws attention to and which underlies it.

One can reach the same characterization of law as consisting in uncontroversial, hard facts by ascribing to legal positivism the epistemological and semantic constraints of logical positivism on legal facts. For the logical positivists, moral judgments were meaningless because they could not be verified by a reliable and essentially uncontroversial test. In order for statements of law to be meaningful, they must be verifiable by such a test (the epistemic conception of the rule of recognition). To be meaningful, therefore, law cannot be essentially controversial.

Once positivism is characterized as the view of law as consisting in hard facts, Dworkin's ascription of certain basic tenets to it is plausible, and his objections to them are compelling. First, law for positivism consists in rules rather than principles, because the legality of a rule depends on its formal characteristics—the manner and form of its enactment—whereas the legality of a moral principle will depend on its content. The legality of rules, therefore, will be essentially uncontroversial; the legal normativity of principles will be essentially controversial. Second, adjudication takes place in both hard and simple cases. Paradigm or simple cases are uncontroversial. The answer to them as a matter of law is clear, and the judge is obligated to provide it. Cases falling within the penumbra of a general rule, however, are uncertain. There is no uncontroversial answer as a matter of law to them, and judges must go beyond the law to exercise their discretion in order to resolve them. Controversy implies the absence of legal duty and, to the extent to which legal rules have controversial instances, positivism is committed to a theory of discretion in the resolution of disputes involving them. Third, positivism must be committed to a rule of recognition in both the epistemic and the semantic senses, for the rule of recognition not only sets out the conditions of legality, it provides the mechanism by which one settles disputes about what, on a particular matter, the law is. The rule of recognition for the positivist is the principle by which particular propositions of law are verified. Relatedly, the conditions of legality set forth in the rule of recognition must be ones of pedigree or form, otherwise the norm will fail to provide a reliable principle for verifying and adjudicating competing claims about the law. Finally, law and morality are distinct (the separability thesis) because law consists in hard facts, while morality does not.

Unfortunately for positivism, if the distinction between law and morality is motivated by commitment to law as uncontroversial, hard facts, it must be abandoned because, as Dworkin rightly argues, law is controversial, and even where it is, law may involve matters of obligation and right rather than discretion.

There is no more plausible way of understanding Dworkin's conception of positivism and of rendering his arguments against it (at least those in MOR-I) persuasive. The result is a form of positive positivism that makes an interesting claim about the essence of law—that by and large law consists in hard, concrete facts—a claim that Dworkin neatly shows is mistaken. The entire line of argument rests, however, on ascribing to legal positivism either a programmatic or metaphysical thesis about law. It is the thesis of law as hard facts—whether motivated by semantic, epistemic, or normative arguments—that explains not only positivism's commitment to the separability thesis, but its adherence to other claims about law, that is, discretion, the model of rules, and the noncontentful standard of legality.

The argument for law as hard facts that relies on the positivist program of knowable, ascertainable law is straightforwardly problematic. Legal positivism makes a conceptual or analytic claim about law, and that claim should not be confused with programmatic or normative interests certain positivists, especially Bentham, might have had. Ironically, to hold otherwise is to build into the conceptual account of law a particular normative theory of law; it is to infuse morality, or the way law ought to be, into the concept of law (or the account of the way law is). In other words, the argument for ascribing certain tenets to positivism in virtue of the positivist's normative ideal of law is to commit the very mistake positivism is so intent on drawing attention to and rectifying.

The argument for law as hard facts that relies, not on the programmatic interests of some positivists, but on the semantics and epistemology of logical positivism is both more plausible and interesting. Hart's characterization of his inquiry as an analysis both of the concept of law and of how one determines if a norm constitutes valid law as if these were one and the same thing suggests a conflation of semantic and epistemic inquiries of the sort one associates with logical positivism. Recall, in this regard, Hart's discussion of the move from the "prelegal" to the "legal." The move from the prelegal to the legal is accomplished by the addition of secondary rules to the set of primary social rules of obligation: in particular, by the addition of a rule of recognition that solves the problem of uncertainty, that is, the epistemic problem of determining which norms are law. Moreover Hart's discussion of judicial discretion—that is, the absence of legal duty—as arising whenever the application of a general term in a rule of law is controversial further suggests the identification, for Hart at least, of law with fact ascertainable by the use of a reliable method of verification. Still, in order to justify the ascription to positivism of the view that law consists in hard facts, we need an argument to the effect that part of what it means to be a legal positivist is to be committed to some form of verificationism.

The problem with any such argument is that the separability thesis can stand on its own as a fundamental tenet of positivism without further motivation. After all, verificationism may be wrong and the separability thesis right; without fear of contradiction one can assert both a (metaphysical) realist position about legal facts and the separability thesis. (As an aside, this fact alone should suffice to warrant caution in ascribing logical positivism to legal positivism on the grounds that they are both forms of positivism; otherwise one might be tempted to ascribe metaphysical or scientific realism to legal realism on similar grounds, which, to say the least, would be preposterous.)[6] In short, one alleging to be a positivist can abandon the metaphysics of verificationism, hang on to the separability thesis, and advance the rather plausible position that the motive for the separability thesis—if indeed there is one—is simply that the distinction it insists on between law and morality is a valid one; and, just in case that is not enough, the positivist can point out that there is a school of jurisprudence that denies the existence of the distinction. In effect, the positivist can retreat to negative positivism and justify his doing so by pointing out that the separability thesis needs no further motivation, certainly none that winds up committing the advocate of a sound jurisprudential thesis to a series of dubious metaphysical ones.

While I am sympathetic to this response, it is not going to satisfy Dworkin. There is something unsatisfactory about a theory of law that does not make an affirmative claim about law. Indeed, one might propose as an adequacy condition that any theory of law must have a point about law. Negative positivism fails to satisfy this adequacy condition. Natural law theory satisfies this adequacy condition by asserting that in every conceivable legal system moral truth is a necessary condition of legality—at least for some norms. Since it consists in the denial of this claim, negative positivism makes no assertion about what is true of law in every conceivable legal system. The view Dworkin rightly ascribes to Hart, but wrongly to positivism generally, that the point of positivism is that law consists in hard facts, meets the adequacy condition and makes the kind of claim, mistaken though it may be, that one can sink one's teeth into.

I want to offer an alternative version of positivism, which, like the "law-as-hard-facts" conception, is a form of positive positivism. The form of positive positivism I want to characterize and defend has, as its point, not that law is largely uncontroversial—it need not be—but that law is ultimately conventional: That the authority of law is a matter of its acceptance by officials.

III. POSITIVE POSITIVISM: LAW AS SOCIAL CONVENTION

It is well known that one can meet the objections to positivism Dworkin advances in MOR-I by constructing a rule of recognition (in the semantic sense) that permits moral principles as well as rules to be binding legal standards.[7] Briefly the argument is this: Even if some moral principles are legally binding, not every moral principle is a legal one. Therefore, a test must exist for distinguishing moral principles that are legally binding from those that are not. The characteristic of legally binding moral principles that distinguishes them from nonbinding moral principles can be captured in a clause in the relevant rule of recognition. In other words, a rule is a legal rule if it possesses characteristic C; and a moral principle is a legal principle if it possesses characteristic C_1. The rule of recognition then states that a norm is a legal one if and only if it possesses either C or C_1. Once this rule of recognition is formulated, everything Dworkin ascribes to positivism, other than the model of rules, survives. The (semantic) rule of recognition survives, since whether a norm is a legal one does not depend on whether it is a rule or a principle, but on whether it satisfies the conditions of legality set forth in a rule of recognition. The separability thesis survives just so long as not every conceivable legal system has in its rule of recognition a C_1 clause; that is, a clause that sets out conditions of legality for some moral principles, or if it has such a clause, there exists at least one conceivable legal system in which no principle satisfies that clause. Finally, one argument for judicial discretion—the one that relies not on controversy but on the exhaustibility of legal standards—survives. That is, only a determinate number of standards possess either *C* or C^1, so that a case may arise in which no legal standard under the rule of recognition is suitable or adequate to its resolution. In such cases, judges must appeal to nonlegal standards to resolve disputes.[8]

Given Dworkin's view of positivism as law consisting in hard facts, he might simply object to this line of defense by noting that the "rule of recognition" formed by the conjunction of the conditions of legality for both principles and rules could not be a rule of recognition in the positivist's sense because its reference to morality would make it inherently controversial. Put another way, a controversial rule of recognition could not be a rule of recognition in the epistemic sense; it could not provide a reliable verification principle. For that reason, it could not be a rule of recognition in the positivist sense. Interestingly, that is not quite the argument Dworkin advances. To be sure, he argues that a rule of recognition of this sort could not constitute a rule of recognition in the positivist's sense. Moreover, he argues that such a rule would be inherently controversial. But the argument does not end with the allegation that such a rule would be controversial. The controversial character of the rule is important for Dworkin, not because it is incompatible with law as hard fact or because a controversial rule cannot be a reliable verification principle, but because a controversial rule of recognition cannot be a social rule. A controversial rule of recognition cannot be a conventional one, or one whose authority depends on its acceptance.

At the outset of the essay I distinguished between two kinds of constraints that might be imposed on the rule of recognition: those having to do with substantive conditions of legality and those having to do with the authority of the rule of recognition itself. The difference between Dworkin's arguments against positivism in MOR-I and MOR-II is that, in the former essay, the version of positivism he objects to is constrained in the first way—legality must be determined by a noncontentful (or pedigree) test—whereas the version of positivism he objects to in MOR-II is constrained in the second way—the rule-of-recognition's authority must be a matter of convention.

Against the law-as-convention version of positivism, Dworkin actually advances four related arguments, none of which, I want to argue, is ultimately convincing. These are what I will refer to as: (1) the social rule argument; (2) the pedigree argument; (3) the controversy argument; and (4) the moral argument.[9]

A. The Social Rule Argument

Legal obligations are imposed by valid legal norms. A rule or principle is a valid one provided it satisfies the conditions of legality set forth in the rule of recognition. The question Dworkin raises in MOR-II concerns the nature of duties under rule of recognition itself. Does the rule of recognition impose duties on judges because they accept it or because the rule is defensible within a more comprehensive moral theory of law? For Dworkin this is the question of whether the rule of recognition is a social or a normative rule.

Dworkin's first argument in MOR-II against law-as-convention positivism is that the social rule theory provides an inadequate general theory of duty. The argument is this: According to the social rule theory an individual has an obligation to act in a particular way only if (1) there is a general practice of acting in that way; and (2) the rule that is constructed or built up from the practice is accepted from an internal point of view. To accept a rule from an internal point of view is to use it normatively as providing reasons both for acting in accordance with it and for criticizing departures from it. But, as Dworkin rightly notes, there may be duties even where no social practice exists, or where a contrary practice prevails. This is just another way of saying that not every duty is one of conventional morality.

If the positivist's thesis is that the social rule theory provides an adequate account of the source of all noninstitutional duties or of the meaning of all claims about such duties, it is surely mistaken. Not all duties imposed by rules are imposed by conventional rules. Fortunately, the law-as-convention version of positivism makes no such claim. The question is not whether the social rule theory is adequate to account for duties generally; it is whether the theory accounts for the duty of judges under a rule of recognition. An inadequate general theory of obligation may be an adequate theory of judicial duty. Were one to take the social rule argument seriously, it would amount to the odd claim that the rule of recognition cannot be a social rule and, therefore, that obligations under it could not be ones of conventional morality, simply because not every duty-imposing rule is a social rule.

B. The Pedigree Argument

The first serious argument Dworkin makes against the social rule theory of judicial obligation relies, in part, on the arguments in MOR-I. In meeting the objection to MOR-I, I constructed a rule of recognition that set out distinct conditions of legality for both rules (C) and moral principles (C_1). Let us abbreviate this rule as "C and C_1." Dworkin's claim is that such a rule cannot be a social rule.

The argument is this: The truth conditions in "$C + C_1$" make reference to moral principles as well as to legal rules. Unlike legal rules, moral principles cannot be identified by their pedigree. Because to determine which of a community's moral principles are legal ones will rely on the content of the principles, it will be a matter of some controversy. But it there is substantial controversy, then there cannot be convergence of behavior sufficient to specify a social rule. The social rule theory requires convergency of behavior, that is, a social practice. A nonpedigree standard implies controversy; controversy implies the absence of a social practice; the absence of the requisite social practice means that the rule cannot be a social rule. A rule of recognition that made reference to morality—the kind of rule of recognition we constructed to overcome Dworkin's objections in MOR-I—could not be a social rule and, therefore, could not be a rule of recognition in the positivist's sense.

The argument moves too quickly. Not every reference that a rule of recognition might make to morality would be inherently controversial. It does not follow from the fact that $C + C_1$ refers to moral principles that this rule cannot determine legality in virtue of some noncontent characteristic of moral principles. For example, C_1 could be an "entrenchment" requirement of the sort Rolf Sartorius has proposed, so that whether a moral principle is a legal principle will depend on whether it is mentioned in preambles to legislation and in other authoritative documents: The more mentions, the more weight the principle receives.[10] Or C_1 could state that a moral principle is a legal principle only if it is widely shared by members of the community. In short, the legality of a moral principle could be determined by some of its noncontentful characteristics. In such cases, to determine which moral principles are legally binding would be no more troublesome or controversial than to determine which rules are legal ones.

Though not every reference to morality will render a rule of recognition controversial, some ways of identifying which of a community's moral principles are law will. Suppose C_1 makes moral truth a condition of legality, so that a moral principle could not be part of a communty's law unless it were true. Whereas its entrenchment is not a controversial characteristic of a moral principle, its truth is. Any rule of recognition that made moral truth a condition of legality would be controversial. A controversial rule of recognition results in divergence of behavior sufficient to undermine its claim to being a social rule. If a rule of recognition is not a social rule, it cannot be a rule of recognition in the positivist's sense.

Not every possible rule of recognition, therefore, would be a social rule. For example, "the law is whatever is morally right" could never be a rule of recognition in the positivist's sense. Because positivism of the sort I want to defend holds that law is everywhere conventional—that (in the language of this discussion) the rule of recognition in every community is a social rule—it must be mistaken.

C. The Controversy Argument

Dworkin's view is that the rule of recognition in any jurisdiction is either a social rule or a normative rule; it imposes a duty, in other words, either because it is accepted or because it is true. Law-as-convention positivism is the view that, in every community, the rule of recognition is a social rule. At this level, negative positivism is the view that, in at least one conceivable community, the rule of recognition is a social rule. Natural law theory would then be the view that, in every conceivable legal system, the rule of recognition is a normative rule. Dworkin's claim is that the rule of rcognition is a normative rule, and therein lies the justification for placing him within the natural law tradition.

The argument in the previous section is compatible with some rules of recognition being normative rules and others being social rules. For example, a rule of recognition that made no reference to morality or, if it did, referred only to noncontentful features of moral principles, might, for all that the previous argument shows, still be a social rule. If it were, Dworkin's arguments, based on the controversial nature of rules of recognition that refer to morality, would be inadequate to establish the normative theory of law.

What Dworkin needs is an argument that no rule of recognition can be a social rule: That regardless of the conditions of legality it sets forth, no rule of recognition can account for certain features of law unless it is a normative rule. Dworkin has such an argument and it appears to be this: Regardless of the specific conditions of legality it sets forth, every rule of recognition will give rise to controversy at some point. For example, a rule that made no reference to morality could still give rise to controversy concerning either the weight to be given to precedent, or the question of whether—and if so, to what extent—the present legislature could bind a future one. Though the rule itself would not be controversial, particular instances of it would be. Were the rule of recognition a social rule, it could not impose duties on judges in such controversial cases. The existence of judicial duties in controversial cases can only be explained by interpreting the rule of recognition as a normative rule.

This argument relies on the fact that even rules of recognition which are by and large uncontroversial will have controversial applications. In those controversial cases, the social rule interpretation of the rule of recognition could not account for the rule's imposing an obligation on judges. That is because, in the social rule theory, obligations derive from convergent practice; and in both the controversial, as well as the as yet unresolved, cases there exists no convergent practice or opinion from which an obligation might derive.

The rule of recognition is either a social rule or a normative rule. If it imposes obligations in controversial cases, it cannot be a social rule. Therefore, if the rule of recognition imposes a duty upon judges in controversial cases, it must be a normative rule. Because the rule of recognition in every community is a normative rule, the obligations of judges under it are ones of critical rather than conventional morality; and the ultimate authority of law is a matter of morality, not convention.

The argument from controversy presupposes that judges are bound by duty, even in controversial cases, under the rule of recognition. Positivism, it appears, is committed to judicial discretion in such cases and is, therefore, unable to explain either the source or nature of the duty. Because the social rule theory of judicial obligation is unable to explain the fact of judicial obligtion in controversial cases, it must be false and, therefore, its alternative, the normative rule theory, true.

One response a positivist might make to Dworkin's argument is to deny that in such cases judges are bound by duty, in which case the failure of the social rule theory to account for judicial duty would not be troublesome. Dworkin quickly dismisses the plausibility of this response with the offhand remark that such a view likens law to a game in which the participants agree in advance that there are no right answers and no duties where sufficient controversy or doubt exists regarding the requirements of a rule. The analogy to a game is supposed to embarrass positivism, but it need not. Anyone even superficially familiar with Hart's work knows that the bulk of examples he draws upon to illustrate his claims about rules, law, and the nature of adjudication are drawn from games like baseball and chess. So the positivist might welcome, rather than eschew, the analogy to games.

Whether it is advanced to support or to criticize positivism, the alleged analogy to games is unsatisfying. The more interesting tack is to suppose along with Dworkin that judges may be obligated by a rule of recognition, even in its controversial applications, and then ask whether, in spite of Dworkin's arguments to the contrary, the social rule theory can explain this feature of law.

D. The Moral Argument

That Dworkin takes judicial obligations in cases involving controversial applications of the rule of recognition to be ones of critical morality rather than conventional practice is illustrated by the moral argument. Unlike the previous arguments I have outlined, the moral argument is direct and affirmative in the sense that, instead of trying to establish the inadequacies of the social rule theory, its purpose is to provide direct support for the normative interpretation of the rule of recognition. The argument is simply this: In resolving hard or controversial cases that arise under the rule of recognition, judges do not typically cite the practice or opinions of other judges. Because these cases are controversial, there exists no convergent practice among judges to cite. Instead, in order to resolve these disputes, judges typically appeal to principles of political morality. For example, in determining how much weight to give precedent, judges may apply alternative conceptions of fairness. If, as the social rule theory claims, the source of a judge's duty depends on the rule or principle he cites as its basis, the sources of judicial obligation in these controversial cases are the principles of political morality judges cite as essential to the resolution of the dispute. The duty of judges in controversial cases can only be explained if the rule of recognition is a normative one whose authority depends on its moral merits; whose normativity, in other words, depends on moral argument of precisely the sort judges appear to engage in.

E. Summary

Dworkin has three distinct, powerful arguments against law-as-convention positivism. Each argument has a slightly different character and force. The point of the pedigree argument is that a rule of recognition that makes reference to the content of moral principles as a condition of their legality will spur controversy and, because it will, it cannot be a social rule, or, therefore, a rule of recognition in the positivist's sense. The argument is weak in the sense that, even if sound, it would be inadequate to establish the normative account of the rule of recognition. Only controversial rules of recognition fail to be social rules; for all the argument shows, uncontroversial rules of recognition may be social rules.

The more general argument from controversy appears to fill the gap left by the pedigree argument. Here the argument is not that every rule of recognition will be systematically controversial. Instead, the argument relies on the plain fact that even basically uncontroversial rules of recognition will have controversial instances. The social rule theory cannot account for judicial obligation in the face of controversy. If the rule of recognition imposes an obligation on judges in controversial cases, as Dworkin presumes it does, the obligation can be accounted for only if the rule is a normative one whose capacity to impose a duty does not depend on widespread convergence of conduct or opinion. The point of the argument can be put in weaker or stronger terms. One can say simply that obligations in controversial cases exist and positivism cannot account for them; or one can put the point in terms of natural law theory as the claim that the duties that exist are ones of critical morality, rather than conventional practice.

The point of the moral argument is that, in resolving hard cases, judges appear to rely on principles of political morality rather than on convergent social practice. Judges apparently believe that they are bound to resolve these controversies and, more important, that their duty to resolve them in one way rather than another depends on the principles of morality to which they appeal.

IV. CONVENTION AND CONTROVERSY

Each of the objections to the social rule theory can be met.[11] Consider the pedigree argument first, that is, the claim that a rule of recognition which refers to morality—which has a C_1 clause satisfied by some norm—will be controversial and, therefore, cannot be a social rule of recognition. Suppose the clause in the rule of recognition states: The law is whatever is morally correct. The controversy among judges does not arise over the content of the rule of recognition itself. It arises over which norms satisfy the standards set forth in it. The divergence in behavior among officials as exemplified in their identifying different standards as legal ones does not establish their failure to accept the same rule of recognition. On the contrary, judges accept the same truth conditions for propositions of law, that is, that law consists in moral truth. They disagree about which propositions satisfy those conditions. While there may be no agreement whatsoever regarding which standards are legal ones—since there is no agreed upon standard for determining the truth of a moral principle—there is complete agreement among judges concerning the standard of legality. That judges reach different conclusions regarding the law of a community does not mean that they are employing different standards of legality. Since disagreement concerning which principles satisfy the rule of recognition presupposes that judges accept the same rule of recognition, the sort of controversy envisaged by the pedigree argument is compatible with the conventionalist account of the authority of the rule of recognition.

Notice, however, that were we to understand the rule of recognition epistemically, as providing a reliable test for identifying law, rather than as specifying truth conditions for statements of law, the sort of controversy generated by a rule of recognition like the law is whatever is morally right would be problematic, since the proposed rule of recognition would be incapable of providing a reliable test for identifying legal norms. This just draws our attention once again both to the importance of distinguishing between the epistemic and semantic interpretations of the rule of recognition, and to the necessity of insisting upon the semantic interpretation of it.

Even on the semantic interpretation, the phrase "controversy in the rule of recognition" is ambiguous. Controversy may arise, as it does in the previous case, over which norms satisfy the conditions of legality set forth in the rule of recognition; or it can arise over the conditions of legality set out in the rule of recognition. Cases of the first sort are the ones Dworkin envisions arising from a rule of recognition that includes a clause specifying legality conditions for moral principles. These cases are not problematic because controversy presupposes agreement about and acceptance of the rule of recognition. In contrast, the claim that every rule of recognition will be controversial in some of its details is precisely the claim that, in some cases, controversy will arise over the content or proper formulation of the rule of recognition itself. The question that these cases pose is not whether judges agree about which norms satisfy the same rule of recognition; rather, it is whether judges can be said to be applying the same rule. Since the social rule theory requires of the rule of recognition that its formulation be specified by convergence of behavior or belief, the controversy concerning the proper formulation of the rule means that the rule cannot be a social rule and, therefore, not a rule of recognition in the positivist's sense.

One way of interpreting Dworkin's claim is that, wherever controversy exists in the proper formulation of a rule, the rule cannot be a conventional or social rule. This is counterintuitive, since all rules—those of conventional as well as critical morality—are vague at points and, therefore, their application in some contexts will be controversial. If we take Dworkin to be making the argument that the existence of controversy is straightforwardly incompatible with the idea of a social rule, then no rule could ever be a social rule. Certainly, in spite of the controversial nature of all rules governing behavior, we are able to distinguish (at least in broad terms) the conventional rules from those whose authority depends on their truth.

A more sympathetic and plausible reading of Dworkin is that he does not mean to contest the existence of social rules. Instead his claim is that social rules cannot account for duties beyond the range of convergent practice. Social rules cannot explain duties in controversial cases. With respect to the rule of recognition, the social rule theory cannot account for the obligation of judges to give the correct formulation of the rule of recognition in its controversial instances. On the assumption that judges have such an obligation, the social rule theory fails. Only a normative interpretation of the rule of recognition can explain the duty in cases of divergent opinions or conduct, since the duty, according to the normative theory, does not derive from convergent practice but from sound moral argument.

Schematically, Dworkin's argument is as follows:

1. Every rule of recognition will be controversial with respect to its scope and, therefore, with respect to the nature and scope of the obligations it imposes.
2. Nevertheless, in resolving disputes involving controversial aspects of the rule, judges are under an obligation, as they are in the uncontroversial cases, to give the right answer.
3. The social rule theory which requires convergence of behavior as a condition of an obligation cannot account for the obligation of judges in 2.
4. Therefore, positivism cannot account for judicial obligation in 2.
5. Therefore, only a normative theory of law in which the duty of judges depends on moral argument rather than convergent practice can account for judicial duty in 2.

As I suggested earlier, a positivist might respond by denying the truth of 2, that is, that judges are obligated in controversial cases in which behavior and opinion diverge. Hart, for one, denies 2, and he appears to do so because he accepts 3. That he denies 2 is made evident by his characterizing these kinds of cases as involving "uncertainty in the rule of recognition" in which "all that succeeds is success." If a positivist were to deny 2 to meet Dworkin's objections on the grounds that he (the positivist) accepts 3, it would be fair to accuse him of begging the question. He would be denying the existence of judicial obligation simply because his theory cannot account for it. Moreover, from a strategic point of view, it would be better to leave open the question of whether such duties exist, rather than to preclude the very possibility of their existence as a consequence of the theory; otherwise any argument that made the existence of such duties conceivable would have the effect of completely undermining the theory. Notice, however, that Dworkin is led to an analogous position, since his argument for the normative theory of law (i.e., 5) requires that judges are under obligations in every conceivable controversial case (i.e., 2). The social rule theory logically precludes judicial obligation in such cases; the normative theory requires it. Both theories of law will fail, just in case the existence of judicial duty in controversial cases involving the rule of recognition is a contingent feature of law. In other words, if it turns out that in some legal systems judges have an obligation to provide a particular formulation of the rule of recognition when controversy arises over its proper formulation, whereas in other legal systems no such duty exists and judges are free to exercise discretion—at least until one or another formulation takes hold—both the theory that logically precludes judicial duties in all controversial cases, and that which logically entails such duties, will fail.

Denying the existence of the duties to which Dworkin draws attention is a strategy that will not serve the positivist well. One alternative would be to admit the existence of the duty in some cases, but to give up the social rule theory according to which the nature and scope of a duty are completely specified by convergent practice in favor of some other theory concerning the way in which conventional or social rules give rise to duties. This is a promising line of argument I am not prepared to discuss here. However, it seems to me that the discussion of conventions in David Lewis's brilliant book, *Convention,*[12] might provide the theoretical foundations for an alternative to the standard social rule theory. Briefly, the idea is that the duties imposed by social rules or conventions are the results of expectations that arise from efforts to coordinate behavior. Vested, warranted expectations may extend beyond the area of convergent practice, in which case the obligations to which a social rule gives rise might cover controversial, as well as uncontroversial, cases.[13]

Another alternative strategy, the one I have been trying to develop, follows the social rule theory in restricting the duty imposed by a conventional rule to the area of convergent practice. In this view, if controversy arises in the rule of recognition itself, it does not follow that the judges are free to exercise discretion in providing a formulation of the rule. What counts is not whether controversy exists, but whether there exists a practice among judges of resolving the controversy in a particular way. And to answer the question of whether such a practice exists, we do not look to the rule of recognition—whose conditions of legality are presumably in dispute—but to the social rule constituted by the behavior of judges in applying the rule of recognition. Whether a duty exists will depend, in part, on whether the judges have developed an accepted social practice of resolving these controversies in a particular way.

Suppose that, in applying the rule of recognition, judges have developed a practice of resolving controversial instances of it. Suppose further that in some jurisdictions, for example, the United States and England, judges, by and large, resolve such disputes, as Dworkin believes they do, by providing arguments of principle; so that in determining, for example, whether and to what extent the Supreme Court can review the constitutionality of federal legislation, judges argue from principles of political morality, for example, the separation of powers and so on. According to Dworkin, we would have a controversy in the rule of recognition itself that judges would be required to resolve in the appropriate way; and the obligation of judges would derive from principles of morality that constitute the best argument. This is the essence of what I referred to as the "moral argument," and it would show that the rule of recognition is a normative, not a social, rule.

For the traditional positivist, we would have a case in whch no obligation existed, where all that succeeded was success: A case in which the judges' recourse to the principles of political morality necessarily involved an exercise of discretion.

Both of these positions are mistaken. If, as Dworkin supposes, judges as a general rule look to moral principles in resolving controversial features of the rule of recognition, then there exists a practice among them of resolving controversial aspects of the rule of recognition in that way; that is, as the moral argument suggests judges in the United States and Britain do. If this is, in fact, the practice of judges in constitutional democracies like ours—as it must be if Dworkin's arguments are to be taken seriously—and if the practice is critically accepted by judges, then there is a legal duty even in controversial cases: A duty that does not derive from the principles judges cite (as in Dworkin) but from their acceptance of the practice of resolving these disputes by offering substantive moral arguments. All Dworkin's arguments really show is that judges have adopted critically the practice that the best moral argument wins, which explains both their appeal to substantive moral principles and, contrary to the traditional positivist, their duty to do so.

What, in Dworkin's view, is evidence for the normative theory of the rule of recognition—that is, general and widespread appeal to moral principle to resolve controversies in it—is, in my view, evidence of the existence of a social practice among judges of resolving such disputes in a particular way; a practice that specifies part of the social rule regarding judicial behavior. The appeal to substantive moral argument is, then, perfectly compatible with the conventionalist account of law.

To argue that the appeal to moral argument is compatible with the conventionalist account is not to establish that account, since the appeal to moral argument as a vehicle of dispute resolution is also consistent with the normative theory of law. One could argue that, at most, my argument shows only that Dworkin's arguments, which rely on both the controversial nature of law and the appeal to moral principle to resolve controversy, are inadequate to undermine positivism. We need some further reasons to choose between the normative and conventional theories of law.

Dworkin has taken the "acid test" for positivism to be whether it can account for judicial behavior in jurisdictions, such as the United States and England, in whch both prospective litigants and judges believe that disputes which arise because of controversy in the rule of recognition are to be resolved, not by discretion, but by principled argument. His arguments are all to the effect that positivism cannot account for either the expectations of litigants or the behavior of judges, because positivism is committed to discretion whenever controversy arises. If controversy arises in a rule subordinate to the rule of recognition, positivism is committed to discretion in virtue of the theory of language it adopts that makes so much of the difference between "core" and "penumbra" instances of general terms. If controversy arises in the rule of recognition itself, positivism is committed to discretion because the rule of recognition is a social rule specified by the behavior of judges; and a social rule can impose an obligation only to the extent behavior converges, that is, only in the absence of controversy. I have argued that, contrary to Dworkin, positivism can, in fact, account for the obligations of judges in controversial instances of the rule of recognition, since the existence of controversy does not preclude the existence of conformity of practice in resolving it. If I am correct, neither the existence of controversy nor the appeal to moral argument in certain jurisdictions as necessary to its resolution are incompatible with law-as-convention positivism. What then is the acid test?

For the normative theory of law to be correct, judges must be under a legal obligation to resolve controversies arising in every conceivable rule of recognition by reliance on substantive moral argument. That is because Dworkin's version of the normative theory entails the existence of judicial duty in all cases, and because the resolution of the dispute must involve moral argument. After all, if the rule of recognition is, as Dworkin claims, a normative rule, then its authority rests on sound moral argument and the resolution of disputes concerning its scope must call for moral argument. Were judges to rely on anything else, the authority of the rule of recognition will not be a matter of its moral merits; or if they appeal to nothing at all, then in such jurisdictions we would have reason to believe that judges are under no particular obligation to resolve a controversy in the rule of recognition.

The real acid test seems to be not whether positivism of the sort I am developing can account for judicial obligations in the kinds of cases we are discussing, but whether these obligations constitute a necessary feature of law which, in every jurisdiction, is imposed by moral principle. As long as the existence of such duties is a contingent feature of law, as is the duty to resolve disputes by appealing to moral argument, the normative theory of law is a less plausible account than is the conventionalist theory. Indeed, it seems straighforwardly false, since we can imagine immature legal systems (which are legal systems nonetheless) in which no practice for resolving disputes in the rule of recognition has as yet developed—where all that succeeds is success. Or we could imagine the development of considerably less attractive practices for resolving such disputes, for example, the flip of a coin: heads, defendant wins; tails, plaintiff does. In the first sort of legal system, it would seem odd to say judges were legally bound to resolve such disputes (though they might always be morally bound to do so), since no practice had as yet developed. Eventually, such a practice is likely to develop, and the range of judicial discretion will narrow as the practice becomes widespread and critically accepted. As the second example shows, the practice that finally develops need not conform to judicial practice in the United States and England. Though judicial discretion narrows as the range of judicial obligation expands, it may do so in a way that is considerably less attractive than the moral argument envisions; in a way that is, in fact, less attractive than a system in which all that succeeded was success.

Unlike traditional positivism, which has trouble explaining judicial behavior in mature legal systems, and the normative theory of law, which has difficulty explaining developing and immature legal systems (for the reasons that the first precludes obligations in controversial cases, while the second requires them), law-as-convention positivism understands such duties to be a contingent feature of law that can be explained as arising from the critical acceptance of a practice of dispute resolution, rather than from the principles of morality which judges under one kind of practice might cite.

V. CONCLUSION

Dworkin makes three correct observations about the controversial nature of some legal standards.

1. A legal system can (and does in the United States and Britain) recognize certain standards as part of the law even though they are "essentially controversial" in the sense that there may be disagreements among judges as to which these are, and there is no decision procedure which, even in principle, can demonstrate what they are, and so settle disagreements.

2. Among such essentially controversial legal standards are moral principles owing their status as law to their being "true" moral principles, though their "truth" cannot be demonstrated by any agreed upon test.

3. The availability of such controversial principles fills the "gaps" left by ordinary sources of law, which may be partially indeterminate, vague, or conflicting. So that, at least with respect to the resolution of disputes involving standards subordinate to the rule of recognition, a judge never has to exercise lawmaking power or "discretion" to fill the gaps or remove the indeterminacy if such moral principles are a part of the law.

In this essay, I have drawn distinctions among three versions of positivism and have discussed their relationship to Dworkin's claims: (1) "Negative positivism," the view that the legal system need not recognize as law "controversial" moral standards; (2) "positive, hard-facts positivism," the view that controversial standards cannot be regarded as law and, hence, rejects Dworkin's three points; (3) "positive, social rule positivism," which insists only on the conventional status of the rule of recognition but accepts Dworkin's three points.

Since the inclusion of controversial moral principles is not a necessary feature of the concept of law, Dworkin's arguments to the effect that such principles figure in judicial practice in the United States and in Britain, are inadequate to undermine the very weak claim of negative positivism. On the other hand, if Dworkin is right—and I am inclined to think that he is—in thinking that controversial moral principles sometimes figure in legal argument, then any form of positivism that is committed to the essentially noncontroversial nature of law is mistaken. Finally, what I have tried to do is to develop a form of positivism which accepts the controversial nature of some legal reasoning, while denying that this is incompatible with the essential, affirmative claim of the theory that law is everywhere conventional in nature. If I am correct, there is a form of positivism which can do justice to Dworkin's insights while rendering his objections harmless.

NOTES

1. Dworkin's claim that positivism is committed to a pedigree standard of legality is too narrow. What he means to argue, I believe, is that positivism is committed to some form of "noncontentful" criterion of legality, of which a pedigree standard would be one. For ease of exposition, I will use "pedigree test" broadly to mean any sort of noncontentful criterion of legality.

2. The phrase "truth as a moral principle as a condition of legality" does seem a bit awkward. However, any other phrase, such as "morality as a condition of legality" or "moral contents as a condition of legality," would be ambiguous, since it would be unclear whether the separability thesis was a claim about the relationship between law and critical morality or between law and conventional morality. My understanding of the separability thesis is a denial of a constitutive relationship between law and critical morality.

3. This seems to be in the form of positivism David Lyons advances to meet Dworkin's objections to positivism. Cf. David Lyons, "Review: *Principles, Positivism, and Legal Theory*," *Yale Law Journal* 87 (1977): 415.

4. But see Rolf Sartorius, "Social Policy and Judicial Legislation," *American Philosophical Quarterly* 8 (1971): 151; Jules Coleman, "Review, *Taking Rights Seriously*," *California Law Review* 66 (1978): 885.

5. The following characterization of positivism in virtue of motivations for the separability thesis was developed after numerous discussions with Professor Dworkin. I am particularly grateful to him for remarks, but it is likely that I have not put the characterizations as well as he would have.

6. That is because legal realism is skeptical about the existence of legal facts. Legal facts are "created" by official action; they are not "out there" to be discovered by judges. Scientific or metaphysical realism maintains exactly the opposite view of facts.

7. See note 4.

8. Often overlooked is the fact that there are two distinct arguments for discretion: One relies on the controversial nature of penumbra cases involving general terms; the other relies on the finiteness of legal standards. The first argument is actually rooted in a theory of language; the second, which would survive a rejection of that theory, relies on gaps in the law. See Coleman, "Review, *Taking Rights Seriously*."

9. Dworkin does not explictly distinguish among these various arguments, nor does he label any of them. The labels and distinctions are mine.

10. Sartorius, "Social Policy," p. 151; Dworkin himself discusses, but wrongly rejects this possibility; see "Model of Rules I" in *Taking Rights Seriously* (1977), p. 977. See also C. L. Ten's useful discussion, "The Soundest Theory of Law," *Mind* 88 (1979): 522.

11. There are two ways in which we might understand the notion of a social rule. Under one interpretation, not every rule of recognition would be a social rule; under the other, each would be. As both Hart and Dworkin use the term, a social rule is specified by behavior. It cannot be formulated in the absence of a practice, and the nature of the practice determines the scope of the rule and the extent of the duties it imposes. The rule that men must doff their hats upon entering church is a social rule in this sense. Not every rule of recognition, however, is a social rule in this sense for two reasons. First, at least in some jurisdictions, the content of the rule may be specified prior to the existence of an appropriate practice. For example, the formulation of the Constitution of the United States did not require the existence of the relevant judicial practice; it preceded the practice. No doubt ambiguities and other uncertainties in the rule are resolved through judicial

practice; nevertheless, the general form and nature of the rule had been specified without regard to practice. Second, whereas Dworkin's contrast between social rule and normative rule theories of law turns on the manner in which legal rules give rise to duties, the rule of recognition is not itself a duty-imposing rule. We might construct a broader notion of a social rule. In this sense a rule will be a social rule if its existence or authority depends, in part, on the existence of a social practice. Here the requirement is not that the rule's proper formulation be specified by practice. Instead, the claim is that the authority of the rule depends on the existence of a practice. The rule itself may be specifiable, at least in general terms and at some points in time, without regard to the practice. However, in the absence of the practice, the rule is empty in that it is incapable of providing justifications for action. In short, its normativity depends on the practice, though its content need not be specified by it. Every rule of recognition for the positivist is a social rule in this sense.

12. David Lewis, *Convention: A Philosophical Study* (1969).

13. Gerald Postema has been trying to develop an alternative to the social rule theory that relies heavily on Lewis's theory of conventions. See Gerald J. Postema, "Coordination and Convention at the Foundations of Law," *Journal of Legal Studies* 11 (1982): 165.

3
Moral Aspects of Legal Theory

David Lyons

The "separation" of law and morals is a dividing line in legal theory: legal positivists are supposed to embrace the doctrine and natural lawyers to reject it. But the meaning of the doctrine and its relation to legal theories are not as clear as this assumes.

Many who endorse the doctrine employ the formula suggested by Hart: "that there is no necessary connection between law and morals or law as it is and ought to be."[1] No one denies that law and moral beliefs influence each other, so this formula is taken to mean that there are no conceptual connections between law and moral principles.

But Hart's formulation seems unsatisfactory. Hart himself appears to argue, for example, that a principle of justice concerning the application of the law to particular cases can be derived from the concept of law, and thus he seems to assert a conceptual connection between law and moral principles.[2] But this does not temper Hart's endorsement of the separation thesis. If Hart is not inconsistent, the doctrine must be understood differently.

Most defenders of the separation thesis rely on the possiblity or actual examples of immoral laws. If this is the foundation of the doctrine, it cannot claim very much. It might be understood to say that law is subject to moral appraisal and does not automatically satisfy the standards by which it may properly be judged. In brief, law is morally fallible. I shall call this the Minimal Separation Thesis.

The Minimal Thesis fails, however, to distinguish legal positivists from natural lawyers, few of whom hold that law is morally infallible. Aquinas, for example, quite plainly says, "Laws framed by man are either just or unjust."[3] This seems to place no strain on his theory of law. And the same applies to other natural lawyers, such as Fuller.[4]

The Minimal Thesis might nevertheless be thought to have some special relation to positivistic thinking about the law. Positivism might be thought to offer a distinctive rationale for the doctrine, while natural law merely accommodates it. That is the possibility I shall explore.

Reprinted from "Moral Aspects of Legal Theory," *Midwest Studies in Philosophy,* Volume 7, 1982. Used by permission of the author and the editors. (Sections 3–6 of the original are reprinted here.)

I. ANALYTIC JURISPRUDENCE AND THE MINIMAL THESIS

Individual positivists have had specific theories about the nature of law that might warrant their support of the Minimal Separation Thesis. If law is believed to be determined by conditions such as Austin or Hart identified, for example, then one might well be justified in thinking that law is morally fallible. Take Austin as a case in point. Austin claims that something is required by law just when it is coercively commanded by some determinate individual or set of individuals, whose coercive commands are generally complied with by the members of a community, and who do not generally comply with the coercive commands of any other human being. This imposes no recognizable moral conditions on what can count as law, and Austin clearly intends his theory to allow that laws be either just or unjust.

It seems reasonable to suppose that Austin is right—that such coercive commands might be either just or unjust. But we must be careful here, since this does not follow from the Austinian analysis alone. For all we can tell so far, the conditions that determine when something is required by law might imply conditions that determine when something is good, right, just, or the opposite. We need more than a theory of law to generate the separation thesis. We need some information about the relations between the conditions that are supposed to determine law and the conditions that determine moral value. I shall return to this point a bit later.

Even if we could infer a separation thesis from specific theories of law, such as Austin's, that would not provide us with the answer to our original question, which concerned the relations between legal positivism as a general type of theory and that doctrine. We need to consider what is distinctive of and also common to positivistic thinking about the law.

It is not easy to define legal positivism, to identify its central tenets or assumptions. Hart offers us some help when he surveys several doctrines that have been associated with positivism. He points out that some are not accepted by all positivists. The residue might help us understand what positivism represents.

Hart's survey includes the following five doctrines: (1) the imperative theory of law, or the idea that law is a coercive command; (2) the separation of law and morals; (3) a distinction between the analytic study of legal concepts (which we can call analytic jurisprudence) and other studies of law, such as inquiries concerning the history of law, the relation between law and other social phenomena, and the normative standards to be used in appraising law; (4) formalism, or mechanical jurisprudence, which holds that a given body of law at a given time is capable of providing a unique answer to every legal question that arises and "in which correct legal decisions can be deduced from predetermined legal rules by logical means alone"; and (5) moral skepticism, or the idea that "moral judgments cannot be established, as statements of fact can, by rational argument, evidence or proof."[5]

Three of these doctrines cannot be used to define legal positivism. The imperative theory of law, though advanced by Bentham and Austin, is rejected by Hart and other positivists; few positivists have been moral skeptics; and few, if any, positivists endorse mechanical jurisprudence.

The only two doctrines that survive Hart's survey are the separation thesis and the distinction between analytic jurisprudence and other inquiries concerning law. These are accepted by Hart and, apparently, by positivists generally. But these two doctrines seem incapable of defining a school of legal theory. They tell us little about the law or how to go about understanding it. Hart's survey seems to leave the idea of legal positivism with too little content. Is there anything else that we can add?

One point that Hart fails to mention is what might be called the social conception of law. This idea, which seems central to legal positivism, is, very roughly, the notion that law is firmly rooted in social facts. Let us add this to our list and consider its relations to the separation thesis.

First let us consider the relations between the Minimal Separation Thesis and analytic jurisprudence. The latter is concerned with distinctively legal concepts, including the concept of law itself, as well as the nature and essential structure of legal systems. The idea that there can be such an inquiry, distinct from a study of, say, the standards that may be used in appraising law, tells us nothing about the separation of law and morals. And it would seem contrary to the spirit of such an inquiry to assume that law and other legal concepts have no significant connections with moral concepts. For that is precisely what such an inquiry is supposed to determine.

It is sometimes suggested that analytic jurisprudence must be value-neutral, but it is unclear what this should be taken to mean. It might mean that we should not enter upon such an inquiry with the assumption that law has any special relations to morality. But neither should we assume the contrary. So far as the idea of analytic jurisprudence is concerned, the possibility of conceptual relations between law and morals is an open question.

The idea that analytic jurisprudence should be value-neutral might also be taken to mean that one can engage in the study of legal concepts without considering any substantive moral values. But it is unclear why one should wish to do this, especially if one wishes to determine whether there are any significant connections between law and morality.

Positivists have generally presented their theories of law as if they were trying to describe the concept of law, the essential nature of law, or something else similarly given. If one believes that morality is not similarly "given," then one might think it appropriate to proceed by ignoring moral issues in the analytic study of law. But this would be mistaken, in two ways.

First, it would be a mistake to assume that morality, in the relevant sense, is not similarly "given." If there are true as well as false, correct as well as incorrect, sound as well as unsound answers to moral questions, then morality is as much a "given" as anything else that might be investigated. There seems no reason to assume the contrary here, and only a radical moral skeptic should be tempted to do so. Since moral skepticism is not a defining feature of legal positivism or a position endorsed by most positivists, this is not an approach that should be identified with positivistic theory.

Second, it may turn out that moral notions, or notions that are common to both law and morality, are needed for a proper understanding of law. Consider, for example, the idea of a justified judicial decision. This is a problematic notion, which may be given a weak or a strong interpretation. On the weak interpretation, justifying a legal decision is like placing a mere label on past or future conduct. It has no implications concerning how one should behave or should have behaved beyond, perhaps, what considerations of prudence might determine. One whose past or future conduct has been so labeled may proceed, in good conscience, to ignore such declarations. On the strong interpretation, justifying a legal decision is establishing how someone should behave or should have behaved, in good conscience. On this interpretation, a justified judicial decision is not a morally neutral matter. To justify a decision, in the strong sense, one must appeal to considerations that are capable of determining how people should behave. If one assumes that a judicial decision can be justified only by appeal to law, justification in the strong sense requires that legal considerations be capable of determining how people should behave. They cannot be morally neutal.

Dworkin, for example, has such a view of law.[6] He regards law as a system with moral pretensions, since it claims to justify what it does to people as well as the judgments that it makes of their behavior. For this reason, Dworkin seems to hold, legal justification aspires to be justification in the strong sense, and it succeeds only if it provides such justification. This is not just a theory about how decisions ought to work, when viewed from a detached moral point of view, but involves a claim about how to understand the nature of judicial reasoning when it is most successful from a strictly legal point of view. Dworkin argues, for example, that only if we view the law in such a way will we be able to understand the judicial techniques of statutory interpretation and the use of judicial precedents.

Dworkin claims that moral values are implicated in judicial reasoning in two ways. It first assumes the idea of fairness in the sense of treating like cases alike. New cases must be dealt with on the basis of the same general considerations that determined how past cases were treated. Second, in identifying these general considerations one must go beyond the authoritative texts that emerged from past legislative and judicial decisions and be guided by their rationales and by the reasons for a system in which both legislation and judicial precedents have such authority. These underlying principles must fit together into a coherent system and reflect the deep values of the community, but they must also be capable of justifying (in the strong sense) decisions that are made in the name of the law.

This theory is not obviously sound, but neither is it obviously crazy. In order to appraise it, not only must one entertain possible connections between law and morals but one's inquiry must be informed by an adequate understanding of the relevant moral values. One of the problems to be considered, for example, is the possible role of fairness in motivating judicial decisions. Dworkin appears to believe that considerations of fairness always argue that new cases be dealt with like past cases in all legal contexts. But it is not clear that this is so. If a legal system is not terribly unjust, both substantively and procedurally, then considerations of fairness may require that new cases be treated like past cases. But if the law of a community is sufficiently corrupt and past cases have been dealt with in a sufficiently immoral manner, then I think fairness cannot require that new cases be treated similarly, though the law may require it. One's view of this matter will turn on one's view about fairness, as well as the possibility that the only plausible account of the underlying rationales of past legislative and judicial decisions yields principles that are morally indefensible. It might turn out, in other words, that Dworkin does not succeed in showing that law presupposes the relevant moral values, but only that legal systems that satisfy some moral minima do so.[7]

It is worth mentioning that positivists typically suggest modes of thinking about the law that are not far removed from Dworkin's. I have in mind especially the way in which positivists distinguish between moral and legal concepts such as obligation. There is clearly a close relation between the concepts of legal justification and of legal obligation, since judgments of obligation are one of the principle subjects of judicial decisions.

The usual positivistic idea is that legal and moral obligations are conceptually distinct and have independent existence conditions. The necessary and sufficient condition for the existence of a legal obligation is that one be required or forbidden by law to behave in a certain way, and this is assumed to imply no moral conditions. But the typical mode of analysis of legal and moral obligations to be found in positivistic theory puts them on a par as two species of a single genus with parallel implications. If one is under an obligation, moral or legal, then one's behavior may be criticized accordingly. One may be held at fault for failing to live up to a legal obligation just as one may be held at fault in the moral case. Or one may be held to have a reason to behave in the way the law requires in just the same sense in which one may be held to have a reason to behave in the way that morality requires. The two reasons, modes of criticism, or obligations may be given different labels, but on these theories that seems to be the only difference between them.

When positivists think of legal obligations in this way, as strictly parallel to moral obligations, their thinking about the relations between law and morality reflects assumptions like those that underlie Dworkin's theory. It appears to be assumed that law, no less than morality, has a kind of legitimate authority to determine how we should behave and how we and our conduct may properly be appraised. I believe this is mistaken, and also that it is an inappropriate position for legal positivists to take. But my objections turn on substantive matters of moral theory and would not show that such an idea about the legitimate authority of law is unintelligible. This may perhaps reinforce the point that, although a theory like Dworkin's can reasonably be doubted, it cannot be discounted at the outset of an inquiry into the nature of law and its relations to morality. Furthermore, such theories cannot properly be appraised without the benefit of insight into moral as well as legal matters.

II. THE SOCIAL CONCEPTION OF LAW AND THE MINIMAL THESIS

Our next question is whether the separation of law and morals can be derived from the social conception of law. Our first task is to decide how the social conception of law is to be understood—the general idea, as distinct from specific theories that link law to specific social conditions.

The general idea is something like this: the existence and content of law is determined by some range of facts about human beings in a social setting—facts about their behavior, history, institutions, beliefs, and attitudes. The relevant range of facts may concern moral convictions, but we are concerned with such matters only so far as they are facts that happen to be relevant to what law is. Joseph Raz has expressed this general idea in the following way:

> A jurisprudential theory is acceptable only if its tests for identifying the content of the law and determining its existence depend exclusively on facts of human behaviour capable of being described in value-neutral terms, and applied without resort to moral argument.[8]

Raz calls this the "strong social thesis," which can be seen to have two distinct parts. One is that law is determined by social facts; the other is that law is not determined by moral considerations. Let us take them in that order.

What if anything follows about the separation of law and morals from the idea that law is completely determined by facts about human behavior that are capable of being described in value-neutral terms? To answer this question, we must look at the possible relations between social facts on the one hand and law and morality on the other.

According to the social conception of law described by Raz, law is completely determined by some range of facts. But Raz leaves open the nature of the relation between propositions of law and the relevant factual propositions. If one thinks of a theory about what law is as analyzing the concept of law, this relation is, presumably, conceptual, and the theoretical claims connecting propositions of law with relevant factual propositions will purport to be analytic truths. But one may wish to allow the possiblity that a theory about law is not analytic but rather describes in most fundamental terms the basic features of law or of a legal system, so that the most general propositions of such a theory are synthetic, just as the most general propositions of a scientific theory may be classified as synthetic rather than analytic.[9] In either case, however, we may understand this sort of theory as claiming that law is determined by some range of social facts.

The same possible relations might obtain between social facts and moral judgments. If ethical "naturalism" in the narrow sense defined by G. E. Moore were correct, moral judgments would be entailed by factual propositions, which might well include facts about human beings in a social setting. But even if naturalism in this sense is incorrect, and no moral judgments are entailed by factual propositions, naturalism in a wider sense might be correct. Some moral principles would be true, though they would not be true "by definition," and moral judgments would be determined by certain factual propositions. There is of course a third possibility, namely, that no factual propositions are capable of determining any moral value. This third possibility amounts to the truth of radical moral skepticism.

The social conception of law is compatible with each of these three possibilities, including both forms of ethical naturalism. There might be morality-determining facts as well as law-determining facts. And, so far as we can tell, law-determining facts might amount to or entail morality-determining facts. That is, the social facts that determine the existence and content of the law (if the social conception of the law is right) might be capable of supporting and might even entail moral judgments about the law and about conduct performed under the law. The social conception of law does not exclude this possiblity. For this reason, the social conception of law seems to tell us nothing about the moral fallibility of law. For all it tells us, the very facts that determine the existence and content of law might also determine that law is always just or that it is always unjust.

This conclusion does not depend on the abstractness of the social conception of law. The same results would follow if we considered any specific social conception of law, such as Austin's or Hart's. This is because the issue concerns not just the idea that law is determined by social facts but also the relationships between facts and moral value. Since the social conception of law is silent on the relations between facts and moral value, it has no implications concerning the separation of law and morals. Without the benefit of moral theory we can draw no relevant conclusions.

If one believes that the separation of law and morals follows from the social conception of law, this is probably because of considerations like the following. Law is shaped by human actions and decisions and is subject to deliberate control by human beings. For example, we tend to think of law as shaped significantly by legislative and judicial decisions that are made by ordinary mortals. This may seem to lead directly to the separation thesis. Since human conduct is morally fallible, it is natural to suppose that law is likewise fallible.

It is worth mentioning, however, that this line of reasoning can probably be attributed to those natural lawyers who accept the moral fallibility of law. When they think of ordinary law in such terms, they are undoubtedly thinking of law as shaped by human actions and decisions and as subject to deliberate control by human beings. Human beings are fallible, and the law they develop is accordingly fallible too.

But this line of reasoning is too quick. Not everything that is shaped by human actions and decisions and that is subject to deliberate control by human beings is usually regarded as morally fallible in the way that law is. Machines, for example, are created and controlled by human beings, but they are not usually thought of as just or unjust. Nevertheless, we do sometimes think of human creations, such as life-saving inventions and instruments of destruction, in moral terms, at least as good or bad. But when we do, it seems unclear that we assume some substantive moral notions, such as the value of human life, welfare, or dignity. What this suggests is that the social conception of law does not by itself entail the separation thesis, but that the argument linking them assumes some substantive moral values. We cannot even begin to understand why and how law is subject to moral appraisal without some substantive conception of what may be taken as relevant from a moral point of view. We prize human dignity, welfare, and fairness, and it is the conviction that these values are not automatically respected by the law that leads one to suppose that law is morally fallible.

I do not mean to suggest that such values are inherently arbitrary or incapable of rational defense. My point is that these values are not implicit in the idea that law is a social phenomenon. So the mere idea of law as social does not provide sufficient basis for inferring that law is morally fallible.

Let us turn now to the second part of Raz's strong social thesis, which claims that law is not determined by moral argument. Raz does not mean that legislation is never motivated by moral considerations, that courts never engage in moral reasoning, or that moral language is never found within the law. His point is that, once the law-determining facts have been taken into account, we have reached the outer boundaries of existing law. So, for example, when courts use moral arguments but are not simply deducing conclusions from moral ideas already placed within the law by legislative or judicial decisions, they must be understood as making new law.

This part of Raz's thesis is independent of the first, the social conception of law. For the thesis takes no stand on moral theory, so it must be compatible with ethical naturalism—the idea that moral value is determined by natural facts (which can presumably be described in value-neutral terms). But ethical naturalism entails that moral argument amounts at bottom to the marshaling of facts. The effect of adding the second part to the strong social thesis is to exclude such facts from the range of facts that are allowed by the thesis to determine law. It means that no facts of basic moral relevance (if there are any) can help determine that something is the law.

So according to the strong social thesis, the class of law-determining facts cannot include any morality-determining facts. This comes very close to implying that law is morally fallible. The intuitive idea at work here is that law has whatever value it has, not by virtue of its very nature, but rather by virtue of its contingent content (perhaps in relation to the social circumstances). But the strong social thesis does not quite yield the Minimal Separation Thesis. This is because it implies nothing of moral significance and does not even imply that law is subject to moral appraisal. The strong social thesis tells us at most that *if* law is subject to moral appraisal, its morality is an open question.

Even if the strong social thesis provided some foundation for the Minimal Separation Thesis, one would not wish to base the latter on the former. For the latter is much less controversial and more plausible. We can appreciate the character of the strong social thesis by considering the narrowest sort of disagreement that might develop around it.

An example is provided by the Due Process Clause of the U.S. Constitution, which says that no person may be deprived of life, liberty, or property without due process of law. The Constitution does not tell us what constitutes due process of law. If there is a general answer to this question, it can presumably be reached only by moral argument that goes beyond mere deductions from authoritative legal texts. Therefore, Raz must hold that a court faced with the task of initially interpreting this legal provision must go beyond existing law and make new law. Once a court that is empowered to issue authoritative interpretations of the U.S. Constitution interprets this clause, the clause acquires new content that enables future courts to render judicial decisions under the clause without making new law. But the initial interpretation involves judicial legislation.

Now consider Dworkin's understanding of the Due Process Clause.[10] On the most natural interpretation, the clause requires that certain legal procedures be fair. But the Constitution does not explicitly tell us what counts as a fair procedure, and it is arguable that the criteria of fair procedures are not implicit in terms like "due process" or "fair procedure." So when a court is called upon to apply this clause (at least prior to its first authoritative interpretation), it must go beyond the text of the law and its strict logical implications. It does not follow, however, that there is no right answer to the legal question that the court must decide. Suppose there is a right answer to the moral question, what constitutes a fair procedure. That is a substantive problem for moral theory, but one for which there may well be a solution. When the Due Process Clause invokes the concept of a fair procedure without specifying criteria, it seems to assume that there is a right answer to the moral question. If this assumption is correct, a court that is called upon to apply the Due Process Clause must engage in substantive moral argument in order to arrive at an appropriate conception of fairness and apply it to the case at hand. If the court's moral reasoning is sound and it reaches the right answer to the moral question, it will be in a position to reach the right answer to the legal question with which it is faced. In Dworkin's view, this will not involve going beyond the law, for if there is a right answer to the moral question, a court that finds it has simply provided the only right interpretation of the clause. It will have done just what the framers of the Due Process Clause imply can be done and require to be done. On this view, there is no good reason to regard the court as legislating, as making new law. On Raz's view, however, even in this sort of case a court must be understood as making new law, just because it is obliged to go beyond the authoritative text and engage in substantive moral argument. Raz is committed to this conclusion even in those cases where there is a single right answer to the moral question which determines the right answer to the legal question and the court correctly identifies both.

This difference between Raz and Dworkin concerning the character of court decisions that interpret moral language in the law involves a further difference in their attitude toward subsequent judicial decisions. Since Raz will not recognize a moral argument as helping to interpret the law, but regards it only as adding content to existing law, he cannot appeal to such an argument in criticizing from a strictly legal point of view the actual interpretations that courts place on such legal provisions. Once a court has provided an authoritative interpretation of such a provision, Raz seems committed to placing great weight on that reading of the law. In Dworkin's view, subsequent decisions must take into account past judicial decisions, and so must give some weight to prior interpretations of such language. But since in Dworkin's view there can be a right answer to the moral question which determines the correct interpretation of the clause, any past interpretation of the clause cannot be taken as decisive. Dworkin's reasoning would justify a court's rejecting a prior interpretation of the clause in a way that Raz's reasoning would not. In this way, Raz seems committed to attributing greater legal significance than Dworkin is to certain "facts of human behaviour capable of being described in value-neutral terms."

It seems to me that Dworkin has the better of this argument, at least as it concerns the initial interpretation of undefined moral language in the law. If there is a right answer to the moral question that such language poses, there seems no reason to deny that this answer provides the right interpretation of the law. But if so, courts interpreting such law cannot be understood as making law. They are making law only if they reach the wrong conclusion and their interpretation nevertheless has precedential effect.

So one would not wish to use something like the strong social thesis as a basis for the Minimal Separation Thesis. It should also be mentioned, finally, that Dworkin's view of the matter does not exclude the fallibility of law, and so is at least compatible with the Minimal Separation Thesis, which he otherwise accepts. For Dworkin's argument does not assume that there is always undefined moral language in the law.

III. THE EXPLICIT MORAL CONTENT THESIS

Our findings so far indicate that the separation of law and morals is an axiom rather than a corollary of positivistic thinking. At the same time, the minimal idea that law is subject to moral appraisal and does not automatically merit good marks is not the exclusive property of legal positivism. This suggests the question whether positivism endorses some distinctive version of the separation thesis.

Raz's strong social thesis suggests such an idea. Hart suggests a similar idea (and implies it is more widely accepted within the positivistic tradition) when he approvingly describes Bentham's and Austin's version of the separation thesis as follows:

> What both Bentham and Austin were anxious to assert were the following two simple things: first, in the absence of an *expressed* constitutional or legal provision, it could not follow from the mere fact that a rule violated standards of morality that it was not a rule of law; and, conversely, it could not follow from the mere fact that a rule was morally desirable that it was a rule of law.[12]

Hart's wording here implies not that law is morally fallible but rather that law has no moral content or conditions save what has been explicitly laid down by law. I shall call this the Explicit Moral Content Thesis.

The Explicit Moral Content Thesis is different from the Minimal Separation Thesis. The latter does not entail the former: one might hold that law has moral content or that there are moral conditions on what can count as law, though they are not explicitly laid down by law, and still hold that law is morally fallible.

This is what Dworkin, for example, appears to hold. On Dworkin's theory, as we have seen, the content of the law is determined by legally sound judicial decisions that have been or could be made. But past decisions, which are not assumed to be morally infallible, act as moral constraints upon new decisions. The argument from fairness assumes that morally imperfect past decisions can have a proper influence on current ones, though that influence is moderated in two ways. First, it is interpreted in terms of principles that provide the best justification of those decisions, so that the surface language of past decisions (such as the language of statutes), while important, will not always be decisive. Second, some past judicial decisions must be regarded as mistaken from a legal as well as from a moral point of view and therefore as deserving only minimal respect. This theory does not imply that law is morally infallible, though it does imply that there are significant connections between law and morals—connections that have never been laid down explicitly as law. Law is determined, in part, by considerations of fairness. Sound legal decisions must pay due respect to past legislative and judicial decisions, so that the decision it is fair to reach, in light of the actual history of the system, may be different from the decision it would be fair to reach if that history had been different and morally more satisfactory.

As I have already suggested, I do not think this can be part of a sound general theory of law, because I do not believe that fairness can play such a role when past legislative and judicial decisions were sufficiently unjust. In that case, whatever argues from a legal point of view that current cases be treated like past cases cannot be fairness. But this objection rests on substantive moral claims, and Dworkin's theory cannot be discounted at the outset. Dworkin's theory thus illustrates that the Minimal Separation Thesis does not entail the Explicit Moral Content Thesis, which would exclude the idea that moral notions like fairness contribute to the content of the law, even though that idea has not been laid down as law in an explicit, authoritative manner.

Hart's suggestion of the Explicit Moral Content Thesis is not misleading. For it is a corollary of a more general Explicit Content Thesis that Hart defends.

Hart argues for the Explicit Content Thesis in his discussion of judicial discretion, or judicial decision making in the absence of sufficient legal guidance.[13] Hart's official purpose in that discussion is to mark out a sensible middle ground between what he regards as the unacceptable extremes in legal theory of formalism, or mechanical jurisprudence, and rule skepticism. Formalism holds that law provides a complete, consistent, mechanical decision procedure, so that sound answers to legal questions can always be deduced from existing law and no room is left for the exercise of judicial discretion, whereas rule skepticism holds that there is always insufficient law prior to a judicial decision, so that judges always exercise judicial discretion. Hart argues, in effect, that formalism is mistaken because there are gaps between laws and that rule skepticism is mistaken because there are laws between the gaps.

Judicial discretion in the relevent sense exists when the law provides insufficient guidance to decide a case, so that no collection of factual findings will enable a court to reach a decision that is uniquely determined by existing law. This might seem to happen when, for example, statutes are poorly drafted. But Hart argues that judicial discretion is an unavoidable feature of law that results primarily and most directly from limitations of language. The terms we use in making law are "open textured": they have a "core" of determinate meaning, represented by cases to which they clearly and uncontroversially apply as well as cases to which they clearly and uncontroversially do not apply, but also a "penumbra" of uncertain meaning, represented by cases to which they neither clearly apply nor clearly do not apply. Hart concludes that laws are "open textured" too, by which he means they have a core of determinate meaning and a penumbra of indeterminate meaning. Hart strongly suggests that laws can be applied syllogistically within the range of their determinate meanings, so that legally sound decisions can be conclusively established. Otherwise, the law is not determinate enough to decide cases and courts have no choice but to make new law as they render decisions. This is the area of unavoidable judicial discretion. It can be reduced by further judicial decisions that add more determinate content to the law, but it can never be completely eliminated. Sometimes the explicit language of the law can be supplemented by the evident aims or purposes of the law in question, and in this way courts may be able to render decisions without exercising judicial discretion, even though the language of the law is somewhat indecisive. But our aims as well as our explicit language are "open textured" too, so that the added appeal to aims or purposes that are evident in the law cannot eliminate judicial discretion entirely.

The importance attached to explicit language in the law is shown by Hart's contrasting treatment of legislation and judicial decisions. Modern legislation provides us with authoritative texts employing language that allows us to infer general rules. Hart accordingly regards the rules created by legislative enactments as determinate just to the extent that the words used have clear meanings and their purposes are helpfully clear. But judicial precedents are regarded differently by Hart, because their language does not similarly allow us to infer general rules for all cases to which they are applied. Precedents that decide cases in relation to specific sets of facts about them can generate rules for a narrow range of cases just like the ones that have been decided. But precedents are also appealed to for guidance in a much wider range of cases, where it is unclear what should be inferred from the prior decisions. Hart treats this as the absence of an "authoritative or uniquely correct formulation" of a rule covering the wider class of cases, and holds that any such use of judicial precedents involves the exercise of judicial discretion.[14]

Similar considerations govern Hart's treatment of moral language in the law. He assumes that terms like "fair rate" and "safe systems of work" have a core of determinate meaning, represented by cases to which such terms uncontroversially apply or do not apply, plus a penumbra of uncertain meaning, represented by cases in which such terms apply only controversially. It should also be mentioned that Hart regards the criteria of existing law as "open textured" too. In a given legal system, a "rule of recognition" determines which other rules have legal standing. The rule of recognition is determined by agreement among officials as to what counts as law, and it is determinate only so far as there is very precise agreement on such matters.

Hart seems to conceive of the law as consisting of rules identified chiefly in linguistic terms. This may seem perfectly natural, in view of the importance generally attached to the language of statutes and decisions. Thus Hart infers that law is gappy because of the "open texture" of language. But this inference is strictly invalid. Suppose it is granted that linguistic expressions are "open textured" or unavoidably somewhat vague. It does not follow that there are determinate facts only where our current linguistic resources enable us straightforwardly to express them. The same applies to the law. Even if we assume that legal formulations are unavoidably somewhat vague, we cannot infer from this alone that the law is indeterminate whenever legal formulations have indeterminate implications. For this ignores the possibility that law has further resources which help to determine how to decide cases when the language of the law is unclear.

Hart ingores, for example, the sort of possibility that Dworkin finds within the law. Dworkin seems to hold that the content of the law is identical not with a set of canonically formulated rules but with what it would be fair for courts to find in cases given relevant past decisions. Arguments from fairness can overcome the indecisiveness of language. Hart's exclusion of such possibilities suggests that he conceives of the law essentially in linguistic terms—as a collection of rules with canonical formulations, which are based either on explicit legislation or on "very general agreement"[15] among officials about the specific import of judicial precedents and other aspects of the law.

The notion of "open texture" suggests a more fundamental assumption about the law. The idea of "open texture" assumes that linguistic terms are applied by reference to a set of criteria, all of which are clearly satisfied in some (core) cases, but which conflict in other (penumbral) cases. Within the core meaning of a rule, it can be applied syllogistically. Within a rule's penumbra, however, it cannot be applied syllogistically, for considerations can be adduced on both sides of the linguistic issue. This suggests another contrast within the law—between cases that can be decided uncontroversially because legal considerations fall overwhelmingly on one side and cases that are controversial because legal considerations can be adduced on both sides of the issue. The more fundamental assumption about the law that may underlie Hart's theory of judicial discretion, then, is this: the law is determinate when, and only when, reasonable disagreement about it is absent. When the identification and implications of a rule of law are uncontroversial, there is no judicial discretion. But when law is controversial, when competent lawyers can develop plausible arguments on both sides of a legal question and a decision cannot be made mechanically but must involve weighing reasons on both sides, then the law must be regarded as indeterminate in the sense that there is scope for judicial discretion. Judges can decide such cases only by adding determinate content to the law, by engaging in "creative judicial activity" that amounts to legislation.[16] Law is determinate just where it is uncontroversial.

A linguistic version of this idea would be the Explicit Content Thesis, that law has no content or conditions save what has been explicitly laid down as law (or is precisely agreed upon by competent officials). A corollary of this view, already expressed in Hart's discussion of moral language in the law, is the Explicit Moral Content Thesis, that law has no moral content or conditions save what has been explicitly laid down by law (or is precisely agreed upon by competent officials). This doctrine goes considerably further than the Minimal Separation Thesis, as we have seen.

Our consideration of the strong social thesis gave us no reason to suppose that there cannot be inexplicit moral content in the law. If there is a right answer posed by undefined moral language in the law, for example, then we have no reason to regard judges who interpret such language as exercising judicial discretion.[17]

The Explicit Moral Content Thesis seems, however, to be suggested by a number of legal positivists. Hart offers a linguistic argument for that thesis, but nonlinguistic considerations might well provide the deeper motivation. That is the possibility we must now explore.

IV. THE MODEL OF RULES

According to Dworkin, legal positivism holds that law consists of standards, which he calls "rules," that are identifiable by their "pedigree" (or social origins) rather than their "content" (or moral acceptability); that these rules can be identified, interpreted, and applied more or less "mechanically" (by syllogistic reasoning); and that in cases which cannot be so decided judges can reach decisions only by exercising "discretion" and making new law. This is what Dworkin calls "the model of rules."[18]

Dworkin argues that these claims are false because the law is not exhausted by "rules" but includes standards that he calls "principles," which are determined in part by their content; these principles cannot be identified, interpreted, or applied mechanically; and principles help decide cases, so that judicial decisions can be fully based on law even when rules have been exhausted (sometimes even when rules must be changed) and decisions can only be justified by nondeductive arguments.

Dworkin's attack on legal positivism appears initially to fail because it is unclear why positivists should be thought committed to the model of rules. Let us suppose that positivists do conceive of the law as determined by what Dworkin calls "pedigree," since this is, roughly speaking, the social conception of law. The model of rules goes much beyond this: it conceives of law as a codelike collection of hard and fast rules that can be identified mechanically and that are capable of deciding cases either mechanically or else not at all. But the notion of pedigree does not seem to entail this conception of law. Positivists recognize legislation, and legislatures are capable of laying down legal standards that cannot be and are not meant to be applied mechanically.

Despite this, if positivists accepted the Explicit Content Thesis, Dworkin's objections would have some point. It may initially appear that they do not do so. Hart, for example, claims that rules are somewhat vague, which suggests that he does not regard law as equivalent to a codelike collection of hard and fast rules. But this is misleading, since Hart regards the law as having determinate content, sufficient to decide cases that arise, only insofar as it resembles such a collection of rules. All the rest is mere penumbra.

Suppose that Hart's view represents the positivistic tradition. The question we then face is, why should positivists conceive of law in this way—as limited to the explicit language of its authoritative texts, supplemented by agreement on some matters among officials?

Dworkin has offered an answer to this question:[19]

> The important question is not, however, whether Hart or any other particular legal philosopher is committed to the thesis that the test for law must make law reasonably demonstrable. That thesis is connected to a more general theory of law—in particular to a picture of law's function. This is the theory that law provides a settled, public and dependable set of standards for private and official conduct, standards whose force cannot be called into question by some individual official's conception

> of policy or morality. This theory of law's function acknowleges, as it must, that no set of public rules can be complete or completely precise. But it therefore insists on a distinction between occasions on which the law, so conceived, does dictate a decision and occasions on which, in the language of positivists, the judge must exercise his discretion to make new law just because the law is silent. This distinction is vital, on this view of law's function, because it is important to acknowledge that when reasonable men can disagree about what the law requires, a judicial decision cannot be a neutral decision of the sort promised in the idea of law. It is more honest to concede that the decision is not, in this case, a decision of law at all.[20]

According to Dworkin, then, the model of rules is tied to legal positivism because it is "a necessary part" of "a political theory about the point or function of law" that is embraced by positivists.[21]

This first claim that Dworkin attributes to positivists is connected to a second claim, which involves the notion of pedigree. According to Dworkin, positivists hold that

> The truth of a proposition of law, when it is true, consists in ordinary historical facts about individuals or social behavior including, perhaps, facts about beliefs and attitudes, but in nothing metaphysically more mysterious.[22]

On this view, what law is can turn on the moral beliefs that people have, but not on the truth of a moral proposition. For that would make law turn on "moral facts," and Dworkin believes that the empiricist leanings of legal positivists make them regard "moral facts" as metaphysically suspect. That is one reason why positivists tend to "reduce" propositions of law or their truth conditions to "ordinary historical facts."

This explains why Dworkin believes that his criticisms of the model of rules, with its attendant theory of judicial discretion, are effective against legal positivism in general. But Dworkin's explanation needs careful scrutiny, because it is not obviously valid and imputes to positivists very questionable modes of reasoning.

Consider Dworkin's claim that one of the factors influencing the development of legal positivism is reductionistic empiricism. Dworkin holds that this leads positivists to think of truth conditions for propositions of law in terms of "ordinary historical facts about individuals or social behaviour including, perhaps, facts about beliefs and attitudes." But, he claims, this attitude leads positivists to reject the idea that the truth of a proposition of law might depend on the truth of a moral proposition because as empiricists they tend to regard such "moral facts" as "metaphysically mysterious."

Dworkin may be right that positivism has been strongly influenced by reductionistic empiricism, but his particular way of construing that influence seems falsified by the evidence. Unlike logical positivists, legal positivists (with a few noteworthy exceptions) have generally regarded moral questions as objectively, empirically decidable. This holds not just for the utilitarians, such as Bentham and Austin, but also for those with conventionalistic moral theories such as Hart. These major figures within the positivist tradition lack the reason that Dworkin claims they have to regard "moral facts" as metaphysically suspect.

The empiricism that is generally associated with legal positivism might, however, be relevant in another more general way. A reductionistic empiricist could be expected to regard the law as reducible to observable phenomena. It would be natural for him or her to place great weight on such things as authoritative decisions and the texts that they spawn, and perhaps to regard the substantive content of the law as chiefly determined by the words of those texts. Even so, this is a highly speculative interpretation of the impact of empiricism on the development of legal positivism. It might help to account for Bentham's views, but it is unclear that it applies to positivists generally, including Hart.

In any case, according to Dworkin, the chief factor shaping positivistic theory is not metaphysical but "a political theory about the point or function of the law." This holds "that law provides a settled, public and dependable set of standards whose force cannot be called into question by some individual official's conception of policy or morality." On this theory, Dworkin says, "it is important to acknowledge that when reasonable men can disagree about what the law requires, a judicial decision cannot be a neutral decision of the sort promised in the idea of law" and so should not be considered a decision determined by existing law. When law is controversial, it must be regarded as indeterminate—not merely unclear, but not yet fully formed. Real law is clearly identifiable, and in particular is not subject to moral interpretation.

There is evidence that one or two legal positivists have viewed the law in some such way—not only have they embraced the model of rules, but their ideas seem to have been shaped by some ideas about how law ought to be. There is evidence, for example, that Bentham wished to conceive of law in codelike terms (much like the model of rules) because he thought that law would best serve utilitarian ends if it took such a form.[23] More recently Joseph Raz endorsed an argument like the one that Dworkin attributes to positivists.[24] But it is unclear that other legal positivists have looked at the law in any such way or that they would welcome any such suggestion. Hart, for example, does not seem to use or endorse such an argument, and it is not clear that he could consistently do so.

Dworkin claims not merely that positivists have both a theory of what law is and a theory of how law ought to function but also that their theory about what law is has been shaped by their theory about how law ought to function. There is little evidence of this. Bentham notwithstanding, positivists have generally presented their theories of law as if they were trying to describe the concept of law, the essential nature of law, or something else similarly given. They do not say, "this is the way I conceive of the law because law so conceived is capable of functioning as it ought to function."

Hart, for example, contrasts "wider" and "narrower" concepts of law, where the narrower concept places moral conditions on something's being the law. He believes that the wider concept makes moral criticism of law possible. But Hart does not embrace the wider concept on the ground that law would better serve its purpose if it were that way. He clearly believes that the wider concept is the one we have—that he is faithfully describing our shared concept of law.[25]

One can imagine a positivist reacting to Dworkin's diagnosis as follows: "If we are right and law is (as you put it) 'reasonably demonstrable,' then of course it will have the merit of certainty, as compared with informal standards. And if law were not reasonably demonstrable, then of course it would not have this merit. But you have put the cart before the horse in claiming that our conception of the law is shaped by our prizing clear public rules. Our point is that law can serve this important purpose just because that is, as a matter of fact, part of its nature. To suppose that we are led to this view of law's nature by our desire for law to provide clear public rules is ungenerously to imply that we have indulged in wishful metaphysical thinking."

We should look once more at Raz's strong social thesis, which includes the Explicit Moral Content Thesis. For one of Raz's arguments for his thesis resembles the argument that Dworkin attributes to positivists generally.

Raz first claims that the strong social thesis "reflects and systemizes several interconnected distinctions embedded in our conception of the law.[26] We distinguish, for example, between the legal skills of judges, which are engaged when they apply the law, and their moral characters, which are at work when they develop law. We also make a distinction between settled and unsettled law, the latter but not the former comprising cases in which moral arguments are employed.

I find this argument unpersuasive. It does not provide sufficient reason to reject Dworkin's approach to the interpretation of moral language in the law, as exemplified in the Due Process Clause.

Raz also claims that these distinctions and his thesis "help to identify a basic underlying function of the law: to provide publicly ascertainable standards by which members of the society are held to be bound so that they cannot excuse non-conformity by challenging the justification of the standard."[27] The point of all this is to make possible a system of cooperation, coordination, and forbearances, which, Raz says, "is an essential part of the function of law in society."[28]

Raz's second argument is more directly relevant to our immediate concerns. But it turns out that his use of it does not support Dworkin's diagnosis. For Raz does not argue that we should conceive of law in this way because law so conceived performs a desirable function. His first argument tries to show that law in fact has such a character, while the second argument connects that character with a desirable social function.

It may nevertheless be useful to examine Raz's second argument, since it offers a rationale for the Explicit Moral Content Thesis.

His argument goes something like this: The social order is liable to break down if substantive moral arguments used in adjudication are counted as helping to interpret the law, because that would encourage members of the society to break the law in hopes of avoiding the legal consequences by "challenging the justification of the standard."

Let us assume for the sake of argument that a society needs a system of forbearances, cooperation, and coordination and that it is one of law's principal functions to secure this by providing publicly identifiable standards. The question that we face is whether such a system would be weakened if the moral arguments used in adjudication were to count as contributing to the interpretation of the law.

It may seem at first as if Raz's thesis has no practical implications, but only concerns how we describe the results of litigation. If that were right, it would seem implausible to claim any connection between that thesis and the maintenance of social stability. But I think Raz's thesis makes a difference to litigation itself. I shall consider two sorts of cases, one in which Raz and Dworkin might well agree, at least initially, and one in which they might be expected to disagree.

The first sort of case involves the explicit use of undefined moral language in the law, as in the Due Process Clause. If there is a right answer to the moral question posed by that clause, Raz would presumably wish a court to reach a decision that is informed by that answer. I say "informed by that answer" because, for reasons already given, Raz and Dworkin may disagree about how much weight later courts should give to an earlier reading of the clause that was based on an unsuccessful moral argument or a defective theory of interpretation. Even given this difference between their views, however, it is difficult to understand why Raz believes the social order is liable to break down if we view the law as Dworkin does. We have no evidence that a social order has broken down or is likely to break down if courts read moral language in the law as Dworkin recommends.

One might believe that moral language would best be excluded from laws so that they might have greater clarity and certainty. But this line of reasoning is irrelevant to our present concerns. Moral terms are found in legislative and judicial language, and the issue here is whether its application involves interpreting or adding to the law.

The main area of disagreement between Raz and Dworkin is suggested by the case of *Riggs* v. *Palmer,*[29] which was used by Dworkin in his attack on legal positivism. Elmer Palmer murdered his grandfather in order to inherit property under his grandfather's will. The statutes governing wills made no explicit exception for such a case, and it was arguable that Palmer should be confirmed as heir. Other relatives challenged this reading of the law, the New York State Court of Appeals found sufficient reason to consider their appeal, and ultimately found in their favor. Although the court was divided, there was no disagreement about the language and the literal reading of the statutes. Disagreement centered on whether to engage in "equitable construction" in the light of conflicting legal doctrines, such as the common law maxim that no one should be permitted to profit from his own wrong.

Dworkin seems to imply that even in such a case a court can be considered as discovering law, whereas Raz suggests that he would regard the *Riggs* court as having changed the law because it did not follow the literal reading of the statute but was diverted by moral arguments. If Raz does not believe this, his thesis has little practical effect and cannot be thought to make much difference to social stability. So let us assume that Raz believes the *Riggs* court changed the law. This suggests that he would have endorsed the opposite finding, which would have secured the inheritance to the murderer. It is difficult to see how this would promote social stability by reinforcing the relevant forbearances.

Cases will undoubtedly vary, so that following Raz's recommendations might sometimes favor social stability. But Raz has given us no reason to believe that a concept of law which excludes nonexplicit moral content systematically promotes social stability.

To return to Dworkin's argument: why should he believe that a theorist might be led to a conception of law by a political theory about the proper function of law? Wouldn't this manifest theoretical confusion?

Dworkin sometimes suggests that there is an intimate connnection between analytic and normative jurisprudence—between theories about what law is and theories about what law ought to be—but he has never made the connection clear. It is true that his "rights thesis," which holds that "judicial decisions in civil cases . . . characteristically are and should be generated by principal not policy,"[30] couples a normative with a descriptive claim, and his argument for that thesis seeks to show that moral notions are needed for a proper understanding of successful judicial decisions. But this result, if achieved, would not mean that descriptive theories are impossible unless coupled with normative claims, or that moral notions cannot be avoided in any plausible account of judicial decision making. Dworkin has defended a particular theory; he has not defended any relevant meta-theoretical claim.

Our examination of the separation thesis does suggest that there may be some connections between analytic and normative jurisprudence that legal positivists tend to ignore. We have found, for example, that the separation thesis, which has helped to shape positivistic legal theory, is not a morally neutral doctrine but represents a detached, critical attitude toward the law. But this does not tend to show that legal theory is impossible without a normative foundation.

One might try reasoning as follows. Certain officials play a decisive role in determining what counts as the law of a community. In systems like ours these are preeminently judges of the highest courts within their respective jurisdictions. Judges refer to statutes and cases when deciding what counts as the law of their jurisidictions, but they do more than that. They are also required to say what law is when statutes and cases conflict or are unclear or when no established rule of law seems to exist. To do this, they must work with a conception of what counts as law—what considerations are relevant to a legal determination. Indeed, this is required even for them to use statutes and cases in the way that they do. This amounts to a theory of law—a theory about how law is to be determined.

This line of reasoning suggests that what counts as law is theory-dependent. But there are different views of the matter. On one view, when judges are guided by unequivocal statutes and cases they are simply doing what the law plainly requires them to do, and when they go beyond the reach of unequivocal statutes and cases they are going beyond the law. On this way of thinking about the law—suggested, as we have seen, by Hart and others—theory plays no essential role in law. Judges may have theories to help them when law fails them, but they do not need theories when the law is clear. On this view, law is not theory-dependent. Furthermore, the argument we have sketched says nothing about the character of the theory that judges use; for example, why it should be considered a normative theory, a theory about how law ought to be, as opposed to a theory about the nature of law. Even if law were theory-dependent in something like the sense suggested, it would not follow that what counts as law is dependent on a conception of what law ought to be.

Dworkin may be understood as arguing that law is theory-dependent because law does not stop when cases are hard. Theory plays an essential role in law because judges do not inevitably make law but rather are capable of finding law when they are obliged to go beyond unequivocal statutes and cases, which they cannot do without a conception of what counts as law. More generally, his argument is that this sort of theory determines what considerations are binding on a judge. A theory of law is a theory of (among other things) judicial duty. The law of a community is represented by the sound judicial decisions that might be made; these decisions presuppose a theory about how judges are required to decide cases; and theories of this kind are subject to appraisal just like theories of any other kind. So on Dworkin's view the law of a community is dependent on a true theory of law—the theory that is capable of generating uniquely sound judicial decisions.

This tells us something about Dworkin's attitude toward theories of law. But it does not tell us why we may not think of such a theory as internal to a legal system, insulated from, say, moral considerations. A possible answer may be suggested as follows. Court decisions succeed in identifying and interpreting law when they are justified. But the idea of a justified judicial decision is a "contested concept." On one view, as we have seen, a decision can be justified only if it provides an adequate basis for the determination of obligations and provides reasons for the behavior of those whose conduct is at issue. Any attempt to defend a theory about justified decisions cannot ignore such claims, so the foundation of any theory of law must involve issues of moral theory. Judicial decisions determine the law, but these decisions must be informed by a theory that can be defended only in the light of substantive political considerations. Positivistic theory regards it as politically desirable that the determination of law be conducted in a morally neutral manner. Dworkin disagrees. But both approaches presuppose an answer to the question, what is a justified judicial decision, and this involves moral argument.

This is but the crudest sketch of an argument that seeks to show how analytic and normative jurisprudence are inseparably connected. It may help to explain why Dworkin believes it is not unreasonable for positivists to be guided by a political theory when arriving at a theory about what law is. The development of such an argument and its appraisal must be postponed for another occasion.

NOTES

1. H. L. A. Hart, "Positivism and the Separation of Law and Morals," *Harvard Law Review* 71 (1958): 601, note 25; compare Hart, *The Concept of Law* (Oxford: Clarendon Press, 1961), p. 253. (These works are referred to hereafter as "Separation" and *Concept,* respectively.)

2. "Separation," p. 623f; *Concept,* p. 155f. I discuss this argument in "Formal Justice," *Cornell Law Review* 58 (1973): 833–61.

3. Thomas Aquinas, *Summa Theologica,* I–II, Q. 96, Art. 4. This translation is from *Basic Writings of Saint Thomas Aquinas,* edited by Anton C. Pegis (New York: Random House, 1945), Vol. 2, p. 794.

4. Lon Fuller, "Positivism and Fidelity to Law—A Reply to Professor Hart," *Harvard Law Review* 71 (1958): 630–72; Fuller, *The Morality of Law* (New Haven: Yale University Press, 1964).

5. "Separation," loc. cit.; cf. *Concept,* loc. cit.

6. Ronald Dworkin, *Taking Rights Seriously* (Cambridge: Harvard University Press, 1978), Chap. 4.

7. Dworkin's view is not entirely clear. In "Hard Cases" he assumes that a legal system (or the "political scheme" determined by the constitution) "is sufficiently just to be taken as settled for reasons of fairness" (*Taking Rights Seriously,* p. 106), but he also assumes that the relevant conditions were satisfied in Nazi Germany and are satisfied in contemporary South Africa (ibid., p. 326–27). Dworkin and I may differ about the conditions required for an argument from fairness. In any case, Dworkin does not assume that such considerations of fairness, represented by law, exhaust the relevant moral considerations to be taken into account by judges or other officials. They determine what counts as law, but sometimes a judge should not follow the law.

8. Joseph Raz, *The Authority of Law* (Oxford: Clarendon Press, 1979), pp. 39–40.

9. One might also wish to leave this matter open, of course, because of doubts about the contrast between analytic and synthetic statements, and especially the application of that distinction to the fundamental principles of a theory.

10. Dworkin, *Taking Rights Seriously,* pp. 131–40.

11. Raz, *The Authority of Law,* p. 40.

12. "Separation," p. 599 (emphasis added).

13. *Concept,* Chap. 7; see also Hart's article, "Philosophy of Law, Problems of," in *The Encyclopedia of Philosophy* (New York: Macmillan and Free Press, 1967), Vol. 6, pp. 268–72.

14. *Concept,* p. 131.

15. Ibid.

16. Ibid.

17. If the Explicit Moral Content Thesis is implausible, then so is the more general Explicit Content Thesis. If the Explicit Content Thesis is tied to the notion that law is determinate insofar as it is capable of providing syllogistic arguments for judicial decisions, it seems vulnerable to Dworkin's criticisms of the model of rules. For part of Dworkin's point is that judicial decisions can be sound from a strictly legal point of view even when they are nondeductive, taking into account considerations on both sides of a legal issue. I discuss a logical version of the Explicit Content Thesis (a "formalistic model" for legal justifications) in "Legal Formalism and Instrumentalism—A Pathological Study," *Cornell Law Review* 66 (June 1981): 949–72.

18. Dworkin, *Taking Rights Seriously,* Chaps. 2-3.

19. In the revised version of Dworkin's "Reply to Critics," published as an Appendix to the Harvard University Press (1978) edition of *Taking Rights Seriously.*

20. Ibid., p. 347.

21. Ibid.

22. Ibid., p. 348.

23. See Gerald Postema, "The Expositor, the Censor, and the Common Law," *Canadian Journal of Philosophy* 9 (1979): 643–70; and "Bentham and Dworkin on Positivism and Adjudication," *Social Theory and Practice* 5 (1980): 347–76.

24. Raz, *The Authority of Law,* pp. 50–52, discussed below.

25. "Separation," pp. 620–21; *Concept,* pp. 202–07.

26. Raz, *The Authority of Law,* p. 52.

27. Ibid.

28. Ibid., p. 51.

29. 115 N.Y. 506, 22 N.E. 188 (1889), discussed in *Taking Rights Seriously,* chap. 2.

30. Dworkin, *Taking Rights Seriously,* p. 84.

PART TWO
The Judicial Decision

4

Legal Principles and the Limits of Law

Joseph Raz

PRINCIPLES AND LIMITS OF LAW

By the thesis of the "limits of law" I mean the position that there is a test which distinguishes what is law from what is not. Professor Dworkin's writings in effect contain three arguments, each of which is partly dependent on his theory of principles, against the thesis of the limits of law.[1] While only two of these arguments are explicitly directed against this thesis, all of them, if valid, undermine it. In the remainder of this article I shall show that each of Professor Dworkin's arguments must fail and that there is good reason to persevere in the attempt to construct a test for distinguishing what is law from what is not. I hope in the course of this discussion to throw some light on how such seemingly disparate matters as the thesis of the limits of law, the nature of rules and principles, the role of judicial discretion, and the criterion of the identity of a legal system are related.

A. Judicial Discretion

Professor Dworkin's first argument is a result of his theory of judicial discretion.[2] He distinguishes three senses of discretion. In the two weak senses "discretion" means "judgment" and "finality." "Sometimes," explains Professor Dworkin,

> we use "discretion" in a weak sense, simply to say that for some reason the standards an official must apply cannot be applied mechanically but demand the use of judgment . . . .
>
> Sometimes we use the term in a different weak sense, to say only that some official has final authority to make a decision and cannot be reviewed and reversed by any other official . . . .
>
> I call both of these senses weak to distinguish them from a stronger sense. We use "discretion" sometimes . . . to say that on some issue [an official] is simply not bound by standards set by the authority in question.[3]

From *The Yale Law Journal* 81, no. 5 (April 1972), 842–54 (Section II of the original article). Reprinted by permission of the author, *The Yale Law Journal,* and Fred B. Rothman and Company. The Postscript has been written especially for this volume and is printed here with the permission of the author.

The thesis that judges have discretion in the strong sense[4] means that there are cases which they are legally entitled to decide and in which no one correct decision is determined by standards of law. The thesis of judicial discretion does not entail that in cases where discretion may be exercised anything goes. Such cases are governed by laws which rule out certain decisions. The only claim is that the laws do not determine any decision as the correct one.

Professor Dworkin argues that (1) the law includes some principles as well as rules. From this he concludes that (2) the courts never have discretion in the strong sense. It follows, though he does not draw the conclusion at this point, that (3) the thesis of the limits of law is wrong. I shall argue that (3) does indeed follow from (2), but that (2) does not follow from (1) and is in any case wrong.

If courts are never entitled to exercise discretion (in the strong sense) it follows that all the reasons, rules, and principles which they are entitled to rely on are part of the law. There is one important exception to this conclusion: those standards which are applied because they are the standards of some other legal system or organization, the standards of which the law respects and enforces, are not part of the law. The exception covers those laws of other states which are recognized and enforced according to the rules of private international law. It also extends to contracts and the rules of voluntary associations recognized by law, and to social, moral, and religious standards of individuals and communities which are taken into account for some legal purposes (such as mitigation of punishment or exemption from military service) or as creating presumptions of fact as to the behavior or intention of litigants. When referring to such standards in their judgments the courts quite clearly do so not because they are part of the law but because the law makes it its business to recognize and give support, to a certain extent, to standards of other organizations, communities or individuals.[5]

This exception apart (and, however important, it does not affect Professor Dworkin's case against the thesis of the limits of law), it follows from Professor Dworkin's views on judicial discretion that all the reasons which the courts are entitled to use in justifying decisions are part of the law. All the reasons for a decision are legal reasons, for the law uniquely determines which decision is the correct one.[6] Now it seems to me true that on various occasions the courts are entitled to rely on every reason which is endorsed by part of the community for some purpose or other. It follows, therefore, from Professor Dworkin's view on judicial discretion that the thesis of the limits of law is wrong at least to the extent to which it claims that it is possible to distinguish between the law and non-legal social standards.

If, on the other hand, courts do have discretion, then in cases in which they are entitled to exercise discretion they act on standards which are not part of the law. Therefore, though every social standard may figure in a court's decision, it does not follow that all of them are laws. The opportunity is given to those who support the thesis of the limits of law to draw a distinction between the standards used by courts which are law and those which are not. How is one to decide whether courts do or do not have discretion?

Professor Dworkin is primarily concerned to argue that there are legally binding principles. But this has never been denied by anyone, least of all by the positivists. Indeed, Austin could not have denied that some principles are legally binding while remaining true to his theory of law. The most fundamental tenet of his theory is that the commands of a sovereign are law, and there is nothing to prevent a sovereign from commanding that a principle shall be binding. Professor Dworkin's mistake lies in assuming that when Austin was talking about commands he was referring to what Professor Dworkin calls rules. But this is not the case. Neither does Hart use "rules" in the same sense as Professor Dworkin. By "rules" he means what Professor Dworkin seems to mean by "standards," namely rules, principles, or any other type of norm (whether legal or social.).[7]

The crux of the argument lies in the inference that since some principles are law, judicial discretion does not exist. Professor Dworkin says very little on this. The reason, I suspect, is that he rightly sees that other theorists, not only the positivists, exaggerated the scope of judicial discretion because they failed to attend to the role principles play in the law. They tended to assume that whenever a rule is vague the court has discretion and did not see that sometimes the rule when read in light of some principles is not vague and does not leave room for discretion. "A set of principles," as Professor Dworkin reminds us, "*can* dictate a result."[8] But that it sometimes can does not mean that it always does. And it is this that Professor Dworkin has to establish to make his case against judicial discretion. Unfortunately, he does not even try to establish this point.

I suppose that there might be a legal system which contains a rule that whenever the courts are faced with a case for which the law does not provide a uniquely correct solution they ought to refuse to render judgment. In such a system there would be no judicial discretion. But, whether or not such a system can exist, few if any legal systems in fact contain such a rule. In most legal systems there are at least three different sources of judicial discretion. Let me survey them briefly.

1. *Vagueness.* Vagueness is inherent in language. It is a problem courts have to face very frequently. As noted above, principles as well as rules of interpretation can sometimes solve problems of vagueness without leaving room for discretion. But principles themselves are vague, and discretion in cases of vagueness cannot be dispensed with so long as courts are entitled to render judgment in such cases.

2. *Weight.* Though principles sometimes limit the scope of the courts' discretion, they tend on the whole to expand it. For reasons noted earlier, the law usually determines with precision the relative weight of rules. Not so with principles. The law characteristically includes only incomplete indications as to their relative weight and leaves much to judicial discretion to be exercised in particular cases. The scope of discretion is in fact doubly extended, since not only must the relative importance of principles be determined, but also the importance relative to each principle of deviating from it or of following it on particular occasions. This matter is usually entrusted to judicial discretion.

That courts have discretion as to weight does not, of course, mean that the law has nothing to contribute to the solution of the case. It contributes some of the elements for a solution, but not all the elements necessary to dictate a uniquely correct solution. In such cases the law dictates what considerations have to be taken into account, but not what weight to assign to each of them or to actions in accordance with or contrary to each of them in particular cases.

3. *Laws of discretion.* Most legal systems contain laws granting courts discretion, not only as to the weight of legally binding considerations, but also to act on considerations which are not legally binding. Such discretion may be, and usually is, guided by principles. These principles, however, do not dictate the considerations to be taken into account, but merely limit the range of the considerations.

One may distinguish between substantive principles, which dictate a goal to be pursued or a value to be protected, and principles of discretion, which guide discretion by stipulating what type of goals and values the judge may take into account in exercising his discretion. Compare the following two sets of hypothetical principles. (a) "Car manufacturers have a duty to protect the public from accidents." "Increased productivity and efficiency should be the prime objective of public corporations." "The validity of standard contracts is contingent on their not taking advantage of the economic necessities of the weaker party." "The law favors security of title." (b) "The courts will not enforce unjust contracts." "Public corporations should act for the general good." "Whatever is *contra bonos mores et decorum* the principles of our law prohibit." The first group of principles set particular considerations to be acted on. They may be vague and they do not specify the weight to be given to each consideration, but the consideration prescribed is clear enough and is not a matter left to the courts' discretion. Principles of the second group, on the other hand, do not stipulate what considerations should be acted on. They merely specify the type of considerations which may be taken into account and leave the rest to the officials or the courts addressed by the principles. Rather than negating discretion, they presuppose its existence and guide it. What is "unjust" or "for the general good" is a matter of opinion and the courts or officials concerned are instructed by law to act on their own views. The law does not impose its own views of justice on the common good. Rather, it leaves the matter to the discretion of the courts or the officials. Many of the principles governing the action of the courts and the executive are principles of discretion.[9] Such principles, far from proving the absence of judicial discretion, are a manifestation of a legal policy to rely on and make use of judicial and administrative discretion in order to increase the flexibility of the law and improve the procedures for its constant review to meet changes in circumstance and opinion.

We must conclude that legal principles do not exclude judicial discretion; they presuppose its existence and direct and guide it. The argument from the absence of judicial discretion against the thesis of the limits of law must therefore be rejected. It should be noted, however, that judicial discretion is not arbitrary judgment. Courts are never allowed to act arbitrarily. Even when discretion is not limited or guided in any specific direction the courts are still legally bound to act as they think is best according to their beliefs and values. If they do not, if they give arbitrary judgment by tossing a coin, for example, they violate a legal duty. A judge must always invoke some general reasons. He has no discretion when the reasons are dictated by law. He has discretion when the law requires him to act on reasons which he thinks are correct, instead of imposing its own standards. When discretion is denied the law dictates which standards should be applied by all the judges. When discretion is allowed each judge is entitled to follow different reasons but he must believe that they are the best. Otherwise, discretion can be equated only with arbitrariness, whim, and caprice.

B. "Sources" of Legal Principles

Legal principles, like other laws, can be enacted or repealed by legislatures and administrative authorities. They can also become legally binding through establishment by the courts. Many legal systems recognize that both rules and principles can be made into law or lose their status as law through precedent. Rules and principles differ in this respect. A court can establish a new rule in a single judgment which becomes a precedent. Principles are not made into law by a single judgment; they evolve rather like a custom and are binding only if they have considerable authoritative support in a line of judgments. Like customary law, judicially adopted principles need not be formulated very precisely in the judgments which count as authority for their existence. All that has to be shown is that they underlie a series of courts' decisions, that they were in fact a reason operating in a series of cases.

This is recognized by Professor Dworkin. He does, however, add a third "source" of legally binding principles: "judgments of the community at large or some identifiable segment thereof."[10] And he adds in a footnote: "On some occasions, in some kinds of cases, moral principles accepted as standards within the community will figure as good reasons for a legal decision, just as, on other occasions, in other kinds of cases, will standards otherwise established. In this sense, such principles are part of the legal system, if it is helpful to talk about law as a system at all, and the flat statement that law and morals are separate systems is misleading."[11] The morality that Professor Dworkin has in mind consists of those moral views which became social norms in the community. No supporter of the thesis of the limits of law has ever denied that some social norms can be legal norms as well. The legislator can make a social norm into law either by direct enactment or by stipulating that social customs of a certain type should be binding as law. By the doctrine of precedent the courts can do the same. To admit as much does not weaken in the least the thesis of the limits of law.

To challenge the thesis it has to be established that all social norms are automatically (without prior legislative or judicial recognition) binding as law at least to the extent to which they do not conflict with laws created by legislation and precedent. If this were the case in all legal systems the thesis of the limits of law would indeed be badly shaken and would need a far-reaching reformulation. In his subsequent remarks Professor Dworkin implies that this is in fact the case.[12] I think that he is mistaken, and it is worth pausing to examine the source of his mistake.

In most countries one of the most general principles restraining judicial discretion enjoins judges to act only on those values and opinions which have the support of some important segment of the population.[13] There are various grounds on which the principle can be justified, none of which in itself justifies its full scope. It can be justified on democratic grounds; it can be defended by arguing that a judge whose actions affect the fortune of many should not trust his own judgment if it is not supported by learned opinion; it can be argued that laws out of tune with community values are unlikely to achieve their aim or will have some undesirable consequences. Each of these justifications, and others that can be used, interprets the principle somewhat differently. A close study of the matter will no doubt distinguish between various related principles which sometimes reinforce each other and sometimes conflict, or which apply to different situations. All these principles restrain but do not exclude judicial discretion. They do not oblige the courts to enforce any specific social norms. They limit their freedom to act on what they think is right by making it conditional on their ability to show that they are not alone in that opinion. There is, therefore, no reason to regard these principles as converting all social morality into law or as undermining the thesis of the limits of law.

They have, however, a curious, though perhaps not surprising, effect on judicial rhetoric in some countries and especially in the United States. As they should, courts tend to justify judgments based on discretion by arguments designed to show that the decision is a good one,[14] and by other arguments to show that the decision conforms to the views of some segment of the population. Unfortunately, some judges like to claim that the values they endorse are not merely the values of some but embody the national consciousness, represent the national consensus, are universally acknowledged, etc. This is perhaps harmless rhetoric if it is understood as such. Professor Dworkin, however, urges us to give literal interpretation to such pronouncements from the bench. The courts apply what they think are community values. It follows that it is wrong to regard them as acting on their own beliefs as legislators do. They may be wrong in their views of what the values of the community are, but if so they are wrong on a point of law, for since they are bound to apply community values these are part of the law.

This literal interpretation of judicial rhetoric is made possible only if one is prepared to join the courts in endorsing two really harmful myths. One is the myth that there is a considerable body of specific moral values shared by the population of a large and modern country. The myth of the common morality has made much of the oppression of minorities possible. It also allows judges to support a partisan point of view while masquerading as the servant of a general consensus. The second myth is that the most general values provide sufficient ground for practical conclusions. This myth holds that, since we all have a general desire for prosperity, progress, culture, justice, and so on, we all want precisely the same things and support exactly the same ideals, and that all the differences between us result from disagreements of fact about the most efficient policies to secure the common goals. In fact, much disagreement about more specific goals and about less general values is genuine moral disagreement, which cannot be resolved by appeal to the most general value-formulations which we all endorse, for these bear different interpretations for different people.

The courts tend all too often to claim that a specific policy is entailed by belief in some general value, thus avoiding a concrete justification of their decision, maintaining the rhetoric of common goals and community values, and endorsing partisan positions without admitting it. Some judges may themselves be captives of the myths they help to perpetuate. But the fact that they are misled should not mislead us. Occasional deviations from the canons of good reasoning can be dismissed as mistakes, but when constant use is made of a pattern of argumentation completely devoid of logical validity, it is time to distinguish between myth and rhetoric on the one hand and reality on the other. And the law should be understood to encompass reality, not rhetoric.

C. The Possibility of a Criterion of Identity

If the thesis of the limits of law is right, there must be a criterion of identity which sets necessary and sufficient conditions, satisfaction of which is a mark that a standard is part of a legal system. Austin's criterion of identity was that all and only the general commands of one sovereign are part of one legal system. Hart has criticized this criterion and suggested another. According to his theory every legal system contains a rule of recognition directed at the courts and imposing on them an obligation to apply those standards which fulfill various criteria set out in the rule.[15] The rule of recognition is a customary rule arising out of the behavior of law-enforcing officials through a period of time. The rest of the laws of the system are valid because they fulfill the conditions set out in the rule of recognition. The general criterion of identity of all legal systems is that each contains a rule of recognition and all those laws satisfying the conditions it stipulates.

Professor Dworkin claims that no adequate criterion of identity can be formulated and that therefore the thesis of the limits of law must be rejected. He directs his attack against Hart's criterion and employs two arguments to show that neither Hart's nor any other criterion of identity can account for the existence of legal principles. I shall argue that one of Professor Dworkin's arguments contains a valid criticism of Hart but does not bear on the possibility of formulating a somewhat different criterion of identity, whereas his second argument fails altogether.

"Hart's sharp distinction between acceptance and validity," the first argument runs, "does not hold. If we are arguing for the principle that a man should not profit from his own wrong, we could cite the acts of courts and legislatures that exemplify it, but this speaks as much to the principle's acceptance as its validity. (It seems odd to speak of a principle as being valid at all, perhaps because validity is an all-or-nothing concept, appropriate for rules, but inconsistent with a principle's dimension of weight."[16] The concept of validity is said to be inconsistent with the principle's dimension of weight on the ground that one establishes a principle's validity by showing that it has "institutional support"; but the amount of support a principle enjoys determines its weight and is a matter of degree: "[T]he more support we found, the more weight we could claim for the principle."[17] But this is surely mistaken. A principle might have been referred to frequently by the courts as binding, but have little weight. The degree of support may sometimes be evidence for a principle's weight, but it need not be and the two notions are not logically related.

Legal principles may be valid in precisely the same way that rules are. They may, for example, be enacted in the constitution or in a statute, as some of Professor Dworkin's own examples show. It is true, though, that some legal principles are law because they are accepted by the judiciary. But this is true of rules as well as principles. It is, however, an important point which does necessitate a modification of Hart's criterion of identity. But here again Professor Dworkin claims too much. He claims that if the master rule says merely that whatever other rules the community accepts are legally binding, then it fails to act as an identifying criterion distinguishing between law and social norms.[18] Had all social customs in all countries been legally binding, this would have been a valid criticism. Some countries, however, do not recognize custom as a source of law at all. Those legal systems which do regard customs as legally binding do so only if they pass certain tests. These tests, if they are not set out in a statute or some other law, are laid down by the rule of recognition, which determines under what conditions social customs are binding in law.

The rule of recognition, therefore, does serve to explain the legal status of general community customs. It cannot, however, explain in the same way the legal status of judicial customs. Since it is itself a judicial custom it cannot confer any special status on other judicial customs. Judicial rule-making, as I indicated above, differs in this respect from the evolution of principles by the courts. A rule becomes binding by being laid down in one case as a precedent. It does not have to wait until it is accepted in a series of cases to be binding. It is binding because of the doctrine of precedent which is part of our rule of recognition. Principles evolved by the courts become binding by becoming a judicial custom. They are part of the law because they are accepted by the courts, not because they are valid according to the rule of recognition.

Hart's criterion of identity must be modified. A legal system consists not only of one customary rule of the law-enforcing agencies and all the laws recognized by it, but of all the customary rules and principles of the law-enforcing agencies and all the laws recognized by them.[19] This is an important modification, but it preserves the fundamental point underlying Hart's criterion and shared by many: namely, that law is an institutionalized normative system and that the fact that the enforcement of its standards is a duty of special law-enforcing agencies is one important feature which distinguishes it from many other normative systems. The importance of this feature of law is made manifest by distinguishing between legal and nonlegal standards according to whether or not the courts have an obligation to apply them, either because they are themselves judicial custom or because judicial customs make their application obligatory.

Professor Dworkin has a second argument disputing the possibility of formulating an adequate criterion of identity. "True," he says, "if we were challenged to back up our claim that some principle is a principle of law, we would mention any prior cases in which that principle was cited, or figured in the argument . . . . Unless we could find some such institutional support, we would probably fail to make out our case . . . . Yet we could not devise any formula for testing how much and what kind of institutional support is necessary to make a principle a legal principle."[20] In this passage Professor Dworkin is rejecting not merely Hart's version of the thesis of the limits of law but all versions of this thesis. He agrees that if legal and nonlegal standards can be distinguished, this could only be done by relying on the fact that only legal standards have adequate institutional support in the practice of the courts. He denies, however, the possibility of a general explanation of what counts as adequate institutional support. It follows that it is impossible to provide a general account of the difference between legal and nonlegal standards and the thesis of the limits of law must be abandoned. What is the force of this argument? If a legal system consists, as I have suggested, of those standards which the courts are bound to recognize, we must agree with Professor Dworkin that we need a general explanation of what counts as adequate institutional support. For laws are binding on the courts either because judicial customs make their recognition obligatory or because they are themselves judicial customs. Thus the acceptability of the thesis of the limits of law depends on our ability to explain the concept of a judicial custom. But judicial customs are but a special case of social customs.

What we need is an adequate explanation of the concept of a customary norm. Once we have it we will know what judicial custom is and will have a complete criterion of identity. Hart has provided such an explanation. No doubt it is possible to improve on it, but there is no reason to suppose that the concept of a customary norm defies analysis. It is true that an analysis of the concept does not give us a decision procedure determining for every principle or rule whether or not it has sufficient support to be regarded as a judicial custom.[21] Borderline cases will remain; they must remain, for customary norms evolve gradually. But Dworkin's is a very weak argument, which rejects a distinction because it admits the existence of borderline cases.

A POSTSCRIPT

In 1967 Ronald Dworkin published an article, "The Model of Rules," in which he challenged what he took to be a dominant view in legal philosophy, legal positivism, whose most prominent spokesman was H. L. A. Hart. That view regards the law as a normative system the content of which is determined exclusively by factual social criteria. I shall call this the sources thesis. It is agreed by Dworkin and the legal positivists that if the content of the law is exclusively determined by social facts, then the law is gappy; that is, there are legal statements which are neither true nor false. I shall call this the indeterminacy thesis.[22]

Dworkin claimed that both positivists' theses stem from one mistake—the failure to notice that the law consists of standards of two kinds, not one. In this article Dworkin called them rules and principles, and claimed that the positivist mistake is the belief the law consists of rules only. The distinction between the two kinds of legal standards is that one applies in an "all-or-nothing" way, whereas the other "has a dimension of weight." This means, as Dworkin explains, that in any case in which an "all-or-nothing" standard is supposed to apply, the result ought to be as it dictates. When a different result is reached, either the law is violated or it is changed, or both. This suggests that "all-or-nothing" standards establish conclusive reasons for action. The other kind of standard has weight but not infinite weight. It argues for a result but it does not absolutely require it. It may be overridden by contrary considerations of greater weight. The second kind of legal standard, in other words, establishes a *prima facie* reason for action.

In the first part of my article, the second part of which is reproduced above, I suggested that we do not normally use the rule/principle distinction to mark the difference between *prima facie* and conclusive reasons or between the standards which establish them. In his article "Hard Cases" (1975) Dworkin has abandoned this use of "principles." Instead he now calls "a principle" any standard which establishes a right. Rules are hardly ever mentioned in "Hard Cases." But it is clear that they can no longer be contrasted with principles in their new (equally idiosyncratic) sense. Surely some rights are conclusive reasons for action. Therefore, some principles are conclusive reasons, i.e., some principles are rules.[23] To avoid confusion I shall stick to the terminology of conclusive and *prima facie* legal standards.

The part of the article here reproduced argues that the fact that the law includes standards setting *prima facie* reasons for action is compatible with both the sources and the indeterminacy theses. The existence of *prima facie* legal reasons no less than that of conclusive legal reasons can be established by social facts, and if anything it lends greater credibility to the view that the law contains gaps. Even though today I might have put some of the detailed points differently, I still believe that the argument is sound. I do not believe, however, that my argument is relevant to the assessment of Dworkin's current views on the law and on legal positivism. Nowhere in "Hard Cases," Dworkin's most systematic treatment of the general questions of legal philosophy, or since has Dworkin relied on any of the arguments of "The Model of Rules." Furthermore, it is difficult to fit the old arguments into the framework of the new theory.

My purpose in this note is to explain how Dworkin's argument shifted. It may help to begin by commenting briefly on two important bones of contention between Dworkin and legal positivists not mentioned so far. At the time I wrote my article in 1972 I believed that Dworkin's "The Model of Rules" was meant to challenge not merely the sources thesis but the very thought that the law has limits, i.e., that there are any tests or criteria which can determine the content of the law and distinguish between, e.g., a person's legal rights and his rights which are not legal rights. I have to admit that when I first read the article I didn't see it in this light. But listening to Dworkin's lectures in Oxford in 1970–72 convinced me that this was indeed his intention. The main thrust of "Hard Cases," however, is precisely to develop such a test. The law is there conceived as the institutional morality of the courts, and the bulk of the article is an attempt to develop and explain a set of tests by which an ideal court (better known as "Hercules") determines the contents of the law. In reviewing Dworkin's *Taking Rights Seriously,* I welcomed this change of view on Dworkin's part and his endorsement of the thesis of the limits of law.[24] However, there are signs that Dworkin's true intentions still elude me. In his "Reply to Seven Critics" Dworkin states that "I do wish to reject, however, the picture of 'existing law' . . . [according to which] . . . the law of a community is a distinct collection of particular rules and principles (and heaven knows what else) such that it is a sensible question to ask whether, at any given moment, a particular rule or principle belongs to that collection."[25] This reads like a renewed rejection of the very idea that there are tests of identity demarcating the limits of law.[26] I find this view hard to reconcile with the doctrine of "Hard Cases."

Much of Dworkin's attack on legal positivism has been and remains directed at the view that courts have discretion to use extra-legal standards in settling disputes. It is true that the indeterminacy thesis leads to the conclusion that courts have discretion. But the two theses should be very carefully distinguished. The fact is that the discretion allowed in most legal systems is much in excess of that required to deal with the inevitable indeterminacy of any legal system. Most legal systems introduce deliberate indeterminacy into many of their rules in order to leave certain issues to the discretion of the courts. This practice should not come as a surprise. We know that in many matters individuals may, and are often encouraged by law, to agree to refer their disputes to arbitrators who are often allowed to apply nonlegal standards. Similar considerations would suggest that on certain issues it is best to leave the law indeterminate and compel the parties to litigate before courts, which will be bound by law to apply nonlegal standards. On other occasions the legislator may lack the political power or will to decide an issue and may prefer to leave it for judicial determination.

These cases of deliberately created discretion do, nevertheless, arise out of (deliberately created) indeterminacy in the law. But much judicial discretion relates not to resolving indeterminacies but to the courts' power to change a determined and clear law. The most dramatic case of such discretion in English law is the power of the House of Lords to overrule both itself and the Court of Appeal. The Common Law consists of decisions of the House of Lords and the Court of Appeal. But all these can be changed by the House of Lords. When deciding whether and how to change the law, it acts predominantly on nonlegal reasons, i.e., it exercises discretion.[27] It is regrettable that so much of the debate about the existence or nonexistence of judicial discretion appears to take it for granted that the fate of the view that courts have discretion depends entirely on the indeterminacy thesis.

Dworkin's antidiscretion arguments in "The Model of Rules" are essentially arguments against indeterminacy only. His later arguments (with the exception of the first one mentioned below) are addressed against discretion regardless of whether its source is indeterminacy or a power to change the law. But what are the new arguments and why is the doctrine of "Hard Cases" difficult to reconcile with the antipositivist arguments of "The Model of Rules"? Dworkin has, so far as I can see, five arguments against the discretion thesis. One, developed in "No Right Answer?," is that it is incoherent. Two others regard the thesis as offensive to our democratic beliefs and to our condemnation of retroactive legislation. The fourth is that if courts have discretion then we would expect their reasoning, as set out in their judgments, to divide into two parts, a legal and a discretionary one. But in fact no such division is to be found. The fifth argument claims that courts in their judgments deny that they have discretion and attorneys arguing before courts address them as if they have no discretion. To claim that despite these facts they have discretion is to subscribe to an improbable conspiracy theory of the law.

I and others expressed doubts about these arguments before,[28] and I will not repeat them here. It is the last of these arguments which I find the most persuasive. It fails in part because the alleged facts are not there. Many judges both in Britain and the U.S. are willing to talk of the court's function in developing the law, adapting it to contemporary conditions, and changing and molding it in various ways. If lawyers address the court as if their sole business is to apply preexisting law, they all too often advise their clients that the law is unsettled and it all depends on the judge's political or personal orientations. Furthermore to regard the law as undetermined does not involve belief in a conspiracy to deceive the people. We are all familiar with ceremonial and ritual forms of address and discourse which are preserved despite a common belief in their literal falsity. The law and the legal profession are notorious for their tendency to preserve archaic, though possibly attractive, rituals. It would be surprising indeed if those were to express themselves exclusively in gowns and wigs and the like, and not in the rhetoric of legal argument. Ultimately the issue rests on the methods of reasoning employed by the courts, and their correct analysis is a matter on which legal scholars are as competent, if not more so, to adjudicate than judges.

To a considerable degree Dworkin's case against the discretion and the indeterminacy theses rests not on any of the above arguments but on his success in developing a view of the law which is inconsistent with them. It is here that the careful reader who is familiar with the debate around Dworkin's views on judicial discretion is due for a surprise when he turns to a careful study of Dworkin's writings themselves. Contrary to expectations encouraged by commentators and critics alike, the view that courts have no discretion is not, in Dworkin's own theory of law, a conclusion arrived at by a long chain of reasoning. It comes very near to being the unargued-for starting point of the theory. The law is conceived as the institutional morality of the courts. It consists in nothing more nor less than those standards which the courts should rely upon when deciding cases. This is the starting point. It is taken by Dworkin to be so intuitively obvious that it is never argued for nor even stated. His main effort is dedicated to an explanation of how the fact that a person acts as a judge make him subject to somewhat different considerations from those which he and others should be governed by in other circumstances. This he hopes to do by showing how, to use his own terminology, the institutional history of the courts (i.e., the fact that they have in the past applied statutes and precedents and developed certain doctrines) affects the way in which background morality (i.e., those considerations which apply to anyone regardless of his circumstances) bears on the courts.

This is a highly fascinating question.[29] But we need not go into it. The denial of judicial discretion was assured even before it was raised. It is a direct and trivial result of Dworkin's starting point, i.e., of the view that the law is the sum total of standards which the courts should rely upon.[30] Since a court has discretion if it is required by law to use nonlegal standards and since, by Dworkin's fundamental assumption, whatever standards the law should apply are by this very fact legal ones, it is clear that courts have no discretion.

This remark is not meant to trivialize the argument. It merely shows that the disagreement between Dworkin and many of his critics cannot be profitably studied by examining the argument about discretion. That argument is a mere reflection of a more fundamental disagreement about the nature of law, a disagreement which is masked by Dworkin himself since he did not state and defend his starting point.

But what precisely is the fundamental disagreement. It is quite separate from any disagreement about the rights thesis. This thesis does not affect at all the range of questions we are considering: the limits, sources, indeterminacy, and judicial discretion theses. A legal positivist who accepts all four of these theses may add to them a belief in the rights thesis. He may believe that courts do always decide cases on the basis of the rights of the litigants. He will deny that all the rights are legal rights. He will contend that sometimes courts are bound to exercise discretion and resort to nonlegal standards. But he will agree that these nonlegal standards may only be those determining the rights of the parties.

Nor is the fundamental disagreement between Dworkin and the legal positivists in the greater role allowed by the latter to judges' personal inclinations and views. This point is worth emphasizing if only because it is so often misunderstood. Many think that the disagreement is primarily between a conception which emphasizes government by judges (the legal positivists) and one of government by abstract principle (Dworkin). It is true that Dworkin's theory of law is committed to moral cognitivism whereas legal positivism is compatible with any coherent view of morality. But legal positivism, no less than Dworkin's theory, requires judges to act on reasons. Both theories rely on the personal views of judges to the extent that both entrust them with the responsibility to find out which reasons are good and valid grounds for their action. Both, however, deny that the fact that a judge holds a certain view makes it a valid ground for action. Both theories maintain that judicial activity is a reasoned activity and therefore judges aim at standards which are not of their own arbitrary invention, and can be criticized if they fail to meet them.[31]

The similarity between Dworkin and the positivists is indeed much greater than is often realized. Both contend that courts are legally required to apply source-based standards and both claim that they are legally required to follow certain moral standards, even when these are not source-based. Both further agree that the source-based standards determine which nonsource-based standards should be applied by the courts and when. Some theorists who are positivists may disagree with Dworkin as to the nature of this determination. But this disagreement does not derive from their positivist articles of faith nor does it threaten them. The only disagreement between Dworkin and the positivists is that the latter regard only source-based standards as law. They regard moral considerations as law only if incorporated through (in the U.K. and the U.S.) legislation or precedent, or if they form judicial customs. According to the positivist, to say of a standard that it is law is to say that it received actual recognition in the society whose law it is through the activities of certain of its institutions (those we normally call its legal institutions). According to Dworkin, to say of a standard that it is law is to say that it is morally right for the courts to apply it.

I have tried to capture the essence of the disagreement in a couple of sentences. It will take much longer to explain its significance. To do that we have to place it in the context of our attitudes to governments and our understanding of the relations between the activities of governments and other aspects of social life. This is not a task to be undertaken here.[32] My present purpose was simply to explain how far removed Dworkin's present criticism of legal positivism and the disagreement between his present views and those of the positivists are from the criticism expressed in "The Model of Rules" and refuted in my article above.

Do the interesting arguments and issues raised by Dworkin's "Hard Cases," and in more recent articles, supersede the arguments of "The Model of Rules" as I have claimed? Or do they merely add to them? One may say that the new arguments build on and add to the earlier ones. In "The Model of Rules," Dworkin conceded that positivists got their account of conclusive legal standards right and claimed they have a blind spot toward the existence of *prima facie* legal standards. Later he claimed that positivists fail to understand the nature of conclusive legal standards as well.[33] But to say this is to underestimate the force and originality of Dworkin's theory of law. For him a statute is law not just because it enjoys the recognition of legal institutions. It is law because (and to the extent that) morality requires courts to follow and apply standards which enjoy such recognition. That is why the more recent Dworkin condemns the positivist treatment of both conclusive and *prima facie* legal standards. The thought that the positivists are better able to account for conclusive legal standards depends on accepting the positivist source-based analysis of such standards as much as on denying their ability to explain *prima facie* standards. The new Dworkin denies that the positivists can explain anything. To defend such a claim, the old distinction between conclusive and *prima facie* reasons is of no help, and the old arguments based on it have no room in the new armory whose new weapons belong to a different era.

NOTES

1. "The Model of Rules" is perhaps not altogether clear that all forms of the thesis of the limits of law are to be rejected, though it plainly opposes one version of the thesis by rejecting the tenet "that the law of a community is distinguished from other social standards by some test in the form of a master rule." Dworkin, "The Model of Rules," *University of Chicago Law Review* 35 (1967): 14, 45, reprinted under the title "Is Law a System of Rules?" in *Essays in Legal Philosophy,* edited by R. Summers, (1968), pp. 25, 59. "Model of Rules" is also reprinted in Dworkin, *Taking Rights Seriously* (Cambridge: Harvard University Press, 1978). Professor Dworkin has, however, confirmed to me in conversation that these arguments are directed against the thesis of the limits of the law generally and has taken such a position in his lectures at Oxford University in 1971.

2. See Dworkin, "Judicial Discretion," *Journal of Philosophy* 60 (1963): 624. Professor Dworkin has reformulated his theory in "The Model of Rules," pp. 32–40 to meet some of the objections raised by G. C. MacCallum, Jr., in his reply to Dworkin's first paper. See MacCallum, "Dworkin on Judicial Discretion," *Journal of Philosophy* 60 (1963): 638.

3. Dworkin, "Judicial Discretion," pp. 32–33.

4. I shall henceforth be concerned only with "discretion" in this sense, and only this sense is involved in what I shall call the "thesis of judicial discretion."

5. On this problem see Joseph Raz, "The Identity of Legal Systems," *California Law Review* 59 (1971): 795, reprinted in Raz, *The Authority of Law* (Oxford: 1979).

6. The courts may occasionally rely on the wrong reasons. I am concerned here only with the reasons which they are entitled to use.

7. Of course both Austin and Hart would maintain that *some* principles are not part of the law. But this is no more than to say that they believe in the thesis of the limits of law. It should be noted

that I am using "standards" to cover not only norms but also generally accepted reasons for action.

8. Dworkin, "Judicial Discretion," p. 36.

9. Many of the principles mentioned by Professor Dworkin are of this kind.

10. Dworkin, "Judicial Discretion," p. 635.

11. Ibid., p. 635, note 9.

12. Ibid., p. 635ff.

13. The main device controlling courts' values and ideology is, of course, not this principle, but the methods of appointing or electing judges.

14. Though judges are entitled, sometimes, to act as they think best, that they believe the decision is a good one is never a reason for it; they must have reasons for their beliefs.

15. For arguments supporting this interpretation of Hart's doctrine, see Raz, "Identity of Legal Systems," pp. 807–8, and notes 23–24.

16. Dworkin, "Judicial Discretion," p. 42.

17. Ibid., p. 41.

18. Ibid., pp. 43–44.

19. For a more precise formulation of the criterion and a more detailed examination of the problem, see Raz, "Identity of Legal Systems," p. 795.

20. Dworkin, "Judicial Discretion," p. 41.

21. It is worth reminding ourselves that not every principle is evolved by the courts; many result from legislative action.

22. I have tried to explain why the sources thesis leads to the indeterminacy thesis in essay 4 of *The Authority of Law* (Oxford; 1979). For Dworkin's attack on the indeterminacy thesis see his "No Right Answer" in P. M. S. Hacker and J. Raz, eds., *Law, Morality and Society* (Oxford; 1977).

23. It would seem that in the terminology coined in "Hard Cases," what was called in "The Model of Rules" a principle is now called a relatively abstract principle, whereas what was then called a rule is now a very concrete principle.

24. "Professor Dworkin's Theory of Rights," *Political Studies* 26 (1978).

25. *Georgia Law Review* 11 (1977): 1256. This reply is included in the 2nd edition of *Taking Rights Seriously.*

26. Needless to say, the thesis of the limits of law does not insist on a sharp boundary to the law, a limit which lacks all vagueness. This would be inconsistent with the positivist thesis of the indeterminacy of the law.

27. In "Law and Value in Adjudication" (in *The Authority of Law*) I argued that all cases of distinguishing earlier decisions are cases of changing the law involving the exercise of discretion. This, rather than the more dramatic overruling, is the most common way in which English courts exercise discretion by changing existing law.

28. Dworkin's argument for the incoherence of the indeterminacy thesis is in "No Right Answer." The other arguments are expressed or implied in "Hard Cases" and elsewhere. For my attempts to refute these points see, on the first argument, essay 4 of *The Authority of Law,* on the second and third, "Professor Dworkin's Theory of Rights," ibid., and on the fourth, essay 10 in *The Authority of Law.*

29. It is also one to which, as "A Reply to Seven Critics," p. 1252 shows, Dworkin has not yet given an answer.

30. Dworkin's fundamental assumption, the starting point of his theory of law, namely the claim that the law is just the standards that courts ought to follow, is also a rejection of the sources thesis. It, like the discretion thesis, is rejected outright. Dworkin's theory is not an argument for their rejection. It is constructed on the basis of the claim that they are wrong.

31. To be a moral noncognitivist is not to identify morality with the whims or personal inclinations of judges. Such a view of morality is incoherent.

32. For my own defense of positivism, see essay 3 of *The Authority of Law* as well as pp. 210–11 of *The Concept of a Legal System,* 2nd edition. (Oxford: 1980).

33. This change in his position precedes "Hard Cases" and is first evident in "The Model of Rules II," first published in 1972.

5

Policy, Rights, and Judicial Decision

Kent Greenawalt

A SUMMARY OF DWORKIN'S VIEWS ON PRINCIPLES AND POLICIES AND INSTITUTIONALIZED RIGHTS

According to Professor Dworkin, arguments of principle "justify a political decision by showing that the decision respects or secures some individual or group right";[1] such arguments are appropriately relied upon by judges. Arguments of policy "justify a political decision by showing that the decision advances or protects some collective goal of the community as a whole";[2] generally judges do not appropriately rely upon such arguments. Dworkin asserts that his distinction between principles and policies affords a description of how judges do decide cases and gives a normative account of how they should decide cases.[3] He commences his argument against judicial reliance on policy by examining two arguments against judicial originality, or lawmaking: first, that judges are not responsible to the electorate and, therefore, should not make new law; and, second, that because judicial decisions have retroactive effect it is unfair to the losing party to base a decision on newly made law. These arguments, Dworkin states, are powerful if one focuses on policies. Decisions upon policy grounds involve "a compromise among individual goals and purposes in search of the welfare of the community as a whole . . . . Policy decisions must therefore be made through the operation of some political process designed to produce an accurate expression of the different interests that should be taken into account."[4] And, Dworkin urges, legislatures are much better equipped for this task than judges. The retroactivity argument is also powerful if one considers decisions based on policy; "it does . . . . seem wrong to take property from one individual and hand it to another in order just to improve overall economic efficiency."[5]

Neither the democracy nor the retroactivity argument against judicial originality has much force, Dworkin asserts, if decisions are based on principles. Arguments of principle do not often rest "on assumptions about the nature and intensity of the different demands and concerns distributed throughout the community"; and a judge "insulated from the demands of the political majority" may be in a good position to evaluate such arguments.[6]

From *Georgia Law Review* 11, no. 5 (September 1977), 993–96, 1003–35, 1047–53. Reprinted by permission of the author and *Georgia Law Review*.

Since an argument of principle claims that a right already exists, the person who loses a case on the basis of principle has no complaint of unfair surprise.

Dworkin suggests a further distinction between principles and policies. Judges are expected to decide with "articulate consistency."[7] They are supposed to decide like cases alike and to base particular decisions on reasons they would be willing to apply to other cases that the reasons cover.[8] In Dworkin's view, decisions based on policy may not require consistency. A strategy may be pursued involving unequal distribution; a subsidy to one aircraft manufacturer or city need not be followed by a similar subsidy to all similar aircraft manufacturers or cities. If judges could decide on the basis of policy, then they would not have to hold to the standard of articulate consistency. Since judges are expected to make decisions on grounds they would follow in other cases and to be guided by cases already decided, it follows that they should be deciding on the basis of principles, not policies.

Legislatures, within constitutional bounds, are free to pursue the general welfare as they choose; they appropriately give weight to arguments of policy as well as arguments of principle in deciding what statutes to pass.[9] The role of courts is different. Courts are supposed to give effect to rights; they are not supposed to decide whether a claim of right comports with the general welfare but whether that claim is given recognition by the institutions of which the court is a part.[10]

Exactly what constitutes an institutionalized right is a complex matter, but that notion is meant to exclude not only the alternative that judges decide on the basis of their evaluation of what will serve the general welfare but also the alternative that judges give effect directly to moral rights.[11] A southern judge in the pre-Civil War United States might, for example, have believed that slaves had a moral or "background" right to be free; but as a judge he had to implement many institutionalized rights of slave owners.[12]

How the ideal judge determines institutional rights varies somewhat depending on whether the issue is statutory, constitutional, or one arising under the common law, but in all three contexts difficult cases require him to construct a political theory that places the particular issue in a broader context. In statutory cases, judges are supposed to implement rights given by the legislature. Any argument about rights the legislature has granted is an argument of principle.[13] In cases as to which the statute is unclear, courts are not supposed to imagine how the legislators might in fact have answered the question if they had thought of it,[14] but rather are to construct and rely upon "a special political theory that justifies this statute, in the light of the legislature's more general responsibilies, better than any alternative theory."[15] In constitutional cases, the task is similar, though constitutions, much more frequently than statutes, contain broadly worded moral concepts, e.g., "equal protection of the laws," "cruel and unusual punishment." As to these, courts are supposed to develop the concepts formulated in the Constitution, even when a developed understanding of those concepts leads to a conclusion different from that the framers would have reached themselves (e.g., a modern court more fully understanding the concept of "cruel and unusual" punishment might hold capital punishment unconstitutional though the framers clearly thought it was not "cruel and unusual").[16] In developing one constitutional concept, the ideal judge, whom Dworkin names Hercules, would also give due regard to the rest of the Constitution.[17] In deciding common law cases, judges also give effect to institutionalized rights. Since fairness requires treating like cases alike, considerable weight must be given to precedent, even when an earlier decision is not directly on point but deals with issues hard to distinguish on morally acceptable grounds from those in the present case.[18] Because decisions based on policies do not have "gravitational force," the gravitational force of precedents is limited to the principles necessary to justify those precedents.[19] In difficult cases, Hercules must rely on a political theory that best justifies existing legal institutions and the rules of common law and those rules of constitutional law and statutory law that are based on principles.[20] This theory will enable him to resolve cases that do not fall within established rules and also to decide when existing common law rules should be modified or abandoned because of their inconsistency with broad common law or constitutional principles.[21]

This account of Dworkin's overall theory gives us a basis for analyzing his thesis about principles and policies as well as his thesis that judges should always try to give effect to institutionalized rights. The parts of the account that require elaboration or qualification are dealt with more fully in the sections that follow.

POLICY AND JUDICIAL DECISION

I turn now to decisions by judges in a complex legal system like that of the United States. This part of the article is divided into four main sections. The first deals with common law adjudication. The second, which is relevant both to common law adjudication and to statutory and constitutional adjudication, considers the ways in which the interests of nonparties figure in judicial decisions. The third and fourth sections are specifically addressed to judicial interpretations of statutes and constitutions, respectively. My analysis leads to the following conclusions: first, as Dworkin develops his own theory, there are some circumstances in which it is hard to see how a judge who relied directly on policies would act differently from one who relied exclusively on principles, as Dworkin understands principles. Second, Dworkin inadequately attends to the interests of nonparties, and what he does say about them borders on being inconsistent. If we interpret Dworkin's theory to provide reasonable responses to questions of how courts are supposed to weigh interests of nonparties, the distinction between principles and policies becomes much more blurred and almost vanishes. Finally, Dworkin's arguments for the proposition that judges should not rely directly on policy arguments are unpersuasive.

Common Law Adjudication

I must now reexamine the "democracy" and "retroactivity" arguments against judicial originality, as well as the requirement of articulate consistency, to see if Dworkin is right in saying that they provide powerful support for a rejection of judicial use of policies in common law adjudication.

Democracy.—Dworkin's first argument is that judicial reliance on policies is not consistent with the democratic premise that policy determinations should be made by a politically responsible body. Because they are responsible to the electorate, legislatures properly make decisions about general welfare and, being sensitive to contending political forces, are better equipped to make such decisions than courts.[22] The problem with this argument is that a legislature simply does not have the time or interest to engage itself in establishing rights for every area of the common law. It leaves certain areas substantially to the development of courts. We may assume that if the legislature got involved in those areas it would pay close attention to what rules would promote the general welfare. Can it be that if it leaves these areas to courts, courts should not pay any attention at all to such considerations? A court in these areas is acting much like the football referee deciding on the forward pass or the council in a society with no legislature. It is not at all obvious that legislatures are better able to decide all questions of general welfare than the courts.[23] Some issues of policy as well as principle may lend themselves better to the reasoned deliberation of the judicial process than to the rough give-and-take of the legislative process.[24] But even if legislatures were always more adept, that would hardly be reason for courts to eschew policy altogether when legislators have declined to get involved. It cannot sensibly be argued that legislative abstinence shows that the politically responsible body has decided that a particular area of law is best developed in terms of principles rather than policies, since legislators are not often likely to focus on that particular issue. Legislative uninvolvement more realistically reflects either lack of political interest or some vague sense that the problems are being adequately handled by courts. Thus, the existence of a democratically elected body with power to pass general legislation does not provide firm support for the argument that judges should rely solely on principles.

Retroactivity.—Dworkin's second argument against judicial reliance on policies is that it is unfair for the losing party to suffer because of a fresh policy determination. Recall, however, that (as indicated in the football example) "hard cases" are those in which rights are uncertain at the outset. It may be questionable whether it is sensible to speak of a retroactivity problem in this setting: certainly the problem is less severe than if clearly held rights are taken away on that basis. And it is not at all clear that exclusive reliance on principle will produce fewer defeats for reasonable expectations than partial reliance on policy.[25] Furthermore, it is plausible to suppose that people understand that recognition of their uncertain claims of right will depend on consistency with the general welfare, especially when claims are made in the context of complex social institutions governing all areas of life rather than in the context of a narrowly constructed game. If people are aware that their right to do some act may sometimes be contingent on the act's not being inconsistent with the general welfare, it is no more offensive to deny their claim on the basis of the general welfare than on the basis of some arguable principle. In addition, not every judicial judgment involves damages or punishment. If a judgment simply tells someone to stop doing something in the future, it is no more retroactive in effect than ordinary legislation. Injunctions and various other remedies are not retroactive in the special sense Dworkin finds objectionable. Of course, any change in the rules of behavior may have adverse consequences for those who have planned on the basis of earlier rules, but this cost occurs with legislative changes as well as judicial decisions. Even when monetary damages would be the typical remedy, courts sometimes make their decisions prospective only,[26] in order to avoid unfair retroactive effects.[27]

It should also be recognized that, even if instances of unfair retroactivity were a cost of judicial reliance on policy, the cost would sometimes be acceptable. This general point is buttressed by the fact that the legal system clearly tolerates retroactive effects in two other sorts of instances. First, legislatures have the power to change rights in pending cases, so long as they do not violate entrenched constitutional rights.[28] This means that in some cases the legislature will take away a right that existed when the relevant transaction occurred and even when litigation started. Dworkin discusses at length an English case called *Spartan Steel*,[29] in which the issue was whether a defendant who negligently destroyed the cable of a power company was liable in damages to another company that suffered losses because its power was cut off. If, after litigation started, the Parliament, whether on grounds of principle or policy, had passed a statute clearly precluding the recovery of damages for this sort of plaintiff, and it had meant that statute to be applied to all pending cases, a court would have denied recovery regardless of the view it might have taken in the absence of a statute. An American court would reach the same result, since the plaintiff company could not convincingly argue that legislative elimination of its expectation of recovery deprived it of property without due process of law.[30]

Second, claims in pending cases can be altered by new precedents. We can imagine that two cases are pending, and the highest court, relying solely on principles but less able than Hercules, makes a mistake and decides for the wrong party in the first case. Lower courts are bound to follow the mistaken decision. Even if the second case gets to the highest court and, with intervening personnel changes, a majority of the highest court thinks the original decision was wrong, as long as the majority thinks the first case was "close" and the decision only slightly wrong, it may decide that it should follow precedent. The end result is that the party in the second case who started out his litigation with a "right" to win lost that right to win because of an intervening mistaken decision. Surely his complaint about retroactive loss of rights is at least as great as that of a party who loses a case because of a reliance on wise policies.

If the defeat of uncertain but justified pending claims is an acceptable price for the doctrine of precedent, and the defeat of even certain pending claims is an acceptable price for legislative supremacy, we must conclude, given the powerful reasons for some judicial reliance on policy, that the retroactivity argument is not in itself a sufficient basis for rejecting such reliance on policy, even assuming that that argument has more force than the earlier discussion suggests.

Articulate Consistency.—There remains Dworkin's argument that principles generate demands for equal treatment in ways that policies do not and that the critical status of precedents in common law adjudication helps to establish the inappropriateness of judicial reliance on policy argument. Dworkin's argument in this respect seems so clearly mistaken, one wonders if one fully understands it. Dworkin says:

> The gravitational force of a precedent may be explained by appeal, not to the wisdom of enforcing enactments, but to the fairness of treating like cases alike . . . .

> [The judge] must limit the gravitational force of earlier decisions to the extension of the arguments of principle necessary to justify those decisions. If an earlier decision were taken to be entirely justified by some argument of policy it would have no gravitational force.[31]

The reasons courts follow precedents are numerous. In addition to the notion of justice that like cases should be treated alike, some of these, as Llewellyn suggests, are convenience, reliance on accumulated experience, and the usefulness for planning of being able to predict what a court will decide.[32] These reasons sound more like intelligent collective policies than principles asserting rights. But whether the underlying reasons for following precedents are themselves reasons of principle or policy or both, the main point is that the reasons for following a particular decision apply even if that decision is initially based on policy. The conferral of benefits for policy reasons typically gives rise to a substantial claim of justice to equal treatment on behalf of those similarly situated. Thus, even if Dworkin is right that the doctrine of precedent is based mainly on considerations of justice, he is certainly wrong that decisions based on policies have no gravitational force as precedents.

Indeed, when Dworkin chooses to illustrate the thesis that decisions based on policy have little or no gravitational force, he turns to legislative subsidies.[33] We may grant that a legislature has the freedom to pursue many kinds of collective goals by selective benefits and that it can subsidize one enterprise and decline to subsidize a similarly situated enterprise. Courts are not engaged in granting subsidies. Nor, when rendering common law decisions, can they conduct controlled experiments. They cannot treat like cases differently on the ground that they would be economically beneficial or would increase scientific understanding of social problems. Courts deciding issues of law must be willing to decide one case in the way they would decide similar cases, and they also have some duty to lay down rules of general application in justifying their decisions.[34]

Legislatures also adopt rules of general application, however, and it is this legislative function, rather than subsidies, that more nearly resembles the business of common law courts. Dworkin does not doubt that legislatures are properly guided by policies in passing general legislation. A moment's reflection is enough to suggest that when a legislature grants rights to one group of people, even if it does so on policy grounds, other groups that are not justifiably distinguishable have a strong claim of fairness to similar treatment. Because of the supposed political checks on most sorts of arbitrariness and because of supposed judicial incompetence to evaluate legislative categorization, courts ordinarily sustain legislative distinctions against claims that they are so unfair they deny equal protection of the laws;[35] but this judicial passivity is hardly a sign that legislatures have no serious responsibility to treat like cases alike.[36] Since judicial authority rests so heavily on the process of reasoned elaboration for decisions, the demand for equal treatment and sensible distinctions is even stronger and forms a more central basis for judicial decision. But the demand for articulate consistency is quite consonant with the appropriateness of reliance on policy arguments.[37]

Negligence, Nuisance, and Some Other Common Law Areas.—We have found that Dworkin's general arguments against judicial reliance on policy are weak and so should not be surprised to learn that courts frequently do rely on arguments that a particular decision will serve the collective welfare in some respect. Dworkin examines some areas of law for which this is often said to be so and concludes that a deeper understanding of what is going on reveals that arguments of principle are really being employed. As we examine the power of his claims, we need to keep in mind not only the question whether his thesis is defensible but also the question whether his defense of it largely undermines its significance.

Professor Dworkin is aware of writing that suggests that most common law rules can be justified on the economic ground that they promote the most efficient allocation of scarce resources.[38] He acknowledges that a direct judicial appeal to overall economic efficiency as the basis for decisions would be inconsistent with his thesis, since such an appeal would be to the policy of promoting the general welfare rather than to institutionalized rights. But he argues that even if courts do engage in economic analysis they may be working out the application of a principle rather than applying a policy directly. An examination of Dworkin's argument in connection with negligence and nuisance exposes the difficulty of distinguishing arguments of principle from ones of policy and illustrates the general acceptance of judicial reliance on arguments of policy.

Dworkin summarizes Learned Hand's theory of negligence as follows: "The test of whether the defendant's act was unreasonable, and therefore actionable, is the economic test which asks whether the defendant could have avoided the accident at less cost to himself than the plaintiff was likely to suffer if the accident occurred discounted by the improbability of the accident."[39] Although this test seems to make the decision turn on whether "the collective welfare would have been advanced more by allowing the accident to take place or by spending what was necessary to avoid it,"[40] Dworkin urges its consistency with his thesis. It is the responsibility of courts to make abstract rights concrete and to resolve in specific cases competing claims of abstract rights.[41] In some cases, "the argument from competing abstract principles to a concrete right can be made in the language of economics."[42] The relevant principle may be that "each member of a community has a right that each other member treat him with the minimal respect due a fellow human being";[43] the proper balance of liberty and restraint may be determined by the collective utility of the pair of people involved. What at first glance appears to be use of a policy is in fact a concrete application of a principle.

Dworkin says "Hand's test [is a method] of compromising competing rights" which considers "ony the welfare of those whose abstract rights are at stake. They do not provide room for costs or benefits to the community at large except as these are reflected in the welfare of those whose rights are at question."[44] If Dworkin means to suggest that any comprehensive statement of a test of negligence would take account only of the welfare of the parties involved, he is obviously wrong. Defendant *A*, driving carefully, sees a live baby on the road in front of him; he swerves to miss it and unavoidably smashes into plaintiff's parked car. Defendant *B*, also driving carefully, sees a dead rabbit on the road and, since he hates to run over dead animals, swerves and unavoidably smashes into plaintiff's parked car. Defendant *A* is not negligent and Defendant *B* is negligent precisely because the welfare of the live baby made *A's* act of swerving reasonable while the welfare of the dead rabbit was not enough to make *B's* act reasonable. Firemen, policemen, and ambulance drivers often drive their vehicles in ways that would clearly be negligent for the ordinary citizen; their acts are not negligent because the welfare of others depends heavily on their getting someplace quickly. It is patently clear, therefore, that within the law of negligence the welfare of members of the community at large, as well as the collective utility of the parties, can be of vital concern.

This concern is even more pervasive for the law of nuisance; whether an activity asserted to be a nuisance is tortious or not will often depend on whether it is inconsistent with community welfare. According to the *Restatement (Second) of Torts,* "[a]n intentional invasion of another's interest in the use and enjoyment of land is unreasonable [and therefore actionable] . . . if (a) the gravity of the harm outweights the utility of the actor's conduct . . . ."[45] It is even harder to say about nuisance what Dworkin says about negligence—that the law is based entirely on a principle of reasonable behavior toward fellow men. A person can act perfectly reasonably by starting in a remote area a business that necessarily involves offensive odors of air pollution. As long as the surrounding population remains small and the damage to each landowner is not very great, no one may have a right to have the business stopped. But if, even for fortuitous and unforeseeable reasons, the area becomes heavily populated, the business can become a nuisance, and each surrounding homeowner, or the municipality, may have a right to abate it, even though no more damage is done to each affected person than was done to those who lived nearby when the population was very small.[46] Now it might be said that when population density reaches a certain level the owner should terminate his business because his continuing use is unfair to his fellow citizens. To stop use may mean very severe economic loss,[47] but under the traditional law of nuisance, society requires him to bear that loss because the social welfare requires it.[48] It would be stretching matters to say that mandatory abatement is simply the application of a principle requiring decent respect for others.

How might a defender of Dworkin's basic thesis try to deal with those points? He might say that a principle of "minimal respect" does encompass the welfare of nonparties or that the common law contains some principles that simply call for behavior consonant with the general welfare. However, as we have already seen, if every argument of policy can be transformed into an argument of principle of equal force, the thesis that judges must rely on principles becomes insignificant. If the thesis is to retain significance, it must be argued either that the areas of tort law just discussed are atypical or that whatever reliance on nonparty interests is justified is somehow different from reliance on collective welfare. The possible attempt to distinguish legitimate reliance on nonparty interests from inappropriate reliance on the general welfare is discussed in the next section. Here, I examine briefly the second possible argument.

Once we have determined that in very important respects one's rights depend heavily on whether one's activities conform with community welfare, we will be skeptical of any claim that, in other areas in which an applicable legal standard gives no clear answer, the consistency of one's claim with the general welfare is irrelevant. And if we look closely at some other areas of common law adjudication in which community welfare is less obviously at the forefront, we also see policies being given weight.[49]

The New York Court of Appeals has indicated that in choice-of-law cases an important factor is the residence of the parties at the time of judicial decision.[50] If the defendant (or presumably the plaintiff) moves to New York after a negligently caused injury has occurred in another state, that is a factor to be weighed by New York courts in determining whether a limitation on damages in the other state will be respected in New York. It is hard to see how arguments of principle about the institutionalized rights of the parties should be affected by a party's move to New York after the accident. Yet a case may arise in which the New York court may apply New York law even though it would have applied the law of another state if the parties had remained residents of another state.

In contract cases, courts have refused to order specific performance in circumstances when that would be economically wasteful,[51] a consideration that seems more directly one of policy than of principle.

Common law rules about standing, ripeness, and mootness, which limit the circumstances in which legal rights may be adjudicated, appear to be another instance in which courts rely on policies, in this case the policies of efficient administration. Dworkin considers these rules justified on the basis of principle because if a court were to allow many suits "it would lack the time to consider promptly enough other law suits that are aiming to vindicate rights that are, taken together, more important than the rights it therefore proposes to bar."[52] As long as judicial resources are irrevocably limited by outside constraint, this justification serves fairly well. But it is obvious that even if the judiciary could command from the rest of society as many resources as it could possibly use, and do so without diminishing the quality of justice in cases now taken, limits on adjudication would be appropriate. It would be a misallocation of social resources to expend substantial time and money establishing rights that may well make no practical difference because the "conflict" is moot or may never ripen. It would be much better to put those social resources to other uses, such as hospitals. It might also be thought that too generous encouragement of litigation would have the socially undesirable effect of educating people not to settle their own problems. Thus, it is too facile to suppose that the reasons for "jurisdictional" limitations have only to do with vindicating rights in other cases and nothing to do with desirable allocations of social resources in some more general sense.[53]

As we have seen, policies appropriately do underlie common law decisions in areas as disparate as torts, contracts, conflict of laws, and "jurisdiction," and there is good reason to suppose that close examination would reveal their appropriate use in any other areas that might be examined.[54]

The Interests of Nonparties

As the previous discussion illustrates, the interests of nonparties figure importantly in the decision of many common law cases, and since the same is true of constitutional and statutory cases, the analysis in this section does not draw distinctions among the three kinds of cases.

At some points in his article, Dworkin appears to come close to suggesting that arguments based on the interests of nonparties are not arguments of principle. We have already looked at his emphasis on the limitation of an economic test for negligence to the collective utility of the parties. And in a brief discussion of the exclusionary rule, his assertion that the government has no "right" to conviction of the guilty leads the reader to suppose that the government may not marshal arguments of principle on its side.[55] But when he explicitly addresses the issue, Dworkin acknowledges that giving weight to the interests of third parties may sometimes be consistent with relying only on principles. His justification of common law limits to jurisdiction rests on the vindication of rights in other cases. When he discusses possible arguments against desegregation, he indicates that the assertion that people would lose their lives in ensuing riots would be an argument of principle.[56] More generally, he says, "[i]f a judge appeals to public safety or the scarcity of some vital resource, for example, as a ground for limiting some abstract right, then his appeal might be understood as an appeal to the competing rights of those whose security will be sacrificed, or whose just share of that resource will be threatened if the abstract right is made concrete."[57]

On the fairest reading of Dworkin, and certainly the only reading that preserves any plausibility for his thesis about principles and policies, arguments about the rights of third parties can count as arguments of principle. Since many arguments about the general welfare can be cast in terms of the rights of nonparties, it might be thought that this concession undercuts the distinction between principles and policies.[58] But Dworkin says, "it is a fallacy to suppose that because some argument of principle can always be found to substitute for an argument of policy, it will be as cogent or as powerful as the appropriate argument of policy would have been."[59] For example, according to Dworkin, although the argument against desegregation that people would lose their lives in riots would be one of principle as well as policy, the argument that people would suffer discomfort from desegregation would be only one of policy. The full weight of arguments against judicial desegregation is therefore weakened, in his view, if courts cannot rely on policies.

What Dworkin fails to do is elucidate how precisely the line is to be drawn between arguments on behalf of nonparties that count as arguments of principles and those that do not. He also fails to indicate in any systematic way why typically the substitute argument of principle will be less weighty than the argument of policy for which it substitutes. In analyzing this problem, it is helpful at the outset to understand some different ways in which the interests of nonparties can figure in legal argument.

(1) It may be argued that behavior was legally justified because the contrary behavior would have violated or risked damage to the established legal rights of nonparties. The driver of a car who swerves to avoid the live baby can argue that if he had not swerved he would have violated the baby's right. Conversely, it might be argued that behavior was unjustified because it violated, or risked damage to, the established rights of third parties.

(2) It may be argued that behavior was justified because it promoted the important interests of potentially affected persons more than alternative behavior would have. The heart attack victim riding to the hospital in an ambulance may have no legal right to get there quickly; thus, an ambulance driver

who obeyed the speed limit might not violate anyone's legal rights. Nevertheless, if he speeds to save the victim's life, he may be neither negligent nor guilty of a traffic offense.[60] In the nuisance cases, whether the perpetrator of the supposed nuisance can continue or not may depend upon the total impact of his activity upon all affected persons.

(3) It may be argued that allowing behavior of a particular type will result in injury to the interests of persons situated similarly to plaintiff by persons situated similarly to defendant. Ordinarily such an argument does no more than suggest a case's general importance; if *B* has a better claim to win than *A*, then ordinarily people situated like *B* would also have a better claim to win than people situated like *A*. But sometimes *A* may have peculiar characteristics that make his claim less appealing than the claim of people situated like him, in which case his appeal to their interests may make a difference. Let us suppose, for example, that a state court is deciding whether to adopt a tort right of privacy for some publications of true facts and that it fully accepts Harry Kalven's contention that injured people who really care about privacy will not sue and thereby republicize the embarrassing facts.[61] If only people who are really indifferent to privacy would recover, that is certainly a good reason for not establishing this branch of the privacy tort, especially when the interest in freedom of the press is weighed on the other side. But the court must consider whether a rule of recovery will deter invasions of the privacy of the genuinely shy. Since the press may not know in advance which people care about privacy and which do not, it may, if potentially liable, refrain from invading the privacy of many persons who in fact would not bring suit. Thus, the claim of *A*, the plaintiff who does not really care about privacy, is strengthened by reference to others who would be situated like him under the rule for recovery he proposes. A similar argument can be made if a court is deciding whether to uphold *A's* claim in a criminal case to have his wife barred from testifying against him when she is eager to do so.[62] Even if a court supposes that the wife's eagerness to testify shows that this particular marriage is beyond repair, it may believe that a rule barring testimony will promote the health of marriages that have not reached the breaking point, thereby protecting the interest in the marital relationship of men situated like *A*.[63]

(4) It may be argued that if certain practices are prohibited or allowed the indirect result will likely be fewer violations of legal rights of nonparties. Interestingly, powerful arguments for and against the exclusionary rule take this form. An argument forbidding admission of illegally acquired evidence is that such a rule will deter the police and thus reduce future violations of persons' constitutional rights to be free of unlawful searches and interrogations. A contrary argument is that if the admission of such evidence is not permitted obviously guilty persons will be freed immediately and many of them will repeat their criminal acts, violating the rights of innocent victims.

(5) It may be argued that if certain practices are prohibited or allowed the indirect result will likely be fewer impairments of important interests of nonparties. Thus, it might be argued that a rule imposing a stringent safety requirement on subway operation will probably diminish injuries.

(6) It may be argued that if certain practices are prohibited or allowed there will be a sort of pervasive educational effect that will promote general respect

for rights and legitimate interests. One argument for the exclusionary rule is that if government, the "omnipresent teacher," seeks to benefit from its own wrongdoing, citizens will both respect the government less and be more inclined to commit wrongs against others when they can gain by them.

(7) It may be argued that if certain practices are prohibited or allowed social resources will be saved that could be used more sensibly to protect other legal rights or to produce other social benefits. The argument that a particular proposed rule would be too expensive to administer is implicitly an argument about saving social resources.

(8) It can be argued that if certain practices are prohibited or allowed there will be too many situations in which courts will be unable fairly to determine and administer legal rights. The contention that a proposed rule of law is unadministrable often boils down to the assertion that courts cannot evenly apply the rule because its crucial factors are too difficult to ascertain and that injustice to parties in subsequent cases would be a likely consequence.

This is not a complete catalogue of the way the interests of nonparties figure in litigation, but it is sufficient to suggest the diversity of such arguments and the inadequacy of any distinction between principles and policies that does not develop more fully which nonparty interests count for arguments of principle.

There are two possible lines that might be taken by one who wishes to preserve a distinction of critical importance between arguments about rights and arguments about the collective welfare. The more promising would seem to be to draw some line between the kinds of interests that count for arguments about rights and those that do not; and this is indeed the line Dworkin suggests when he says that it is an argument of principle against desegregation that people may be killed in riots but only an argument of policy that people may be caused discomfort.[64] The second possible line would be in terms of the closeness of the relationship between the case at hand and the interests of nonparties supposedly affected. I shall consider the second possibility briefly before considering the first at greater length.

One might suggest that rights and interests of nonparties can count only if they are directly implicated in the litigation before the court. Thus the interests of those directly touched by behavior claimed to be tortious might be made the basis of an argument of principle. Perhaps the interests of persons situated similarly to the parties whose legal rights would be directly affected by a proposed rule of law (as in the right of privacy example) would also qualify. But arguments that a particular decision or rule of law would lead by a chain of causation to impairments of the interests of nonparties would not be considered arguments of principle. Two things may be said about this possible distinction between direct and indirect effects on nonparties. First, it seems arbitrary. It is not clear exactly how one would draw such a line and why one should draw it. It is sensible to say that courts are not particularly well suited to deciding empirical disputes about remote effects and that they should decline to give great weight to doubtful empirical assertions; but it is quite another thing to say they should treat as irrelevant any argument cast in terms of indirect effects, however powerful and well supported by evidence the argument may be. Second, this is plainly not the line that Dworkin himself wishes to pursue. The argument that persons will die in riots if schools are desegregated is one of indirect causal effect, and Dworkin treats it as an argument of principle. The argument that if moot cases are adjudicated the courts will handle more pressing cases less well or less quickly is also one of indirect causal effect, and Dworkin treats it as an argument of principle. Though more might be said on this subject, we can abandon a possible attempt to exclude some arguments about the interests of third parties on the basis of indicia of remoteness to the litigation at hand; such an attempt seems unpromising and, in any event, not reflective of Dworkin's views.

The other possibility is to distinguish some interests of nonparties that count as rights (and can thus be the basis for arguments of principle) from other interests that do not count as rights (and thus can be the basis only for arguments of policy). Under this approach, since some considerations relevant for the argument of policy may be excluded from the argument of principle, the position would still be defensible that a substituted argument of principle might not be as powerful as the argument of policy for which it substitutes. Therefore, it would matter whether courts could consider arguments of policy; if they could only consider arguments of principle, many contentions would be weaker in the form in which they were presentable to the judiciary than in the form in which they were presentable to the legislature.

The first thing to notice about this approach, which Dworkin's desegregation example suggests, is that it concedes that if every relevant aspect of a general welfare argument can be broken down into an argument about the rights of nonparties, the argument of principle will be just as powerful as the argument of policy. Thus in the privacy case, the power of a plaintiff's argument for protection would not depend on whether it was cast in terms of the rights of those who care about privacy or the general interest in preserving privacy.[65] And some "policy" arguments for and against the exclusionary rule would not lose much, if any, force if put in terms of the protection of the rights of citizens against the depredations of known criminals and overzealous policemen. In those cases in which all arguments of general welfare are reducible to arguments about the protection of legal rights of nonparties, the acknowledgment that arguments of principle can include arguments about the rights of nonparties does eliminate any practical importance to the distinction between principles and policies. Nevertheless, the distinction could retain general importance if interests calculable as part of the general welfare are frequently not usable as the basis for an argument of principle. Dworkin offers discomfort likely to be suffered from desegregation as an example of such an interest, but he leaves it for the reader to try to figure out how the line is to be drawn between interests that count for arguments of principle and those that do not.

We might start with the assumption that an argument that a particular decision or rule of law is likely to lead to violations of legal rights of nonparties is an argument of principle. In the desegregation example, it might be said that innocent people have a legal right not to be killed by rioters. In the privacy example, it is not initially clear whether nonparties who really care about privacy have a legal right to be free from some embarrassing publications of true facts, but a court could first preliminarily resolve that issue (on the basis of relevant arguments of principle) and then decide whether the plaintiff who does not care about privacy should be afforded relief.

Even understood broadly enough to include the privacy case, however, there are some startling defects in the suggestion that arguments about the interests of nonparties must be cast in terms of likely violations of their legal rights. The most obvious defect is that when the sacrifice of vital interests is asserted as a likely effect, it would be absurd to say that a court can take the effect into account only if it involves the violation of the prospective victims' actual legal rights. Some people who die in riots may be rioters who are justifiably killed by policemen or by private citizens acting in self-defense or to prevent crimes. Even some innocent people who suffer death as a consequence of a justifiable use of deadly force may technically have suffered no violation of their legal rights. Surely it cannot be that a court contemplating a course of action that may lead to riots can consider only the likely deaths of persons whose legal rights are violated. The likelihood that people will be killed is a relevant argument for judicial consideration even when none of those killed will have suffered a legal wrong. A citizen may have no legal right against an invading enemy[66] or his own inadequately prepared government, yet few would doubt that a substantial "national security" argument should be given some weight. Likewise, few would doubt that an argument that a safety procedure would save many lives would be entitled to some weight by a court deciding whether or not to require the safety procedure, even if it were clear that those who would otherwise die would have no legal claim to relief. Thus, if Dworkin's position is to remain plausible it must admit as arguments of principle arguments in terms of important interests of nonparties that enjoy substantial legal protection even when the expected impairment of those interests will not actually violate legal rights.

Now the problem is to determine which interests enjoy substantial legal protection and which do not. Some laws that are designed to protect individual interests do not give rise to individual claims for damages. Individuals adversely affected may not be able to recover, for example, if others violate laws making criminal the blocking of public highways or strikes by school teachers and subway conductors. Is the interest of the driver, parent and child, or subway rider to count for a right in Dworkin's terms? It would not be sensible to make the propriety of judicial consideration of an argument based on the interest of a nonparty turn on whether the invasion of that interest typically gives rise to civil damages. For example, it cannot be crucial when an arguable application of an antipollution law is at issue, or where the constitutionality of such a law is in question, whether the legislature has decided to create a civil remedy as well as a criminal sanction for the forbidden activities.

There are other interests that enjoy a kind of legal recognition but are neither the basis for prohibitory statutes nor grounds for individual claims to civil relief. What are we to make of "rights" to decent food, decent housing, decent health care, employment, and fair opportunity? Let us assume that our society, as reflected in legal materials including prologues to various welfare statutes, recognizes these as genuine rights. That is to say, in Dworkin's terms, it is accepted that a general improvement in housing conditions, for instance, would not justify depriving some people of minimally acceptable housing. The "right to decent housing is viewed as having substantial "trumping power" over claims of general welfare.[67] Yet we have not reached a point of development at which one's failure to get decent housing gives him any legal claim to relief or necessarily indicates that anyone has committed a legal wrong. Suppose a common law case arises regarding the rights of mortgagees and it is claimed that if the poor mortgagor wins the consequence will be that fewer mortgages will be given to poor people and fewer of them will have decent housing.[68] It would be strange to say that this is not an argument of principle simply because the law has not conferred a legally enforceable right to decent housing.[69]

So far, we have seen that it is not at all easy to deny the status of arguments of principle to many arguments about the interests of nonparties. What interests are left that figure only in arguments of policy? Dworkin has offered the avoidance of discomfort at desegregation as an interest that is not a right and cannot be the basis for an argument of principle. But discomfort of various sorts can underlie claims that a defendant has created a nuisance or is guilty of intentional infliction of emotional distress; it can also constitute the basis for divorce on grounds of incompatability. It is impossible to say that avoidance of severe discomfort is not a concern of the law; indeed, it may be relevant even in constitutional cases. Even most of the dissenters in *Paris Adult Theatre I* v. *Slaton*,[70] who argued that obscene materials could not constitutionally be suppressed, assumed that the discomfort many people experience when forced to view obscenity is a sufficient basis for banning public displays of obscene pictures, though a ban of public displays of many other kinds of communications would violate the first amendment. The literal language of the equal rights amendment would seem to bar restrooms segregated by gender, but supporters have urged that it would not be so interpreted, largely because a court would recognize that the considerable discomfort that would be caused to many people by integrated restrooms would far outweigh any thin claim to nondifferentiation in the use of toilet facilities.[71] And suppose, in the desegregation example, school authorities had asserted that the discomfort most black students would suffer from integration would be so severe that their learning capacities would be far less than in segregated schools. Would this not have been an argument of principle for preserving segregated schools or at least permitting substantial segregation through "freedom of choice" plans? There may well be reasons that lie in the intent of the equal protection clause and the history of segregation that make white discomfort of little or no relevance in a suit for desegregation; but it cannot blithely be assumed that "discomfort" can never underlie arguments of principle.

Perhaps an asserted increase in general economic welfare is the strongest candidate for classification as an argument of "mere" policy, but an increased income for some families will spell the difference between inadequate and barely decent housing, between sickness and health, between ignorance and education. In a society that takes seriously notions like "rights to decent housing and fair opportunity," it is apparent that general economic prosperity contributes to the satisfaction of these rights. And a stimulus to the economy may create jobs for persons whose social "right" to be employed is then unrealized. If it is proper for a court to consider improvements in economic welfare to the extent these will contribute to the satisfaction of social "rights" to minimum treatment, it is a little hard to say that possible improvements beyond the minimum level are totally irrelevant to judicial decision. Yet if these are allowed, the distinction between principles and policies as a guide to judicial action breaks down because every claim about the general welfare would be translatable into an equally powerful argument of principle.

Perhaps with enough ingenuity Dworkin could meet these queries and provide a satisfactory theoretical framework for distinguishing arguments of principle and policy as they relate to interests of nonparties. If his thesis that judges should not rely on policies is to bear any relation to actual and desirable judicial behavior, he must acknowledge that in many circumstances when the legal rights of nonparties will not actually be violated the protection of their interests can count for arguments of principle. Perhaps by some complex procedure he could then assign appropriate differential weights and maintain his thesis that substitutable arguments of principle may be less strong than analogous arguments of policy. But it seems doubtful that what would remain would be much help for sitting judges trying to decide what arguments to consider and how much weight to give them.[72]

We do know that in some cases the crucial issue may be the impact on the welfare of all those affected by a particular activity. In a nuisance case, whether one homeowner will have the right to stop pollution will depend largely on how many other homeowners are suffering in the same way he is and on the broader effect on the community of continuing or stopping the pollution. We cannot talk about the legal rights of parties or nonparties until we estimate the overall effect of the pollution. In this context, an effort to distinguish legally protected interests that count for arguments of principle from other interests that count only for arguments of policy would be misguided. The difficulty of drawing any such line in other contexts as well helps to confirm the suspicion we have already reached on the basis of the weakness of Dworkin's arguments against judicial reliance on policy, namely, that judges do appropriately give weight to considerations of general welfare in resolving genuinely difficult cases.

Judicial Interpretation of Statutes

Dworkin's thesis that judges should consider only arguments of principle seems most plausible when judges interpret and apply statutes, for in such cases the court's role is to give effect to rights that have been created by the legislature. Even if the legislature itself has acted on the basis of policy, once it has acted, it has created rights; and, according to Dworkin, arguments about the content of those rights are arguments of principle. But how are courts to resolve cases when it is not clear what rights the legislature has created? The theory of statutory interpretation that Dworkin sketches virtually obliterates any significant distinction between principle and policy in statutory cases, and so it becomes difficult, or impossible, to describe a case in which Dworkin would foreclose judicial attention to an argument about general welfare that would be appropriate for legislative consideration.

We can identify at least three ways in which policy arguments can be transformed into arguments of principle given Dworkin's theory. First, if the legislature itself adopts a standard that refers a judge to community welfare, then, of course, the judge must consider policy arguments in applying the standard. Legislation might actually say, "Lumberers are free to cut down trees in national forests as long as that is consistent with the general welfare"; more common would be legislative use of a term like "reasonable" or "public necessity and convenience" which directs the courts to consider competing policy arguments in determining rights.[73] Although Dworkin does not actually discuss this possibility, he would almost certainly concede that the legislature could direct courts to weigh competing claims of welfare in resolving cases.

Second, principles can incorporate policies when it is clear that the legislature passed a statute to promote a particular policy. Then resolution of hard cases might depend on judicial determination of the implications of that policy. If a court properly can consider a single policy, it must be able to consider a number of policies when multiple policies have influenced the legislature. Dworkin does not direct himself to cases in which the policy or policies pursued by the legislature are clear from the statute itself or from the legislative history,[74] but we may suppose that in such cases courts should give weight to and attempt to develop the implications of those policies.

One might take the position that courts could rely on policy arguments only when directed to do so by the legislature or when necessary to implement what the legislature intended to accomplish. In this form the thesis that judges should rely on principles would not bar judicial consideration of policy arguments in interpreting statutes, but it would require a showing that the relevant policies were likely to have been given weight by the legislature and would limit their judicial weight to the weight they were apparently given by the legislature. Since legislatures rarely leave reliable guides about the weights assigned to relevant policies, such a standard might not have much practical utility, but at least it would possess theoretical clarity. Courts would have to look to legislative purposes for evaluating policy arguments; the repair of legislative mistakes and the expansion of valuable legislation would be left up to the legislature.[75]

This theoretically straightforward position is not Dworkin's. In a hard case, he says, a court is not supposed to try to determine what the legislature "would have done if it had been aware of the problem presented by the case";[76] the court is to rely on "a special political theory that justifies this statute, in the light of the legislature's more general responsibilities, better than any alternative theory."[77] This means that in difficult cases the courts may interpret legislatively created rights stringently or expansively not because of evidence of legislative intent in respect to the statutes involved but because of the court's view of the consistency of alternative results with the legislature's general responsibilities. These general responsibilities include "some general duty to pursue collective goals defining the public welfare."[78]

By authorizing courts to refer to general legislative responsibilities in every difficult case, Dworkin is authorizing a third form of reliance on policy arguments, since the pursuit of public welfare is a part of legislative responsibilities. In terms of the sorts of arguments that can be presented to courts and the weight they may be given, little, if any, difference apparently remains between Dworkin and the person who simply says that judges should resolve hard statutory cases with an eye to the general welfare.[79] Dworkin's own discussion of the *Charles River Bridge*[80] case indicates how far he is ready to concede the appropriateness of judicial reliance on policy arguments.[81] In that case, the courts declined to find that a grant to build a bridge across the river was meant to be exclusive, although simple analysis of the terms of the grant itself suggested exclusivity. Dworkin approves judicial reliance on arguments that an exclusive grant would be improvident and unreasonable, presumably because it would disserve the general interest in convenient and economical transportation.

There is a point of relatively minor importance on which Dworkin is ambiguous and which suggests that there does remain some difference between him and the advocate of judicial reliance on policy. Dworkin says the court's responsibility is to determine "what rights the legislature has already created."[82] Perhaps he means that a court should interpret the legislation to make it consonant with the performance of the legislature's general responsibilities as properly perceived at the time of enactment. Although this approach might not bar the court from relying on subsequent growth in understanding of the general responsibilities of legislators, it would preclude reliance on changing social facts that alter estimates of behavior likely to promote welfare. If that is Dworkin's position, it does differ from that of someone who urges the court to consider which result in a difficult case comports with present evaluations of how best to promote the general welfare. It would require holding the grant in the *Charles River Bridge* case to be exclusive if at the time of the original charter an exclusive grant appeared a prudent legislative choice to encourage the one bridge that was needed and if the subsequent conflict between public welfare and an exclusive grant could not reasonably have been foreseen. It is doubtful, however, if the decision in the case is supportable on that theory, since exclusivity might well have seemed sensible at the time the original grant was made.[83]

It might be suggested that the reason the courts in the *Charles River Bridge* case may have been justified in giving direct weight to present social needs is that the contracts clause of the federal Constitution rendered the original legislative grant immune from legislative repeal; for more mundane issues as to which legislative alteration is a possibility, perhaps the courts should adopt a perspective based on the time of enactment. Even this position, however, would be inconsistent with actual and sound judicial practice. Suppose the legislature passes a badly drafted antipollution statute leaving coverage of many activities uncertain. A civil suit arises concerning whether a particular form of pollution is prohibited by the statute. Even though a judge might not have found the practice covered soon after the statute was passed, he may now properly find it to be covered because the language can be stretched without much difficulty to reach the practice, and the practice now appears, because of new factual knowledge or greater abhorrence of pollution, to be clearly inconsistent with the general welfare. The legislature must deal with a multitude of problems; it cannot legislate for every detail, and it cannot relegislate every time changing social conditions call for slight alterations. The courts are not usurping legislative power if they step in; they are lending a hand. When the legislature is not continually attentive to issues, it would be unwise to bar courts, just as it would be unwise to bar administrative agencies, from taking account of policy arguments about the general welfare as presently conceived.

Examination has revealed that the thesis that judges must rely exclusively on principles is practically unimportant in statutory cases for the sorts of arguments courts may consider and for the weight they can give those arguments. If the thesis requires the courts to interpret legislation in terms of what would have been most consonant with the legislature's general responsibilities at the time of enactment, it forecloses judicial consideration of changes in factual assessments and social values that courts do, and should, take into account.

Constitutional Interpretation

There are relatively few provisions in the American Constitution whose terms plainly authorize courts to engage in assessments of community welfare. The ban on unreasonable searches and seizures may qualify. Although it may require attention to other factors and may demand a balancing of values that will last over time and not vary from place to place, the standard of "reasonableness" does imply some calculation of social harms and benefits.[84] In any event, there can be no question that if a constitutional provision does authorize such calculations, judicial consideration of relevant arguments of policy is as appropriate as it is for the application of ordinary statutes containing similar authorizing language.

Some provisions of the Constitution may also be thought designed to promote particular policies, for example the standards relating to interstate commerce and import taxes.[85] Again, if judges properly work out the implications of underlying policies in interpreting ordinary statutes, the same approach must be proper when they are interpreting constitutional provisions.

Dworkin's theory of constitutional interpretation in hard cases is complex, and in a subsequent section it is more fully examined. Here it is enough to indicate that this theory parallels his theory of statutory interpretation. An ideal court would not try to figure out how the framers would have answered a particular constitutional issue; it would develop and apply "a full political theory that justifies the constitution as a whole." Just as ordinary statutes are interpreted to fit with the legislature's general responsibilities, constitutional provisions are expansively or restrictively interpreted to fit with other provisions of the Constitution.

I have suggested that pursuit of the general welfare is such a central responsibility of legislatures that courts following Dworkin's theory would treat arguments about welfare pretty much the same way as courts relying directly on policies in hard cases. The matter is somewhat more complicated in the constitutional context. Many constitutional provisions, most notably those protecting individual rights, can be perceived as limitations on the pursuit of general welfare, imposed on the basis of a determination that some moral rights of individuals should override marginal gains to the common good and that these rights should be guaranteed against legislative and executive infringement.[87] Under this view, these constitutional standards, many drawn from the common law, are themselves based on arguments of principle thought to be so important that this special form of institutionalization was deemed appropriate. In a case involving the interpretation of one of these rights, reference to a theory that justifies the whole constitution would not render arguments of policy so obviously relevant as a theory that justifies a statute in light of the legislature's general responsibilities.

Nevertheless, reference to arguments of policy is appropriate in difficult constitutional cases, even those involving guarantees of individual rights. Difficult constitutional cases arise when it is plausibly urged that the apparent coverage of a guarantee should be withheld because of harmful consequences that would ensue or when it is urged that the relevant provision simply does not reach the matter at issue.[88] Dworkin asserts, and I agree, that in respect to many forms of behavior the Constitution establishes protections that cannot be overriden, or at least can be overcome only by a very compelling showing of public necessity. No claim of public necessity would justify convicting someone on the basis of compelled testimony, and only the most compelling public danger can justify penalizing newspapers for publishing truthful information of public concern. Unless rights are absolute, their entrenchment at the expense of claims of public necessity does not establish the irrelevance of policy arguments; it only establishes that arguments of policy must be very powerful to overcome claims of individual right within the scope of constitutional provisions.

In most constitutional cases, the issue is not whether some claim that is of a sort clearly reached by the relevant provision should give way to a claim of necessity; but whether the claim falls within the ambit of the constitutional protection at all. Does the first amendment reach obscenity? Does the probable cause requirement of the fourth amendment relate to the limited invasions of "stop and frisk"? Does the privilege against self-incrimination relate to organizational records? Even if constitutional rights are "absolute," courts must set the boundaries of those rights.[89] Whether explicitly or not, the Supreme Court does consider arguments of policy as well as principle in setting the limits of constitutional rights; it is much less likely to read a guarantee expansively if it thinks an expansive reading would not be conducive to general welfare. In rejecting the claim that an official could refuse to produce an organizational record on the ground that it would incriminate him, for example, the Supreme Court said, "The greater portion of evidence of wrongdoing by an organization or its representatives is usually to be found in the official records and documents of that organization. Were the cloak of the privilege to be thrown around these impersonal records and documents, effective enforcement of many federal and state laws would be impossible."[90]

On a theoretical and normative level, we may say that the Constitution is meant to be the framework for a going social enterprise. The political theory that would best justify the Constitution as a whole would presumably not provide for entrenched rights in a marginal case in which the individual seeking to establish that claim has no powerful moral or social welfare argument in favor and recognition of the right would cause great social damage.[91] At least when arguments of principle are very closely balanced, it is appropriate for courts to give weight to powerful arguments about the general welfare. As long as we can presume that the general responsibilities of those who drafted and approved constitutional provisions included some obligation not to undermine seriously the collective welfare, Dworkin's theory could convert arguments of policy into arguments of principle in the same way it does for ordinary legislation. There remains the question whether judges must adopt the perspective of the time of enactment in considering what would best promote the general welfare or may rely on present evaluations. Since the Constitution is so much more difficult to amend than ordinary statutes, the argument that present evaluation is proper is even more powerful than in the context of a statutory interpretation.

Policies and Judicial Decision: A Summary of Conclusions

No persuasive argument has been given for judicial abstinence from policy considerations, that is, considerations based on the collective welfare. The arguments from democracy, retroactivity, and articulate consistency all fall far short of providing firm support for the thesis that judges should rely exclusively on principles. We have seen that even Dworkin allows judges to rely on policies in some circumstances in which those considerations are turned into considerations of principle. We have also seen that his sparse treatment of the way interests of nonparties can count in litigation leaves us uncertain about what precisely he views as the line between principles and policies and creates skepticism that any line can be drawn that would be helpful for real judges. Dworkin's concessions to use of policies and the unrecognized complexity of distinguishing policies from principles serve to confirm our initial judgment that judicial reliance on policies is warranted.

This conclusion does not affect the validity of two other assertions about judicial decisions that might be made. It can plausibly be argued that judges, because of their training and the manner in which contentions and information are presented in the legal process, are better able to decide whether behavior accords with accepted standards than to weigh instrumental justifications cast in terms of future consequences. This position, which Dworkin might well find congenial,[92] differs from his thesis in "Hard Cases" in two important ways. It does not bar the use of instrumental justifications in all or some kinds of legal cases; it suggests only that such justifications should count for something less in judicial decision than in legislative and executive decision. Nor does this position try to draw a sharp line between arguments about rights and arguments about collective welfare. Dworkin acknowledges that some instrumental arguments are arguments about rights, as, for example, the argument that people may be killed in riots if schools are desegregated, and close examination of cases involving the interests of nonparties has revealed that many other instrumental justifications might be viewed as contentions about rights. The position that courts should give somewhat less weight to instrumental justifications would thus reach both arguments of policies and many arguments of principle.

The second assertion that is not undermined by acknowledgment of the appropriateness of judicial reliance on policy is that judges should generally give more weight to claims of right than to claims of collective welfare when the two conflict. This is certainly a position to which Dworkin subscribes; indeed, it has been a central theme of his writings on constitutional law, summed up by the title of his newly published book, *Taking Rights Seriously*.[93] One may believe that the Constitution institutionalizes many individual rights against claims of collective good, that statutes create rights that judges should not casually cast aside when they believe them to do disservice to collective welfare, and that rights to be found within the common law should not be overriden whenever they are thought to be inconvenient. This view would lead to the conclusion that when one party has a clearly warranted claim of right, it should never be rejected or should be rejected only upon the strongest showing of urgent public necessity. This view might also lead to the conclusion that when arguments of right, though debatable, are in a judge's view tipped strongly in one direction, the judge should rarely, if ever, decide the contrary way. But the notion that judges should give weight to rights does not lead to the conclusion that when arguments about rights are nearly balanced judges should try to decide a case without considering the general welfare at all. It is this conclusion that Dworkin asserts in "Hard Cases" and that the preceding analysis suggests is wrong.

JUDICIAL DECISION AND INSTITUTIONAL GUIDANCE

Are Judges Always Under a Legal Duty to Be Guided by Institutionalized Materials When Those Suggest a Particular Result?

One part of Dworkin's theory that judges decide upon institutionalized rights is that when the theory that justifies existing legal rules points in one direction in a particular case, the judge's legal duty is always to decide the case in that way. That duty excludes decision the contrary way even if the judge has a deep moral sense that the contrary way would be preferable and even if he believes that his moral sense is shared by most members of the general society or professional community. I believe that this conclusion is incorrect and that a judge may properly opt in some difficult cases against what he believes to be the implications of existing legal standards.

We must recognize at the outset that the distinction drawn here is of more theoretical than practical interest, and it is extraordinarily difficult to pose a testing case for a number of reasons. Dworkin says that the judge's own moral and political philosophy will unavoidably have a good bit to do with the theory that he constructs justifying existing standards, so that any particular judge's theory will already bear the stamp of his personal views. Moreover, legal institutions and standards, unlike the analogous characteristics of a game, are immensely complex. In the United States, virtually every strong moral argument against government action can be plausibly cast in constitutional garb, and every widely shared social value is somehow reflected in legal norms. Especially since real judges do not have the theory-making capacities of Hercules, it will be a rare instance in which a judge deciding a difficult case[94] will be able to say that the law points him in one direction but his own moral sense and that of the community points him in another.[95]

Yet it is just such cases that are the payoff for Dworkin's thesis about institutionalization. Legislators are free to act on the basis of their own sense of what is right; judges are guided by institutional norms. If, as applied to difficult cases,[96] the thesis of institutionalized rights is to be more than a myth supporting exercises of judicial power, it must contemplate cases in which a legislator would decide one way and a judge another. In the following paragraphs I shall try to suggest some testing cases for Dworkin's thesis and conclude that judges in difficult cases for which the law provides no clear answer are sometimes warranted in departing from the answer to which present legal materials may point.

In connection with the use of policy arguments, I hypothesized a badly drafted antipollution statute and a civil suit arising some years later over whether a particular practice is covered.[97] Let us suppose that public understanding of relevant facts and moral indignation about pollution have greatly increased since passage of the statute and that the particular practice is now widely condemned as undesirable. We shall assume that the case is a very close one but that at the time of passage a judge would properly have found against coverage. Even if all relevant legal materials have remained unaltered, I think a judge may now properly find in favor of coverage. By the same token, I think judges in very close cases may properly decide common law issues in accord with a widely prevailing sense of what is right even if that contrasts with the result that would be suggested weakly by existing legal materials.

In *City of El Paso* v. *Simmons,*[98] the Supreme Court held that Texas was free to alter its contractual obligations to landholders in a manner that arguably violated the constitutional prohibition on state impairment of the obligation of contracts.[99] Justice Black argued forcefully in dissent that the change in contractual rights was exactly of the sort the framers meant to prevent. Without doubt the force of the obligation of contracts clause is sharply limited after *El Paso*. It is most doubtful if any notion that the framers invited the development of constitutional concepts can cover *El Paso*. The constitutional language does not have the same open-ended character as the ban on cruel and unusual punishment, and it was very evidently intended to bar certain specific kinds of breaches of obligations. Moreover, *El Paso* represents not an expansion of protected rights but a withdrawal of an individual constitutional guarantee that the framers meant to provide, a guarantee they deemed important enough to make one of the few restrictions on state power in favor of individual rights to be found in the Constitution before the post-Civil War amendments. *El Paso* was decided the way it was because reasonable state alterations in contractual obligations, like other government involvements in commercial matters to promote the general welfare, seem much more acceptable now than they did in 1787.

Since the Constitution itself contains nothing inconsistent or even in tension with a much broader reading of the obligations clause, it cannot be said that the document as a whole leads to the narrow reading of *El Paso*. It might be urged that statutory and common law legal standards do reflect the declining importance given to the sanctity of contractual obligations, but this line of argument would authorize the reduction of constitutional rights on the basis of changes in common law and statutory rights, a technique of doubtful propriety given the hierarchical ordering of legal norms accepted by the rights thesis.[100] More fundamentally, we must ask whether judges are really limited to legal institutions and standards in deciding what weight to attach to contractual obligations. Can they appropriately consider relevant evidence about the effect of stringent protection of contractual obligations or community attitudes toward the sanctity of contractual obligations?[101] I should think so. And it is precisely in the situations in which such considerations are appropriate that the Supreme Court brings the Constitution into line with prevailing social values in a way not fully explained by any part of Dworkin's theory.

The most notable instance of inconsistency between legal standards in the United States and moral concepts was long-time legalization of slavery. Dworkin believes, and I agree, that when presented with a slave owner's claim based on an indisputably correct reading of a clearly constitutional statute, the judge's legal duty was to decide in favor of the slave owner[102] (even if the judge might be morally justified either in resigning his office or subverting the law). But what of the difficult case for which existing legal materials gave no clear guidance? Robert Cover's book on the antislavery movement and the judicial process[103] analyzes two judicial attitudes. The first, which predominated, was that judges should further the purposes of the political branches in interpreting slavery legislation like any other legislation; under this view an expansive reading might be given to a fugitive slave act that offended the judge's moral sense and perhaps even the moral sense of most of the national community. The second attitude was that in cases left in doubt by the positive law judges should rely on natural law, bringing the positive law so far as possible into harmony with moral principles;[104] under this view difficult cases would be resolved in favor of slaves and against slave owners.

Dworkin suggests that a failure of jurisprudence contributed to the judicial dilemma of choosing between these two attitudes, a failure that would not have occurred if his rights thesis had been understood. He urges that the rights of slaves were institutional, in large part because "[t]he general structure of the American Constitution presupposed a conception of individual freedom antagonistic to slavery."[105] It is much less clear to me than it is to Dworkin that a judge who took his theory seriously could happily have decided for slaves in every doubtful case. After all, in two places the federal Constitution undoubtedly provides protection for the practice of slavery[106] and in at least one other place it acknowledges its appropriateness.[107] Whether we like it or not, the theory that would best justify the original Constitution might well include the principle that Negroes are not full human beings or at least are not entitled to the rights of other human beings. Certainly a judge in a slave state deciding an issue of state law might be led to the conclusion that in his state slaves were not entitled to rights and that that was consistent with the federal Constitution. A serious attempt to apply the rights thesis might well have led a judge who personally abhorred slavery to resolve many difficult cases against slaves.[108]

Certainly we can imagine a country, even if it is not the United States before the Civil War, in which the thesis that a judge must decide upon institutionalized rights would lead him to decide difficult cases in morally reprehensible ways. I do not think that is a judge's legal duty. When authoritative legal sources leave an issue genuinely in doubt, I think a judge properly decides in accordance with firm convictions of moral rightness and social welfare that command wide support, even if these convictions are at variance with the theory that would best justify existing legal standards. Indeed, if the judge's convictions are very firm and if the issue involved is of great moral or social significance, I think a judge may follow these convictions even if he does not think they are shared by most members of the community.[109] A judge is an agent for change in the law in marginal cases and, just as a legislator, he sometimes may rely on his own strongly held views in preference to those of the community.[110] The process provides some protection against idiosyncratic views, for if a judge sits on an appellate court, his vote alone will not decide an issue, and decisions on the law by lower courts are typically subject to appeal.

It is impossible to state in clean conceptual form precisely what a judge's legal duty is in every case. When authoritative legal materials provide a clear answer, the judge's legal duty is to accept it.[111] In difficult cases, the institutionalization thesis provides a good guide: the judge typically attempts to implement the values reflected in the legal system. Ordinarily he will be unable to distinguish his own personal view of the right result in difficult cases from the view he believes is to be had from consideration of legal values. But a judge is often warranted in drawing from nonlegal sources to resolve issues of moral rightness and social welfare, and sometimes these may outweigh what he thinks are the contrary implications of a fine weighing of all "legal" values. When existing legal standards point in one direction and the judge's sense of moral rightness and social welfare in another, what factors are relevant to deciding which course to take? The weaker the signal given by the existing law, i.e., the closer it is to being completely indecisive, the easier it is for the judge appropriately to override it. Similarly, the stronger the moral and social reasons for overriding, the more appropriate it is. The broader, the more intense, and the more stable the community sentiment supporting the judge's own views, the more easily he can rely on them. Such support both provides some indication of the soundness of his own views and casts him more in the role of an agent for the whole community. Usually a judge will assume his own perspectives have broad support because his own intensive consideration of a problem may seem to him the best indicia of what others think or would think if they gave the problem equally serious thought. But I believe that a judge is sometimes justified in "striking out on his own" even when he recognizes he has little support. That is appropriate, however, only if his convictions are very firm and the issue involved is of great significance.

NOTES

1. Ronald Dworkin, "Hard Cases," *Harvard Law Review* 88 (1975): 1509.
2. Ibid.
3. Ibid, p. 1101.
4. Ibid., p. 1061.
5. Ibid.
6. Ibid., p. 1062.
7. Ibid., p. 1064.

8. See H. Wechsler, "Toward Neutral Principles of Constitutional Law," *Harvard Law Review* 73 (1959); reprinted in H. Wechsler, *Principles, Politics, and Fundamental Law* (1961).

9. Dworkin, "Hard Cases," pp. 1061, 1086.

10. Ibid., p. 1078.

11. Ibid., pp. 1078, 1105.

12. See Ronald Dworkin, "The Law of the Slave-Catchers," *Times Literary Supplement*, Dec. 5, 1975, p. 1437 (review of R. Cover, *Justice Accused* [1975]).

13. Dworkin, "Hard Cases," pp. 1085–87.

14. Ibid., p. 1087.

15. Ibid., p. 1086.

16. Ronald Dworkin, "The Jurisprudence of Richard Nixon," *New York Review of Books* 18 (May 4, 1972): 28.

17. Dworkin, "Hard Cases," pp. 1083–84.

18. Ibid., pp. 1087–96.

19. Ibid., p. 1091.

20. Ibid., p. 1094.

21. Ibid., pp. 1096–101.

22. Ibid., p. 1061.

23. Richard Posner asserts that the common law has promoted efficiency much more effectively than legislation and administrative regulation. See Richard Posner, *Economic Analysis of Law* (1972), § § 23.3–5.

24. For an analysis of the comparative strengths and weaknesses of the two processes, see Cornelius J. Peck, "The Role of the Courts and Legislatures in the Reform of Tort Law," *Minnesota Law Review* 48 (1963): 265. Harry Wellington discounts the typical argument that the legislature usually is better able to determine social desirability than the courts, but emphasizes the legislature's greater ability to implement and monitor many policies and its greater capacity to accommodate conflicting interests. See Harry Wellington, "Common Law Rules and Constitutional Double Standards: Some Notes on Adjudication," *Yale Law Journal* 83 (1973): 221, 240–41.

25. This point is made powerfully in Note, "Dworkin's 'Rights Thesis,'" *Michigan Law Review* 74 (1976): 1167, 1178 (John Umana); and in somewhat different form in Stephen R. Munzer, "Right Answers, Preexisting Rights, and Fairness," *Georgia Law Review* 11 (1977): 1055.

Professor Wellington suggests that policies are less stable than principles and that the likelihood of unfair surprise is greater when courts rely on them (see Wellington, "Common Law Rules," p. 242). If this is true, then the retroactivity problem may be generally greater when courts rely on policies than when they rely on principles, but it would not be greater when courts rely on policies that are relatively stable. Wellington also suggests that when a defendant has committed an act that the law regards as a serious wrong (for example, murder), his possible surprise when certain novel legal consequences are held to flow from his act (for example, his inability to inherit under the victim's will) should not occasion serious concern. See ibid., pp. 233–35. But since many cases in which arguments of principle in Dworkin's sense are decisive do not fit this category, Wellington's point does not establish that as a general matter reliance on principles gives rise to less concern about unfair surprise than reliance on policy.

26. In some cases, courts have even stated that a newly announced rule, instead of becoming immediately applicable, would take effect at some future time. See *Spanel* v. *Mounds View School District,* 264 Minn. 279, 118 N. W. 2d 795 (1962); *Holytz* v. City of Milwaukee, 17 Wis. 2d 26, 115 N.W. 2d 618 (1962).

27. If a plaintiff's argument of principle persuades a court that the plaintiff has suffered a substantial wrong, then there is a powerful reason for providing damages even if the defendant suffers a degree of unfair surprise. This reason does not apply when the plaintiff's argument is that behavior like the defendant's will be harmful to the general welfare if allowed to continue. Wellington, who draws a distinction between arguments that the defendant's act has breached a strong moral duty to the plaintiff, and instrumental arguments that the community will benefit if acts like the defendant's are deemed improper, concludes, for reasons given in this note and two previous notes, that prospective application is particularly appropriate when courts rely unexpectedly on instrumental justifications. See Wellington, "Common Law Rules," pp. 233–35, 254–57. I think this conclusion is sound. But it is important that his distinction between principles and policies is not the same as Dworkin's. Dworkin's principles include many arguments that Wellington would treat as policies, such as arguments based on carrying out the purpose of legislation grounded in policy and arguments about the effects on the rights of nonparties.

28. See *United States* v. *Schooner Peggy,* 5 U.S. (1 Cranch) 103, 110 (1801) in which Chief Justice Marshall wrote for the Court: "[I]f, subsequent to the judgment, and before the decision of the appellate court, a law intervenes and positively changes the rule which governs, the law must be obeyed, or its obligation denied." As Marshall also wrote, in a case affecting private rights, "a court will and ought to struggle hard against a construction which will, by a retrospective operation, affect the rights of parties . . . ." Courts are properly hesitant to read a statute as abolishing rights that clearly existed prior to the statute. See e.g., *Hassett* v. *Welch,* 303 U.S. 303 (1938); *Addiss* v. *Selig,* 264 N.Y. 274, 190 N.E. 490 (1934).

29. *Spartan Steel & Alloy Ltd.* v. *Martin & Co.,* (1973) 1 Q.B. 27. For Dworkin's discussion of this case, see Dworkin, "Hard Cases," pp. 1060–61, 1087–101.

30. Cf. *Hamm* v. *City of Rock Hill,* 379 U.S. 306 (1964). The Court interpreted the public accommodations sections of the Civil Rights Act of 1964 as abating convictions for trespass of persons who had participated in "sit-ins" of luncheon facilities protesting racial segregation. Although the reasoning focuses on abatement of criminal prosecutions, it is likely the same result would have been reached in a pending case involving a civil action for trepass.

31. Dworkin, "Hard Cases," pp. 1090–91.

32. See K. Llewellyn, *The Bramble Bush* (1930).

33. Dworkin, "Hard Cases," pp. 1059, 1068–69, 1091–92.

34. It is disputed how crucial a responsibility is the judicial attempt to state principles of decision in a generalized form.

35. Review, of course, is much more intense if a suspect classification or fundamental right is involved. See generally Kent Greenawalt, "Judicial Scrutiny of "Benign" Racial Preference in Law School Admissions," *Columbia Law Review* 75 (1975): 559, 561–65; Gerald Gunther, "The Supreme Court, 1971 Term—Foreword: In Search of Evolving Doctrine on a Changing Court: A Model For a Newer Equal Protection," *Harvard Law Review* 86 (1972). In a confused footnote, Dworkin suggests that the distinction between "old" (relaxed review) and "new" (strict review) equal protection supports his position that we make "slight demands upon legislatures" when "their decisions are generated by arguments of policy," ("Hard Cases," p. 1091 note 26). He cites language from *Williamson* v. *Lee Optical Co.,* 348 U.S. 483 (1955), indicating that reform can take one step at a time. But this language has also been used with respect to legislation generated by principle. In *Katzenbach* v. *Morgan,* 384, U.S. 641 (1966), the Court considered federal extension of the right to vote in state elections of Spanish-speaking citizens educated in American flag schools; employing a relaxed standard of review, it sustained this reform legislation designed to implement equal protection rights, against the argument that the legislation was invalid because other Spanish-speaking citizens should have been treated similarly.

A much more crucial flaw in Dworkin's analysis is his failure to recognize that a common, perhaps the typical, instance of new equal protection (strict scrutiny) occurs when legislation is generated by policy but attacked as violating a principle. Segregation and voting restrictions were supported by policies, but first involved a suspect classification and the second a denial of a fundamental right. See e.g., *Kramer* v. *Union Free School District,* 395 U.S. 621 (1969); *Reynolds* v. *Sims,* 377 U.S. 533 (1964); *Brown* v. *Board of Education,* 349 U.S. 294 (1955). What these and countless other cases indicate, see e.g., *Shapiro* v. *Thompson,* 394 U.S. 618 (1969), *Skinner* v. *Oklahoma,* 316 U.S. 535 (1942), is that when certain forms of classification are used, legislatures are held to very stringent requirements regarding equal treatment whether the legislation itself proceeds from principle or policy.

Nor can something of Dworkin's point be saved by the suggestion that strict scrutiny occurs whenever those attacking legislation do so on grounds of principle. Persons of classes adversely affected by legislation often make fairly strong arguments of principle that they are victims of a suspect classification or have been denied a fundamental right, but the Court nevertheless uses the relaxed standard of review if it decides no suspect classification or denial of fundamental right is involved. See e.g., *Village of Belle Terre* v. *Boraas,* 416 U.S. 1 (1974); *San Antonio Independent School District* v. *Rodriguez,* 411 U.S. 1 (1973); *Dandridge* v. *Williams,* 397 U.S. 471 (1970). Any equal protection challenge must rest primarily on an argument of principle; the victim is asserting denial of a specific constitutional right and, as under most constitutional provisions, courts are not authorized to overturn debatable legislative judgments about social desirability. See Wellington, "Common Law Rules," p. 267. Nevertheless, arguments that, at first blush at least, appear to be ones of policy may be crucial for a decision. In most "new" equal protection cases, the claimant must answer arguments that a classification is necessary to serve a compelling governmental interest. See *Kramer* v. *Union Free School District,* 395 U.S. 621 (1969); *Korematsu* v. *United States,* 323 U.S. 214 (1944). In "old" equal protection cases a claimant must show that the classification is without "rational basis," that it does not even arguably contribute to social welfare. And in modern equal protection cases purporting to apply the rational basis standard but, in fact, using a more stringent standard of review, the supposed social benefits of a classification are examined more carefully. See *Weinberger* v. *Weisenfeld,* 420 U.S. 636 (1975): *Eisenstadt* v. *Baird,* 405 U.S. 438 (1972); Gunther, "The Supreme Court, 1971 Term."

36. Dworkin does concede that a legislature may act improperly if it makes "grossly unfair distributions" ("Hard Cases," p. 1092).

37. John Umana, who, relying on arguments developed by R. M. Hare and W. Frankena, urges that universalizability is a critical aspect of judical decision and points out that this requirement is quite consistent with reliance on policy. See Note, "Dworkin's 'Rights Thesis,' " p. 1194.

38. See Dworkin, "Hard Cases," p. 1074. Dworkin argues correctly that the mere coincidence of possible economic justifications with common law rules does not undercut the descriptive aspect of his rights thesis, although it might constitute evidence that judicial views of institutional rights are heavily influenced by economic considerations. It is possible that judges who consciously considered only arguments of principle would unconsciously make decisions promoting the policy of economic welfare. However, if the coincidence of economic justifications with existing common law rules is made the basis of a suggestion that courts should aim at promoting efficient resource allocation, which is certainly one of the messages in Richard Posner, *Economic Analysis of Law* (1972), then a challenge is apparently being posed to the normative aspect of Dworkin's rights thesis. Dworkin can successfully meet that challenge only by rejecting the conscious economic approach or by showing that that judicial approach is really consistent with his thesis, the possibility discussed in the text.

39. Dworkin, "Hard Cases," p. 1075. Professor Posner suggests that a more precise formulation would emphasize marginal loss avoidance. See Posner, *Economic Analysis of Law,* p. 69, but a simpler test suffices for our purpose.

40. Dworkin, "Hard Cases," p. 1075.

41. See ibid., pp. 1070, 1075.

42. Ibid., p. 1075.

43. Ibid.

44. Ibid., pp. 1076–77.

45. *Restatement (Second) of Torts* § 826 (Tent. Draft No. 18, 1972); see W. Prosser, *Law of Torts,* 4th ed. (1971), § 89, pp. 597–99. This latest revision of the *Restatement* adds to the earlier formulation, *Restatement (Second) of Torts* § 826 (Tent. Draft No. 16, 1970), the rule that an intentional invasion can also be a nuisance if "(b) the harm caused by the conduct is substantial and the financial burden of compensating for this and other harms does not render infeasible the continuation of the conduct." Thus in some cases in which the utility of the actor's conduct outweighs the harm, he may still be required to pay damages.

46. See *City of Fort Smith* v. *Western Hide & Fur Co.,* 153 Ark. 99, 239, S.E. 724 (1922); *Campbell* v. *Seaman,* 63 N.Y. 568 (1876); *Restatement (Second) of Torts* § 840D (Tent. Draft No. 16, 1970). Given a constant degree of damage to the community, an activity might also become a nuisance because its value to the community declined. And of two activities producing the same damage, one may be a nuisance and the other not because the latter is a valuable community resource. A cheap restaurant indistinguishable from countless others in quality might be required to abate noise and smoke affecting adjoining apartments even if it could show that the cost of abatement would be too prohibitive to allow it to remain in business. A famous restaurant attracting tourists and business to the same area might, upon a similar showing of cost, avoid having the same pollution from noise and smoke declared a nuisance.

47. Cf. *Hadacheck* v. *Sebastian,* 239 U.S. 394 (1915) (sustaining a city ordinance prohibiting the manufacture of bricks against a constitutional challenge).

48. Recently it has been held that in at least some circumstances those who benefit from abatement should share its cost. *Spur Indus., Inc.* v. *Del E. Webb Dev. Co.,* 108 Ariz. 178, 494 P. 2d 700 (1972). In many instances this may well be a fairer way of allocating social costs than to impose the burden solely on the person whose activity has become a nuisance.

49. I have not distinguished cases in which a court applies some broadly worded legal standard to a specific situation from those in which it decides whether to accept a newly formulated legal rule. Dworkin does not appear to believe such a distinction is relevant, supposing that his thesis

applies to both classes of cases. And, since many applications of general standards could also be characterized as the formulation of new substandards, I doubt if it can be asserted that a kind of argument can be relevant for one sort of case but not the other.

50. See *Miller* v. *Miller,* 22 N.Y. 2d 12, 237 N.E. 2d 877, 290 N.Y.S. 2d 734 (1968). But see *Reich* v. *Purcell,* 67 Cal. 2d 551, 432 P. 2d. 727, 63 Cal. Rptr. 31 (1967), rejecting the doctrine that changes in residence after an accident may be relevant.

51. See *Jacob & Youngs, Inc.* v. *Kent,* 230 N.Y. 239, 129 N.E. 889, 186 N.Y.S. Appdx. (1921). Robert Summers uses the case to illustrate "public goal serving" reasons. See his "Two Types of Substantive Reasons—The Core of a Theory of Common Law Justification," *Cornell Law Review* 63 (1978): 707–88.

52. Dworkin, "Hard Cases," p. 1077. Limits on what the courts can handle may affect substantive doctrines as well as jurisdictional doctrines.

53. Jurisdictional limits are, of course, also supported by the notion that courts can more intelligently resolve cases in whch the facts have ripened and there are sharp adversaries, and by considerations concerning separation of powers.

54. In his careful study of common law decisions, "Two Types of Substantive Reasons," Professor Robert Summers has found extensive use of what Dworkin considers to be arguments of policy.

Professor Wellington argues that common law policies must be relatively neutral (see Wellington, "Common Law Rules," pp. 236–42), the courts should not, for example, have a common law policy of promoting collective bargaining, since they should not ordinarily justify rules accepting the demands of one innocent interest group at the expense of another. No doubt courts,unlike legislatures, cannot simply favor one group rather than another; they must put forward a plausible justification in terms of community welfare. But often decisions made on policy grounds do favor one "innocent" group at the expense of another: in nuisance cases courts often favor the interests of one group over the incommensurate interests of another; strict liability favors those affected by an activity at the expense of those engaging in the activity; and implied warranties favor consumers over producers. Perhaps what Wellington's example illustrates is that when the group to be favored closely approximates the typical organized interest group capable of action before the legislature, when the importance and political character of competing policy arguments make eventual legislative resolution likely and appropriate, and when the complexity of the issue and need for accommodations make successful judicial treatment unlikely, courts should refrain from relying on policy arguments. The more these three factors are in evidence, the stronger the reasons against judicial reliance.

55. Dworkin, "Hard Cases," pp. 1077–78. Dworkin suggests that it may be permissible to allow criminal defendants to succeed on policy arguments because the government has no countervailing right.

56. See ibid., p. 1073.

57. Ibid., p. 1077.

58. See Note, "Dworkin's 'Rights Thesis,'" p. 1181.

59. Dworkin, "Hard Cases," p. 1073.

60. On his justificatory defense against a speeding charge, see *Model Penal Code* § 3.02 (1962).

61. See Harry Kalven, "Privacy in Tort Law—Were Warren and Brandeis Wrong?" *Law & Contemporary Problems* 31 (1966): 326.

62. See *Hawkins* v. *United States,* 358 U.S. 74 (1958).

63. A person whose behavior is clearly covered by a statute but who attacks the statute as impermissibly vague on its face may succeed because a court thinks it necessary to protect the many others as to whom coverage is doubtful.

64. See Dworkin, "Hard Cases," p. 1073.

65. An argument of principle may be weakened if there is doubt whether the right asserted has been institutionalized, but the strength of policy arguments might also be affected by degrees of institutional acceptance.

66. I put aside the possibility that the invader violates international law.

67. See Dworkin, "Hard Cases," p. 1069. Dworkin says that a right "has a certain threshold weight against collective goals in general." Ibid. It may give way to goals of special urgency, but if it yields whenever the collective welfare would benefit, it is not a right in a significant sense.

68. This example draws from R. Wasserstrom, *The Judicial Decision* (1961), pp. 140–44.

69. The nonexistence of a legal right in the technical sense may reflect the impracticability of

having such a right, rather than any sense that the social right is less important than many social rights for which enforceable legal claims exist.

70. 413 U.S. 49, 73 (1973) (Brennan, J., dissenting).

71. Of course, given legislative history that gender integration of toilet facilities was not intended, a court might rely on this history rather than independently weighing discomfort against the claim to integration.

72. For an interesting and somewhat different argument that the distinction between principles and policies breaks down, see Note, "Dworkin's 'Rights Thesis,' " pp. 1172–77.

73. Such standards often, but not always, call for initial determination by administrative agencies which have considerable latitude of application as far as the courts are concerned.

74. See Dworkin, "Hard Cases," p. 1086.

75. Insofar as legislation was based on principle rather than policy, it would, according to Dworkin, appropriately influence common law developments. Ibid., p. 1094.

76. Ibid., p. 1087.

77. Ibid., p. 1086.

78. Ibid., p. 1085.

79. See Note, "Dworkin's 'Rights Thesis,' " pp. 1182–83.

80. *Charles River Birdge* v. *Warren Bridge,* 24 Mass. (7 Pick.) 344 (1829), *aff'd,* 36 U.S. (11 Pet.) 420 (1837).

81. See Note, "Dworkin's 'Rights Thesis,' " p. 1086, note 21.

82. Dworkin, "Hard Cases," p. 1089, note 23.

83. It could, of course, be argued that long-term exclusivity is always so risk-laden it is unwise; the majority of the Supreme Court made that assumption in interpreting the charter. *Charles River Bridge* v. *Warren Bridge,* 36 U.S. (11 Pet.) 420, 546–48 (1837).

84. See *United States* v. *United States District Court,* 407 U.S. 297 (1972) (suggestion that probable cause standard may be relaxed for wiretapping of domestic "subversives"); *Terry* v. *Ohio,* 392 U.S. 1, 20–27 (1968) (stop and frisk upheld).

85. U.S. Constitution, Art. I, § § 8, para. 3, 9, para. 2.

86. Dworkin, "Hard Cases," p. 1084.

87. A contrary theory would be that these rights are thought to promote the general welfare and are entrenched only to guard against temporary legislative misjudgments on how to pursue that welfare.

88. Though of some analytical assistance, this distinction is by no means clear-cut. Not only are there difficult borderline cases, almost any argument of one kind can be translated into an argument of the other kind.

89. Justice Black's treatment of some First Amendment issues illustrates clearly that belief in the absoluteness of a guarantee does not necessarily lead to an expansive understanding of its coverage. See e.g., *Cohen* v. *California,* 403 U.S. 15, 27 (1971) (dissent); *Tinker* v. *Des Moines School District,* 393 U.S. 503, 515 (1969) (dissent); *Adderly* v. *Florida,* 385 U.S. 39 (1966).

90. *United States* v. *White,* 322 U.S. 694, 700 (1944). For other cases in which considerations of policy were treated as relevant, see *Terry* v. *Ohio,* 392 U.S. 1 (1968); *Miranda* v. *Arizona,* 384 U.S. 436 (1966); *City of El Paso* v. *Simmons,* 379 U.S. 497 (1965).

91. Dworkin might not accept this formulation since he apparently believes that in every doubtful case, courts should decide in favor of rights asserted against the government. See Dworkin, "Taking Rights Seriously," *New York Review of Books* 15, Dec. 17, 1970, pp. 23, 28. My objections to this position are stated briefly in Kent Greenawalt, "Discretion and Judicial Decision: The Elusive Quest for the Fetters that Bind Judges," *Columbia Law Review 75,* (1975): 243.

92. See Dworkin, "Does Law Have a Function? A Comment on the Two-Level Theory of Decision," *Yale Law Journal* 74 (1965): 640.

93. This was also the title of an earlier article; see note 91.

94. Judges deciding easy cases as to which the law is quite clear may more often find their own views at variance with the decision to be reached by reference to legal materials.

95. I am unaware, for example, of any difficult legal issue on which Professor Dworkin has written as to which his recommended decision differs from his own moral evaluation.

96. For simple cases the theory explains why judges are obligated to follow the authoritative legal norms.

97. See text following note 80 above.

98. 379 U.S. 497 (1965).

99. U.S. Constitution, Article I, § 10.
100. See Dworkin, "Hard Cases," pp. 1094–95.
101. Given the fact that the clause was adopted to prevent legislators sympathetic with debtors from undermining the interests of a smaller number of creditors, the attitudes of an identifiable debtor class should not be controlling, even if debtors constitute a majority of the population.
102. See Dworkin, "The Law of the Slave-Catchers," p. 1437.
103. R. Cover, *Justice Accused* (1975).
104. Wellington, "Common Law Rules," p. 264, takes a similar position concerning legislation that deviates from established moral principles. He says courts should go only as far as the legislature's "clear statement." Wellington's position differs from the natural law position in making the judge's ultimate standard for principles those standards accepted by the community.
105. Dworkin, "The Law of the Slave-Catchers," p. 1437.
106. U.S. Constitution, Article I, § 9, para. 1, protected the slave trade against congressional prohibition until 1808; apart from equal suffrage in the Senate, it was the only unamendable part of the original constitution. Article IV, § 2, para. 3 required interstate rendition of fugitive slaves.
107. Under Article I, § 2, para. 3, a slave counted as three-fifths of a person for the purposes of apportioning Representatives and direct taxes among the states.
108. Dworkin's theory works best in respect to the procedures used to determine if someone was a slave in fugitive slave cases. The theory that would best justify all parts of the Constitution might well lead to the conclusion that a person should enjoy full procedural protections until clearly shown to be a slave, protections woefully absent in the Fugitive Slave Act of 1850. See R. Cover, *Justice Accused,* pp. 175–91.
109. But see Wellington, "Common Law Rules," pp. 243–44, arguing that a court is restricted to conventional morality.
110. The suggestion of M. Kadish and S. Kadish, *Discretion to Disobey* (1973), that various officials occupy recourse roles allowing them to depart from prescribed means for their roles when they are firmly persuaded that these means will not be conducive to prescribed ends, might profitably be applied here. We might think that a judge is bound to a degree to follow the implications of existing legal institutions and standards or at least to follow community notions of moral rightness and social welfare, but concede that when he is very strongly convinced these point in the wrong direction, he may follow his own views.
111. But see ibid., pp. 86–90, suggesting that in some instances, judges may properly depart even from applicable mandatory rules, such as grossly ill-conceived mandatory sentences.

6

Glosses on Dworkin: Rights, Principles, and Policies

Donald H. Regan

A great many people have attempted to explain what is wrong with the views of Ronald Dworkin. So many, indeed, that one who read only the critics might wonder why views so widely rejected have received so much attention. One reason is that, whatever may be wrong in Dworkin's theories, there is a good deal that is right in them. But what is right is not always clear. Important passages in Dworkin can be distressingly obscure, or tantalizingly incomplete.

This essay is a set of loosely connected observations on themes from Dworkin. While I shall add some criticisms of my own to the list of charges against Dworkin, my primary object is to defend and to amplify, clarifying here, filling in gaps there. I shall concentrate on what Dworkin has to say about the nature of rights, principles, and policies. I shall not address directly issues about the relation of law to morality. The omission just indicated makes it clear that I am not engaged in a comprehensive review of Dworkin's position.

It is in the nature of this essay to have no unifying theme. Various parts of the essay do, however, converge in supporting the following observation: Individuals, and relations between individuals, are squarely at the center of Dworkin's picture of the common law. For the most part (not invariably) Dworkin seems to operate with a rather old-fashioned idea of the common law as a system based on fundamental moral principles, understandable by all, regulating intercourse between individuals and referring only incidentally to general social consequences. The centrality of the individual is revealed both in judgments about what are appropriate occasions for judicial intervention and in judgments about what reasons for decision it is appropriate for judges to consider. The suggestion that Dworkin tends to focus on individuals should not surprise anyone who has read his essays. What may be surprising is the number of Dworkin's claims that turn out on analysis to reflect this tendency.

I. RIGHTS

In a recent review of *Taking Rights Seriously,* Joseph Raz devotes considerable attention to Dworkin's view of the nature of rights.[1] After arguing that Dworkin's claims are obscure and apparently contradictory. Raz seems to despair of finding in Dworkin any interesting view at all. My own opinion is that Dworkin's writings contain two distinct interesting views about the nature of rights. Dworkin does not treat these views as distinct, but I shall show that certain of Dworkin's arguments about rights require that the two views be kept separate.[2]

A. Rights as Trumps

On one view, a right is a sort of political trump. The simplest way to elucidate the idea of "rights as trumps" is to sketch a theory about political goals in which such rights figure. The theory I shall sketch is Dworkinian in its basic conception and illuminates various features of Dworkin's views. It may not represent perfectly Dworkin's current theory of political goals. Dworkin's essays, written over a number of years and republished recently without any attempt at harmonization, do not add up to a definitive statement of what Dworkin believes.

According to the theory I shall consider, and to a first approximation, the basic purpose of civil government is to provide for the satisfaction of the preferences of individual citizens.[3] The basic purpose is not to produce great philosophers, nor to advance science or the arts, nor to produce the highest possible level of economic welfare subject to a constraint of precise material equality, nor to approach any other conception of the ideal state. The basic purpose is to let people have and do what they want as fully as possible. Inevitable conflicts between individual preferences are to be resolved along traditional utilitarian lines. Government should seek to maximize the aggregate satisfaction of preferences, taking intensity of preference into account.

So far we have referred to nothing resembling rights. Rights come into this sketch as a refinement of the basic purpose we have postulated for government. *Rights are preferences which are given special weight.* (More accurately, perhaps, rights are special protections accorded certain preferences in the form of extra weighting.) Thus, to say that someone has a right of political expression is to say that his preference for indulging in political expression is given *more weight* than ordinary run-of-the-mill preferences (that is, preferences not protected by rights) of the same intensity. The purpose of government, once rights are taken into account, is to maximize the aggregate satisfaction of preferences where the method of aggregation respects both the varying intensity of preferences *and* the special weights accorded to any preferences because they are protected by rights.

This sketch of the nature of rights[4] makes it clear in what sense rights can override considerations of the general welfare, and why it is appropriate for Dworkin to refer to rights as "anti-utilitarian".[5] If I have no right of political expression, then it is a sufficient justification for forbidding me to speak that the aggregate satisfaction of everyone's preferences (including mine, of course, and taking account of the intensity of all relevant preferences) will be greater if I am silent. But if I have a right to speak, then the same balance of other preferences which was sufficient to outweigh my bare desire to speak may out outweight my desire when it is given the extra weight it acquires by virtue of the right. Thus my having a right may tip the balance against a governmental action which would be justified by reference to the general welfare if the right did not exist.

The preceding paragraph establishes that it is not a sufficient argument for denying a right that the aggregate satisfaction of preferences, measured without reference to the special weight the right confers on certain preferences, would be marginally increased by doing so. A corollary of this proposition is the following: If it *is* a sufficient justification for the government's defeating some preference that the general welfare is marginally served thereby, then the preference in question is *not* protected by a right. This is the basis for what I shall call the "Lexington Avenue argument." Dworkin writes at one point: "I have no political right to drive up Lexington Avenue. If the government chooses to make Lexington Avenue one-way down town, it is a sufficient justification that this would be in the general interest . . . ."[6] The context makes it clear that the second sentence just quoted is intended as a rather elliptical argument for the claim in the first sentence that Dworkin has no right to drive up Lexington Avenue. Our sketch of the nature of rights reveals why, in Dworkin's view, the argument is valid.

I have paused over the Lexington Avenue argument for two reasons. First, I shall use the argument myself against a claim of Dworkin's in the next section of this essay. Second, the argument seems to have occasioned some confusion. Raz, for example, thinks the Lexington Avenue argument must rest on the claim that "rights cannot be defeated by considerations of the general interest or by any other considerations."[7] I do not know why Raz adds the phrase "or by any other considerations," since the Lexington Avenue argument plainly speaks to nothing but the relation between claims of right and the general interest. The important point, however, is that the Lexington Avenue argument does *not* depend even on a claim that "rights cannot be defeated by considerations of the general interest." What the argument depends on is the claim that not just any marginal increase in the general welfare which would flow from denying a right can justify that denial. So long as there is no right to drive up Lexington Avenue, then the possibility of achieving even the slightest increase in the general welfare justifies making Lexington Avenue one-way downtown. If there is a right to drive up Lexington Avenue, however, it takes more than this marginal advantage to the general welfare to justify making the Avenue one-way the other way. In sum, the Lexington Avenue argument does not depend on the claim that rights can *never* be defeated by considerations of the general interest. It depends only on the claim that rights cannot be defeated by the *same* considerations of the general interest that would justify defeating the relevant preferences if they were not protected by rights.[8]

This is an appropriate point at which to call attention to another feature of our sketch. It allows for rights of widely differing importance. To say that there is a right to something is only to say that a preference for that something gets *some* extra weight. It is not to say anything about how much extra weight.

A right which guarantees the preference it protects only a little extra weight is a weak right, but a right nonetheless. The interesting rights, to be sure, are the strong ones, those that confer a great deal of extra weight on the preferences they protect. But the logic of rights does not require that rights be strong, or interesting. Far from suggesting that rights cannot be defeated by considerations of the general interest, our sketch leaves open the possibility that some rights can be denied in order to produce relatively small gains in the aggregate satisfaction of preferences.[9]

The sketch we are considering is a sketch of the logic of rights, no more. As noted in the previous paragraph, it does not tell us how important any particular right is. More generally, it tells us nothing (by itself) about what rights we have. Despite this, the sketch generates some significant arguments. Dworkin employs the central idea of the sketch when he argues in the essay "Taking Rights Seriously" that a right maintains its power to override the general welfare over the whole range of its relevance, or in other words that a right does not just naturally lose its power to override (some) arguments based on the general welfare as the range of cases in which the right is recognized moves further and further beyond the unambiguous "core" cases.[10] Dworkin employs the same idea in his argument that the government cannot justify enforcing a law it had no right to pass in the first place on the ground that nonenforcement will lead to a marginal decrement in respect for law.[11] The same idea is at the center of the argument in "What Rights Do We Have?" that there is no general right to liberty.[12] I do not suggest that these arguments are unproblematic. But they are significant, and they flow directly from the logic of rights embodied in the sketch.

Our sketch also accounts very neatly for Dworkin's apparent view that an individual does not have a right to his own welfare.[13] If Jones has a right to his own welfare, then all of Jones's preferences are entitled to extra weight in the aggregating process. But if Jones has this right, then so does everyone else. (This is an assumption. I assume that if the right to one's own welfare exists, then it is a universal right.) If everyone has the right, then all of everyone's preferences are entitled to extra weight. But if all of everyone's preferences are entitled to extra weight, then in effect no preference is given extra weight, at least on the basis of this particular right. In sum, the very idea of a (universal) right to one's own welfare is incoherent.

Note that the argument just given does not preclude a right to some minimum level of welfare. We could give extra weight to all preferences which must be satisfied if we are to bring everyone up to some specified minimum level of satisfaction. Provided the level specified can be achieved for everyone without exhausting the society's resources, recognition of this right will not result in giving extra weight to all preferences, and so will not lead to incoherence. I suspect that most proponents of a "right to welfare" have in mind a right to some minimum level of welfare. It is a virtue of the sketch that it explains how there can be a right to minimum welfare at the same time that it explains why the notion of a right to welfare in general, not limited at any level of satisfaction, is problematic.[14]

Let me turn now to a few criticisms that are likely to be made of our sketch. It may appear that the sketch, in addition to not telling us what rights we have, falls hopelessly short of accommodating all the rights we think we have, or all the rights Dworkin thinks we have. How, for example, do we fit the right to equal concern and respect, or the right not to be discriminated against on the basis of race, into this picture of rights as specially weighted preferences without gross distortion? There are difficulties here, but they may be less than they appear at first.

As to the right to equal concern and respect, that is not just *a* right in Dworkin's scheme. It is *the* right, the foundation of everything else. This right is not one to be analyzed as a specially weighted preference. Rather, this right is embodied in the very structure of the scheme, in the idea that the basic purpose of government is to promote the satisfaction of preferences, some of them, perhaps, given special weight. Equal concern is reflected in the fact that everyone's preferences are counted equally, and some degree of respect is reflected in the fact that counting only preferences excludes governmental enforcement of ideals which are not widely shared by the citizenry.[15] A further degree of respect can be guaranteed, and in a fully spelled-out theory presumably would be guaranteed, by the assignment of special weights to certain preferences (such as that for free speech or for particular forms of sexual expression) which we think cannot be denied without invading the personality of the individual.[16]

As to the right not to be discriminated against on the basis of race, matters are more complicated. We must consider just what we mean by this right. If we mean a right not to have one's preferences ignored or discounted because of one's race, then of course the right to non-discrimination so understood is embodied in the sketch as one way of specifying the general right to equal concern and respect. If, on the other hand, we mean a right not to have race used as a basis for any legal classification, then I doubt that there is such a right at the most fundamental theoretical level. We are rightly suspicious of any use of racial classifications, both because we think race is presumptively irrelevant to most problems the law deals with, and because racial criteria have been appallingly misused. But I do not see how it can be said that race could never be an appropriate basis for classification in a scheme that maximized satisfaction of everyone's preferences, correctly weighted and aggregated. (Lest it be objected that the last sentence simply demonstrates the inadequacy of the whole maximizing-of-satisfaction approach. I will say that I do not see how race could be *absolutely* forbidden as a basis of classification on any plausible political theory.) The sketch I have offered is intended to capture the logic of theoretically fundamental rights, and if the "right" not to have race used as a basis for classification is not such a right, it is no objection to the sketch that it cannot accommodate it. Note that accepting the sketch as a sketch of the logic of fundamental rights does not exclude the possibility of stringent constitutional rules, such as a flat ban on the use of race as a classification, if such rules are desirable in practice as protection against abuse of political power.[17]

Another possible criticism of our sketch is that it allows any right to be overriden by a sufficiently strong argument based just on the general welfare. No matter how much extra weight is given to any particular preference (provided it is not an infinite weight, which would involve us in other difficulties), it is logically possible that the balance of other relevant preferences should be enough to outweigh that one preference. This may be a defect of the sketch. It will appear to some readers that while any right must give way in the face of some imaginable disasters, yet there are some rights that cannot be violated just to produce an *increase* in general welfare (assuming we are already above some reasonable minimum) no matter how great that increase might be. Dworkin himself might take this view. We could make selected rights impervious to supposed justifications for denial based on increases (of whatever magnitude) in the general welfare by according lexicographical priority to certain preferences in certain circumstances. I shall not pursue this complication, which would have little or no effect on the rest of this essay.

There may be readers who wonder whether the sketch I have offered is defensible as an interpretation of Dworkin. The sketch does not employ Dworkin's concept of "external preferences." For reasons discussed in a footnote, I tend to regard the essays on external preferences as interesting digressions from the main current of Dworkin's theorizing.[18] Aside from that, the sketch captures neatly the idea of rights as trumps, and it allows us to account crisply for some claims Dworkin leaves incompletely justified.

There is another respect in which the sketch is thoroughly Dworkinian. Reading Dworkin's essays together, one cannot overlook the fact that, however complex some of his arguments, Dworkin wants to make the basic structure of his scheme of fundamental political values as simple as possible. The desire for simplicity and liberal predispositions together lead Dworkin to want to do just what our sketch does, namely, to put individual preferences at the center of things, with as little supporting machinery as possible.[19]

B. Trump-Rights and Private Litigation

One of Dworkin's central claims is that all litigation, properly understood, is about rights. So far as I am aware, Dworkin never specifically claims that all litigation involves "trump-rights," rights which satisfy the logic of rights developed in the preceding section. But he does sometimes seem to suggest this. For example, in rejecting the claim that Learned Hand's formulation of the test for negligence[20] is a common-law doctrine based solely on the policy of efficiency, Dworkin asserts that Hand's test is a method of compromising competing abstract rights of the parties.[21] Furthermore, the most explicit notion of rights in Dworkin is the notion of rights as trumps. If it is not trump-rights that are supposed to be involved in all litigation, Dworkin makes little effort to tell us explicitly what sort of rights he has in mind.

In this section I shall show that, despite the suggestions in Dworkin, much common-law litigation cannot be understood as being about trump-rights. More specifically (and this specification is important in case the sketch of trump-rights in the preceding section is not fully acceptable to Dworkin), much common-law litigation cannot be understood as being about rights which obey a logic justifying what I have referred to above as the "Lexington Avenue argument."[22] The discussion which follows will center around negligence litigation and the Hand test. Other critics have objected to Dworkin's treatment of negligence, saying that if we sometimes compromise competing rights by appealing to policies, as we seem to do in this area, then the claim that litigation is always about rights loses its interest.[23] I think that objection is somewhat off the mark, for reasons which will appear later in this essay. My own objection is stronger and narrower: stronger because I propose to show that as a logical matter we simply cannot view some areas of common-law litigation as involving trump-rights; narrower because I am prepared to admit, indeed to argue, that there may be other interesting senses in which common-law litigation is about rights after all.

Before proceeding, I should like to eliminate two possible sources of confusion. One is an argument that, for Dworkin, all litigation is about trump-rights. The other is an argument that private litigation could not possibly be about trump-rights.

As to the first, it might be suggested that in Dworkin's view a court is always obligated to pronounce whatever decision is required by the existing legal institutions. Furthermore, a court may not depart from whatever decision is required by existing institutions just because the general welfare (including the welfare of the parties to the case) would be marginally increased by doing so. In every case, then, the party who should prevail under existing institutions has a trump-right that the court decide in his favor. The party who should prevail has a trump-right that the judge enforce the law.

The argument just described does suggest a sense in which (at least for Dworkin, who believes in right answers) litigation always involves trump-rights. But Dworkin surely means more than this when he says that litigation involves rights. For one thing, if this is all he means, then his claim that litigation is about rights bears no relation to the idea that litigation is about rights *more than about policy*. We could perfectly well assert on the one hand that some party has a trump-right that the law be enforced and on the other hand that the law involved even in private disputes is based exclusively on policy. If we want further evidence that Dworkin means something more than that one party has a trump-right that the law be enforced, we have only to look at what he says. In responding to the claim that the Hand test for negligence is based on policy instead of rights, Dworkin does *not* say, "Ah, but even so the party who should win under the Hand test has a right to a favorable decision." What he says is that the Hand test *itself* is a method of compromising competing rights.

As to the second possible confusion, it might be suggested that private litigation could not possibly involve trump-rights, because trump-rights are rights against the state. Dworkin says that the notion of rights as trumps "marks the distinctive concept of an individual right against the State which is the heart . . . of constitutional theory in the United States."[24] It might seem that unless trump-rights are involved in private litigation in the manner we have just rejected, that is, as rights against the judge that the law be enforced, then they cannot be involved at all. But there is another way in which trump-rights can be involved in private litigation. Consider the law of assault. It seems plausible to suggest that an individual, in addition to having a trump-right not to be assaulted by agents of the state, also has a trump-right to be protected by the state from at least serious assaults by other citizens. If this is so, then the private law of assault presumably reflects that trump-right, at least in part, and litigation arising from private assaults will involve questions about the scope and implementation of that trump-right. It is in this sense, it seems to me, that Dworkin suggests trump-rights are involved in negligence litigation.[25]

We are now ready to consider the principal question, whether the common law of negligence can be understood as involving rights as trumps. Learned Hand's famous test for negligence was laid down in the *Carroll Towing* case.[26] The issue in that case was whether a barge-owner could be held negligent on the ground that its bargee was not present on a barge moored to a pier, where the absence of the bargee was a contributing factor to damage that occurred after the barge slipped or was torn from its mooring.[27] Hand's answer was that behavior is negligent if and only if it fails to maximize utility. Hand did not state his view in just those terms, but that it how he has been widely understood, and that is how Dworkin understands him. In effect, then, Dworkin says that even though the test of a defendant barge-owner's negligence is not having a bargee on board a moored barge is whether, in the circumstances, it would have been more productive of utility to have a bargee on board than not to, this test can still be understood as a method of compromising the competing abstract trump-rights of the barge-owner and others whose property an errant barge might damage. In this Dworkin is mistaken.

It is clear, I take it, that an appropriate legislative body could adopt the rule that a barge-owner is required to have a bargee on board a moored barge at all times. It is also clear, I assume, that the legislative body could adopt this rule with no other justification than that it marginally served the general interest. If these propositions are granted, then the barge-owner has no trump-right to dispense with a bargee on board. That is just an application of the Lexington Avenue argument.[28] If the presence of a bargee can be required just to promote (marginally) the general welfare, then there is no trump-right to dispense with a bargee.

It is tempting to respond that Dworkin never claims there is a trump-right to dispense with a bargee. He relies rather (the response goes) on some broad abstract trump-right of the barge-owner to operate his barge, or more generally to manage his business or to use his property, as he sees fit. The fact that this abstract right may be subordinated to the general welfare in the specific context of the bargee-on-board problem does not mean that the abstract right does not exist. This response, while superficially plausible, is either mistaken or beside the point. Assuming for the moment that the abstract right to operate one's barge as one sees fit (or whatever grander abstract right we might rely on) exists, either it is implicated in the bargee-on-board problem, or it is not. If it is not, then of course no solution of the bargee-on-board problem represents a compromise between abstract trump-rights, since one of the rights which is supposedly implicated is not implicated after all. If the right *is* implicated, then it cannot be denied just because denying it would be in the general interest. The reason is that if an abstract trump-right is implicated at all, it must be implicated as a trump-right, which means that it must retain the power to override some arguments based on the general interest. (Dworkin is fully aware of this, since this is a central argument of the essay "Taking Rights Seriously."[29]) In sum, if the bargee-on-board can be legislatively solved by a rule whose justification is simply that having a bargee on board at all times promotes the general welfare, then the bargee-on-board problem does not implicate any abstract trump-right of the defendant, of any description.

We have established that the bargee-on-board problem does not implicate any trump-right of a defendant barge-owner. That proposition has a further interesting consequence: If the bargee-on-board problem can properly be dealt with by applying Hand's "maximum-utility" test for negligence, then it does not involve any trump-right on the plaintiff's side either. Under Hand's test, defendant loses if his behavior is not calculated to promote the general welfare. But also under Hand's test, defendant wins, and plaintiff loses, if defendant's behavior *is* calculated to promote the general welfare. Whatever interest plaintiff has is subordinated to marginal considerations of the general welfare. Therefore, by an application of the Lexington Avenue argument, whatever interest plaintiff has is not a trump-right. It turns out that the bargee-on-board problem involves no trump-right on either side.

Note that the argument that plaintiff has no trump-right depends on the prior conclusion that defendant has no trump-right. If there were a trump-right of defendant's involved in the case, we could say plaintiff's right was being subordinated to the right of the defendant. But since there is no trump-right on the defendant's side, the plaintiff's supposed trump-right is being subordinated to the general interest alone (including, of course, the "general interest" of the defendant) and is shown not to be a trump-right by that fact.

We have just seen that the argument that plaintiff has no trump-right depends on defendant's having none. That suggests a possible objection to the original argument that defendant has no trump-right. The original argument turned on the assumption that defendant could be required to have a bargee on board *on the sole ground that such a requirement would marginally promote the public interest.* It might now be objected that this assumption was unjustified. To be sure, the objection runs, defendant can be required to have a bargee on board. But our clear intuition that this is possible implicitly assumes that the point of the requirement is to protect the rights of potential plaintiffs not to suffer damage from errant barges. Our intuition that the regulation is justifiable is therefore not an intuition that the regulation can be justified by appeal solely to the general welfare.

This objection is formally on point. If our belief that the defendant can be required to have a bargee on board depended on the implicit assumption that this was being done to protect the trump-rights of potential plaintiffs, then the argument that defendant had no trump-right would collapse. But reflection will reveal that we do not think the requirement of a bargee on board can be justified only as a protection for potential plaintiffs in damage suits. Even if there were no significant risk of damage caused by having no bargee on board, the presence of a bargee could be required if it would merely facilitate the movement of traffic in and out of slips where barges are moored. For that matter, the legislature could require the presence of a bargee on board just as a feather-bedding measure passed at the behest of the bargemen's union. We conclude that there is indeed no trump-right which protects the barge-owner's preference for not having a bargee on board.[30]

We have shown that there are no trump-rights, not even abstract ones, at issue in private litigation where plaintiff's claim is based on defendant's alleged negligence in not having a bargee on board a barge. The same argument would suffice to show that there are no trump-rights at issue in many, if not most, ordinary negligence cases. I believe that the same argument could be used to show that no trump-rights are implicated in much private litigation over property rights. Dworkin has admitted that conflicts between "rights" arising in connection with the institution of property are often settled by appeals to the general welfare.[31] This fact by itself does not show that the "rights" at issue are not trump-rights. But it does show that they are not trump-rights if it is also true that the defendant's behavior is of a sort which could be regulated by statute just to produce a marginal increase in the general welfare.

I think we are justified in concluding that there are large areas of traditional private litigation which do not involve trump-rights at all. If all private litigation involves "rights," as Dworkin claims, then they must be "rights" of some other sort.[32]

C. *Rights as Individuated Claims*

If we return to our text, we will discover that there is an aspect of rights which Dworkin emphasizes nearly as much as the idea that rights are trumps. That is the idea that rights are individuated political aims.[33] In saying that rights are individuated political aims, Dworkin seems to mean something more than the truism, as Raz calls it, that rights have right-holders. Does this suggest anything about the sense in which private litigation involves rights?

It is a fact, a fact so obvious as to be easily overlooked, that in the standard common-law case the plaintiff comes before the court citing a specialized harm to himself, either accomplished or threatened. For example, every law student learns that a cause of action in negligence requires "[1] a breach [2] of a duty that [3] causes [4] *harm.*" Similarly, every law student learns that physical harm is not required in cases involving intentional torts like assault because of the injury to plaintiff's dignity; or that in many kinds of defamation cases damage is presumed, whereas in a few it must be proved;[34] or that actual harm is not required in cases of trespass to land because of the need for an action to try title. The paradigm seems clearly to be that in order to state a cause of action plaintiff must explain (among other things) how he has suffered from defendant's behavior. In the case of a plaintiff whose leg was broken in an automobile accident, there is no problem. In the case of a plaintiff who has been assaulted but not injured physically, we make special mention of a less obvious injury, to plaintiff's dignity. In defamation cases in which proof of harm is not required, it is not because harm is irrelevant, but because it is "presumed." In the case of trespass to land, we recognize the need for an explanation of why there is a cause of action even when there is no harm of any usual sort, either actual or presumed.

Needless to say, if there is a statute authorizing actions by plaintiffs who have suffered no special harm, or who can prove none, then there is no bar to the court's hearing a case brought under the statute. Indeed, the court must do so.[35] Dworkin rarely focusses on statutory problems, and he plainly assumes that the claim that statutory litigation is about rights is not controversial. I am not entirely comfortable with that. I should like to know more about just how statutes create rights, and just what sort of things statutory rights are. But Dworkin is probably correct that few of his readers would object to the idea that statutes create rights. I shall therefore concentrate, in the remainder of this section, on plaintiffs who do not rely on a statute.[36]

We can find more evidence for the claim that common-law causes of action normally require a showing of specialized harm to the plaintiff if we return to the *Carroll Towing* context. Suppose that the absence of bargees from moored barges creates no significant risk of damage to any property, but that it does injure the general welfare by slowing somewhat the movement of harbor traffic. If there is no relevant statute or port authority regulation, an ordinary citizen of the harbor town, one who has no special connection with the operations of the harbor, cannot go to court and seek an injunction requiring some named barge-owner to man his moored barges. Nor, for that matter, can a ship-owner whose vessels use the harbor regularly. If all the plaintiff ship-owner can say is that everything would run a bit more smoothly if defendant manned his moored barges, and that plaintiff is inconvenienced by defendant's refusal in the same manner and measure as everyone else who uses the harbor, then plaintiff will be held not to have raised an issue which makes a claim on the court's attention (beyond the attention required to dismiss the complaint). Plaintiff cannot come before the court and argue simply that defendant's behavior is inefficient or otherwise damaging to the general welfare.

Note that I do not say plaintiff must claim a harm to himself which is greater than or different from the harm to anyone else. I say only that plaintiff must claim a harm to himself which is greater than or different from the harms distributed over society at large. This is obviously a matter of degree, and there are borderline cases. But the basic point is clear. Courts do not exist for the redress of claims based solely on considerations of the general welfare.[37]

It is worth asking why courts do not listen to plaintiffs who base their claims solely on the general welfare. The most obvious answer is that we do not think courts are well suited to deal with questions about what promotes the general welfare. But this answer ignores what even Dworkin admits, that courts do and should decide cases on policy grounds if these grounds are somehow implicated in questions about "rights."

A somewhat more sophisticated answer is that we do not need courts to listen to "nontraditional" plaintiffs, plaintiffs who claim no specialized harm. If the only losses from defendant's behavior are relatively slight ones spread widely over the citizenry (and this is the practical precondition for the absence of a "traditional" plaintiff who has suffered specialized harm), then either the legislature will be moved by broad-based political pressure to do something about defendant's behavior, or else the problem is not serious enough to worry about.[38]

Another possible reason for not listening to a plaintiff who claims no special harm (and who does not rely on a statute) is that the defendant is specially likely to be surprised if a court rules against him at the instance of such a plaintiff. The reason is not just that defendant will be surprised if the court entertains a case against him by a nontraditional plaintiff when nontraditional plaintiffs are not generally listened to. Surprise from this source can be avoided by making it clear that nontraditional plaintiffs will be heard. The reason is that even if it is understood that nontraditional plaintiffs will be heard, it may be harder for defendant to anticipate that his behavior will create a case for a nontraditional plaintiff than to anticipate that it will create a case for a traditional plaintiff. Defendants may not be as well-placed to identify the general social consequences of their behavior as they are to identify significant threatened harms to individual potential plaintiffs. Courts cannot always avoid surprising litigants, but surprise is a bad thing, and in addition to being more likely, it may be less defensible where the only harm defendant does is to general social interests.[39]

I have pointed out that courts do not ordinarily listen to plaintiffs who claim no special harm to themselves, and I have offered some suggestions about why this might be so. We can interpret Dworkin's assertion that private litigation is about rights as an assertion that private litigation is based on individuated claims, claims arising either from specialized harm or else from a statute.[40] There is a problem with this, however. It does not follow from the fact that courts may not entertain claims based on the general welfare (that is, based neither on specialized harm nor on a statute) that courts may not attend to any and all *arguments* based on the general welfare in those cases which merit their attention for other reasons. The assertion that private litigation is about rights as individuated claims seems to be an assertion about "standing" which tells us nothing about what arguments are admissible, or about what a court is supposed to do with a standard "hard case." I think there is more than we have yet discovered in the idea that private litigation involves rights as individuated claims, but whatever else there is is elusive. I shall not try to pin it down just yet.

It is appropriate to conclude this part of the essay by noting a few connections, more phenomenological than logical, between the idea of rights as trumps and the idea of rights as individuated claims.

First, there is a natural tendency to slide from the perception that private litigation involves rights in the sense of individuated claims to the notion that private litigation involves rights in the sense of trumps. A private plaintiff who sues a private defendant ordinarily has suffered or is threatened with some significant harm. Now, it is widely felt that avoiding harm is more important than promoting increases in welfare. In particular, it is widely felt that it is unfair to require a few individuals to suffer significant specialized harms in order to produce widespread benefits, even if the total benefit exceeds the total harm. In a theory which reflects these feelings, the "right" not to suffer harm functions as a trump. Preferences for not suffering particularized harms are accorded special weight. Because of this special weight given to avoiding harm, rights in the sense of individuated claims are also rights in the sense of trumps. I shall refer to this connection by the convenient, if crude, sobriquet "lumps as trumps."

It may seem that by introducing the idea of lumps as trumps, I have given a reason to believe that all ordinary common-law litigation, based on particularized harms, involves trump-rights after all, and that I have thereby contradicted the conclusion of the previous section. That is not the case. What I have shown is that in a legal regime which fully respected the intuition that avoiding harm deserves special weight, all common-law litigation would involve trump-rights. But, precisely because of elements like the Hand test for negligence, our present regime does not fully respect that intuition. Under the Hand test, if defendant's behavior promotes the general welfare, the costs are allowed to fall where they may. Probably we are moving in the direction of greater respect for the intuition that avoiding harm deserves special weight. An important factor (not necessarily the most important factor) in the rise of strict liability has been that it tends to treat lumps as trumps. But even if it is dying, the Hand view is not yet dead. It is not yet the case that common-law litigation always involves rights as trumps.

The idea of lumps as trumps suggests an insight into Dworkin's claim, which has troubled critics, that when an argument of policy is translated into an argument of principle it ordinarily loses force in the translation.[41] Dworkin's point, I suggest, is quite simple. If we are considering a policy argument about a complex matter with widespread social ramifications, then most of the harms or benefits which figure in the policy argument will be small and ordinary. They will not involve preferences which are protected by trump-rights such as the right to speak or the right to have an abortion. Furthermore, to the extent the argument depends on avoidance of harms, most of the harms involved will not be sufficiently large or specialized to involve rights as individuated claims, even if the relevant political theory has a principle about avoidance of large harms which transforms rights as individuated claims into rights as trumps. In short, most of the harms and benefits which figure in the policy argument drop out when we consider the rights-based argument that can be manufactured from the same social consequences, and the extra weight that some of them acquire when treated as trumps is not enough to make up the difference.

I have one final observation, unrelated to the "lumps as trumps" idea. I have noted previously that there is no abstract trump-right to use one's property as one sees fit (or that if there is one, it is not implicated in many concrete situations where the breadth of the rubric would lead us to expect it to be implicated).[42] We are nonetheless strongly inclined to talk as if there were such a right. The idea of rights as individuated claims may explain why. It may be that when we say an owner has the right to use his property as he sees fit, we are calling attention to the fact that (in the absence of a statute) no other private individual will be heard to complain about how the property is used unless that other individual has been specially harmed. This is a significant protection for the property-owner, even though it falls short of being a trump-right.

II. PRINCIPLES AND POLICIES

The principal results of the discussion to this point are the following: (1) we have sketched the logic of rights as trumps; (2) we have shown that not all private litigation involves trump-rights; and (3) we have suggested that all private litigation may involve rights understood as individuated claims created either by statute or by the occurrence of specialized harm. We have also observed that even if private litigation involves rights in the sense of individuated claims, it is not obvious that anything follows about what arguments judges may appropriately consider in deciding hard cases. The notion of rights as individuated claims speaks to the issue of what cases courts should hear, and not, it would seem, to the issue of how courts should decide the cases they do hear.

This brief summary indicates a new problem. Dworkin claims that judges must consider only arguments of principle, not arguments of policy, and he defines arguments of principle as arguments about rights.[43] But what we have learned so far about rights is not an adequate basis for any distinction between arguments of principle and arguments of policy. We have seen that the rights involved in common-law cases are not limited to trump-rights. That means that if common-law adjudication relies only on arguments of principle, then arguments of principle must include more than arguments about trump-rights. How much more? The only other notion of rights we have uncovered is the notion of rights as individuated claims. Now, if all private litigation is about rights provided it involves individuated claims, and if any argument offered on the issue of whether someone has a right is an argument of principle, it might seem to follow that *any* argument made to a court in litigation arising from an individuated claim is an argument about rights and becomes *ipso facto* an argument of principle. We need not pause over the somewhat dubious logic of this suggestion. Plainly it is not what Dworkin has in mind. But it does pinpoint the problem. Dworkin defines arguments of principle as arguments about rights, but the only notion of rights we have found so far that is consistent with his claim that private litigation is about rights is a notion which is of no use when it comes to admitting some arguments and excluding others.

If we are going to make sense of Dworkin's principle/policy distinction, we must infer what the distinction is from his arguments about why it matters. With that in mind, we shall plunge ahead into Dworkin's arguments about why courts rely only on principle, even though these arguments assume a distinction we do not yet understand. If we succeed in making something of the principle/policy distinction, we will presumably be uncovering a new notion of rights at the same time. Or at least, and I think I prefer this characterization, we will be giving some new content to the ideas of rights as individuated claims.

A. Principles, Policies, and Consistency

There is an argument in Dworkin which runs as follows: Courts are subject to a strong requirement of articulate consistency. They must explain, without relying on arbitrary distinctions, how their decisions treat like cases alike. In general, political decisions based on principle must treat like cases alike, but political decisions based on policy need not (or need not to the same extent). If courts could properly base their decisions on policy, then it would be impossible to account for the importance we attach to articulate consistency in judicial decision. Therefore it must be that courts can properly base decisions only on arguments of principle. Q.E.D.[44]

Undeniably courts are subject to a strong requirement of consistency. Also undeniably, legislatures (or legislators, if that is the appropriate comparison) are not held to the same standard. Why there should be this difference is an important question. But the argument just outlined is a very problematical answer because of its reliance on the notion that decisions based on policy need not treat like cases alike.

Dworkin's claim that decisions made on grounds of policy need not treat like cases alike is puzzling, and it has not gone uncriticized. Unfortunately, both Dworkin and his critics rely largely on assertion and on examples which are either flatly unconvincing or else leave one wondering whether they really go to the heart of the problem. I think there is some truth on both sides. To see why, we must spend some time clarifying the issues.

First off, we note that Dworkin acknowledges a variety of restrictions on decisions based on policy: (1) they must not be irrational; (2) they must not violate independent rights (as would a program providing a subsidy only to newspapers with certain political views); (3) they must not be used as a cover for discrimination against weak or unpopular groups [this restriction could be viewed as included in (2), but Dworkin mentions it separately]; (4) they must not impose excessive burdens on particular individuals or particular sections of the community.[45] But Dworkin goes on to say that:

> If a legislative decision benefits some particular group, not because that group is thought entitled to the benefit, but because the benefit is a by-product of a scheme thought to advance a particular collective goal, then others have no political right to the same benefit, *even if providing that benefit for them would, in fact, advance that same collective goal even further.*[46]

In short, there seems to be no right that like cases be treated alike in the distribution of benefits to which the recipients are not entitled (or to which they are not entitled independently of the legislative decision in question). The problem we shall focus on, then, is the problem of fairness in the distribution of benefits incidental to the promotion of some general social goal.

We should also keep in mind that Dworkin's real position is less extreme than he sometimes suggests. There are passages, including the passage just quoted, in which Dworkin intimates that there is no requirement of consistency in decisions of policy conferring benefits.[47] But when he is being careful he says rather that the requirement of consistency in such decisions is "relatively weak"[48] or makes "slight demands."[49] Indeed, Dworkin and his critics seem to agree that at some level the proposition that like cases should be treated alike is a truism.[50] Even so, there is disagreement about the strength of the requirement of consistency. Against Dworkin's claim that the requirement is "relatively weak," Greenawalt says that "[t]he conferral of benefits for policy reasons typically gives rise to a *substantial* claim of justice to equal treatment on behalf of those similarly situated."[51] Raz writes that "the requirements of consistency apply with equal force and in the same way to rights and goals."[52]

Even if we keep in mind the points made so far, there are respects in which Dworkin's arguments and examples tend to confuse as much as they clarify. One problem is that Dworkin, since he believes that only legislatives should make decisions based on policy,[53] considers as examples of decisions based on policy only decisions made by the legislature. The result is that even if we agree that the requirements of consistency are weak in Dworkin's exemplary situations, we may feel that what is manifested is not a weak requirement of consistency for decisions made on the basis of policy, but rather a weak requirement of consistency for decisions made by the legislature. This objection might be answered if Dworkin compared with his examples of legislative policy decisions some examples of legislative decisions based on principle. But he does not do this, or does not do it explicitly enough.

It is clear that we *do* expect less consistency from the legislature than from courts. And this fact requires some explanation. We could possibly construe Dworkin as arguing that we should accept, as the most plausible explanation for this undoubted fact, a package of *two* propositions, namely (1) that courts, unlike legislatures, are restricted to arguments of principle and (2) that decisions based on principle are intrinsically more subject to the requirement of consistency than decisions based on policy. If this were Dworkin's argument, then it would be formally unimpeachable, but it would reveal its weakness on its face. There is a limit to how much we will swallow all at once on the basis of a "most plausible explanation" argument. Instead, Dworkin plainly intends at some points to be giving independent evidence for the second of the two propositions mentioned above, so that only the first proposition will have to be accepted on "most plausible explanation" grounds. But his examples are unconvincing as evidence for the second proposition precisely because they may be evidence of nothing more than the as-yet-unexplained difference between legislatures and courts.[54]

Another difficulty with Dworkin's discussion is that many of his examples involve the issue of whether the granting of a benefit to one person or group requires the granting of a similar benefit to a different person or group *at a later time.* This is problematic because we may feel that all kinds of political decisions (decisions of principle as well as decisions of policy) are subject to weaker requirements of consistency-over-time than of consistency-between-different-persons-at-the-same-time. Thus, in discussing his "theory of mistakes," Dworkin writes:

> [T]he main force of the underlying argument of fairness is forward-looking, not backward-looking. The gravitational force of Mrs. MacPherson's case depends not simply on the fact that she recovered for her Buick, but also on the fact that the government proposes to allow others in just her position to recover in the future. If the courts proposed to overrule the decision, no substantial argument of fairness, fixing on the actual decision in the case, survives in favor of the plaintiff in [a later similar case].[55]

Here, of course, Dworkin is denigrating the importance of consistency-over-time even in the application of principle. I do not mean to suggest that there is no requirement of consistency-over-time, either in decisions of principle or in decisions of policy. I suggest only that time is a complicating factor and that Dworkin's frequent inattention to the importance of time makes it harder to decide just what he manages to prove.

Despite my objections to Dworkin's exposition, I think he has a point, which I shall attempt to elucidate by discussing some examples of my own. Note that what follows is not a complete discussion of the extent to which decisions of policy are constrained by the requirement of consistency. What I offer is only a suggestion about what Dworkin might plausibly mean when he says that decisions of policy and decisions of principle differ in respect of this requirement.

Let us suppose a kingdom in which there are ten thousand subjects, ruled by Rex. One day Rex says to us: "The economy is in need of stimulation. I have decided to select a thousand of my subjects at random and give each subject so selected a thousand dollars." We might suggest that it would be fairer to give a thousand dollars to all ten thousand subjects, instead of giving that amount to only one thousand subjects selected at random. Or we might suggest that if Rex has only a million dollars to distribute, he would do better to give each of his ten thousand subjects one hundred dollars. But Rex might respond:

> It is a well-known economic fact, in my kingdom, that a windfall of less than a thousand dollars will not affect the spending of any subject, though the effect of a thousand dollars is significant. Because of threshold, it is not possible to stimulate the economy at all, at least in the short run, with gifts of under a thousand dollars. On the other hand, the total stimulation that is required is only a million dollars' worth. Greater stimulation would cause the economy to "overheat," as my advisers are fond of saying. So I have proposed the most equitable distribution of largesse possible consistent with the needs of the economy and the possibilities for influencing it.

At this point we might try to convince Rex that equal treatment of his subjects is more important than either stimulating or not overheating the economy, and that he should for that reason either give nothing or else give the same thousand dollars to each of his subjects. But we would recognize that Rex's position has a satisfactory internal logic of its own. If he disagrees with us about the relative importance of equal treatment and of effective fiscal policy, we would not regard him as irrational.

Let us now compare with this economic stimulation program a different program from exactly the same source. One day Rex says to us: "I have just realized that there is a moral right of free speech. I have decided to select a thousand of my subjects at random and protect them in the exercise of that right." This would be exceedingly odd. It seems to me that Rex's free-speech proposal is not merely unfair, but downright irrational. I hope the reader will at least agree with me at the outset that the free-speech program seems *somehow* more objectionable than the economic stimulation program. If the existence of some difference between the programs is conceded, I can attempt to explain what the difference is.

To say that there is a right of free speech is to say that for each individual subject, there is a reason for protecting that subject in his desire to speak. If there is a reason for protecting each individual subject in his desire to speak, then it is irrational (absent some citation of countervailing reasons) to protect a thousand subjects and ignore the other nine thousand. Indeed, it would be irrational to protect nine thousand nine hundred ninety-nine and ignore the other one. There is a sense in which the need for economic stimulation also provides a reason for giving a thousand dollars to each individual subject (assuming that all subjects have the same propensity to spend windfall income). But there is a difference between the sorts of reasons involved in the two cases. The reason for giving money to each subject in the economic stimulation program is what we might call an "index-dependent reason." The strength of the reason for giving money to any particular subject depends on the number of other subjects to whom it has already been decided that money shall be given. In the precise case before us, the reason for giving out money vanishes entirely at some point, to be replaced by a reason for *not* giving out any more. Rex's reason for protecting speech, however, is what we might call an "index-free reason." The strength of the reason is the same for the ten-thousandth subject as for the first.[56]

I have said that Rex's reason for protecting speech is an index-free reason, and I think that is the natural way to take the statement I put into Rex's mouth describing his free-speech proposal. I do not assert that all possible reasons for protecting speech are index-free. If the reason for protecting speech is to promote the discovery of truth, or to provide a check on governmental misbehavior, then it is likely that the return from protecting the last thousand subjects is less than the return from protecting the first thousand. These reasons for protecting speech are index-dependent. But if the reason for protecting speech is either of those suggested, then we have not really recognized a *right* to speech at all. We have decided to protect speech in the pursuit of a social goal. To recognize a *right* to speech, as we ordinarily use the term, is precisely to posit an individual-centered reason for protecting speech, a reason which does not diminish in strength as more and more individuals are protected. In sum, speech may be protected without being recognized as a right; but if it is recognized as a right, then the reason for protecting speech represented by the right is index-free.[57]

Just as there can be index-dependent reasons for protecting speech, so there might, at least as a theoretical possibility, be index-free reasons which do not apply to all persons. It is conceivable (though unlikely) that someone could establish the existence of a right to free speech belonging, say, to all persons over six feet tall and to no one else. The reason for protecting speech provided by such a right would not be index-dependent, since the strength of the reason would not depend on the number of persons protected. On the other hand, if Rex's reason for protecting speech were the existence of this right, then he would not be behaving irrationally if he protected only those of his subjects whose height was over six feet. In suggesting that Rex cannot rationally protect the desire to speak of some of his subjects without protecting the same desire for all of them, I have been assuming that any right to speak must be a universal right. It must belong to all Rex's subjects or to none of them.[58]

It may strike the reader as odd that I now say I have been assuming that the right to speak is a universal right. I set out a few paragraphs back to explain why it is irrational for Rex to protect only a thousand subjects in his free-speech program. It might seem that if I had just begun by pointing out my assumption that the right to speak was universal, then, aside from the possibility of questioning the assumption, nothing more need have been said. Plausible as this sounds, it suggests that matters are simpler than they are.

Our original goal, remember, was to explain the difference between Rex's economic-stimulation plan and his free-speech plan. The universality of the right to speak is not enough to explain this difference. The assertion that the right to speak is a universal right would seem to mean that, with regard to the right to speak, all Rex's subjects are indistinguishable. Whatever differences there may be between subjects, those differences are not relevant to who should be allowed to speak and who should not. But the reason for giving each subject a thousand dollars under the economic-stimulation plan was also a "universal" reason. We assumed that there were no differences between individual subjects in their propensity to spend windfall income.[59] In other words, subjects were indistinguishable with regard to the assignment of roles in the economic-stimulation program until Rex (justifiably) created some distinctions by his random selection process. That Rex was justified in creating some distinctions in one program but not in the other reflects, of course, a genuine difference between the programs. But the difference is not the universality of the right to speak.

In general, if Rex sets out to pursue a social goal like economic stimulation, he cannot safely assume *either* that all of his subjects are indistinguishable with respect to the roles they can play in a program for promoting the goal *or* that all subjects who are indistinguishable (prior to any creation of distinctions by a selection process) should be treated the same. If Rex sets out to protect a right, however, we would normally expect *both* that all subjects are indistinguishable with respect to possession of the right *and* that all subjects who are indistinguishable should be treated the same. All subjects will be indistinguishable if the right in question is universal; and all subjects who are indistinguishable should be treated the same because the reason for political decision provided by the existence of a right is index-free.[60] The example of Rex's economic-stimulation program shows that it is possible to have a reason which is universal but not index-free. The example of a hypothetical right to speak belonging only to persons over six feet tall shows what it would be to recognize a reason that was index-free but not universal. Index-free-ness and universality are distinct and independent properties. The source of the difference between Rex's economic-stimulation program and his free-speech program is just what we said it was in the first place. It is the index-free-ness of reasons based on rights.[61]

I have devoted some pages to arguing that Rex's free-speech program is irrational in a way his economic-stimulation program is not. Although I have considered only legislative programs, I have compared a legislative program based on policy with a legislative program based on rights. We can be certain that any difference we have discovered depends on the nature of the programs and not on the branch of government involved.

There may still be readers who think that the difference between the programs is more a matter of fairness than of rationality. Some readers, for example, may think that both programs are unfair and that the reason the free-speech program seems more objectionable is because fairness is specially important in the distribution of fundamental rights such as the right to speak. I shall not repeat the arguments I have already made about why I think the difference is more than this. I would make two new points: First, if fairness is specially important in the distribution of fundamental rights, then that alone is a partial justification for Dworkin's claim that consistency is more important in decisions of principle than in decisions of policy. Second, it is *only* a partial justification. "Fundamental rights" are presumably limited to trump-rights, and if fairness is specially important only in connection with trump-rights, Dworkin is left with no explanation of the strong requirement of articulate consistency which applies to courts in private litigation not involving rights as trumps. I shall explain presently how my own suggestion about the difference between Rex's programs allows us to account for the importance of consistency in cases involving rights which are not trump-rights.

Other readers may feel that the main objection to Rex's free-speech program is one which falls right on the borderline between a claim of unfairness and a claim of irrationality. It is that Rex makes distinctions in the conferring of benefits without offering any reason at all. I agree that this is a strong objection to the program. I disagree only in thinking that it does not reflect the full measure of the program's faults. The free-speech program is not only worse than the economic-stimulation program we have described. It is worse than a program in which Rex gives pure gifts of a thousand dollars, unmotivated by any consideration save generosity, to one-thousand randomly chosen subjects and nothing to the rest. The problem is therefore not simply that Rex makes a distinction without having any reason for it. The problem is that in not protecting some of his subjects in their desire to speak, he ignores a positive reason for protecting them which his use of the idea of rights commits him to.[62]

I have been suggesting that what is special about rights is that they constitute index-free reasons for political decisions. The example of a right I have relied on so far, the right to speak, is one which most people would regard as a trump-right. But the idea that rights are index-free reasons applies also to rights as individuated claims. Any argument for a political decision which begins from the consequences for an individual, as opposed to beginning from the desirability of promoting some general social goal, posits a reason which is index-free.

Consider one of Dworkin's favorite cases, *MacPherson* v. *Buick*.[63] Regardless of whether Mr. MacPherson has a trump-right not to suffer on account of the negligence of Buick, if the argument for compensating MacPherson for his injuries begins from the desirability of making him whole, then there must be an analogous argument for making whole any other plaintiff who has suffered a similar injury. To be sure, there may be differences in the cases which eventually lead us to deny recovery to the other plaintiff. Real decisions about how far to extend rights, and about how to mesh the protection of rights and the pursuit of policies, are vastly more complex than my Rex examples suggest. But the basic point remains. If it is a good to compensate MacPherson, it is *prima facie* a similar good to compensate other plaintiffs who have suffered similar harms.

Actually, I have just muddled together the universality and the index-freeness of rights. There are two aspects, which ought to be distinguished, to the justification of the claim that if it is a good to compensate MacPherson, it is *prima facie* a similar good to compensate other plaintiffs who have suffered similar harms. One aspect is the assumption that if harm to MacPherson counts as a bad, then a similar harm to someone else counts as a bad also; or in other words that MacPherson is not distinguishable from other persons with regard to the importance attached by our political theory to his and their interests. In effect, this is the assumption that the right to be protected from physical injury occasioned by another's negligence, even if it is not a trump-right, is universal. The other aspect of the justification of the claim above is the assumption that a later plaintiff who has the same sort of interest as MacPherson, while he may benefit from the analogy to MacPherson, cannot be prejudiced by the fact that MacPherson has already sued and won. We assume that the force of the reason for allowing plaintiffs like MacPherson to recover has not been exhausted by his recovering. We assume, in other words, that the reason underlying MacPherson's recovery is index-free. That, indeed, is why we unhesitatingly call it a "right."

Observe that the reason underlying MacPherson's recovery might, logically, have been a reason that was not index-free. It would not have been illogical for the court which decided in favor of MacPherson to have done so on the ground that too large a fraction of the nation's wealth was owned by corporations, and that a transfer from Buick to MacPherson would be good social policy. This reason would be index-dependent. It would not follow from MacPherson's winning on this ground that there is any reason at all for a later plaintiff to win. MacPherson's recovery might have exhausted the force of the reason on which it was based. The transfer to MacPherson might have been just the transfer away from corporations that was needed. If so, later plaintiffs, even if they are totally indistinguishable from MacPherson in every respect except that they sue after him, should lose.[64]

It may seem odd to suggest that the court might logically have decided for MacPherson on the basis of a reason which would provide no support at all to a later plaintiff who was indistinguishable from MacPherson except in being later. Indeed, I hope it does seem odd. That oddity, I believe, is precisely Dworkin's point.

When we look at how courts behave, we see that they generally attempt to discover and to extrapolate the reasons for prior decisions. They do not ordinarily ask themselves whether the force of any particular reason has been exhausted by the decisions that reason has already been used to justify. But if the reason in question was index-dependent, that inquiry would be indispensable. A court wondering whether to follow or extend the rule of *MacPherson* does not ask whether whatever the decision in *MacPherson* was meant to accomplish was fully accomplished so far as it was desirable by that decision itself. But if the court thought the decision in *MacPherson* might have been based on the desirability of reducing the wealth of corporations, it would have to consider that question.

In sum, the standard judicial approach to common-law precedent indicates that courts view common-law decisions as based on arguments that begin from the interests of individuals.[65] Such arguments posit reasons for political decisions which are index-free. This is why precedents have "gravitational force." This is an important sense in which common-law adjudication is about rights.[66]

I shall close this section with three further observations. First, I do not think either the principle/policy distinction or the distinction between index-free and index-dependent reasons is "the key" to understanding common-law adjudication. The patterns of judicial reasoning are much more complicated than any attempt that has yet been made to describe them. I do think, however, that the distinction between index-free and index-dependent reasons is a significant one, which helps to make sense of what courts do and of what Dworkin says about them.

Second, it may be that the most important line suggested by this section is not really between rights and policies, but between rights and a certain kind of policy on the one hand and a different kind of policy on the other. The crucial point, it seems to me, is the point I have attributed to Dworkin about how courts view the reasons relied on in prior cases. Courts assume (in general) that whatever was a good reason in an earlier case is still a good reason if it is relevant to the present case. Now, even though the policies of economic stimulation or decreasing corporate wealth do not generate reasons which behave this way, there may be other policies which do. For example, the policy of economic efficiency may generate reasons which behave this way. It seems plausible to suggest that whatever we would do in one case on the ground that it promoted efficiency, we would also want to do in later similar cases. The goal of efficiency is not inherently limited in the way the goal of economic stimulation is.

I shall not attempt to describe more carefully this suggested difference between efficiency and economic stimulation. One reason is that the concept of efficiency is widely invoked and widely misunderstood, and this is not the proper occasion for plunging into that morass. Another reason is that if we looked more closely we would quickly discover other types of policy intermediate in their characteristics between efficiency and economic stimulation. If I may nonetheless give names to the two sorts of policy I have indicated, I would call economic stimulation a "satiable" policy (since it is a good thing which it is possible to have too much of) and efficiency a "nonsatiable" policy (since it really is not possible to have too much of efficiency, properly defined, though it may be possible to have too much of certain supposed expedients for achieving it). Ignoring the fact that the family of possible policies does not divide up quite so neatly as this language suggests, I think it is worth considering whether the most important demarcation in the class of political aims, at least for purposes of understanding what courts do, might not be between rights and nonsatiable policies on the one hand, and satiable policies on the other.

Third, the distinction between satiable and nonsatiable policies may be the key to solving another puzzle about Dworkin's theory. Dworkin does not doubt that when a court decides a case under a statute, it must consider whatever policy the statute embodies. It may seem that because of Dworkin's holistic approach to legal questions—his assumption that the law is a seamless web, every part of which is connected to every other part—any policy that is part of the justification for any statute becomes relevant to the decision of all legal questions, including common-law questions. If this were so, then the distinction between principle and policy would be of little practical importance, since almost any policy a court might wish to rely on in deciding any case would be part of the justification for some feature of some statute. Plainly Dworkin does not intend this wholesale invasion of the common law by statutory policies. An explanation of why all policies embodied in statutes do *not* automatically become relevant to common-law questions is provided by the distinction between satiable and nonsatiable policies. If the legislature has passed a statute based on a satiable policy, there is no reason to assume that they have not pushed the policy as far as they think it should be pushed. Therefore legislative action based on a satiable policy does not ordinarily invite further judicial action (outside the range of cases in which the statute is directly implicated) in pursuit of the same policy.

B. Principles, Policies, and Right Answers

There is a possible argument for the proposition that judges should consider only arguments of principle, which runs as follows: Questions of principle have right answers; questions of policy do not. Judges deal only with questions that have right answers. Therefore, judges must deal only with questions of principle.

Dworkin does not make this argument in so many words. He might disown it in the form I have just given it. On the other hand, the argument as stated is suggested by Dworkin's "democratic-theory" argument for the proposition that judges should rely on principle. The version of the democratic-theory argument that appears in "Hard Cases" may seem quite different from the argument I have given, but the democratic-theory argument of "Hard Cases" is untenable as it stands, since it apparently depends on the assumption that judges enforce only trump-rights.[67] That assumption, as we have seen, is mistaken. In "Seven Critics" the democratic-theory argument is restated in such a way as to eliminate explicit reference to trump-rights and to bring the argument closer to the argument I have given.[68] Whether the argument I have given is Dworkin's or not, it is an argument which would occur to any reader of Dworkin, and it is worth brief consideration.

For many readers, the most problematic part of the argument will be the second premise ("Judges deal only with questions that have right answers"). Despite the controversy about whether questions properly presented to judges always or almost always have right answers, I shall not dispute the second premise in this essay. For the moment I am interested in the first premise, in whether it is plausible to suppose that questions of principle and questions of policy differ in the extent to which they have right answers.[69]

Dworkin is ambivalent about whether questions of policy have right answers. Sometimes he suggests that legislation by a representative body should be viewed as a form of "procedural justice", by which he means what Rawls calls "pure procedural justice". That is, he suggests that there is no noninstitutional criterion for right decisions about the general welfare; all we can say is that decisions on policy are right, or just, or acceptable, if they are produced by a democratically constituted representative body.[70] Sometimes, however, Dworkin seems more willing to accept that there may be correct decisions about the general welfare, at least in theory, and to defend the democratic legislative process on the ground that, under suitable restrictions, it is the best means we can devise for generating correct decisions.[71]

If Dworkin wished to maintain that questions of policy do not have right answers even in theory, he would have some scrambling to do. He has made it clear that questions requiring consideration and evaluation of general social consequences, questions we would ordinarily speak of as questions of policy, must be decided by courts if they are made relevant by a statute, or by community morality, or by the "point" of a social institution such as the institution of property.[72] If courts must sometimes consider these questions about policy, and if all questions considered by courts have right answers, then some questions about policy must have right answers. If some such questions have right answers, it is difficult to see why all such questions do not have right answers, at least in theory.[73]

In sum, Dworkin seems to be committed to the idea that questions of policy do have right answers in theory. This is perfectly consistent with a claim that legislatures will decide some questions better than courts and that courts will decide others better than legislatures. But it makes it impossible to argue that judges are limited to questions of principle because those questions and only those have right answers.

It may seem that we have moved too fast and that we have ignored a difference between the way we talk about questions of principle and questions of policy. Dworkin's argument for the existence of right answers has never amounted to much more than assertions about the way we think and talk. (His recent essays focusing on the "right answer" problem consist primarily of rebuttals to various possible arguments for the claim that there are not right answers.[74]) Accepting for the moment that we frequently talk as if there are right answers to questions of principle, even in hard cases, it might be suggested that we do not talk the same way about questions of policy. If we talk as if there are right answers to questions of principle, and if we do not talk as if there are right answers to questions of policy, then perhaps there is a difference after all. If the difference is not immediately apparent, we may need to look harder.

Unfortunately for this line of argument, it is far from clear that we really talk about questions of policy differently from the way we talk about questions of principle. Even in the area of policy, we talk as if there are right answers more often than not. People who argue in favor of more military spending ordinarily talk as if there is a right answer to the question whether more military spending is desirable. So do people who argue against more military spending. People who argue in favor of strict environmental protection laws talk as if the question whether such laws are a good thing on balance has a right answer. So do people on the other side. People who argue that we should have tax deductions for three-martini lunches and people who argue that we should devote more resources to energy research or to support of the arts are all alike in talking as if these policy questions have right answers.

This is connected with a point I made in a footnote in the first section of this essay.[75] The legislative process in this country may weigh and compromise competing interests. But it does not merely weigh and compromise what Dworkin calls "personal preferences," as opposed to "external preferences." An important function of public political debate is to line up support for various positions among persons who are not directly affected. The appeal to these disinterested parties is ordinarily based on claims that certain political decisions are either more just or more conducive to the general welfare than others. Even when the claims are about the general welfare, they assume that some answers to questions about how to promote the general welfare are right and others wrong. It is not easy to imagine how else one could try to enlist support for political decisions among parties not directly affected.[76]

The political process and public political debate are complex affairs, and I have oversimplified egregiously. But my point about discussions of policy is just Dworkin's point about discussions of cases at law. If we look at what we do and say, ignoring any preconceived idea that legislative questions lack right answers, we will discover that more often than not we talk as if there are right answers to these questions. So much the worse, some readers will say, for the attempt to draw inferences from the way we talk. Perhaps that reaction is the right one. But it is no comfort to anyone who would demonstrate a difference between policy and principle by pointing to differences in the way we talk about them.[77]

If we take it as established that questions of policy and questions of principle are not distinguishable in respect of having right answers, then the argument I stated at the beginning of this section—that judges are limited to questions of principle because those questions and only those have right answers—cannot be maintained. There is, however, a possible fall-back position for the proponent of the argument. Still drawing inspiration from the way we talk, he could point out that we do not ordinarily say a legislator has a "duty" to vote for correct legislative outcomes. That suggests the following reformulation of the argument: Our system imposes no political duty on officials to produce correct policy decisions. Our system imposes a duty on judges to decide each case correctly. Therefore judges' decisions cannot be policy decisions.

As with the original formulation of the argument, I shall concede, for purposes of this essay, the second premise ("Our system imposes a duty on judges to decide each case correctly") and focus on the first. The first premise ("Our system imposes no political duty on officials to produce correct policy decisions") is based on the observation above that we do not ordinarily talk of a legislator's "duty" to vote for correct decisions. But in passing from that observation to the first premise of the argument, the observation is transformed in two ways. First, it is changed from a statement about the way we talk to a statement about what duties our system imposes. Second, it is changed from a statement about legislators to a statement about officials generally, including judges. Both changes are problematic.

As to the first change, it is true that we do not ordinarily speak of a legislator's "duty" to vote for correct decisions. But that may be only because we normally reserve the word "duty" for obligations that are relatively clear. Even if there are right answers to policy questions, it is usually far from obvious what the right answers are. It would seem odd to many people to speak of the legislator's "duty" to vote for the correct outcome in a case where the identity of the correct outcome was highly controversial. I do not mean to claim that duties cannot be controversial. I mean only to point out that our disinclination to speak of legislator's duties may reflect nothing more than a general speech habit of not calling obligations duties when they are controversial. Now, the argument in which the premise we are analyzing appears does not respect this speech habit. The second premise of the argument asserts in effect that judges have many controversial duties. It may well be that, as the word "duty" is used in the second premise, legislators *do* have a duty to vote for correct policy decisions. In sum, it may well be that if the word "duty" is used consistently throughout the argument, the first premise is false even as applied to legislators. In any event, the first premise, even as applied to legislators, is not adequately supported for purposes of inclusion in this argument by the observation about the ordinary use of "duty" which inspired the argument.

The second change, it will be recalled, transformed the observation about legislators' duties into a premise about the duties of officials generally. Even if we assume *arguendo* that our system imposes no duty on legislators to produce correct policy decisions, the extension of this claim to cover officials generally is unjustified. We would be justified in extending the claim if the only plausible reasons for legislators' having no duty to vote for correct policy decisions applied with equal force to all officials. But as it happens, the most plausible way of explaining the absence of legislators' duties in this regard has no application to judges.

We are still assuming that there are right answers to policy questions. If this be granted, why might we deny that legislators have a duty to vote for correct outcomes? We might deny it if we thought that the best way for a legislature to go about generating correct decisions of policy was for each legislator to vote in response to his mailbag. It is not clear that we do think this. The question whether a legislator should vote his constituents' views or his own is an ageless one about which our political culture is schizophrenic. But, as I say, we might believe that each legislator has a duty to vote his mailbag, on the ground that that approach, generally followed, will produce the best approximation to correct answers which fallible mortals can achieve. If this is why we believe that legislators have no duty to vote for correct policy decisions, then obviously the argument does not establish that judges have no duty to make correct policy decisions. Judges do not participate in a process calculated to combine many votes not based on views of correct policy in such a way as to produce decisions which reflect correct policy nonetheless. All of this may be a reason to prefer that policy issues be decided so far as possible by legislatures rather than by courts. That I do not deny. My point is just that the reformulated argument we are discussing, depending as it does on the premise that no officials have duties to make correct policy decisions, begs the question as to judges instead of proving anything about them. It says nothing against the possibility that there are some genuine policy questions which we prefer to leave, or at least are content to leave, to judges, and as to which we think judges have a duty, albeit a controversial one, to produce correct decisions.[78]

It has not been my object in this section to prove that judges ought to make policy decisions. I have attempted to demonstrate only that the conclusion that judges are limited to arguments of principle cannot be based (at least without further argument) either on the premise that policy questions lack right answers or on the premise that no official has any duty to decide policy questions correctly.

C. Principles and Policies in Practice

There is a passage in "Seven Critics" in which Dworkin undertakes to explain why it matters in practice whether we instruct judges to consider only arguments of principle.[79] If we are in doubt about just what Dworkin intends by the principle/policy distinction, we might hope to learn something about what the distinction is from a discussion of why it matters. As it turns out, only a part of Dworkin's discussion sheds light on the principle/policy distinction. However, the part which is unhelpful on this point is interesting in itself.

Dworkin begins by describing five possible theories of rights which a judge might hold (other than a "strict deontological theory"). The first three theories are different utilitarian theories of rights. The fourth theory is a theory based on an abstract "right to the concern of others."[80] The fifth theory is a theory of "institutional rights" based on "reasons of fairness [which] require that settled institutions be administered in accordance with their rules and with the expectations these rules generate."[81] Dworkin apparently believes that a judge who accepts any of these five theories will decide cases differently if he is instructed to consider only arguments of principle (that is, arguments about rights) than he will if he is allowed to consider arguments of policy.[82] But what Dworkin devotes most attention to is the claim that a judge who holds either of the last two (nonutilitarian) theories will decide cases differently if he considers only arguments of principle. It is Dworkin's argument in support of this claim that we shall consider.

Dworkin hypothesizes a judge who is required to develop a scheme of riparian water rights without significant help or interference from the legislature, and he suggests a variety of things the judge might do if he were guided solely by policy. The judge might, for example, take as one of his aims the reduction of food prices relative to the prices of manufactured goods. Alternatively, the judge might divide the state into two distinct areas, with one set of rules to govern riparian water use in one area, and a different set of rules in the other. Or he might announce rules which are to be effective for a certain number of years but which are to be replaced by different rules when the effects desired from the first set have been achieved. All of these things Dworkin says the judge might do if he were free to decide on the basis of policy; none of them, according to Dworkin, would be appropriate if the judge must decide on principle and if he holds one of Dworkin's nonutilitarian theories of rights.[83]

I should like to set aside for the time being Dworkin's suggestion that a judge deciding cases on principle could not take as one of his aims the reduction of food prices. This is the part of Dworkin's argument which I think *does* tell us something about the principle/policy distinction. For that reason, I shall postpone consideration of it until we have dealt with Dworkin's other claims.

Dworkin says that a judge deciding cases on principle could not introduce different rules for different parts of the state or announce rules which were to be effective for only a predetermined time. I think he is right that we would regard a judge's attempt to do either of these things as decidedly odd.[84] But I doubt whether this tells us anything at all about what arguments judges are entitled to consider.

We must distinguish between what I shall call "input restrictions" and what I shall call "output restrictions." An input restriction is a restriction on the kinds of argument a judge may consider. Thus, the requirement that a judge consider only arguments of principle (assuming we know what those are, and assuming that some arguments are not arguments of principle) is an input restriction. An output restriction is a restriction on the kinds of results a judge can announce. Thus, if we believe that judges must announce only rules possessing some minimum degree of generality, or if we believe that judges must announce only rules which are to apply throughout their territorial jurisdiction, those would be output restrictions.

Now, an important point is this: Any output restriction is logically consistent with the total absence of input restrictions. We might, as a logical matter, say that judges are free to consider whatever arguments they regard as relevant to the problem before them, provided only that when they announce results, or rules, or whatever, they must observe certain output restrictions such as those we have already mentioned (and perhaps others). Indeed, it is possible that the actual constraints on common-law decision-making are better described in terms of output restrictions than in terms of input restrictions. Some critics of Dworkin have suggested just that.[85]

With the distinction between input and output restrictions in mind, let us consider Dworkin's claim that a judge making decisions on principle could not announce different rules for different parts of his jurisdiction, or different rules for different (future) times. The purported object of the passage in which this claim occurs is to explain why the input restriction to arguments of principle makes a practical difference. Yet it seems that all Dworkin does is to remind us of the existence of two output restrictions which are generally recognized as binding courts. An unsympathetic reader might plausibly complain that Dworkin says nothing at all to the point.

A more sympathetic reader might say that Dworkin at least suggests an argument—he suggests that *if* the input restriction to arguments of principle is observed, then the aforementioned output restrictions must be satisfied. Thus the input restriction does make a difference. There are two problems with this defense of Dworkin. First, Dworkin does not argue that if the input restriction is observed, the output restrictions we have identified must be satisfied. He simply asserts that a judge who was concerned only with fairness between the parties would not produce different rules for different parts of the state, or different rules for different (future) times. This may be true, but it is not so obvious that it can be granted without argument.[86] Second, even if it is conceded *arguendo* that an input restriction to arguments of principle would guarantee outputs consistent with the output restrictions we have identified, this may not mean that the input restriction "makes a difference." What we have conceded *arguendo* implies that *in the absence of any output restrictions* the input restriction would make a difference. But if we are committed to the output restrictions regardless of whether we accept any input restrictions, then an input restriction is not shown to make a difference in practice by being shown to restrict possible outputs in the same way as certain independently recognized output restrictions.

Dworkin might still argue that the input restriction makes a difference because we do not accord the output restrictions independent validity. He might suggest that the only plausible way of accounting for the output restrictions is by viewing them as a check on whether the input restriction is complied with. Thus, if we assume that there is an input restriction to arguments of principle, and if we assume that from such arguments only results consistent with the specified output restrictions can follow, then we can explain the output restrictions as a handy means for catching violations (or, in the course of the judges' own reasoning, incipient violations) of the input restrictions. Of course, the output restrictions would not catch all violations. Inadmissible arguments might be used to justify admissible outputs. But they would have some value, since inadmissible outputs would certainly indicate that inadmissible arguments had been considered. A problem with this suggestion is that, even if the output restrictions so far identified can be regarded in this light, there are other output restrictions we recognize which cannot, because they impose restrictions on possible results over and above those entailed by the supposed input restriction to arguments of principle. The existence of some output restrictions which cannot be accounted for by reference to this input restriction raises serious doubts about whether any output restrictions are best accounted for in the manner suggested.

An example involving an output restriction which cannot be explained by an input restriction to arguments of principle has already been described in a footnote to an earlier section.[87] We observed that a legislature could adopt the rule of *MacPherson* v. *Buick* for automobiles and at the same time explicitly forbid applying the rule to washing machines. We observed also that the distinction could well be justified solely on grounds of principle. The legislature, taking into account the reluctance of automobile manufacturers to settle morally meritorious claims, the willingness of washing-machine manufacturers to settle such claims, and the litigiousness of washing-machine purchasers, might arrive at the specified result even though it had no purpose except to protect the rights of all parties concerned. But, as we have previously noted, this result, which is acceptable when announced by the legislature, would not be acceptable if announced by a court on the same grounds. There is apparently an output restriction on the courts whose existence cannot be accounted for by an input restriction to arguments of principle.

If we are not to oversimplify, we must look more closely at this supposed output restriction. Observe that there is no general output restriction which would prevent courts from developing one rule for automobiles and a different one for washing machines in an appropriate context. The area of products liability might even be the appropriate context. It is not inconceivable that the courts should have developed the "inherently dangerous" rationale relied on in *MacPherson* and should ultimately have decided that while automobiles are inherently dangerous, washing machines are not. Even if such a result would have been mistaken, it would not have been objectionable in the way different rules about water use for different parts of the state would be objectionable if announced by a court. It might be suggested that if courts can draw a line between automobiles and washing machines on some grounds (for example, the ground of inherent dangerousness) but not on others (relating to the behavior of various classes of persons in the management of disputes), then it is really an input restriction we are dealing with after all. It must be that in formulating rules courts are forbidden to consider the proclivities of classes of persons with regard to dispute management. But this is surely false. Many common-law rules are shaped in part by judicial consideration of the likelihood of satisfactory extra-judicial dispute adjustment or to the danger of spiteful litigation. For example, reasons of this sort presumably underlie the common-law refusal to enforce most promises made without consideration. If the restriction manifested in our automobile/washing-machine example is not a pure output restriction, it is not a pure input restriction either. It is a hybrid. Certain sorts of argument, not inadmissible in themselves, may not give rise to certain sorts of distinction, also not inadmissible in themselves. This suggests that the original distinction between input and output restrictions was too simple, but not that it is useless. It is a first step to understanding, even though it is not fully adequate to deal with the complexity of the restrictions courts labor under.[88]

Further discussion of this complicated and, I think, important topic would take us far beyond our text. By bringing in output restrictions, Dworkin raises interesting issues, but it is doubtful that he advances or clarifies his position concerning what arguments courts may consider.

We turn now to Dworkin's suggestion about judicial attention to food prices. As we have noted previously, Dworkin says that a judge holding a theory of rights based on the right to the concern of others would regard as "irrelevant" the aim of lowering food prices relative to prices of manufactured goods.[89] Here, just as in his reference to output restrictions, Dworkin appeals to an intuition which I assume is widespread. We would think it odd for a judge to announce a rule of water law and explain that the rule was justified because it would tend to encourage agriculture at the expense of manufacturing. Unfortunately, Dworkin says nothing about why this judicial behavior would strike us as odd. Other social consequences not obviously different in kind from a lowering of food prices, such as a local economy's loss of jobs, are treated by Dworkin as relevant to what is required by concern for others.[90] Perhaps our intuition that judges should not worry about food prices is mistaken and should be abandoned.

I think our intuition about the irrelevance of food prices can be defended. The first step is to recognize what sort of intuition it is. It is not an intuition that lowering food prices could never be a goal in common-law adjudication. It is only an intuition that lowering food prices is not an appropriate goal of common-law adjudication in our society. Suppose, by way of contrast, a society in which food is scarce, in which food production is difficult, and in which guaranteeing an adequate diet for the population demands that practically all of the community's resources he devoted to agriculture. In such a society any use of land which impeded or displaced agricultural production would, at least *prima facie,* display a lack of concern for others. In such a society, a judge who regarded himself as charged with implementing a right to the concern of others would be fully justified in formulating water law designed to encourage agriculture and lower food prices.

We see that whether it is appropriate for a judge to consider food prices depends on the general state of society. That is a proposition I assume Dworkin would have no difficulty with. But Dworkin's critics may still be dissatisfied. They may feel that while it is all very well to say food prices are relevant sometimes and not others, still it is not very helpful and not very enlightening so far as the principle/policy distinction is concerned unless we can be a little more specific. Fortunately, we can be just that—a *little* more specific.

Dworkin is suggesting, none too clearly, that judges ought to decide common-law cases by standards which focus on the relations between individuals and which are available to the understanding of the individuals themselves.[91] Whatever standards we think the parties should appeal to in deciding how they ought to behave or in criticizing each other's behavior, those are the standards we expect the court to apply in deciding cases. What these standards are will vary from society to society. In our society it is perfectly appropriate for the legislature to promote agriculture or manufacturing or to adjust the balance between these sectors in the pursuit of general economic welfare. But there is no such present imbalance between the satisfaction of needs for food and the satisfaction of needs or wants for manufactured products that any individual should regard himself as morally constrained to worry about the consequences of his own behavior for the balance between agriculture and manufacturing in general.[92] That, I take it, is why food price policy is not relevant in our society to the implementation of the "right to the concern of others."

Right or wrong, the idea that courts should appeal in common-law adjudication only to standards which we would expect the individuals involved to appeal to is an important and interesting idea which Dworkin suggests without making it explicit and which others have not commented on.[93]

CONCLUSION

I began by promising a disjoined essay, and that promise I have surely fulfilled. I do not propose to summarize all my conclusions. I do want to point out a common thread which ties together the principal conclusions regarding the nature of common-law adjudication. Let me begin by reminding the reader of the conclusions I refer to.

First, we saw that although private litigation does not always involve trump-rights, it does always involve rights as individuated claims. In common-law cases, where the individuated claim cannot be based on a statute, the source of the individuated claim is always a particularized harm. Second, we saw that there is some sense to the idea that the requirement of consistency in decision-making is specially strong in decisions based on principle, which is to say, on rights. The reason is that arguments beginning from the desirability or undesirability of some consequence for some individual have a sort of guaranteed relevance to later similar cases which (most) arguments beginning from the desirability or undesirability of general social consequences lack. Third, we found in Dworkin's comment about food prices the notion that judges ought to decide non-statutory cases by standards which are accessible to the understanding of the individuals concerned. Judges should appeal to the same standards we would expect the individuals themselves to appeal to in deciding how they ought to behave or in criticizing each other's behavior.

The common thread is the centrality of the individual. The occasions for common-law adjudication are those where there is special harm to individuals; the preferred reasons for common-law decisions are reasons founded directly on consequences to individuals;[94] and the standards applied by common-law judges ought to be standards which the parties might have apprehended and applied to themselves.

As I noted in the opening paragraphs of this essay, a central theme in Dworkin's theory of adjudication is a rather old-fashioned idea of the common law as a system of fundamental moral principles, accessible to all, and regulating intercourse between individuals, with only occasional and incidental reference to general social consequences. The methods for the elaboration of these principles are analysis of precedent and consideration of hypothetical cases, methods peculiarly appropriate for dealing with "individual-centered" reasons for political decisions. The primary agents for the elaboration of these principles are judges, who we think are better suited than legislatures to engage in the careful parsing of relatively bounded dispute situations, repetitive in their general outlines but infinitely variable in detail, which these methods require.

I have referred to this individual-centered picture of the common law, which motivates many of Dworkin's arguments, as old-fashioned. That is not to say that it is dead or that it has lost its appeal to all but Dworkin. The idea of the common law as a set of fundamental propositions about how individuals should comport themselves towards one another, even if it is a little embarrassing to many in this post-realist era of economic and policy analysis of law, has never been expunged from the thinking of lawyers, or of judges, or even of most law professors. Dworkin's unusually forthright allegiance to this idea is an important source of the appeal of his theory, as well as of the air of unreality which (for some) surrounds it.

Unfortunately, the idea of the common law may be becoming less and less suitable to the society in which we live. It assumes that we can approach the settlement of legal disputes by asking what concern a person owes his neighbor. But whose neighbor is the manufacturer of a freon-powered aerosol deodorant, or the dumper of toxic wastes into the ocean? And what concern does an automobile manufacturer owe its purchasers in the design of its cars for crashworthiness or in the design of its purchase contracts with regard to warranties of the same? In our society it is true of more and more disputes that neither the circumstances from which they arise nor the effects of their resolution are likely to be localized in space and time. Maxims like *sic utere tuo* are less and less helpful in deciding cases.

If the range of cases to which traditional common-law methods are appropriate is shrinking, it is unclear what judges should do. One possibility is that they should recognize explicitly the changed nature of the problems with which they are being asked to deal and should plunge ahead as legislators *pro tempore*. This seems to be what Greenawalt would recommend.[95] The other possibility is that they should do their best to treat new problems by the old judicial methods and should count on the legislature to intervene when the results thus produced are unacceptable. This seems to be what Dworkin has in mind. I shall not argue here for either choice in this dilemma. But I think the dilemma is a real one, despite the fact that, were it not for Dworkin, we might almost succeed in ignoring it.

One final point. I have referred to Dworkin's conception of the common law as being based on fundamental moral principles, accessible to all. The reader may think that by introducing "fundamental moral principles" into the discourse without making clear just what I mean, I fudge deep and important questions. The reader is absolutely right. But the questions I fudge are questions on which Dworkin seems thoroughly ambivalent, and I propose to leave them, at least in this essay, just where he leaves them. If Dworkin is ambivalent, that is as much a sign of virtue as a defect. He is ambivalent largely because he is less inclined than his contemporaries to flinch and look away from the most difficult questions about the relation of law to morality, questions no one has yet produced satisfactory answers to.[96]

NOTES

1. Joseph Raz, "Professor Dworkin's Theory of Rights," *Political Studies* 26 (1978): 123.

2. I wrote this essay before I had access to Dworkin's own response to Raz, which appears in the expanded R. Dworkin, *Taking Rights Seriously* (paperback ed., 1978), p. 364. Had I had Dworkin's response in hand, I might have written Part I.A somewhat differently, but I think no changes are required, and I have made none in the text. I have added some footnotes.

It seems to me that Dworkin's response to Raz confirms many of my suggestions about Dworkin's meaning and disconfirms none of them. There is this principal difference: Dworkin continues to assume an unanalyzed notion of rights as trumps and emphasizes that rights as trumps may exist in political systems which recognize various general background justifications for political decisions. I provide a more detailed sketch than Dworkin does of how rights as trumps might be built into a system which takes as its background justification a utilitarian notion of the general welfare. Most of Dworkin's writings, focusing as they do on American and British political theory, are about such systems.

My treatment in Part I.A supplements Dworkin's response to Raz; it suggests, in the digressive note 18, some criticisms of Dworkin's position which differ from Raz's; and it provides the foundation for the argument in Part I.B that Dworkin needs some notion of rights, in addition to the notion of rights as trumps, if he is to maintain his claim that all private litigation involves rights.

3. I shall simply ignore, here and elsewhere, the genuine and significant issue of how a government ought to behave toward noncitizens, whether within or without its territorial jurisdiction.

4. It will occur to some readers at this point that the sketch in the text makes no use of Dworkin's concept of "external preferences." My reasons for essentially ignoring that concept are explained in note 18.

5. See, e.g., R. Dworkin, *Taking Rights Seriously* (hardback ed., 1977), p. 269. The paperback (see note 2) and the hardback editions are identical in content and pagination, except that the paperback has an appendix which is a revised and expanded version of Dworkin's article, "Seven Critics," which first appeared in *Georgia Law Review* 11 (1977).

6. Dworkin, *Taking Rights Seriously* (hardback), p. 269.

7. Raz, "Dworkin's Theory of Rights," p. 126.

8. There is an ambiguity in natural language which contributes to confusion about the Lexington Avenue argument. Dworkin says that there is no right to drive up Lexington Avenue because it is a sufficient justification for making the Avenue one-way downtown that that would be in the general interest. If I am correct, what Dworkin means is that there is no right because the supposed right can be denied in order to secure *any* net advantage to the general interest, however small. That is a perfectly natural construction of what Dworkin says. But it is also possible to construe Dworkin's words as Raz does, that is, as saying that there is no right because there is *some* advantage (perhaps very large) to the general interest which would justify making the Avenue one-way downtown. I think my interpretation of Dworkin makes better sense than Raz's interpretation. But I recognize the ambiguity. Indeed, I am especially sensitive to it because I shall from time to time appeal to the Lexington Avenue argument in what follows. The reader should bear in mind that when I make assertions like Dworkin's in the Lexington Avenue argument, I mean those assertions to be construed as I construe Dworkin's.

9. Dworkin sometimes speaks as if rights must always be important or weighty. There are two possible explanations for this which would not undermine what I suggest in the test about the logic of rights. First, for purposes of thinking about practical problems, the only rights which make a difference are rights which confer *considerable* extra weight. The discriminations we can make in practice about the balance of preferences are not sufficiently fine to notice any rights but these. Second, Dworkin plainly thinks that the rights he is most interested in—the right to free speech, the right to follow one's inclinations in private sexual behavior, and so on—are among those rights which confer on the preferences they protect substantial extra weight. To establish this requires argument about more than the logic of rights, and I do not think Dworkin establishes it. But he expects his readers to share his intuitions, and probably most of them do.

10. Dworkin, *Taking Rights Seriously* (hardback), pp. 197–204.

11. Ibid., p. 193.

12. Ibid., pp. 266–72.

13. Cf. ibid., pp. 266–72 (arguing against a general right to liberty).

14. Compare Dworkin's new discussion of rights to welfare and of rights to minimum welfare. Ibid. (paperback), pp. 366–67.

Dworkin's discussion suggests a qualification to the argument in the text. The idea of a universal right to general welfare is *incoherent* only in the context of a theory in which the basic goal of government, which the existence of rights modifies, is the satisfaction of individual preferences. In the context of a different sort of theory, such as the theory that government exists to promote religious salvation, the idea of a universal right to general welfare would not be incoherent, but it would tend to supplant the other basic purpose of government. There is more to be said about this than Dworkin says, or than I am prepared to say here. As I pointed out in note 2, this essay assumes, as Dworkin usually seems to assume, that the "unrefined" basic purpose of government is to promote the satisfaction of individual preferences.

15. Ibid. (hardback), p. 274.

16. Compare *Taking Rights Seriously* (paperback), p. 368 (quoting *Taking Rights Seriously* (hardback), p. xv): The right to be treated as an equal is "so fundamental that it is not captured by the general characterization of rights as trumps . . . because it is the source both of the general authority of collective goals and of the special limitations on their authority that justify more particular rights."

17. Compare Dworkin's recent suggestion that the right of nondiscrimination is not theoretically fundamental, *Taking Rights Seriously* (paperback), p. 365:

> The claim that members of some minority have particular rights in such a society (like the right to an integrated education, possibly) will appear to features [of the society] not necessarily present elsewhere. But many rights are universal, because arguments are available in favour of these rights against any collective justification in any circumstances reasonably likely to be found in political society. It is these that might plausibly be called human rights.

18. External preferences, as defined by Dworkin, are preferences about the degree to which preferences of *other* persons (that is, persons other than the possessor of the "external" preference in question) should be satisfied. *Taking Rights Seriously* (hardback), pp. 234–35. Dworkin suggests that certain rights are best understood as protection against legislation which is likely to be passed (if it is passed at all) in response to external preferences. See generally ibid., pp. 235–39, and for a more pointed statement, ibid., pp. 277–78.

My principle objection to the external preferences analysis is this: Dworkin suggests that we want to prohibit "decisions that seem, antecedently, likely to [be] reached by virtue of the external components of the preferences democracy reveals." Ibid., p. 277. He then specifically defends minimum-wage legislation on the ground that it is *not* antecedently likely to give effect to external preferences. Ibid., p. 278. But I should think that in a populous and heterogeneous democracy like our own, almost every law is passed in response to external preferences and that these preferences are crucial as often as not. Surely most minimum-wage legislation, like most other legislation protecting specific groups, depends for its passage on the existence of widespread external preferences. Persons not directly affected seek such legislation to promote what they perceive as a more just distribution of income or of the benefits of social life generally. Indeed, it seems to me that Dworkin concedes this in the newly added appendix to *Taking Rights Seriously*. He says: "[People] will vote their external preferences; they will vote for legislators, for example, who share their own theories of political justice. How else should they decide for whom to vote?" *Taking Rights Seriously* (paperback), p. 358. I do not know how Dworkin would attempt to reconcile this with his suggestion that minimum-wage laws are not antecendently likely to give effect to external preferences. The assertion just quoted seems to me to make it impossible to argue that any right at all exists *simply* by virtue of the fact that legislation inconsistent with the supposed right would probably reflect external preferences.

There are other less important reasons for de-emphasizing the external-preference analysis. For one thing, the theory sketched in the text makes rights more fundamental. It seems truer to common intuitions about the reasons for protecting speech to say we protect it because the desire to speak is especially important than to say we protect it because laws restricting speech are especially likely to be passed for the wrong reasons. In practice, of course, most people support a constitutional protection for speech both because the desire to speak is special *and* because laws against speech are likely to be passed for the wrong reasons. But if we must choose between these arguments in defining the structure of our views at the most fundamental level, I suspect most people who "take rights seriously" would prefer the first explanation of rights to be second. (I do not mean to *assert* that we must choose. Perhaps the best theory of the sort we are considering will turn out to be one which both excludes certain preferences, such as external preferences, and gives certain other preferences special weight.)

The sketch in the text also makes better sense than the external-preferences approach of Dworkin's claim that rights are "anti-utilitarian." In the sketch, the existence of rights modifies the maximand of the utilitarian approach. In discussing external preferences, however, Dworkin suggests that the exclusion of external preferences is required by a correct understanding of utilitarianism itself. If that is so, then rights based on the external-preference argument are not really anti-utilitarian at all. They are practical protections against persistent political tendencies to depart from what utilitarianism requires.

19. Compare Dworkin, *Taking Rights Seriously* (paperback), pp. 367–68, where Dworkin suggests that the familiar antagonism between rights and collective welfare is a superficial manifestation of a fundamentally unified theory based on treatment as equals. Dworkin's notion of equality generates both the idea that everyone's preferences count and count equally (the goal of collective welfare) and the idea that certain preferences specially linked to individual dignity and autonomy deserve special weight (the goal of protecting rights).

20. *United States* v. *Carroll Towing Co.,* 159 F. 2d 169 (2d Cir., 1947).

21. Dworkin, *Taking Rights Seriously* (hardback), pp. 98–100.

22. See text at notes 6–8.

23. E.g., Kent Greenawalt, "Policy, Rights, and Judicial Decision," *Georgia Law Review* 11 (1977): 991, 1010–14, 1021–22; Note, John Umana, "Dworkin's 'Rights Thesis,'" *Michigan Law Review* 77 (1976): 1167, 1179–83.

24. Dworkin, *Taking Rights Seriously* (hardback), p. 269. It is perhaps worth noting that there can be nonconstitutional and nontrump-rights against the state, or at least against the government, such as the statutory rights at issue in much administrative-law litigation.

25. I do not suggest that all trump-rights against the state are or ought to be reflected in private litigation. It seems likely that in an affluent society with large disparities of wealth and income there is a trump-right to some degree of redistribution. Even so, we would think it improper for a judge to decide for the plaintiff in a private-law case just because the defendant was rich and a transfer of wealth from defendant to plaintiff would produce a more satisfactory distribution.

26. *United States* v. *Carroll Towing Co.,* 159 F. 2d 169 (2d Cir., 1947).

27. It was a *plaintiff* barge-owner whose ability to recover despite the absence of the bargee was at issue in *Carroll Towing,* but Hand obviously intended his test to be decisive of the negligence of a defendant barge-owner as well. Dworkin deals with Hand's formulation as a test of defendant's negligence, and so, for convenience, shall we.

28. See text at notes 6–8.

29. Dworkin, *Taking Rights Seriously* (hardback), pp. 197–204.

30. The objection considered in the text does suggest an interesting point. If there were a regulation requiring a bargee on board, and if it were clear that this measure had been passed solely for the convenience of traffic, or for feather-bedding, then the regulation might well not be regarded as making the absence of a bargee negligence *per se* in a private suit for damages from an errant barge. This insulation of private litigation from the effects of some rules adopted solely to promote the general welfare is an interesting phenomenon, and it may well be related to other features of private litigation discussed in the remainder of this essay. But it has no effect on the argument that defendant has no trump-right and that plaintiff therefore has none either.

31. Dworkin, *Taking Rights Seriously* (paperback), pp. 300–301; Dworkin, "Seven Critics," p. 1211.

32. The following point is worth noting: While Dworkin says that the plaintiff's right involved in cases like *Carroll Towing* is the right to be treated with the minimal respect due a human being (*Taking Rights Seriously* [hardback], p. 98), he does not specify what right of the defendant is supposed to be in issue. The closest he comes to specifying the defendant's right is a reference to the "liberty of those from whom [is demanded] an unstated level of concern and respect." Ibid. But it is a central contention of "What Rights Do We Have?" that there is no trump-right to liberty in general. Ibid., p. 266–72. The argument in "What Rights?" is correct. Dworkin does not point to any genuine trump-right of defendant which is involved in *Carroll Towing* because, as we have seen, there is none.

It might be suggested that there is a quite different right of defendant involved—the right not to have money taken from him to enrich someone else. It is true that we think the government could not order defendant to pay plaintiff a specified sum *simply* because the transfer would promote the general interest. In that sense there is a trump-right not to have money taken. But we have no doubt that defendant can be required to pay for damage *he has* (proximately?) *caused* in cases like *Carroll Towing* if a rule imposing liability would promote the general interest. Somehow, then, the trump-right not to have money taken away is not implicated when the question is whether money should be taken from defendant to compensate plaintiff for harm defendant has caused. There are interesting complications here which I shall not pursue, since Dworkin nowhere clearly relies on defendant's right not to have money taken away. The fleeting suggestion of such a right (ibid., p. 85) raises more problems than it settles.

33. E.g., ibid., p. 91.

34. The test describes the state of the law of defamation before *Gertz* v. *Robert Welch, Inc.,* 418 U.S. 323 (1974). I make no attempt to assess the impact of that case, beyond noting that it extends the requirement of proof of harm.

35. It might be suggested that a statute authorizing suit in a court of the United States by a private individual who had suffered no harm would raise constitutional problems. The constitutional law of standing involves complexities which are obviously not relevant here, and I shall ignore this matter.

36. It is perhaps worth noting that even though statutes can create causes of action in plaintiffs who have suffered no harm, they rarely do so. Most statutory causes of action, at least against private defendants, either require a showing of harm or else stipulate as the basis for liability behavior from which some harm is easily presumed. It is an interesting question why this should be so, why we make so little use of "private attorneys general." The principal reasons I shall suggest below for requiring plaintiffs to show specialized harm in the absence of a statute do not support the same limitation on statutory causes of action.

There are a number of possible reasons for the general requirement of harm even in statutory cases. One is that the legislature is concerned to prevent wasteful or spiteful litigation. Another is that the legislature is influenced, consciously or unconsciously, in the formulation of statutory causes of action by the paradigm of a "standard" common-law cause of action.

Yet another possibility is that even statutes are often not intended as firm rules for how persons shall behave so much as they are intended as negotiable (in effect) rules for localized "sub-games" in the large game of social behavior. The much-maligned "zone of protected interests" test for standing to complain of administrative decisions (see generally, J. Vining, *Legal Identity* [1978], pp. 34–39) may be explained on that ground. If the legislature contemplates that the process of administrative oversight of a regulated activity will be one of bargaining and give-and-take between the agency and the parties regulated, then allowing unregulated parties only incidentally affected to challenge administrative decisions might upset a delicate balance for no reason the legislature regards as significant. This is not a standard view of the administrative process, but it is a realistic one in some respects and may be part of a better theory than any we now have.

37. Needless to say, a plaintiff who relies on a statute does not rely solely on the general welfare, even if that is what the statute is based on.

38. The argument I suggest in the text about why courts do not hear claims based solely on the general welfare is the same argument the Supreme Court used to deny standing in *United States* v. *Richardson,* 418 U.S. 166 (1974), and *Schlesinger* v. *Reservists Committee To Stop the War,* 418 U.S. 208 (1974). I feel constrained therefore to explain why the argument is *not* a good one in the context in which the Court applied it, that is, when the issue is standing to raise a constitutional question.

The argument I made in the text assumes that the legislature can be counted on to pursue the general welfare. But with regard to any particular prescription for legislative behavior which is included in the Constitution, the mere fact of inclusion suggests that the prescription in question is one which the legislature cannot be counted on to follow if left to its own devices. Furthermore, although we tend to think of constitutional provisions as intrinsically anti-majoritarian and to regard provisions which do not protect particularized interests as being of secondary importance, this view is too narrow. The Framers of the Constitution were interested in protecting the majority as well as minorities. The fear in pre-Revolutionary times of "corruption" of the legislature by the executive is well-documented, and the recognition by 1787 of the need for an executive branch with substantial powers hardly suggests that that fear was forgotten. The provisions at issue in *Richardson* and *Schlesinger* (especially the latter) can be seen as aimed at least in part at preventing this corruption. If that is the point of the provisions, then leaving the enforcement to Congress is like leaving a suggestible child to guard the cookie-jar against a smooth-talking older sibling who offers to share the booty from an illicit raid.

39. I confess that although I have the feeling that surprising the defendant is more objectionable where the defendant harms only the general interest, as opposed to inflicting a specialized harm on some particular plaintiff, I am not sure why this should be so. The one possible reason that occurs to me is the following. Where there is a plaintiff who has suffered specialized harm, that plaintiff has in all probability been "surprised." The choice then is either to leave the loss on the surprised plaintiff or else to transfer it to a surprised defendant. If, on the other hand, there is no plaintiff who has suffered specialized harm, then the total surprise is minimized by avoiding surprise to the defendant.

It might be said that surprise to the defendant can be avoided by making the court's decision prospective. Indeed, it might be said that if there is no traditional plaintiff, the only likely remedy is an injunction. But even injunctions, though they are prospective in a sense, controlling only future behavior, alter the returns from past behavior and injure expectations. And money may be at stake if the defendant is liable for attorney's fees or costs.

40. I ignore the possibility of claims against private individuals based directly on the Constitution. After *United States* v. *Guest,* 383 U.S. 745 (1966) (the Constitution protects the right to travel against private interference), and *Bivens* v. *Six Unknown Named Agents,* 403 U.S. 388 (1971) (the Constitution itself creates action for damages against federal officials for Fourth-Amendment violations), the possibility of an action against a purely private defendant based directly on the Constitution cannot be dismissed. But any such cause of action would be a curiosity.

41. For Dworkin's claim, see his *Taking Rights Seriously* (hardback), p. 96. For a troubled critic, see Greenawalt, "Policy, Rights, and Judicial Decision," pp. 1016–26.

42. See text accompanying notes 28–30; see also note 32.

43. Dworkin, *Taking Rights Seriously* (paperback), p. 297; "Seven Critics," p. 1207. See also *Taking Rights Seriously* (hardback), p. 100. In elaborating the claim that courts should consider only arguments of principle, Dworkin admits that judges may sometimes consider arguments about widespread social consequences and other arguments based on what we would normally regard as policies. E.g., ibid., p. 107–10, (policy embodied in statute); *Taking Rights Seriously* (paperback), pp. 300–301; "Seven Critics," p. 1211, (policy made relevant by conventional morality); *Taking Rights Seriously* (hardback), pp. 314–15; "Seven Critics," pp. 1226–27, (policy part of point of a social institution). But he insists that as long as the underlying question is one of rights, the "policy" considerations are transformed into arguments of principle.

44. The variants of this argument include but are not limited to Dworkin's arguments about the "gravitational force" of precedent.

45. Dworkin, *Taking Rights Seriously* (paperback), pp. 320–21; "Seven Critics," p. 1233.

46. Dworkin, *Taking Rights Seriously* (paperback), p. 321; "Seven Critics," pp. 1233–34.

47. See also Dworkin, *Taking Rights Seriously* (hardback), p. 113 (the full paragraph in mid-page).

48. Ibid., p. 88.

49. Ibid., p. 113.

50. For Dworkin, see *Taking Rights Seriously* (paperback), p. 319; "Seven Critics," p. 1232. For the critics, see passages cited in text at notes 51–52.

51. Greenawalt, "Policy, Rights, and Judicial Decision," p. 1008.

52. Raz, "Professor Dworkin's 'Theory of Rights,'" p. 135.

53. Perhaps it would be more accurate to say that, for Dworkin, only the legislature should make decisions based on "pure" policy, since courts may consider arguments of policy in contexts which make them "really" arguments of principle. See note 43.

54. Note that the criticism in the text is not the same as Greenawalt's complaint that Dworkin used examples involving legislative subsidies. Greenawalt, "Policy, Rights, and Judicial Decision, pp. 1008–9. Dworkin's response that *any* benefit conferred as a by-product of an attempt to promote the general interest, even under rules of general application, is in effect a subsidy, (*Taking Rights Seriously* [paperback], p. 320; "Seven Critics," pp. 1232–33) is persuasive against Greenawalt's criticism. But it has no force against mine, since the examples Dworkin uses against Greenawalt still all involve legislative decisions.

Lest my criticism be thought captious, I shall give an example which reveals a difference between what we expect from legislatures and what we expect from courts that plainly does not depend on any difference between principles and policies. Supposing *MacPherson* v. *Buick Motor Co.*, 217 N.Y. 382, 111 N.E. 1050 (1916), had not been decided, the legislature could enact the rule of *MacPherson* for the automobile industry without enacting a similar rule for washing machines. They could do this on the sole ground that they had special evidence of the irresponsibility of automobile manufacturers in refusing to settle morally meritorious claims out of court, a ground which surely would not justify a court in having a special rule for automobiles. Indeed, if the legislature were concerned lest the pressure of common-law development under the influence of the new statutory rule for automobiles should eliminate the distinction between automobile and washing-machine manufacturers, they could, at the same time they enact the new rule for automobiles, enact the old rule (of manufacturer nonliability in the absence of privity) for washing machines. They might do this on the ground that washing-machine manufacturers had a good record of satisfying morally meritorious claims without litigation, while purchasers of washing machines were demonstrably prone to bring unfounded and spiteful suits against their vendors. All of the reasons for legislative action which I have mentioned involve the protection of rights, either the rights of purchasers or the rights of manufacturers. Nonetheless, we would not think it appropriate for a court to draw a line between automobile manufacturers and washing-machine manufacturers and justify it on these grounds. We see that even in the pursuit of rights, the legislature can appropriately draw lines in a way the courts cannot.

55. Dworkin, *Taking Rights Seriously* (hardback), p. 118.

56. I ignore, for the sake of simplicity, the possibility that there might be index-dependent *costs* associated with protecting speech, that is, that the marginal social cost of protection might vary with the number of speakers who are protected.

57. It might be objected, against what I say in the text, that some people would justify some constitutional rights, including perhaps the right to speak, entirely in terms of social goals such as the discovery of truth, and that people who take this line are not talking nonsense, so that my equation of "rights" with individual-centered or index-free reasons is incorrect. The objection is misguided. If we give speech constitutional protection in order to achieve general social goals, we are not recognizing a theoretically fundamental right to speak. We are posing a right to speak at the level of constitutional analysis. But *at that level* we are also committed, by our use of the language of rights, to regarding the posited reason for protecting speech as index-free. Some further complications are dealt with in the text which follows, but I believe the reader will see that the objection outlined at the beginning of this note vanishes if we are careful to check the designation of something as a right against its operative logic at the same level of analysis.

58. I ignore the problem of children, incompetents, and so on. Compare Dworkin's assumption that all political rights are universal, *Taking Rights Seriously* (hardback), p. 94, note 1.

59. Indeed, that assumption is necessary to make Rex's *random* selection of beneficiaries rational in terms of the natural goal of achieving the desired stimulation at minimum cost to Rex or the fisc. Of course it might be that there are small differences in propensity to spend windfall income and that the random selection of beneficiaries was a limited departure from rationality to promote perceived fairness.

60. I continue to assume that the costs of protecting the right are not index-dependent.

61. Essentially the same point about the difference between Rex's programs can be made in another way which some readers may find helpful. As I observed earlier, Dworkin and his critics apparently agree that it is in some sense a truism that like cases should be treated alike. Consistently with this, we can suggest that the difference between the economic-stimulation program and the free-speech program is in what makes cases like or unlike.

In the economic-stimulation program, the effect on the economy of subsidizing any particular subject depends on the number of other subjects being subsidized. Two subjects are therefore "like" for purposes of this program only if, from the point of view of the two, the same number of "other" subjects have been chosen to receive subsidies. In the free-speech program, on the other hand, the effect on the underlying goal of protecting any particular subject does not depend on who else is being protected. All subjects are therefore "like" for purposes of this program regardless of how many are protected.

The reader may have noticed that, as I have defined "likeness" in the economic-stimulation context, it is tautologically true in that context that like cases *are* treated alike. If we consider any pair of subjects and any possible scheme for distributing subsidies, the two subjects in question will be "like" in the number of "others" (from the point of view of each) who receive subsidies under that scheme if and only if they are themselves treated the same by that scheme—if and only if they both receive a subsidy or both receive none. The requirement that like cases be treated alike therefore imposes no effective constraint on the design of the economic-stimulation program. (It would do so, of course, if we introduced some further factors relevant to "likeness," such as a varying propensity to spend. We shall not pursue that possibility.) With regard to the free-speech program, however, the requirement that like cases be treated alike does impose an effective constraint. Because all subjects are "like" regardless of who is protected, the requirement of treating like cases alike limits the possible designs of the program to two, that in which no one is protected and that in which everyone is.

It may seem odd that the requirement of treating like cases alike has no force at all in the first context and considerable force in the second, but that is the truth of the matter. The artificial simplicity of our examples contributes to the starkness of the contrast, but we see that the requirement that like cases be treated alike has much greater impact on a program to protect rights than on a program to promote a general social goal.

The reader will find a fuller treatment of a problem which is structurally analogous to the problem of what it means to treat like cases alike in Chapter 6, "Utilitarian Generalization," of my *Utilitarianism and Cooperation* (Oxford: Clarendon Press, 1980).

62. I must admit that Dworkin tends to refer to the strong requirement of consistency in dealing with rights as a matter of fairness, even though I have suggested that it is primarily a matter of rationality. Perhaps I have not been explicating Dworkin's point at all. But there are other possible explanations for his greater emphasis on fairness. One possible explanation is that he has conflated the point I have been expounding with the separate point that fairness is especially important in the distribution of fundamental rights. Given Dworkin's unclarity about the relevance of trump-rights to private litigation, this seems quite likely. Another possibility is that Dworkin does not recognize any distinction between constraints of fairness and constraints of rationality as these apply to governmental behavior. The "constructivist" view of political morality which is manifested in "Justice and Rights" seems to suggest that for Dworkin the only reason to care about rationality in governmental behavior is because fairness requires it. *Taking Rights Seriously* (hardback), pp. 159–68.

63. *MacPherson* v. *Buick Motor Co.*, 217 N.Y. 382, 111 N.E. 1050 (1916).

64. It may seem implausible to suppose that the transfer to MacPherson was, all by itself, just the transfer that was needed, but the basic point remains. After some number of plaintiffs have recovered, corporate wealth will have been decreased enough. After some number of cases follow MacPherson's case, the reason on which they were all based will vanish utterly, even though similar plaintiffs continue to appear. As I explain in the text that follows, courts do not talk as if the reasons they rely on behave this way.

65. Lest I be misunderstood, let me make it clear that distinguishing between arguments which begin from the consequences for an individual and arguments which do not is perfectly consistent with the belief that all political goals are ultimately validated by their contributions to individuals' welfare. Even if we do not regard economic stimulation or the containment of corporate powers as intrinsic goods, even if we regard them as desirable only to the extent that they ultimately make individuals better off, still, in positing such a goal as economic stimulation we do not focus directly on the ultimate distribution of the benefits we expect to flow from it. Under some program designs, the individuals we propose to affect directly will not even be the individuals who will reap the final benefits. Because the direct effects of the program do not represent the final goal, there is no reason to assume that everyone should be directly affected in the same way. If we were in a position to control precisely the *final* effects of the program, then perhaps the presumption would be that we would want to affect everyone the same way at that level, but ordinarily the details of the final effects are largely uncontrollable. On the other hand, when (or to the extent that) we are protecting rights, even rights as individuated claims which are not trump-rights, the direct effect is the final goal. The presumption therefore is that everyone similarly situated should be directly affected in the same way.

66. I have claimed that courts talk as if they *do* consider only (or primarily) arguments about rights. I have not, as it turns out, said much about whether they *should* consider only arguments about rights. Anyone who has read this far can plug in some standard arguments about why questions like how far to press a program of economic stimulation are less apt for judicial decision than questions about rights. In my terminology, the idea is that courts are good at elaborating and weighing index-free reasons, but weak at figuring out just how index-dependent reasons depend on the relevant index. I shall not consider further in this section the question of what courts *should*

do, first, because I have nothing now to add to the standard arguments and, second, because Dworkin's arguments seem more relevant to the descriptive than to the prescriptive claim.

67. Dworkin, *Taking Rights Seriously* (hardback), p. 85.

68. Dworkin, *Taking Rights Seriously* (paperback), pp. 322–24; "Seven Critics," pp. 1235–37.

69. Even this issue I shall treat superficially. What is really needed, both for present purposes and for more general purposes in the investigation of the relation of law to morality, is a plausible explanation of what a right answer *is*. Dworkin does not provide this explanation, nor shall I, at least in this essay.

70. See note 68.

71. E.g., Dworkin, *Taking Rights Seriously* (hardback), pp. 276–77.

72. See note 43.

73. Admittedly, a court considering a policy question will ordinarily, or perhaps always, confront a narrower range of possible decisions on the basis of the relevant policies than the legislature confronts. But if there are policy questions that have no right answers, there is no obvious reason to expect that the narrowing of possibilities that accompanies the transfer of the question from the legislative to the judicial realm will always bring it about that just one answer among those that remain is correct. In other words, if we believe that policy questions always have right answers in the form in which courts consider them, the only plausible explanation of this fact would seem to be that policy questions always have right answers, period.

It is perhaps worth noting that the most common reason for doubting that policy questions have right answers (at least for persons who, like Dworkin, believe that government should promote the satisfaction of individual preferences) is worry about interpersonal comparison of utility. But this reason ought to affect all questions or none. Genuine scruples about interpersonal comparisons would make it impossible even to compare benefits and disadvantages to two parties, which Dworkin undeniably contemplates that courts shall sometimes do in implementing the right to the concern of others. E.g., Dworkin, *Taking Rights Seriously* (hardback), p. 99.

74. "Can Rights Be Controversial?" Ibid. (hardback), pp. 279–90; R. Dworkin, "No Right Answer?" *New York University Law Review* 53 (1978): 1 (reprinted, in revised form, from P. Hacker and J. Raz eds., *Law, Morality, and Society: Essays in Honor of H. L. A. Hart* [1977].

75. Note 18.

76. I note again that Dworkin seems to agree with me about this. See note 18. It might be suggested that another way of lining up support for a position among persons not directly affected is by log-rolling ("You vote for my bill, I'll vote for yours"). Undeniably, log-rolling goes on in legislatures. To some extent it is a good thing. But for the most part the goals legislators pursue via log-rolling are the goals favored by their constituents, and the constituents choose among goals in large part on the basis of their own external preferences.

77. It might be objected that even if public debate is based on the supposition that there is a right answer to such questions as whether we should have strict environmental protection laws, no ones supposes that there is a right answer to every question of detail about how the laws should work. I think this objection is mistaken. It is true that public debate about matters such as environmental protection rarely focuses on questions of detail. But that is just because large questions must be settled first. Once they are settled, other large questions have a stronger claim on the general attention than the questions of detail which follow upon the resolution of the original large questions. When questions of detail (relatively speaking) like the question of the tax deduction for the three-martini lunch are publicly debated, they are debated as if there were a right answer.

78. It might be suggested that a judge can have no duty to decide a policy question correctly because no individual has a right to correct policy decisions. This assumes what I think is surely false, that no duty can exist without a correlative right. Is it not plain that a judge can sometimes have a duty to decide a criminal case against the defendant, even if no one has a right that the case be so decided? Even denying that there can be a duty to decide against a criminal defendant would not help the proponent of the argument currently under consideration in the text. The second premise of that argument is that our system imposes a duty on judges to decide each case correctly. If there can be no duty to decide a case against a criminal defendant, and if there is always a duty to decide correctly, then a decision against a criminal defendant can never be correct. This cannot be.

79. Dworkin, *Taking Rights Seriously* (paperback), pp. 311–17. "Seven Critics," pp. 1223–29.

80. Dworkin, *Taking Rights Seriously* (paperback), pp. 314; "Seven Critics," p. 1226.

81. Dworkin, *Taking Rights Seriously* (paperback), pp. 314–15' "Seven Critics," p. 1226.

82. Dworkin, *Taking Rights Seriously* (paperback), p. 317; "Seven Critics," pp. 1228–29.

83. Dworkin actually makes this argument only about the fourth theory. But he prefaces it and follows it with claims about both the fourth and fifth theories. He plainly assumes that the "institutions" presupposed by the fifth theory would not allow the judicial decisions he puts beyond the pale. Since Dworkin obviously believes in general that the institutions of the common law are based on a theory which gives a central place to the "right to the concern of others," his tendency to conflate his fourth and fifth theories is understandable.

84. Courts have occasionally been known to announce that they would continue to enforce an existing common-law rule only until some specified date and that if the legislature did not revise the rule by then, they (the courts) would revise it themselves. This behavior, while it may be justified in some cases, is pathological in terms of our standard views about the judicial role. Furthermore, it is probably best understood not as an announcement that the court is going to recognize a new common-law rule in the future, but as saying that the old rule is already undeserving of enforcement and will be continued in effect for some brief time only out of respect for reasonable expectations. This is a quite different matter from the different-rules-for-different-times example Dworkin has in mind.

85. See Greenawalt, "Policy, Rights, and Judicial Decision," p. 1010 (citing Note, "Dworkin's 'Rights Thesis,'" p. 1194).

All of the output restrictions so far mentioned have been cast as restrictions on the rules courts can announce. Dworkin might object that in talking about output restrictions, I misapprehend the nature of judicial "output." He might say I assume courts are primarily engaged in announcing rules, whereas in fact they are primarily engaged in deciding cases and giving reasons. This objection is miguided. I do not assume that courts are primarily engaged in announcing rules. I assume only that *to the extent that* courts announce rules, we expect them to announce rules for their entire jurisdiction, and for the foreseeable future, and so on. I do not suggest that courts must decide cases by announcing rules of a certain sort, but only that if they decide a case by announcing a rule, then the rule must be of a certain sort.

86. If the assertion at issue in the text is true, I suspect it is true for reasons like those discussed further on in connection with the inappropriateness of judicial pursuit of lower food prices. Compare note 88.

87. Note 54.

88. The real truth about our example may be that courts are not allowed to consider, or to produce results which suggest that they have considered, certain *information,* in this case information about the comparative dispute-management behavior of automobile manufacturers and washing-machine manufacturers, or automobile purchases and washing-machine purchasers. This is information which a court is not well-suited to collect and which we are not prepared to assume courts just naturally "understand," as we might assume they "understand" how automobiles and washing machines compare in terms of inherent dangerousness. The possibility that courts are constrained not just by what arguments they may consider but also by what information they may rely on is one Dworkin devotes too little attention to. The idea that courts may rely on facts developed in the case at hand or else accessible to the common understanding fits in neatly with the suggestion further on in this section about why (or when) courts should not worry about food prices.

89. Dworkin, *Taking Rights Seriously* (paperback), pp. 316–17; "Seven Critics," p. 1228.

90. E.g., Dworkin, *Taking Rights Seriously* (paperback), p. 296; "Seven Critics," p. 1206.

91. Compare Dworkin, *Taking Rights Seriously* (paperback), p. 317; "Seven Critics," p. 1229.

92. On a strict act-utilitarian theory, of course, the individual must regard the consequences of his behavior for the balance between agriculture and manufacturing as theoretically relevant to what he ought to do. But probably few of my readers are thorough-going act-utilitarians. The text is written with "standard" intuitions in mind. Even for the act-utilitarian, if there is not noticeable imbalance between agriculture and manufacturing, and if markets for labor and other resources are functioning tolerably well, it is very likely that a rule-of-thumb which directs one not to worry about the effect of one's private choices on the balance between these major sectors of the economy is a good rule-of-thumb. Thus, one need not worry about this balance in practice.

93. It is interesting to speculate about the extent to which this Part, suggesting that courts can consider any policy we would expect individuals to consider in making their own decisions, and Part II.A, suggesting that perhaps courts can consider nonsatiable policies, pick out the same policies for judicial consideration. If we regard as nonsatiable any policy which is nonsatiable over

the range of circumstances which members of a society at a given time are likely to confront, I suspect the suggestions of these two sections reinforce one another to a considerable degree.

94. I ignore here, and in the remainder of this Conclusion, the possibility that reasons based on nonsatiable policies may be appropriate for judicial consideration. I am here summarizing what we have learned about Dworkin. The suggestion about nonsatiable policies was a frolic of my own.

95. Greenawalt, "Policy, Rights, and Judicial Decision," pp. 1051–52 (judge as "agent for change").

96. What I perceive as ambivalence may be revealed as single-minded adherence to a new and important meta-ethical theory if Dworkin ever produces a satisfactory elucidation of what he calls "a special kind of intellectual activity, . . . defending a particular conception of a concept." Dworkin, *Taking Rights Seriously* (paperback), p. 351. Dworkin admits that he has not yet given "an adequate or even clear account of that activity." Ibid.

7
The Third Theory of Law

John Mackie

I have resisted the temptation to entitle this paper "Taking Rights Seriously and Playing Fast and Loose with the Law." But it will become plain, as I go on, why I was tempted.

Professor Dworkin's theory of law is now well known, especially since the publication of his book, *Taking Rights Seriously.*[1] But it may be as well to review it, and show how some of his main theses fit together.

I call it the third theory of law because it contrasts both with legal positivism and with the doctrine of natural law, and is in some ways intermediate between the two. The natural law doctrine is well summarized by Blackstone: "This law of nature being coeval with mankind and dictated by God himself is of course superior in obligation to any other. It is binding over the whole globe, in all countries and at all times. No human laws are of any validity if contrary to this, and such of them as are valid derive their force and all their authority, mediately or immediately, from this original."[2] This entails that a judge, relying on his rational knowledge of natural law, may overrule even what appears to be the settled law of the land—unambiguous and regularly enacted statutes or clearly relevant and unopposed precedents—and declare that the apparently settled law is not the law. Against this, I think that Professor Dworkin would concede that all law is made somehow by human beings, and that the (detailed) question, What is the law? makes sense only if construed as asking, What is at a certain time the law of England, or of France, or of the United States, or of South Dakota? The validity of a law is wholly relative to the legal system to which it belongs. Consequently the finding out of what is the law is an empirical task, not a matter of a priori reasoning. But, this being conceded, Professor Dworkin stresses a series of contrasts between his view and legal positivism, even such a cautious form of positivism as Professor Hart's.

First, he holds that the law consists not only of rules but also of principles, the distinction between these being logical: "Rules are applicable in an all-or-nothing fashion," whereas principles have the extra dimension of weight (*TRS*, pp. 22–28).

Secondly, he rejects the positivist notion of a single ultimate or fundamental test for law, such as Professor Hart's "rule of recognition." In its place

---

he puts the sort of reasoning that he ascribes, in "Hard Cases," to his imaginary judge, Hercules. Some parts of the law in a certain jurisdiction are settled and relatively uncontroversial, in the constitution or statutes or precedents. Hercules uses these as data, seeking the theory, in terms of further rights and principles, which best explains and justifies this settled law. Having developed this theory, he then applies it to the hard case (*TRS*, pp. 105–23).

Thirdly, and as a result of this method, Professor Dworkin holds that in any sufficiently rich legal system (notably in that of England no less than in that of the United States) the question, What is the law on this issue? always has a right answer, discoverable in principle, and it is the duty of the judge to try to discover it. One of the parties will always have a right to a decision in his favor. "Judicial decisions enforce existing political rights." There is a theoretical possibility of a tie, a dead heat, between competing sets of principles when all relevant considerations have been taken into account, but this is so unlikely that it may in practice be ignored. (See *TRS*, pp. 81, 279–90, esp. 286–87.)

Consequently, and fourthly, though judges in hard or controversial cases have discretion in the weak sense that they are called upon to exercise judgment—they are not supplied with any cut and dried decision procedure—they never have discretion in the strong sense which would exclude a duty to decide the case one way rather than the other (*TRS*, pp. 31–35, 68–71).

Fifthly, though it is really only another way of making the same point, Professor Dworkin holds that even in a hard case one does not reach a stage where the law has run out before it has yielded a decision, and the judge has to make some new law to deal with a new problem. Judges never need to act, even surreptitiously, as legislators, though he has allowed that they may in fact do so as they sometimes do when they make a mistake or when they prospectively overrule a clear precedent.[3]

A sixth point is further consequence of this. If judges were in effect legislating, it would be appropriate for them to do so in the light of considerations of policy—in particular, of utility or the general welfare of the community or the known will of the majority of the people. But if they are not legislating but still discovering an already existing law, they must confine themselves to considerations of principle; if they let policy outweigh principle, they will be sacrificing someone's rights in order to benefit or satisfy others, and this is unjust. There is, however, an exception to this point. It holds uniformly in civil cases, Professor Dworkin says, but only asymmetrically in criminal cases. The accused may have a right to be acquitted, but the prosecution never has a right to a conviction. So a court may sometimes justly acquit, for reasons of policy, someone who is in fact guilty (*TRS*, pp. 82–100).

Seventhly, Professor Dworkin rejects the traditional positivist separation of law from morality. However, this is a tricky issue. The legal positivism he has explicitly taken as his main target is that of Professor Hart, and Professor Hart recognizes many ways in which law and morality are closely linked. For example, he says, "In some systems, as in the United States, the ultimate criteria of legal validity explicitly incorporate principles of justice or substantive moral values . . . . [S]tatutes may be a mere legal shell and demand by their express terms to be filled out with the aid of moral principles; the range of enforceable contracts may be limited by reference to conceptions of morality and fairness . . . . Judicial decision, especially on matters of high constitutional import, often involves a choice between moral values." But one point on which Professor Hart stands firm is that we can sometimes say, "This is law but too iniquitous to obey or apply," rather than, "Because this is iniquitous it is not law." He argues (against supporters of natural law) that it is both more clear-headed and morally better to allow that something can be a valid law and yet evil.[4] It is not clear to me whether Professor Dworkin would deny this. But he makes the following important point. The task which he assigns to Hercules in "Hard Cases" is to find the theory that best explains and justifies the settled law, and to use this theory to decide otherwise unsettled issues. He construes the phrase "best explains and justifies" as including a moral dimension; Hercules has to find the morally best justification of the constitution, statutes, practices, and so on which are not in dispute. In doing this, Hercules must himself make substantive moral judgments, and not merely take account of conventional morality, of widely accepted social rules (*TRS*, pp. 123–28; cf. pp. 206–22).

This third theory of law combines descriptive with prescriptive elements. On the one hand, Professor Dworkin is claiming that it gives the best theoretical understanding of legal procedures and legal reasoning actually at work in such systems as those of England and the United States. But on the other, he wants it to be more explicitly accepted and more consciously followed. He wants it to become a truer description than it yet is, whereas some views that might count as interpretations of the positivist model—for example, the "strict constructionist" view favored by ex-president Nixon—would, he thinks, have deplorable results (*TRS*, pp. 131–49).

It follows that discussion of this theory must also be on more than one level. We are concerned with both its truth as a description and its merit as a recommendation. Let us consider it first as a description. Professor Dworkin argues that courts do, in fact, appeal to principles as distinct from rules and that no coherent description of their procedures can be given by a theory which recognizes only rules as constituting the law. This must, I think, be conceded. But he further maintains that the way in which judges reason in hard cases is some approximation to that which he ascribes to his superhuman judge, Hercules; and such a view is much more controversial. Along with other aspects of his descriptive theory it needs to be checked empirically and in detail. But some general preliminary comments can be made.

First, there is a distinction—and there may be a divergence—between what judges say they are doing, what they think they are doing, and the most accurate objective description of what they actually are doing. They may say and even believe that they are discovering and applying an already existing law, they may be following procedures which assume this as their aim, and yet they may in fact be making new law. Such a divergence is not even improbable, because even where new law is being made, it will seem fairer if this fact is concealed and the decision is believed to enforce only presently existing rights; and because the making of new law will usually mean only that existing rules or principles are extended somewhat beyond their previous field of application.

Secondly, even though legal reasoning in hard cases involves appeals to principles and rights and is affected by "the gravitational force of precedents," it does not follow that it does or must or even should work in terms of a complete theory of the underlying law for the jurisdiction in question. The superhuman Hercules is, as his name indicates, a mythical figure, and human judges will always operate in a more limited way. However, the practical force of Professor Dworkin's account is that it allows and encourages judges to bring to bear upon a controversial case general considerations and notions about rights which are supported by elements in the settled law that are remote from the case in hand. We may or may not want this; but I would stress that this holistic treatment of the law is in no way required by the admission that legal reasoning appeals to principles as well as to rules. That admission allows such remote control, but does not require it.

Thirdly, though legal reasoning in hard cases refers to rights, this does not entail that it can take no account of interests. Admittedly, to take rights seriously is to see them as having some resistance to interests; in particular, it is to recognize that the rights of an individual will often justify a decision in his favor which is against the interests of the community as a whole. However, Professor Dworkin himself does not regard all rights as absolute, but admits that they may sometimes be overruled by community interest. And when rights conflict with one another, interests may help to determine which right is the stronger in the particular circumstances.

There is no doubt that judges sometimes argue in this way, as in *Miller* v. *Jackson and Another,* heard in the British Court of Appeal—reported in *The Times,* 7 April 1977. The plaintiff lived in a house built in 1972 near a village cricket ground which had been used for over seventy years. He sought an injunction to prevent the club members from playing cricket unless they took adequate steps to prevent stray balls from hitting his house and garden. There is a conflict of rights here: prima facie the club has a right to go on playing cricket and the plaintiff has a right to enjoy his home and garden in safety. The court refused, by two to one, to grant the injunction. The judges on the majority side spoke of the public interest and also stressed that the injunction sought was a discretionary remedy. Lord Denning said that the public interest lay in protecting the environment by preserving playing fields in the face of mounting development and enabling our youth to enjoy the benefits of outdoor games, in contrast to the private interest, which lay in securing the privacy of a home and garden without intrusion or interference. Lord Justice Cumming-Bruce said that in considering whether to exercise a judicial discretion to grant an injunction the court was under a duty to consider the interests of the public. That is, they seemed to think that while each part had a prima facie right, when these rights came into conflict the importance of the public interest made the cricket club's right the stronger. Professor Dworkin may deplore such reasoning, but he can hardly deny that it occurs, nor can he argue that it should not occur merely because in a hard case there are appeals to principles and rights.

Fourthly, it would be a mere fallacy (which I want to guard against, but do not accuse Professor Dworkin of committing) to argue from the premise that hard cases should be reasoned (partly) in terms of rights—including prima facie, non-absolute rights—to the conclusion that in such a case one party must have a (final or resultant) right to a decision in his favor.

Fifthly, there is a weakness in the argument that an exactly equal balance between the considerations on either side is so unlikely that it is almost certain that one party will have an antecendent right to win (*TRS*, pp. 286–87). This argument assumes too simple a metric for the strength of considerations, that such strengths are always commensurable on a linear scale, so that the strength of the case for one side must be either greater than that of the case for the other side, or less, or else they must be equal in the sense of being so finely balanced that even the slightest additional force on either side would make it the stronger. But in fact considerations may be imperfectly commensurable, so that neither of the opposing cases is stronger than the other, and yet they are not finely balanced. Consider the analogous question about three brothers: Is Peter more like James than he is like John? There may be an objectively right and determinable answer to this question, but again there may not. It may be that the only correct reply is that Peter is more like James in some ways and more like John in others, and that there is no objective reason for putting more weight on the former points of resemblance than on the latter or vice versa. While we might say that Peter's likeness to James is equal to his likeness to John (because neither is determinately the greater), this does not mean that any slight additional resemblance to either would decide the issue; hence, it does not mean that this equality expresses an improbably exact balance.

Sixthly, we must note an implication of Professor Dworkin's inclusion of a moral dimension in the reasoning he assigns to Hercules. Hercules's judgment about what the law is on some specific issue depends on what he finds to be the best explanatory and justificatory theory of the settled law. So what the law is, on Professor Dworkin's view, may crucially depend on what is morally best—what is best, not what is conventionally regarded as best in that society. Now I would argue, thought I cannot do so here, that moral judgments of this kind have an irreducibly subjective element.[5] If so, then Professor Dworkin's theory automatically injects a corresponding subjectivity into statements about what the law is. Of course, Professor Dworkin is right in arguing that the moral judgments people make—and this may also be true for those that Hercules can be presumed to make—are not, in general, reports of socially established rules or even such reports conjoined with the speaker's acceptance or endorsement of those rules (*TRS* 45–58). Moral judgments typically include what I call a claim to objectivity and to the objectivity precisely of their prescriptive authority. But these claims, I maintain, are always false. Prescriptive moral judgments are really subjective, though those who make them commonly think that they are objectively valid and mean them to be objectively valid. Suppose Hercules and another judge in the same jurisdiction, both following Professor Dworkin's methods, reach different conclusions about what the law on some issue is because each has reasoned coherently in the light of his own moral views. Though each of them will sincerely and consistently believe that the law already is as he determines it, I maintain that they will both be wrong. The grounds on which they rely fail to determine an objective preexisting law. Whichever judge's opinion wins the day in the final court of appeal will become the law and will then be the law. The judges who finally decide the case will have been legislating, though they will sincerely, consistently, and rationally believe that they have not. By making a choice determined by their subjective moral judgments for which they honestly but mistakenly claim objective validity, they will have been making law an issue on which there was previously no determinate law, on which they had no antecedent duty to decide one way rather than the other, and on which neither party had a right to a decision in his favor.

These six general points cast doubt on some parts of Professor Dworkin's descriptive theory, but they should be tested along with the theory, against actual examples of hard cases. I now want to leave the question of description and consider the merits of the third theory as a recommendation. I can do this best by going straight to a concrete example, taken from the legal history of the United States. Professor Dworkin, in a review of Robert M. Cover's book *Justice Accused,* applies his theory to cases which arose before the American Civil War under the Fugitive Slave Acts.[6]

He finds it puzzling that such judges as Joseph Story and Lemuel Shaw, though themselves strongly opposed to slavery, enforced these acts, sending alleged runaway slaves back from states in which slavery was not permitted to states where it still existed and from which they were alleged to have escaped. But why is there a puzzle? Were these judges not, as they themselves said, simply doing their legal duty of enforcing what was then the law of the land, despite the fact that it conflicted with their own moral views? Professor Dworkin argues that it is not so simple. The relevant law was not settled: these cases were controversial. Though the judges in question explicitly denied this, in their deeper thinking they admitted it. But then, being legal positivists, they concluded that they had to legislate, to make new law by their findings. But why, then, did they not make the law in accordance with their moral convictions and their sense of justice? Because, says Professor Dworkin, following Cover, they saw themselves as subordinate legislators only, bound to make the law in harmony with the discoverable intentions of the superior legislators in Congress and, earlier, in the Constitutional Convention. These legislators had, in their several enactments, created and maintained a compromise between the slave states and the nonslave states; therefore, sending an alleged slave back to the state from which he had come was the natural fulfillment of that compromise.

According to Professor Dworkin, the reasoning of these judges was a "failure of jurisprudence." If they had been adherents, not of positivism, but of the third theory, they could have found in the general structure of the American Constitution "a conception of individual freedom antagonistic to slavery, a conception of procedural justice that condemned the procedures established by the Fugitive Slave Acts, and a conception of federalism inconsistent with the idea that the State of Massachusetts had no power to supervise the capture of men and women within its territory." These principles were "more central to the law than were the particular and transitory policies of the slavery compromise."

It is not in dispute that if these judges had been adherents of the natural law doctrine—as evidently they were not—they might have refused to enforce the Fugitive Slave Acts. Then the judges would have held that even if the Acts were settled law in the sense of being unambiguous and regularly enacted statutes, they were not genuine law because they violated principles of justice and natural right which were prior to any man-made system of law. The problem is whether the third theory would have yielded the same result.

First, was the law really not settled? Professor Dworkin says that the (federal) Fugitive Slave Acts "left open many questions of procedure, particularly about the power of the free states themselves to impose restrictions on the process in the interests of the alleged slave." And Massachusetts had enacted such restrictions. However, the judges held that these restrictions were overruled by the federal laws, and this seems to follow from a straightforward interpretation of Article VI of the United States Constitution: "This Constitution, and the laws of the United States which shall be made in pursuance thereof, . . . shall be the supreme law of the land; and the judges in every State shall be bound thereby, anything in the constitution or laws of any State notwithstanding." Professor Dworkin refers also to "narrowly legalistic and verbal arguments" on behalf of the alleged slaves, but arguments of that description, too easily produced, will not show that the law was not, for all that, settled. The only ground on which he can claim, in a way that is even initially plausible, that the law was not settled, is that the procedures laid down in these acts "offended ordinary notions of due process." The federal official who returned the alleged slave to his purported master was "a mere commissioner who received a higher fee if the alleged slave was sent back than if he was not, there was no question of a jury trial, and the defendant was not allowed to contest whether he was in fact a slave, that issue being left to be decided in the slave state after his return."

But it is far from clear that these provisions offend against due process. They would be defended on the ground that these proceedings were only preliminary: the legal issue about the fugitive's status was still to be decided in the state from which he had come, and that, surely, was where witnesses to his identity and status would be available. He was not being deprived of liberty without due process of law; the due process would take place in, say, Virginia. This argument could be rebutted only by casting doubt on the legal respectability of the Virginia courts, and whatever private doubts the Massachusetts judges may have had about this, it was an essential part of the federal compromise that they should not be guided by such doubts in their legal decisions. Article IV, Section I, of the Constitution says that "full faith and credit shall be given in each State to the public acts, records, and judicial proceedings of any other State." The Virginian slaveowner could have argued that if he were not allowed to get his slave back without bringing a large number of witnesses five hundred miles so as to have his claim heard before a Massachusetts jury which was likely to be hostile to the very institution of slavery on which his claim was based, he would be, in effect, being deprived of his property, namely the slave, without due process of law. Article IV, Section 2, of the Constitution is quite explicit: "No person held to service or labor in one State, under the laws thereof, escaping into another, shall, in consequence of any law or regulation therein, be discharged from such service or labor, but shall be delivered up on claim of the party to whom such service or labor may be due."

That, in the face of all this, Professor Dworkin can hold that the law was not settled brings out an important characteristic of his theory, highly relevant to the assessment of its merits as a recommendation: the third theory often takes as unsettled issues which on a legal positivist view belong clearly to the realm of settled law.

But suppose that the law was not settled, and that a judge at the time had tried to decide these cases by Professor Dworkin's method. What conclusion would he have reached? Hercules, being a product of Professor Dworkin's imagination, would no doubt have argued as Professor Dworkin does. But let us invent another mythical judge, say Rhadamanthus.[7] He might have argued as follows:

> What principles that are relevant to this case are implicit in the settled law? The fundamental fact is the Union itself, which arose out of an alliance, against Britain, of thirteen separate and very different colonies. It was recognized from the start that these colonies, and the states which they have become, have diverse institutions and ways of life. The Union exists and can survive only through compromises on issues where these differing institutions and ways of life come into conflict. One salient principle, then, enshrined as clearly as anything could be in the federal Constitution and in various statutes, is that the rights which individuals have by virtue of the institutions of the states in which they live are to be protected throughout the Union. A Virginian slave-owner's property in his slaves is one of these rights; the clear intention of Article IV, Section 2, of the Constitution and of the Fugitive Slave Acts is to protect this right. Therefore, whatever merely technical defects may be found in them the law of the land, as determined by the third theory of law which I hold, is that the alleged slave should be returned from Massachusetts to Virginia, where it can be properly decided, by the evidence of many witnesses, whether he is in fact the slave of the man who claims him.
>
> The contrary view, that the Constitution presupposes a conception of freedom antagonistic to slavery, cannot be upheld. Jefferson, who actually wrote the Declaration of Independence, and who later was mainly responsible for the amendments which most strongly assert individual rights, was himself a slave-owner. The individual freedom which the Constitution presupposes was never intended to apply to slaves. Nor will the requirements of procedural justice, which can indeed be seen as principles enshrined in the settled law, support a finding in favor of the alleged slave. On the presumption that slave-owners have legally valid property rights in their slaves, procedural justice will best be secured by sending the alleged slave back. The conception of federalism does no doubt give the state of Massachusetts the power to supervise the capture of men and women in its territory, but this power must be exercised in ways that respect the institutions of Virginia and the rights of citizens of Virginia, especially as these are further protected by federal law.

Even if Joseph Story and Lemuel Shaw had shared Professor Dworkin's theory of jurisprudence, they might still have followed Rhadamanthus rather than Hercules and, without for a moment abandoning their reliance on principles or their concern for rights, might have reached just those decisions they did reach by a more positivistic route. This brings out a second characteristic of the third theory, highly relevant to the assessment of its merits as a recommendation: the rights thesis, like the natural law doctrine that it in some ways resembles, is a two-edged weapon. It is particularly risky for an opponent of slavery and of racial discrimination to appeal to states' rights within a federal system. The special importance which Professor Dworkin, in his essays on applied jurisprudence (*TRS*, pp. 206–58), gives to the right to equality is not a necessary consequence of the rights thesis as such.

A third important characteristic of Professor Dworkin's theory is that its adoption would tend to make the law not only less certain but also less determinate than it would be on the rival positivist view. Of course, it is never completely determinate. Reasonable judges may well disagree on hard cases, whatever theory of jurisprudence they hold. But the third theory introduces a further source of indeterminancy. It is well known that the inference from a precedent to a general rule supposed to be implicit in it is not watertight; but a much larger degree of freedom is introduced if the judge has to frame hypotheses, not merely about rules which apply directly to cases, but also about far more general and abstract principles of justice and their implications.

Professor Dworkin would deny this. He would say that it is legal positivism that would make the law in hard cases indeterminate, since it envisages situations in which the law as a whole, not merely the settled law, has run out. Judges are then called upon to legislate, bringing in considerations of policy as well as morality, and it tells judges that they thus have discretion in the strong sense. His theory, on the other hand, holds that there is on every issue a determinate and, in principle, discoverable, though perhaps not settled or certain, law.

This is why I am tempted to speak of Professor Dworkin playing fast and loose with the law.[8] The alleged determinacy of the law in hard cases is a myth, and the practical effect of the acceptance of this myth would be to give, in three ways, a larger scope for what is in reality judicial legislation. First, it would shift the boundary between the settled and the unsettled law, it would make what on another view would be easy cases into hard ones. Secondly, this approach would encourage a holistic treatment of the law, letting very general principles and remote parts of the law bear upon each specific issue. Thirdly, it would encourage judges, in this holistic treatment, to rely upon their necessarily subjective views about a supposedly objective morality.

The third theory of law is thus a plea for a more speculative and enterprising handling by judges of their traditional materials and data. Like the natural law doctrine, this theory allows the consciences and the speculations of judges to intervene more significantly between what the legislative and executive branches try to do—or, for whatever reason, leave undone—and the law as it actually operates. We know well that people's prejudices, training, and social position—the movements in which they are caught up and the ideologies linked with these—strongly influence their consciences and their speculations. Whether we consider this a merit or a demerit depends upon our judgment of the judges, and particularly upon comparative judgments we make between them, the legislators, and the holders of executive office. Which of these three, with their characteristic methods and the influences to which they are exposed or from which they are sheltered, are the more to be trusted with the opportunity for partly independent decision in the making and remaking of the law? Should we give up some certainty and determinacy about what the law is, and some freedom for legislators to decide what it shall be, in order to give greater weight to what judges will see as people's rights or just claims? I do not know what answer to give, but I want it to be clear that this is the choice.

NOTES

1. Ronald Dworkin, *Taking Rights Seriously* (London, 1977), hereafter referred to as *TRS*.

2. *Commentaries*, quoted by Julius Stone, *The Province and Function of Law* (Sydney, 1946), p. 227.

3. *TRS,* pp. 82–84. Professor Dworkin gave this clarification in reply to a question from Professor Sir Rupert Cross at a seminar on Hard Cases in Oxford, 12 May 1976.

4. H. L. A. Hart, *The Concept of Law* (Oxford, 1961), pp. 181–207, esp. 199–200 and 205–7.

5. I have argued for this view in Chapter 1 of my *Ethics: Inventing Right and Wrong* (Harmondsworth, 1977).

6. *The Times Literary Supplement,* 5 December 1975.

7. Cf. Plato, *The Apology of Socrates* 40e–41a: "Would it be such a bad journey if one arrived in Hades, having got rid of the self-styled judges here, and found the true judges who are said to have jurisdiction there, Minos and Rhadamanthus and Aeacus and Triptolemus and such other demigods as were just during their lives?"

8. Cf. *Oxford English Dictionary:* "Fast and loose: A cheating game played with a stick and a belt or string, so arranged that a spectator would think he could make the latter fast by placing a stick through its intricate folds, whereas the operator could detach it at once."

PART THREE
The Objectivity of Law

8
No Right Answer

A. D. Woozley

It has long been a commonplace of legal positivism that in a legal system such as our own a case may come before a court for adjudication for which there is no answer which is the one and only answer which the court could give. In the existing state of the law one answer may be more reasonable than others, or more than one may be equally reasonable, or there may be no lead at all given by statute or earlier decisions. Judges, while not, if they find themselves in such a situation as the last, acting as initial legislators (as in some systems, e.g., the Swiss, they could), have to use their discretion: in the absence of a right answer which they might discover from further study of the law they have to do the best they can within the tradition and ethos of their system.

This is a commonplace which, with much else of legal positivism, Professor Ronald Dworkin rejects. And for many years now, from "The Model of Rules" (1967)[1] to "Can Rights Be Controversial?" (1977), he has been arguing against it. The theme runs through several of the essays collected (with some revisions) in his *Taking Rights Seriously*;[2] the two pieces just mentioned are among them. In this article I concentrate on an essay "No Right Answer?", which is not in that book, but which is his contribution to the collection published as a *Festschrift* for Professor H. L. A. Hart.[3] By "the no right answer thesis" I am going to mean what Dworkin does, viz., that in law a question may arise and come up for adjudication to which no answer can be given such that it is *the* right answer and that any different answer would be wrong. He rejects that thesis—or at least he claims to refute the arguments for it. His claim is that "the occasions on which a legal question has no right answer in our own legal system must be much rarer than is generally supposed" (p. 54), and that "for all practical purposes there will always be a right answer in the seamless web of our law" (p. 84). He distinguishes two versions of the thesis, and on behalf of the second version he sets up three different arguments. I am going to concern myself mainly with the third argument for the second version (what he calls "The Argument from Controversy"), because it is the only one I can take seriously. It is to be taken seriously, because it brings out better than any of the others the rationale of the no right answer thesis, and because, as it seems to me, Dworkin's attempt to re-

From *The Philosophical Quarterly* 29 (1979), 25–34. Reprinted by permission of the author and *The Philosophical Quarterly*.

fute it involves a fundamental confusion. What I think I detect is the ghost of a natural law theory which he tries to materialize in the form of a logical theory about truth.

One or two things have to be said about the earlier parts of the article, because they bring out factors which are relevant to understanding and criticism of his handling of the controversy argument. The *first* version of the no right answer thesis which he considers rests on the presupposition that a pair of concepts which appear to be contradictories may turn out not to be, because, although they are mutually exclusive, they are not jointly exhaustive, so that there will be a logical gap between their boundaries. And it might be the case that some pairs of legal concepts are of that kind, so that, e.g., it is both false that a particular contract is valid and false that it is not, both false that a particular act constitutes a crime and false that it does not, etc. As I do not wish to discuss his discussion of this first version, I shall do two things only: (1) applaud his insistence on the need to distinguish between propositions of law and propositions about the duties of judges—and regret that he did not hang on to it himself in the later and more important part of his article; (2) mention an author who, it might be suggested, was an exponent of the first version, or who would have been if he had ever thought about it—Plato. He did realize that there were pairs of concepts of exactly the kind described. "It is not true of everything that there is that the boundary of one thing adjoins the boundary of another, but there are some having a no man's land which lies between them and adjoins the boundary of each of the pair" (*Laws,* 878b, 867a). And the only time (as far as I know) that he made that point was in a legal context, because he thought that at least one such pair was legally interesting: an act, e.g., of killing or wounding, if committed in anger, falls somewhere between being *ἀκούσιον* and being *ἑκούσιον*. But, because his penal code provided specifically for the adjudication of such cases, and because of the way in which it did, he is *not* to be cited as a candidate flagbearer for the first version. What his example brings out is that from the proposition by itself that the concepts F and $\sim F$ have a logical gap between them nothing whatever follows about whether the right answer exists to the question how a decision should go concerning something falling in the gap. Indeed, the question how a decision should go concerning something falling in the gap is ambiguous. That Dworkin has fallen victim to the ambiguity is one of the main failings I find in his general line of argument. My general thesis is going to be that we have on our hands not one question but two, which need to be kept distinct from each other. With regard to a disputed legal issue we have two questions:

(a) What is the law on this issue?
(b) How is the legal issue to be settled?

If we have a clear answer to (a), then we have a clear answer to (b)—but that does not make them the same question. The answer to (b) is that the legal issue is to be settled by the court using whatever specific criteria the system provides for answering questions of law (a). The connection between (a) and (b) is that there are answers to (a) only because courts recognize a duty (b) to settle issues by the specific criteria of the legal system; and that they do recognize the duty is a *contingent* fact about the system. Furthermore, even where we have a clear answer to (b), we may not have a clear answer to (a). That a court goes about settling an issue by whatever the recognized criteria of the system are does not guarantee that there is one and only one answer which it can give—nor even that the answer *could* be known before it had been given. The logical distinction between (a) and (b) can be brought out by imagining a system in which the criteria to be used were such that until they actually had been used in a particular case there *could* be no answer to (a), but only guesses, bets or predictions what the answer to (a) would (or will) be. If the rule, for example, were that in hard cases the issue was to be settled by tossing a coin, we should in a particular case have a clear answer to (b), but no possiblity of an answer to (a) until after the coin had been tossed.

The principles which provided us with a clear answer to (b) might not be legal principles at all: they might, for example, be political principles. Even where they are legal principles, as in Plato's case they were, it cannot be guaranteed that a clear answer to (b) will provide us with a clear answer to (a). But sometimes it will. Similarly with Dworkin's treatment of vagueness, with which I entirely agree. The fact that some language in a statute bearing on a question of law (e.g., whether a given contract is valid) is vague does not determine that the question is also vague whether, given that statute, the contract is valid: there may be principles of law available which enable a judge to settle the question of the contract's validity. If he could settle them that way, then there would be an answer which he could give which would be the right answer. But one cannot generalize from that and say that, whenever there is a correct way for a judge to settle the issue, the way provides an answer which is the right answer to the question what the law is on the issue before him.

To make good my claim, I now turn to consider Dworkin's treatment of the argument from controversy—the third argument for the *second* version of the no right answer thesis. The second version can most simply be contrasted with the first by saying that, while on the first F and $\sim F$, although mutually exclusive, are not jointly exhaustive, so that there is a gap between them into which something might fall (a contract might be neither valid nor not valid), on the second F and $\sim F$, although jointly exhaustive, are not mutually exclusive, so that there is an overlap between them into which something might fall (a contract might be both valid and not valid). That is not quite how Dworkin formulates it—indeed he does not quite formulate it at all—but I think that that is what it comes to.

The argument from controversy rests on what he calls the demonstrability thesis, viz., "if a proposition cannot be demonstrated to be true, after all the hard facts that might be relevant to its truth are either known or stipulated, then it cannot be true. By 'hard facts' I mean physical facts and facts about behavior (including the thoughts and attitudes) of people"; a proposition is demonstrated to be true if backed by arguments such that anyone who understood it and them "must assent to its truth or stand convicted of irrationality" (p. 76). Dworkin agrees that in some legal cases from the hard facts alone no conclusion can be demonstrated to be true, and that, if hard facts are all the facts that there are, then the demonstrability thesis succeeds, i.e., we must accept its consequence that in such legal cases no right answer can be given. But he then proceeds to argue that there are other facts, and suggests two kinds such that, if there are facts of either kind, the demonstrability thesis must fail. The first kind of fact which he suggests is moral facts. The proposition that a disputed contract is valid might be true in virtue of the alleged fact that a judge had the moral duty to enforce it, given the hard facts of the case. Therefore, even after all the hard facts were known or stipulated, it might be rational to debate whether a particular moral fact exists. Even if a proposition cannot be demonstrated from the hard facts, it does not follow that it cannot be true. I am not going to spend any time on that one, because Dworkin does not either. He does not offer a single reason why we should accept a judge's having a moral duty as a moral *fact,* and I do not feel called on to argue against it. Of course, locutions like "it is a fact that the judge's duty is to . . . " and "the fact is that the judge's duty is to . . . " are perfectly good idiomatic locutions; but that we talk that way has no tendency to show that there are, or even that we think that there are, *facts* of a special kind to be called "moral."

I turn now to the other kind of facts which he does think there are; they are brought out in a literary exercise which he describes, and corresponding facts can be revealed by a similar exercise in legal reasoning. The game is this. We ask a question about a character in, say, a novel, a question which is not directly answered by anything that the author writes in the novel. It is the "How many children did Lady Macbeth have?" game, the game that Sherlock Holmes nuts devote such sustained ingenuity to playing. Dworkin's own example is David Copperfield, and the question is whether David had a homosexual relationship with Steerforth. The answer that he did is the right answer, is true, if it gives better consistency than the answer that he did not—i.e., if it provides "a better fit than its negation with propositions already established, because it explains in a more satisfactory way why David did what he did, or said what he said, or thought what he thought, according to the established propositions" (p. 78). So a proposition which does not record a hard fact is true according to Dworkin if it is the proposition required by the combination of (a) the hard facts with (b) the fact of the proposition's success in narrative consistency with the hard facts. An empiricist philosopher comes along and denies that there are such facts as facts of narrative consistency—although why any empiricist philosopher would be so idiotic as to deny that we are not told—and he is then punched all round the ring.

Now this really will not do. If Dworkin wants to equate "the right answer" with "the answer to the question which says what is true," he can. And if he wants to equate "the right answer" with "the most reasonable answer," he can. But he cannot do both, unless he is proposing to redefine "true." If he wants to do that, he can; we must then wave him goodbye and let him get on with his game by himself—because, even if that is what he wants to mean by "true," it is not what *is* meant by "true". This can be shown by looking more carefully at narrative consistency and truth in fiction. The difference between having grounds for asserting *p* and correctly asserting *p* applies within fiction as much as outside. I can have grounds for asserting *p*, even if *p* has *no* truth value, and even indeed if I *know* that *p* has no truth value, because the author has not yet given it one, nor decided which one to give it. This is going to be relevant to the legal analogue. Reasonable, hardheaded lawyers can properly discuss the question (and disagree with each other in their answers to it) what the right answer to a question of law is, even although they agree that there is not a right answer to it—yet. So having grounds for asserting *p* does not imply that *p* has a truth value—unless to say that *p* is true (false) just means the same as saying that we have better (worse) grounds for asserting *p* than for asserting $\sim p$. But it quite obviously does not. We can play Dworkin's literary game (in its third form) if we want to, but do not let us think that we must be playing a truth-game—or that we can, by analogy, say of a corresponding answer to a correspondingly inconclusive question of law that it is true. That the hard facts of the case combine with the fact that *p* fits the hard facts better (even much better) neither constitutes nor entails the truth of *p*. It may come nearer to it in law than it does in fiction, but it does not quite get there.

Before arguing my case for a new look at the literary game, let me just mention the case of counterfactual conditionals, because Dworkin brings them in in his (not altogether accurate) allusion to Dummett's "Truth"[4] and to the question whether, and under what conditions, it could be true that Jones was brave, given that he was never in his life exposed to a situation requiring bravery. Could "If Jones had encountered danger, he would (would not) have acted bravely" be true? Could "Either Jones was brave or he was not" be true of such a man? Now, some counterfactuals can be said to have a truth value, because we have facts of a kind which provide overwhelmingly good grounds for asserting (denying) them—for example (pretending that Hitler did *not* in fact overrun Luxembourg): "If Hitler had tried to invade Luxembourg in 1940, he would have succeeded." Others cannot be said to have a truth value, *either* (i) because we do not know enough, or there is not enough for us to know, to provide overwhelming good grounds for assertion (denial)—e.g., "If Hitler had tried to invade Britain in 1940, he would have succeeded"; *or* (ii) because we do not know anything at all, or there is not anything at all for us to know, which would provide a ground for assertion (denial)—e.g., in the Dummett example, if there was no fact of Jones's life such that if we know (or knew) of it we would have any reason for asserting (denying) that we would have acted bravely in a situation of danger. So here "Jones was brave," "Jones was not brave," and "Either Jones was brave or he was not" all lack truth value: in the case of each of them there is nothing such that, if we knew of it, it would count in favour of it. Counterfactuals, being the logically queer things that they are, can only be said to have a truth value in the case where their narrative fit with the hard facts is overwhelmingly good (bad). They are not going to be any help to Dworkin.

Now, back to Dworkin's literary exercise, and to a different example from his. Suppose that I am reading *Emma* and wondering whether in the end Emma marries Mr. Knightley. Suppose that (although I do not know it) Jane Austen died before she finished writing the novel. In that case the concept of truth does not allow "Emma marries Mr. Knightley" (nor consequently "Emma will marry Mr. Knightley") to have a truth value. The proposition that she marries him is true iff by the end of the novel Jane Austen marries her to him, and is false iff by the end Jane Austen does not marry her to him. But, if Jane Austen dies before getting that far, than neither *p* nor $\sim p$ is true. There is *no* right answer to the question "Does Emma marry Mr. Knightley?" It is not true that she does, nor that she does not, nor that either she does or she does not. But, as I read the novel, still unaware that it is broken off before the end by Jane Austen's death, I can wonder whether Emma will marry Mr. Knightley, and I can have excellent grounds for asserting that she will: the proposition that in the end she marries him may have a far better narrative fit with the hard facts of what Jane Austen did write than the proposition that in the end she does not. What all this shows is that the question whether *p* is true is *not* the question whether *p* gives the best narrative fit with the hard facts. The question whether *p* is true is still left on our hands, even after the question of its narrative fit is settled. Suppose, again, that, instead of dying first, Jane Austen did finish writing the novel, but gave it a different ending, leaving everything as it is, except that at the last minute she marries Mr. Knightley off to Harriet Smith. Up to the end of ch. 54 the narrative fit of "Emma marries Mr. Knightley" is exactly as in the novel as we now have it (and exactly as in the novel as we would have had it, if Jane Austen had died after completing ch. 54 but before beginning to write ch. 55): but the proposition that Emma marries Mr. Knightley is now false. So we have three alternative fates for the novel: in all three of them the narrative fit of "Emma marries Mr. Knightley" is the same, in two of them its truth value is different, and in the third it has no truth value at all. "What is it reasonable to think that Emma will do?" is determined by all that has been written (or read) up to the time of asking the question. "What will Emma do?" is determined by what Jane Austen makes her do in the last chapter (if she gets that far). And, if she unexpectedly makes Mr. Knightley marry Harriet, that will be disappointing to readers rooting for Emma, and will, perhaps, be bad craftsmanship, but, like it or not, it will determine that the right answer is that Emma does not marry Mr. Knightley. Again, if, as I read the novel, I think Emma will marry Mr. Knightley, I do so, not because I think that there is a fact of her marrying him waiting to be disclosed to me (namely Jane Austen's marrying them in the last chapter, which I have not reached yet), but because of such and such (namely all that has happened so far). There is no Emma-marrying-Mr. Knightley waiting for us and Jane Austen in what is going to be the last chapter. If Jane Austen dies before she can complete the novel, there is *nothing* to determine the answer to the question "Will Emma marry Mr. Knightley?" There is then *no* right answer to that question, only a right answer to a different question, viz., "Is there a right answer to that question?"; and the right answer to *that* question is "No."

Now for the law, to which the things that Dworkin says about the literary exercise can be transferred with much more plausibility than they possess in their original setting of the literary exercise; that is because the judge is subject to constraints from which the novelist is free. Nevertheless, enough of the analogy survives to be awkward for Dworkin's case. In some disputes there will be, in advance of the final judgment, no right answer waiting for us in what will be the final chapter. The answer depends on what is written in the final chapter—which has not been written yet. In the case where we cannot say that it is more reasonable that the judge should declare that *p* than that he should declare that $\sim p$, i.e., where *p* does not have a better legal narrative fit with the hard facts than $\sim p$ does, we have no ground for asserting, when he does come down for *p*, that that *had* been the right answer for him to give. In a decently sophisticated legal system there should be a right answer to the question how to settle a disputed question of law (it might be, depending on the character of the society and its institutions, a matter of applying legal principles or of applying extra-legal principles), but that does not mean that there was a right answer to the question of law waiting to be found. It is not difficult to see either of two contrary answers to such an issue as reasonable; and surely such issues occur, especially in as yet little trodden areas of the law. For example, an increase in the number and variety of trans-sexuals is likely to throw up several such issues in the not distant future. They are issues just because there is no clear direction given by the narrative fit of precedent, or priority of rights, or whatever, to what will be the answer; there is not in such a case a right answer already there waiting for the judge to arrive at it or unearth it. And if afterwards we agree with his judgment and say that he gave the right answer, we are not saying anything about *truth*. And we are not entitled to say of our opponents, who disagree with his judgment and say that he gave the wrong answer, that they have somehow failed to see the truth. The judge's answer may have been more reasonable than the contrary answer would have been; and in that case it *was* the right answer for him to have given (he does not enjoy a novelist's freedom), but its having been the right answer for him to have given is not the *same* as its having been the right answer to the question of law. If the judge's answer survives attempts to modify or reverse it, and if it gets absorbed into the body of the law, then there is an answer to the question "What is the law on this matter?" which is the right answer, because that is how the book has been written—but it was not in the book until it was written; and it is not the job of judges to try to make out the invisible words of not yet written books.

Judges, I have said, are under constraints by which novelists are not bound. A novelist may try for narrative fit, and he may fail; or he may not try, he may even, to achieve some effect, go against it. Critics in turn may, justifiably or not, pan him for it. But that will be that: what he wrote is what he wrote. The judge has to try for whatever in his system counts as narrative fit, but if he is thought by higher or later courts to have failed, they will write a different ending. Eventually some ending gets accepted into the legal system, and the statement of that becomes the right answer; it was the answer which sooner or later was given and endured. If the legal system is a good one, the judgment will not be given or endure unless it is one which achieves a reasonable (not necessarily the one reasonable) narrative fit. So the narrative fit is the criterion which the judge should use in making up his mind what judgment to give, and he does not have the license the novelist has to astonish and disappoint or delight us by departing from it; but in both cases the answer is determined by what in the end is written or affirmed. Furthermore, the constraints to which courts are subject are, in a sense, self-imposed; and this brings us back towards the novelist again. It is not (as for Dworkin I think it would be) the "soft" fact of best narrative fit by itself that is a truth condition of a proposition of law, but rather the soft fact of best narrative fit, where that is recognized (hard fact) by the courts as the criterion for themselves to use in deciding cases. One of the ways in which a legal system could be defective would be the failure of courts in it to recognize and carry out the duty of using best narrative fit in deciding cases.

There is a legal analogue to the two kinds of counterfactual mentioned earlier. If we ask the question "What would the law on that be?" about some matter which has never previously been adjudicated, then in some cases a proposed answer would have a truth value (cf. "If Hitler had tried to invade Luxembourg in 1940, he would have succeeded"), and in other cases it would not (cf. "If Hitler had tried to invade Britain in 1940, he would have succeeded"). That a subjunctive conditional of the latter kind may, in some sense, later acquire a truth value does not mean that it had it all along. One can agree what the truth value should be, predict or take bets what it would (or will) be, but one cannot say what it *is*—for, in such a case, there is no "what it is." If it is a case where the hard facts are such that only one specific answer would give the best narrative fit, one is tempted to say that that is what the answer would be. But it would be that answer, only on the assumption that the courts would recognize and use the criterion of best narrative fit. And whether that assumption, which is an assumption about hard facts, was a reasonable one would depend on the standard of intellectual integrity and discipline actually shown by the courts. The theory of American Realism, in overemphasizing that law is what the courts say, underemphasized the constraints from which a judge is never free. Dworkin seems to have committed the opposite error: in overemphasizing the constraints from which a judge is never free he has underemphasized that the law is what the courts say—to which we should add: whatever the courts would say, whenever that claim does have a truth value. If he wishes to claim that in our legal system no cases occur in which the constraints do not compel the judge to one conclusion rather than the other, that is a statement of fact about how things actually are under our system (including a fact about judicial attitudes). I do not know enough about the details of how things actually are positively to deny his statement. But, given the nature of legal reasoning, and the extent of its similarity to nonlegal reasoning, e.g., moral reasoning, I find it hard to believe that his statement is true. When a person is faced with a real moral problem, and with the question "What ought I to do here?," there characteristically is *no* right answer, no answer waiting there, darkly hidden, for him to find it if he can. The answer which he gives after he has done all the honest wrestling that he can with the complexities of his problem, the factors on either side, the advice and judgment of the wisest and most understanding people that he can find, etc., is the right answer—or would be, if it were proper to speak of "right answer" in such a case. It is proper in the literary or judicial case, because the author and court respectively are authorities. In the moral case it is not proper, because there is no authority, nor such a thing as being the authority: for the agent it was the right answer, the only right answer, but he does not, and could not properly, claim that it was the right answer for anybody else, for whom all the relevant considerations were the same, to have given. For him it was the right answer to have given, not because it was the answer which he did give (that would be to overassimilate him to the novelist), but because it is the answer which he did give after recognizing and carrying out the duty of doing all the wrestling with the problem which he could (that is the respect in which he is like the judge). Not that it is always a matter of choosing between a pair of equally reasonable or satisfactory answers. Sometimes we have to choose between two answers, each of which is equally unreasonable and unsatisfactory—deciding one way or the other in a Bakke-type case is surely of that kind—but we do have to choose. And in neither of these hard cases are others, if they agree about the hardness of the case, entitled to say that we took the wrong decision. The moral agent's decision is, in a sense, similar to the novelist's decision how to end the book. As I have tried to indicate, the judge's decision on a hard case of law is in an important way different (although even in that way not totally different), but in another important way similar: he is more exposed to the criticism that he took the wrong decision, but the way the book ends is the way he ends it; and, if the world ends before the book ends, then, although it will not matter any more, the question of law has no right answer.

NOTES

1. *University of Chicago Law Review* 35 no. 1 (1967).
2. Ronald Dworkin, *Taking Rights Seriously* (London, 1977).
3. P. M. S. Hacker and J. Raz (eds.), *Law, Morality and Society* (Oxford, 1977).
4. *Proceedings of the Aristotelian Society* 59 (1958–59).

9
Dwork in as Pre-Benthamite

Neil MacCormick

I. INTRODUCTION: "THE CONSTRUCTIVE MODEL"

Not the least interesting element in Ronald Dworkin's work[1] is his theory as to the nature of ethical theorizing. This he develops from a discussion[2] of Rawlsian "reflective equilibrium." It is the theory that the distinctively moral point of view—morality as against mere mores—is developed by construction of a consistent and coherent set of principles which most adequately justify and make sense of our intuitive moral judgments. The intuitive judgments we make in particular cases, are, in a sense, the data from which moral theory commences. But they are not unquestionable, in the sense that each and every one must be accommodated within the constructed set of principles. We can and should revise our judgments to fit in with the set of principles which best fits the judgments to which we are most strongly committed.

This he calls a "constructive model" of morality, in contrast to the alternative possible "natural model," which would postulate that moral principles are not created but discovered by people, being a kind of description of an objective moral reality. If we adhered to the "natural model" we would not be able to take a high handed way with troublesome intuitions as the "constructive model" authorizes. If these are apperceptions of moral facts, we must stick by them in the hope that we will in the end find the true set of principles which can accommodate all the facts—rather as the natural scientist may not suppress inconvenient data, but must hope that in the long run improvements in scientific theory will enable them to be accommodated within a full understanding.

The correlation of this view of ethical constructivism with the work of Rawls, and indeed with that of now unfashionable "intuitionists" such as W. D. Ross, H. A. Prichard and W. G. Maclagan, is obvious. It gives body to the idea of "reflective equilibrium," of securing that our judgments match our principles and our principles match our judgments. It is also true that it facilitates interesting comparisons between moral argumentation and legal argumentation, and the drawing of analogies further afield in the realms of aesthetics.

In his recent essay "No Right Answer"[3] Dworkin has made that further comparison, pointing out that literary criticism can and does go beyond mere textual criticism concerned with the *ipsissima verba* of the author's text. The critic does and should read a novel with a view to constructing a vision of the world created by the author's text. There can be truths about David Copperfield not stated in the very words of *David Copperfield*; so too can a legal system contain genuine answers to problems which no case has yet directly decided. The ultimate unity of legal and moral deliberation, and the possibility of right answers to questions of right, both of which Dworkin's theory envisages, depend on a fundamental unity of method: the method authorized by the constructive model.

It is convenient for the critic that Dworkin should himself have made the literary analogy, since at the present time a constructive review of his work has to be "constructive" in the Dworkinian sense. *Taking Rights Seriously* has a right to be taken seriously, but it would be only too easy to take it to pieces at the level of textual criticism for inconsistencies and shifts of position. Such are inevitable in a book which collects together pieces published separately over a decade, ordering them according to theme rather than chronologically. In truth, what is remarkable about the performance is not the inconsistencies but the overall consistency and sense of theoretical unity which the work taken as a whole presents. Even so, much more than would be acceptable in the case of a purpose-written monograph, the reader is left to construct a whole view of the Dworkinian Theory out of what seem to him the main points of the position. On the whole, this view will attempt to come to terms with Dworkinianism benignly constructed, and air objections to that, rather than nit-pick around the text for internal inconsistency. But some adverse criticism of some textual points is necessary and inevitable.

The key fact about Dworkin is that he is a pre-Benthamite; the perspective of jurisprudence since Bentham with its insistence on the separation of expository and censorial jurisprudence, legal facts and legal values, he finds as inimical to grasping the truth as did the pre-Raphaelites find that other perspective which they abandoned in their painting. Dworkin's stated ambition[4] is to restate legal theory in such terms as re-unify exposition and censorship. Legal theory in this programme is not divided from but an intimate part of moral and political theory. As important as anything else in Dworkin's writing are the elements of ethics and politics which he finds essential to the elucidation of laws and of rights.

In my judgment the execution does and must fall short of fulfilling the ambition. But the failure, like others before it, is an enormously instructive one, one which has already revised the agenda for legal philosophy, and one in which those who reject the central tenets cannot but find both a challenge, and a host of valuable insights which any view of law, politics and morality must accommodate or even incorporate. Dworkin has not succeeded in demonstrating (not to me, anyway) that there is no gap between the description of law and the framing of critical principles against which to test the quality of actual laws. But he has succeeded in showing that existing schemata for the analysis and description of legal systems are defective, and he has put forward a version of political liberalism which is interesting and provocative as a critical morality for the criticism or justification of laws and legal institutions.

One reason for the failure is that the constructive model will not take the weight which Dworkin puts upon it. The natural model has a certain attraction in that it founds upon a claim that there is in some sense "an objective 'order of values'" (as W. G. Maclagan put it[5]) to which our specific judgments are oriented and which our statements of principle attempt to capture. Such a model can account for differences of moral view precisely as differences of view, different ways of looking at the same thing, the same order of values. The best view is the one which most fully grasps that objective order. The constructive model retreats from that assertion, beset as it notoriously is with epistemological and ontological problems, to the weaker claim that, as Dworkin puts it: "Men and women have a responsibility to fit the particular judgments on which they act into a coherent program of action, or at least, that officials who exercise power over other men have that responsibility" (*TRS* 160).

This does seem to me a responsibility worth taking seriously, for what it amounts to is an insistence on rationality in practical affairs. Whatever be the variations in possible moral positions which people may have there are criteria of coherence and consistency of judgments and principles which can be and ought to be applied to anything which claims to be a "moral position," as distinct from mere gut-reactions or knee-jerk prejudice. Respect for rationality imposes formal constraints on practical arguments and on practical theories, theories *for* action, whether they be moral, political or legal. Such formal constraints are not intrinsically different from those which respect for rationality imposes upon us in speculative matters such as scientific inquiry.

But ought we in either sphere to observe the constraints imposed by respect for rationality? There are two possible ways of answering such a question as that. One way is to say that rationality is and is perceived by us to be an objective good, to belong within the "objective order of values." The other way is to offer rationality as a value absolute so far as it goes within a *Weltanschauung* the "constructive" nature of which one cheerfully admits, happy in the knowledge that if any one presents *reasoned* arguments against such a position, he is thereby estopped from denying the standing of rationality. The latter is certainly the course which I would take. But then what is one doing? One is offering to others for their adoption a certain form of life which for oneself one finds more acceptable than available alternatives. In the last resort the appeal is to what is experienced as acceptable to this that or another human being.

So far from being a weakness, this seems to me to be truly a strength of what I would understand by the "constructive model." For what we are out to do is to find the way or ways in which we are to live, and that can only be found in terms of what we find by experience acceptable to us as beings endowed with passion and will as well as reason. If what Hume called the "claim passions" are not engaged by such argumentation, it is in the end pointless.

If this be true, one position which cannot be sustained is the position that over and above the various practical theories or systems we may construct, there is some criterion independent of any of them whereby we can judge of one theory or system as better than another. Each of us is committed to the search for what seems to him the best, but it is a delusion to suppose that that which we find to be the best is the best there is for any human being. Only by covertly reverting to the natural model could we sustain that claim.

What has been said of the demands of rationality as a value can in turn be said of anything else, for example, justice, fairness, humanity, which one might present as an important practical value; there is no need to repeat the steps of the argument. If the constructive be preferred to the natural model, whatever is good is apprehended and presented as such within the four corners of that which is experienced as the most acceptable practical theory or system one can construct, and none of us can claim to find an Archimedean point beyond any such theory or system whereupon to lever one theory to a position above others as self evidently or even evidently the best for everyone.

Dworkin's fundamental weakness is a desire to have it both ways. Consider for example the following remark:

> The constructivist model insists on consistency with conviction as an independent requirement, flowing not from the assumption that these convictions are accurate reports, but from the different assumption that it is unfair for officials to act except on the basis of a general public theory that will constrain them to consistency, provide a public standard for testing or debating or predicting what they do, and not allow appeals to unique intuitions that might mask prejudice or self-interest in particular cases [*TRS* 163].

What, we must ask, is the status of the said "different assumption" which the constructivist model makes about the unfairness which would follow from noninsistence on consistency with conviction? Is it a "unique intuition," or is it a considered judgment within the theory "constructed" by Dworkin? If the former, is he not a naturalist after all? If the latter, can constructivism quite so blatantly heave itself up by its own bootstraps?

To raise these questions is to dig out the ambiguity which is at the heart of *Taking Rights Seriously*. The kind of unity—unity in substance, not only in method—of law, politics and morality for which Dworkin argues has hitherto been taken for a hallmark of natural law thought. But in its classical manifestations natural law thought did found on what Dworkin now characterizes as the "natural model" but which he expressly forswears. He cannot in my judgment make the switch to the "constructive model" and at the same time assert that unity in substance and method. Especially he cannot sustain the assertion which has set the jurisprudential community by the ears, the assertion that there is after all in any hard case at law a single uniquely right answer to the points in issue between the parties.

It may be that my own argument to this point is one which manifests a failure properly to grasp Dworkin's conception of the constructive model. But even were that so, I would argue that the most credible version of what he calls "the constructive model" certainly supports the argument I have put. Elsewhere,[6] in analysing the nature of legal arguments, I have tried to show the necessity of the constraints of consistency and coherence in legal argument in a manner which, I discover, chimes closely with Dworkin's account of the constructive model. But in my conception of it, it certainly won't take us to the length to which Dworkin thinks it will. In the next section of this essay, I shall test out the Dworkinian theory as to the adjudication of hard cases to show why that seems so.

II. "HARD CASES"

Dworkin's theory of law has as its nodal point the topic of hard cases and indeed the essay on "Hard Cases."[7] The phrase signifies those litigated disputes in which, even apart from any dispute about the facts of the matter, there is a dispute between the parties as to the bearing of the law on whatever facts can be proven. To take an example parallelling one which Dworkin uses,[8] let us suppose that *X*'s employee has incautiously severed a power cable in the course of roadwork operations, the cable being the property of a public utility corporation. *Y*'s factory has lost production because of a resultant failure in the electricity supply. Founding on the legal doctrine that an obligation of reparation is incumbent on one whose careless act causes reasonably foreseeable damage to another, *Y* sues *X* for damages to cover the cost to him of his lost production. *X* denies liability, founding in turn upon the doctrine that damage of a purely economic character occasioned to one party as a consequence of damage to another's property caused by negligence is "too remote" to be the subject of any obligation of reparation.

In such a case, justification of a decision cannot be achieved simply by subsuming the propositions of proven fact under a governing legal rule and reading off the result. The very point of the dispute is as to what rule or doctrine among rival possibilities governs. Legal theorists such as Kelsen, Bentham, Austin or Hart, positivists to a man, would say that in such a case the judge's decision is necessarily norm-creating, since it involves answering the question what *is to be* the governing rule for such a case. "American realists" would broadly agree, subject to reservations on the question whether cases can ever "turn on" rules and on the question whether all disputes do not leave the judge sufficient of what Karl Llewellyn called "leeway"[9] to make his own ruling for these parties, guided by the traditions of his craft, or whatever.

For Dworkin all such *soi-disant* "realistic" approaches are downright unrealistic. Surely, he insists, the parties have their rights. The law gives or guarantees to citizens certain rights as against each other (Dworkin does not, but we might, call these "primary rights"). As against political institutions such as courts, citizens must then have secondary rights (what he calls "institutional rights") that only such decisions will be given as will secure already vested primary rights. Not least among our institutional rights against courts is that they shall not, no more than legislatures may, create retrospective laws to any citizen's disadvantage. However much a projected legal provision might serve the common interest, it cannot in justice be invented in the course of a litigated dispute and then be applied retroactively to the detriment of one of the parties under a show of upholding a "right" of the other's which by the hypothesis did not exist when the litigation was started, far less when the matters in dispute actually occurred. To tolerate that would be to tolerate using the unfortunate loser as a means to public ends, which is *the* cardinal sin in the Dworkinian calendar.

Dworkin need not—though he seems to[10]—assert that no such intolerable thing ever occurs, for presumably it is always a possibility that rights, even institutional rights, will be infringed. The fundamental point of his argument is not that judges cannot do injustices, but that there is something fishy about any theory of law which presents the systematic infliction of such injustice as a *necessary*, not a possible but regrettable, incident of adjudication whenever a hard case comes to trial.

This, in his view, is a necessary feature of those theories of law which (whatever their detailed content) represent legal systems as comprising nothing other than bodies of socially operative rules whereby citizens regulate their lives and judges judge cases. The problem which he discerns in such theories is the "strong" discretion which they necessarily ascribe to judges in any litigated cases which the rules do not "fit." If the rules are all there is to the law, then in the cases where (because of "vagueness," "open texture," or indeed plain "gaps") the rules don't determine a clear answer, there is nothing for it but that the judge must make law for the case relying on such standards as he thinks right to justify his decision standards which *ex hypothesi* cannot already belong to the law. Hence the ostensible necessity of the injustice of retrospective legislation, and of the systematic infringement of institutional rights which ought to be taken seriously.

Rather than acquiesce in theories which have so distasteful implications, Dworkin invites us to reconsider how a hard case such as that of *Y* v. *X* might really be decided. No statute governs the matter in hand, and by our hypothesis (which is true in fact) there are precedents and legal doctrines which "pull both ways." What then? Dworkin's answer is that we, supposing ourselves faced with the task of judging, not merely spectating, must decide which pulls hardest. How can we find that out? By having, he says, a theory of the law; not, be it noted, a descriptive theory *about* law, but a justifying theory *of* the law.

It seems, though the evidence is here a little obscure, that Dworkin accepts that to have laws and courts at all, we must indeed have the man made rules and humanly established institutions whose anatomy and typology have been so exhaustively explored by positivists. But, he would add, these rules and institutions function intelligibly not because they are there as some kind of brute social fact, but because they are theorized, because social agents operate them through the categories of some normative political and social theory whereby they make sense of them.

At any given point of time, therefore, we can examine a society's established rules and institutions in order to work out by what principles and policies they are animated; that is, if we follow an eccentric stipulation of Dworkin's,[11] we can ask what rights of individuals they are supposed to secure ("principles") and what collective advantages they are supposed to serve ("policies"). By such a procedure, we can work out for any breach of law and, had we but world enough and time, for the whole legal system, a justifying theory. That is, the theory which best makes sense of the law all and whole as an engine for protecting individual rights and beyond that for advancing common public goods. Not every statute and precedent will necessarily be accommodated by such a theory. But the main points of the system as men and women have built it up and tried to live with it will be clarified and in the light of that we will know which precedents and statutes to reject, or at least to confine within a narrow ambit, as "anomalies."

In doing all this, we will necessarily be taking account of the theories which have animated agents working before us within the system. We shall not, however, be simply describing their view of it, for we are now no less engaged than were they. As they did, so must we, construct and act upon the best justifying theory of the system that we can contrive, taking account of but not being enslaved to their theories. In so far as we may be called upon to give advice or make decisions within the system we can properly do so only by reference to the "theorized" system, not just to the inert mass of black letter rules which in Dworkin's opinion positivists have mistakenly supposed to be the whole body of the law.

A particular point of such a theory will be that it goes beyond simply expounding the various principles and policies subserved by the law. It will necessarily rank them in order of priority by assigning "weights" to them, with a generally heavier weighting for principles concerning rights than for pure policies.[12] (The whole point of "taking rights seriously" is that in the areas covered by rights individuals are guaranteed against having their interests postponed to some collective interest in which they may or may not share.)

The last refinement is what gives, in Dworkin's view, the possibility of certainty of decision and rightness of decision in our figured case of *Y* v. *X*. The assignment of relative "weights" to the principles and policies which underly the rules of the law is what enables us to decide who ought to win. For as we saw, *X*'s and *Y*'s sides of the case are each supported by a body of legal "doctrine," which expounds and explains guiding principles and policies of this branch of the law. But once we have assigned weights to the policies and principles, it must appear either that *X*'s principles and policies outweight *Y*'s, or vice versa. (There is, Dworkin concedes, a remote possibility of a tie, but the system can and should incorporate some tie breaking rule.) Accordingly either *X* or *Y* has a right to be granted a decision in his favour, and that decision should be handed down which secures the right of *X*, or, as the case may be, of *Y*. That is to take rights seriously, and it is the reverse of retroactive legislation.

For the decision to be justified in the full, strong sense which Dworkin demands, it is necessary that the theory which authorizes it is the best possible theory of the legal system in question at the time in question. This seems a tall order. Given the Dworkinian prescription for theorizing the law, it would be hard enough for any mere mortal to construct *a* theory of a legal system all and whole, far less to satisfy himself that he had done the best possible job. But Dworkin does not claim that we can be sure that we have achieved the best possible theory. He claims only that we can be sure that the best possible theory is what we must try our best to achieve. Real judges, he claims, are engaged in just that attempt when wrestling with hard cases—and that is what a positivistic legal philosopher would find himself trying to do if he were called upon to be a judge and therefore to abandon that external observational position from which alone the task appears an impossiblity.

To make this point vivid, a demigod *ex machina,* "Hercules J." is postulated,[13] he being endowed with such superhuman mental capacities that he can construct the theory which best justifies and reconciles and conclusively sets the priorities among all the elements of the legal system comprehended together at once. No one can be a Hercules, but the very fact that we can intelligibly postulate such a being justifies the claim that every judge can and should try to get as close to Herculean competence as he can.

This is the very point at which we must cry "halt," and ask whether the thesis holds. The Greeks' Hercules was a handy man at achieving the physically impossible, but has Dworkin not imposed on his own Hercules the altogether taller order of achieving that which is, by his own premises, logically impossible? If the constructive model is the right model for practical reasoning, can it make sense to claim of one constructed theory that it is the best possible, from all possible points of view? Or can such a claim be sustained only by opting for the natural model with all the problems and difficulties which that faces, the model which in face of such problems Dworkin expressly rejects? Such would be my conclusion, and therefore I find Dworkin unable to sustain his conclusion by his premises.

Let us think some more about the nature of the problem in *Y* v. *X*. The court before whom the case is brought must decide it, and must justify its decision.[14] The decision must be justified according to the law. But plainly "according to the law" does not for such a case mean "according to a rule of law uncontroversial in interpretation," for by the hypothesis the case is a hard one.

The very idea of justifying the decision implies that it is to be decided not on a "once-off," "individual merits of the parties" basis. There must be some ruling on the point in issue which is logically universal in the sense that it can cover this and all other like cases which may arise; in this sense the requirement of universalisability applies in legal justification. But that is a necessary, not a sufficient, condition of justifying the decision. In turn the ruling itself must be justified.

But what does that involve? First, there is a requirement of consistency: no ruling can be acceptable which contradicts any previously established rule of law which is binding for that court (what "rules of law" are "binding for the court" depends on detailed provisions of the particular legal system concerning formal sources of law). This is a strict test, but relatively easy to satisfy, given the open texture of law and the leeways of interpretation which it leaves open. But there are further tests which must be applied. A ruling upon law which can be entertained by the court must also be shown to be "coherent" with the rest of the system. That means that it must be shown to be supported by relevant principles of the system, or (what comes to the same thing) to be derivable by analogical extrapolation from the existing body of the law.

From where, then, can we get these "principles" which authorize such rulings and which secure the coherence of the legal system as a rational and intelligibly purposive scheme for the ordering of a society? The answer is that to some extent we find them, and to some extent we make them. We find them, to the extent that previous judges and doctrinal writers have expounded broad statements of general norms which make sense—in their view—of congeries of interrelated rules and precedents. "Making sense" implies showing that there is some value or values which is advanced by adherence to the rules in question. We make them precisely by trying to make our own sense of the rules and precedents which confront us, taking fully into account the efforts of our predecessors, giving them the more weight according to their number and authority.

Even at that, we may often find that in just such a case as that of *Y* v. *X* *both* sides can appeal to settled and sound principles. *Y*, whose factory was plunged in darkness, can adduce the general principle that everyone ought to take reasonable care to avoid inflicting foreseeable harm to others, and to answer for such harm as is caused by failure to take such reasonable care. *X*, who indubitably through his employee caused the harm can adduce principles which have been enunciated as restricting the possible range of liability for negligent acts, in particular the principle that the duty of care is owed only to those upon whom one's acts may forseeably inflict physical harm, whether to their persons or to their property.

What else can come into play at this point of the argument? My answer would be that a characteristically legal mode of consequentialist argument does normally, and should in any event, come into play. A ruling for or against *Y* could be made consistently with the preestablished rules, and adequately supported by one or other of the principles mentioned. But which ruling should be made? Is it not relevant to ask what will be the outcome if it be ruled that all who engage in activities which may cause nonphysical damage to other persons owe to those at risk a duty to take reasonable care, and an obligation of reparation if they cause such economic loss by failure to take reasonable care?

The Courts in practice certainly do ask such questions and, in Britain, in the "economic loss" cases, they have concluded that the potential range of liability which such a ruling would imply in cases such as *X*'s are too extensive and catastrophic to be acceptable. This is partly what lawyers call a "commonsense" point, in the sense that the range of potential plaintiffs is so large that the defendant could not possibly meet or insure against all their possible claims; so imposition of liability would be pointless. It is partly an argument of justice, to the extent that it is held both that so large a burden of damages cannot fairly be imposed on defendants, and that those who are particularly sensitive to loss of electric power can and ought to insure against it, not come against those who could not know of their particular sensitivity. So far, that has been the clinching point of the argument in economic loss cases.

The evaluation of consequences is not by reference to any variant of the hedonistic utilitarian principle, but by reference to such concepts as "justice," "commonsense," "public policy." But it necessarily follows that any judge or critic in making up his mind one way or another at this level of argument is doing so by reference to his conception of "justice," "commonsense," "public policy" and whatever else, reflecting on and advancing from what he takes to be the best conception of the justice (or whatever) that the law serves. In so doing he is *ascribing* weight to this or that of the principles in play, deciding which ought to have priority in such a situation as this now before him.

This brings us back to the very argument I made earlier, leading to the point that: "one position which cannot be sustained is that over and above the various practical theories we may construct, there is some criterion independent of any one of them whereby we can judge of one theory or system as better than another." Of course we do pass judgment on other theories; but we pass judgment from the perspective of one theory or another, from the perspective of that which to us as judges or critics seems to us the most acceptable. The constructive model cannot take us beyond that, nor should it pretend to, and it is a model which well fits the style of legal argumentation—as also, in my opinion, of moral deliberation. Judges do (and ought to) construct theories of the law, and do (and ought to) use the conceptions of legal justice and so on, which seem to them best constructed, in deciding in the last resort to which of two well-founded arguments to give the greater weight. This is not a matter which can be decided in a theory-independent way, nor can the question which is really best among the theories which people think best be answered in a theory-independent way. If "constructivism" is correct, Hercules can finish his job only at the far end of an infinite regress.

That knocks out a main point of Dworkinian legal theory, the "right answer" thesis. Such being knocked out, we are left to conclude that Dworkin has not, in the sense he intended, established the grounds for his pre-Benthamite program. He has not succeeded in demolishing the alleged gap between censorial and expository jurisprudence.

Certainly as the foregoing sketch account of adjudication in hard cases implicitly supposes, there must be more to any account of a legal system than simply an account of different sorts of rules and their interrelations. The making and implementing of such laws presupposes and involves reference to values which can be and sometimes must be rendered explicit in statements of principle or of policy. It would be only a matter of arbitrary fiat answering no good end of understanding if these elements of principle or policy were ruled out in an exposition or description of the law which exists within some jurisdiction.

What that says, however, is only that a good description (or definition) of law must be *expanded* beyond a mere accont of "rules." It does not say or mean that descriptions as distinct from criticism of law is impossible. No doubt the legal system of the Soviet Union or of the Republic of South Africa is pregnant with principles as well as with rules, and should be seen and grasped as such. The principles, however, may be from my point of view very bad ones; I may rightly wish to proceed from description to criticism—and the mere observation that law comprises principles and policies as well as rules in no way impedes that proceeding, nor justifies the thesis that expository and censorial jurisprudence are, after all, identical. The pre-Benthamite program is therefore flawed at the heart.

Moreover, there is a certain sense in which the "rules" have logical primacy. As Hart[15] and others have shown, "developed" legal systems develop precisely by establishing more or less clear criteria as to what counts as a rule of the system. This is essential to law as a common and objective standard of conduct in a complex society. It is quite right to say, as Dworkin in effect does, that this law is "theorized" in action. But the principles which can reasonably be propounded as principles of this or that legal system are limited by the need to fit the more or less objectively established rules. It would be absurd, for example, to suggest that the principle of the equal freedom of all human beings was implicit in the law of the later Roman Republic. Among the reasons why it would be absurd would be simple observation of the clear rules concerning slavery then clearly established in Rome.

Whatever his ambition, Dworkin has added to, rather than subverted, the "ruling theory" which he thinks so inadequate.

III. "RIGHTS"

It may seem unsatisfactory that Dworkin's key argument about "rights" has been passed over. In truth, as will appear, it is the argument itself which is unsatisfactory, both in particular and in general.

The problem about rights in hard cases can be dealt with fairly swiftly. Dworkin argues, fairly enough, that if courts in hard cases are not enforcing rights, they are in effect legislating retroactively. He takes this to imply that in every case one party necessarily has a right to the decision in his favor, and that legal theory is committed either to that "rights thesis" or to the inevitability of retrospection.

This is at best a half-truth. To see why, we need only recur to the definition of a hard case as one in which *both* parties have some doctrine or principle or precedent or such like on which to base their respective cases. Let us suppose that since each party has a principle in his favor, he has a right to something or other as against the other party—, for example, *Y* has a right to damages, *X* has a right to be absolved from liability. (Notice: Dworkin *must* suppose this to be the case, since by his definition principles *always* determine rights; the truth is that *some* principles do.)

Then the problem is that *both* parties have rights, but their rights conflict—this is exactly what makes hard cases hard. The rights conflict because the principles conflict. Therefore, just as Sir David Ross[16] conceived as prima facie obligations those obligations we have under potentially conflicting moral principles, so too we had better adopt "prima facie rights"—or some such phrase—to cover the legal rights which potentially conflicting legal principles vest in us.

Thus a hard case is one in which each party has some ground on which to assert at least a prima facie right. The problem for the court is not one of inventing a right and applying it retroactively. It is a problem concerning *which right to uphold in preference to the other.* In addition to the merit of being true, this actually follows from Dworkin's own definition of principles, and his definition of hard cases as involving a conflict of principles. If we go on and say, along Dworkinian lines, that judges should decide to which right to give preference by making recourse to a kind of "constructive" argument, we are left to conclude that the decisions can only be justified in a theory-relative way. Since there may be honest and rationally irresoluble differences of theory between different judges, the decision contains an irreducibly dispositive element. Each judge tries to work out which right ought to prevail. The court's decision determines which *is to* prevail; it establishes a preference, it does not merely record a preestablished preference of one (prima facie) right over another in the genetic circumstances of the case. That conclusion is probably not startling to, and certainly not radically subversive of the "ruling theory."

This preliminary point may well be thought to show that Dworkin is not fully attentive to all the implications of what he variously says about principles and about rights. Nor is he. But what is worse is that he fails to take "rights" as seriously as he would have us take rights. He variously[17] describes rights as "political trumps held by individuals," as not being "spooky things men and women have in much the same way as they have nonspooky things like tonsils," as being an "individuated political aim" which is "described" (*sic*) by a principle as distinct from a policy; and so forth. He embarks upon an elaborate typology of rights in his essay on hard cases. He distinguishes[18] rights in a "strong sense" and rights in a "weak sense" (the distinction turning on that between what it is wrong to do to somebody and what it is not wrong for somebody to do—rather like Hohfeldian[19] "right" versus Hohfeldian "privilege"). But the nearest he ever really comes to identifying what he calls a right in the strong sense is when he says:[20]

> A man has a moral right against the state if for some reason the state would do wrong to treat him in a certain way, even though it would be in the general interest to do so.

If that is his main view, it is simply not open to him to argue, as he elsewhere does, that some political theories start from rights and derive duties from the basic set of rights, while others do the reverse, his being of the former kind.

What is wrong for the state to do is that which the state has a duty not to do. The definition above quoted therefore defines rights effectively in terms of duties. The position can be saved only if he goes on to say that the wrong or duty in question is founded in some right which the individual has. But on that account the definition is viciously circular. A person has a right if he has a right such that the state would wrong him by taking it away. True. But what's a right?

The lesson from this is that anyone who wishes to give rights the kind of primacy that Dworkin wishes to give them in political theory must think harder than Dworkin has thought about their nature. In my judgment (more fully explained elsewhere[21]) the direction in which such a person must look is that of the traditional "interest theory" as against the "will theory" of rights.

The argument to be made is that rights always and necessarily concern human goods, that is, concern what it is, at least in normal circumstances, good for a person to have. When positive laws establish rights, for example expressly by legislation, what they do is secure individuals (or members of a particular defined set of individuals) in the enjoyment of some good or other. but not by way of a collective good collectively enjoyed, like clean air in a city, but rather an individual good individually enjoyed by each, like the protection of each occupier's particular environment as secured by the law of private nuisance. Such protection is characteristically achieved by imposing duties on people at large, for example, not to bring about certain kinds of adverse changes to the environment of land or premises occupied by somebody else, and further duties, which may be invoked at the instance of any aggrieved occupier, to make good damage arising from adverse environmental change. And there are other ways of securing protection, which I have discussed elsewhere.[22]

One way of conceptualizing "rights" is to conceive them as goods which are in some such way normatively secured to individuals. Another, apparently less profitable way, is to see them simply as the reflex or correlative of the duties for some reason imposed by law, correlativity being determined by the presence or absence in a person of power to waive, or enforce, or demand remedies for breach of such duties. (The latter is the view held by H. L. A. Hart[23] among others.)

Looking at it from a moral or political rather than strictly or narrowly legal point of view, if we wish to use "rights" as a ground for arguing that people have certain moral duties to each other, or ought to have certain legal duties imposed on them, it is obvious that the Hartian conception of rights is unuseful, as he himself states.[24] From this point of view, therefore, a theory which asserts the primacy of rights must necessarily postulate that there are goods or values which in their character as goods-which-ought-to-be-secured-to-individuals therefore count as "rights." That is an analytical apparatus which will enable us to treat of rights as grounds for identifying duties and justifying various kinds of laws and political institutions. For rights so understood can genuinely be presented as logically prior to duties, or at least, some duties; and as grounds for determining *what* it is wrong for the state to do to an individual, or indeed for one individual or group to do to another individual or group. "Or indeed" is important; Dworkin seems far too apt to suppose that rights affect only relations between individuals and the state, which obviously they don't.

I do hold that there are goods which ought to be secured to individuals, goods which it is wrong to withhold from or deny to any individual. To such goods I would say that people have rights, and accordingly I would further say that their having such rights is a good justifying reason for certain duties which I would assert to be incumbent on individuals in their conduct towards others and on the state in its conduct towards individuals. This is perhaps no more than spelling out a more exact meaning for Dworkin's idea of an "individuated political aim"—to reflection upon which I am much indebted. But I do not find in Dworkin any such, or any other, elaborated account of rights.

From this point of view we might say something about the fundamental and about the universal quality (with respect to all human beings) of rights people may have. Goods which are goods for an individual might be ranked by that individual in order from those most valued by him/her to those least valued. To an individual the goods most valued—those least readily given up in competitions with others are the fundamental ones. If these goods belong within the category of goods which ought to be secured to that individual, they are for that individual rights which he/she holds as fundamental.

That would not necessarily make them universal in the sense of belonging to all human beings. There have been slavemasters who have valued their freedom as a fundamental good, and who have held it as a fundamental right; and there have been slave ideologies since at least Aristotle's time which have justified the existence of freedom as a fundamental right for some but not for all human beings. Even apart from that, some rights which we might think fundamental for all children, we would not necessarily think fundamental, or even rights, for all human beings; for example, the right to care and nurture by parents or parent-substitutes.

In short, the account of rights as goods which ought to be secured to individuals is—as it should be—a formal one which does not settle *what* goods should be secured, nor *to whom*. These are vital questions of moral and political substance, not capable of settlement by mere analysis or definitional *fiat*. To answer them calls for the "construction" of moral and political theories. Clear analysis is, however, a prerequisite of the construction of a worthwhile theory; with respect, I find no sufficiently clear analysis in Dworkin, though I suspect that what I have said is more or less compatible with what he does say.

IV. LIBERTY AND EQUALITY

These remarks are an essential preliminary to a consideration of Dworkin's political philosophy, which is an anti-utilitarian restatement of liberalism, in which he gives pride of place to every person's right to equal concern and respect with every other. So far indeed is he insistent upon the egalitarian aspect of his theory that he goes to the length of saying that "In any strong sense of right, which would be competitive with the right to equality, there exists no general right to liberty at all."[25] His argument for this view is that by his definition of "right in the strong sense," there could be a right to liberty in general only if it were wrong for the state to limit any aspect of liberty on simple "general interest" grounds. Yet laws restricting one's liberty to drive down Lexington Avenue and "the vast bulk of the laws which diminish my liberty" are in fact justified "as being in the general interest of welfare."[26]

The point is dubitable on several counts: first, it turns on the inadequate analysis of "right" already castigated above; secondly, it makes the somewhat facile assumption that the sole argument for a one-way street system, or other such legal restrictions, is a general interest one, whereas it might well be argued that traffic regulation systems, for example, are an attempt to balance such rights as the right to free and expeditious movement through cities and the right to bodily security (which is plainly put at some hazard by toleration of the motor car); and finally, most seriously, the argument does not treat on the same footing "liberty" and "equality." Let us see how.

The argument concerning liberty is of the form: if there is a right to liberty in general, then no encroachment by government upon liberty can be justified simply on grounds of general interest. Some encroachments on liberty are justified simply on grounds of general interest. Therefore there is no right to liberty in general. To make out the case that "equality in general" (which would be the relevant comparison) is the subject matter of a right, Dworkin must therefore be prepared to argue that no departure by government from equality of treatment of citizens can ever by justified on grounds of general interest. I do not find him to make such an argument, and it would be difficult indeed to make and sustain argument in relation to such matters as military conscription for defense of a nation, or taxation legislation, or legislation regulating different payment of different public office holders—and so on and so on.

Of course, Dworkin intends no such argument, for his contention is not that people have a right to equality of treatment in every respect, but only that people have a right to treatment as equally deserving an equal measure of concern and respect from the government. In short, he wishes to say that in this crucial matter, everyone has an equal right: an equal right to concern and respect.[27]

I agree with that, but at the cost of disagreeing with his assertion that the right to liberty cannot compete with the right to equality, for it turns out that they are by his lights on a similar footing: in *some* matters, people have a right to liberty; in *some* matters they have a right to equality.

Unlike Dworkin, I would be content with the traditional definition of liberty as what he tendentiously calls "liberty as license"[28] in favor of his "liberty as independence."[29] Liberty, in my judgment, is most simply to be understood as freedom from imposed constraint on one's actions, whether such constraints be normative (for example, laws imposing duties not to do this or that) or factual (for example, handcuffs on a prisoner's hands). To have liberty in some matter is to be free from constraint.

To establish that there is some right to liberty by my account of the matter it is therefore necessary to establish that liberty is a good which individuals ought to have secured to them; and to establish that it is a fundamental right of everyone, it needs to be shown that liberty is a good for everyone, which ought to be secured to everyone.[30]

There is one important reason why we should be inclined to think liberty both a good and a relatively basic good for everyone, namely, the following: people may have many various and mutually differing values, indeed they do; but whatever different things they value, they can pursue whatever values they have only on condition that they are not normatively or factually constrained against pursuing them. So, for everyone, liberty to pursue what they value is a good precisely because it is a condition of getting anything else they think good.

But to say that everyone ought to be free to pursue whatever he/she thinks good is evidently absurd because the satisfaction of some people's ideals or desires may result in the imposition of constraints by them on other people. Therefore it is necessary to stipulate that everyone's liberty should be constrained at least within such limits as prevent the imposition of unequal constraints on others.

This stipulation does indeed turn upon recognition that each person does have a right to equal respect with every other, has indeed an equal right to the conditions of self-respect and of the contentment which resides in the ability to pursue his or her own conception of what is a full and rewarding life. But that is a ground for prescribing the *universality* within a population of the right to liberty, not a ground for perceiving liberty as the subject matter of right. Liberty is not good because people are to be treated as equals. Rather, it is because liberty is a good and because people ought to be treated as equals that there is, with certain qualifications a right to equal liberty.

What then are the qualifications? First, there are exceptions for children and persons of unsound mind justified by reference to the interests of such persons. Secondly, there is the Rawlsian qualification[31] that within a set of institutions designed for the protection of liberty, it may be legitimate to impose special restrictions on and to give special privileges to those who hold particular institutional offices: e.g. judges are (rightly) subjected to restrictions on their political activity and granted special privileges in relation to their utterances in their capacity as judges. Thirdly, there are rights which compete with the right to liberty especially those concerning fair shares in economic goods.

The third of these points is worth pursuing. Liberty is one of the conditions of self-respect and the "pursuit of contentment" as delineated above. But so is life, and so are the means essential to a tolerably commodious existence. A starving peasant may have the fullest possible freedom of speech, but writing letters to the editor of the local paper is not his foremost concern. For him to have an equal opportunity of self-respect with a well-heeled local businessman, it is essential to him to have more money, more food, and the chance to sustain himself reasonably commodiously by his own work.

It is at least open to argument that a legal order which maximises the freedom of property owners to do what they will with their own and which encourages the fullest possible freedom of market transactions will fail to secure for the starving peasant the degree of equality with the businessman which has been postulated. To that extent and within such spheres the right to liberty collides or competes with the right to such a share in general economic resources as in a condition of one's self-respect and pursuit of contentment. Therefore there is good ground for arguing that liberty of property owners and market liberties ought to be restricted to whatever extent is necessary to secure other no less basic rights to individuals.

This can be argued in a different way: the existence of a liberty to do *X* being defined solely in terms of the absence of constraints (normative or factual) against doing *X*, it is evident that one can be free to do *X* without being capable of doing it. I may be free to swim across the Atlantic without being capable of doing it. But a legal order may secure equality of liberty without in any degree securing an equal capability to exercise the liberties secured.[32] Black children of a given level of native intellectual capability may under a particular system of public education turn out to be incapable of exercising the liberty to enter a professional training which some white children may be capable of exercising, not because of greater native endowments but because of better schooling and greater environmental advantage. And so on.

On the basis of either of the foregoing arguments, or both of them, it is possible to argue for some restrictions either on the general scheme of legal liberty, or on the particular exercise of particular liberties, in the cause of securing economic fairness in general and of making fair allowance for socially induced differences of capability to exercise legal liberties. In constructing a fair legal and social order we inevitably find that there are goods other than the liberties of individuals which compete for recognition. But, so far as economic goods are concerned, the range of possible competition is restricted. Freedom of speech, freedom from arbitrary arrest and seizure, freedom of religion, conscience and opinion, freedom to come and go in public places as one chooses, political rights of participation, and such like, are in principle neutral as between different systems and schemes of distribution and allocation of economic goods. Hence it is always a bogus argument that "bourgeois liberties" such as these are inimical to a fair distribution of economic goods, or a fortiori that liberty in these respects is a mere adjunct of a bourgeois system of private ownership of the means of production distribution and exchange. It is an equally bad argument to contend, as some Conservatives appear to do, that liberty in the former respects is logically impossible without the liberties implicit in a private property system.

The rhetoric of the indivisibility of liberty, to which Dworkin objects,[33] makes just that mistake. I wholeheartedly agree with him as to the absurdity of treating liberties connected with property and the market as being essential to a just and liberal ordering of society, but I venture to think that the conclusion he reaches is preferable to the method of his argument for it. Liberty is a good, and people do have a right to it, but only within an order in which each has in principle an equal liberty, subject to the exception for children and other *incapaces,* subject to the Rawlsian qualification, and subject to other requirements of justice, especially economic fairness; but the last qualification, operates only as against those aspects of liberty which can conflict with our favored conception of economic fairness. Certainly, the idea of *equal* liberty for *everyone* requires as a prior postulate an equal right of everyone to self-respect and to respect from others. But to say, or even to seem to say, that that makes liberty in general subordinate to equality in general would be absurd.

Finally, one aspect of Dworkin's argument for the right to "liberty as independence" should be challenged. He argues, in effect, that rights of self-expression always predominate over other rights. This he takes to follow from his interesting distinction between "personal preferences" and "external preferences."[34] Preferences of the former kind concern how I want my life to be, preferences of the latter kind concern how I want other people to live, or what kind of relations I prefer to have with other people. If a person wants to be a lawyer, that is a personal preference. If a person wants all lawyers to be white men, that is an external preference.

One of the quarrels which Dworkin picks with utilitarianism is that in principle it equates personal and external preferences in prescribing principles of governmental action. Thus even if all blacks wanted to be lawyers, a scheme which admitted no blacks to the legal profession would satisfy more preferences if all the whites wanted there to be no black lawyers, and if whites were in the majority. But such a scheme would involve systematically refusing "equal concern and respect" to the minority, in this case an ethnic minority. And so it would be wrong.

Dworkin argues[35] that it would be wrong because it involves a kind of systematic double counting of majority preferences. They get to be what they want to be (or at least get a chance of being it) in virtue of the weight of their personal preferences. But they also stop the minority, or some members of it, from getting to be what they want to be, in virtue of the weight of their external preferences. Since this is unfair, Dworkin argues that in principle all external preferences ought to be omitted in determining any public course of action. But since in a democratic system this is impossible in practice, the device of entrenched rights must be resorted to in order to secure minorities against the baneful restrictions entailed by majorities' external preferences. And, in turn, this leads to particular interpretations of the rights entrenched in the U.S. Constitution.

Thus, in relation to the right of free speech Dworkin in effect argues that short of inflicting physical danger on other people, demonstrators must have the right not only to say what they like but to express their position how they like, however that may be.[36]

> It may be said that the anti-riot law leaves [a person] free to express [his] principles in a non-provocative way. But that misses the connection between expression and dignity. A man cannot express himself freely when he cannot match his rhetoric to his outrage, or when he must trim his sails to protect values he counts as nothing next to those he is trying to vindicate. It is true that some political dissenters speak in ways that shock the majority, but it is arrogant for the majority to suppose that the orthodox methods of expression are proper ways to speak, for this is a denial of equal concern and respect.

This looks like an attractive argument. But how far does it go? What if the majority of people in a town prefer a beautiful old terrace to stand as it is, whereas a property developer wants to tear it down to put up a new office block? The developer is also an architect, and claims that carrying out this piece of building here is essential to his self-expression.

For my part, I would have no hesitation in saying that the property developer has no absolute right worthy of entrenchment as against the wishes of the majority. Yet theirs are "external preferences" and his are "personal preferences" if I have the distinction aright.

The case seems to me to be one which casts doubt on the pleasing simplicity of the "personal" versus "external" distinction as between preferences. We all live in this town and necessarily share in the physical environment which it offers. Either the environment contains these historically interesting and aesthetically pleasing houses, or it contains the office block, but not both. There is as much risk that the property developer will fail to show full and proper respect to his fellow citizens as vice versa. And somebody's preferences are going to lose out in the end.

I cannot bring myself to resist the belief that for each of us a physical and social environment which is pleasing to us is a good of the kind which may properly be the subject matter of rights. So far as concerns public and visible additions to the environment or public actings which necessarily impinge upon all and sundry I cannot see the overwhelming justice of the view which says that everyone must always be free to choose whatever mode of self-expression he or she may choose. Thus for example it appears to me that some forms of obscenity law and of environmental protection law may be justified although they do impose limits on the manner of individuals' self-expression; but they must not limit the substance of what may be said or thought.

This requires an admission that environmental goods may be brought into the balance against the good of freedom of action, which is no doubt dangerous to admit because the admission can readily be abused. But to the extent that constraints are placed only on actings in public and are placed equally on all, such constraints are not inimical to the essential equality of liberty for which I have argued.

With some caution, therefore, I would make that admission. In making it I am driven to conclude that Dworkin's distinction between external and personal preferences, at least as he has so far drawn it, is too crude to be acceptable. Applied to contexts other than those to which he applies it, it appears to yield unacceptable results.

CONCLUSION

This review has on the whole concerned points of disagreement with or criticism of Dworkin's work. But, at least in the last section disagreement has concerned matters on which in the reviewer's opinion there are not conclusive right answers. If nothing else is evident, it ought to be evident that *Taking Rights Seriously* is a book full of stimulation and of interesting arguments. It ought to be taken seriously, which is another way of saying that it ought not to be swallowed uncritically.

NOTES

1. This essay is presented as an extended review of Ronald Dworkin, *Taking Rights Seriously* (Cambridge: Harvard University Press, 1977), pp. xv, 293, hereinafter cited as *TRS*.
2. *TRS,* Chapter 6, esp. at pp. 159–68; see also Chapters 4 and 5.
3. In P. M. S. Hacker and J. Raz, eds., *Law, Morality, and Society: Essays in Honour of H. L. A. Hart* (Oxford: 1977).
4. *TRS*, pp. ix–xi, 7.
5. See W. G. Maclagan, *The Theological Frontier of Ethics* (London: 1961), p. 54.
6. See my *Legal Reasoning and Legal Theory* (Oxford: Clarendon Press, 1978).
7. *TRS*, Chapter 4.
8. Dworkin's example is *Spartan Steel and Alloys Ltd.* v. *Martin and Co.* [1973] 1 Q.B. 27.
9. K. N. Llewellyn, *The Common Law Tradition* (Boston: 1960), pp. 62f., 219f.
10. See *TRS*, Chapter 13.
11. See *TRS*, p. 90. For the eccentricity of the stipulation, see the Excursus to Chapter 9 of my above noted *Legal Reasoning and Legal Theory.*
12. See *TRS*, pp. 116–17.
13. *TRS*, Chapter 4.
14. The following section summarizes some of my main arguments in the above cited book, Chapters 3–9.
15. H. L. A. Hart, *The Concept of Law* (Oxford: 1961), Chapter 5.
16. See W. D. Ross, *Foundations of Ethics* (Oxford: 1939), pp. 84–6; also *The Right and the Good* (Oxford: 1930), p. 19. He was confessedly unhappy with the qualifying phrase *prima facie.*
17. The references are respectively to *TRS*, pp. xi, 139, 90, 91.
18. *TRS*, pp. 188–92.
19. W. N. Hohfeld, *Fundamental Legal Conceptions* (New Haven: 1919). Although a former holder of the Hohfeld Chair at Yale, Dworkin takes no time comparing his taxonomy and analysis of rights with that of his distinguished predecessor.
20. *TRS*, p. 139.
21. MacCormick, Neil, "Children's Rights: A Test Case for Theories of Right," *A.R.S.P.* 62 (1976): 305–17; "Rights in Legislation," in Hacker and Raz, eds., *Law, Morality and Society,* pp. 189–209.
22. Hacker and Raz, eds., ibid., p. 205.
23. H. L. A. Hart, "Bentham on Legal Rights," in A. W. B. Simpson, ed., *Oxford Essays in Jurisprudence,* 2nd series (Oxford: 1973).
24. Ibid.
25. *TRS*, p. 269.
26. Ibid.
27. Ibid., pp. 180–83, 227, 272–78.
28. Ibid., pp. 262, 267–68.
29. Ibid., p. 263.
30. The argument stated here is expanded in my lecture, "Civil Liberties and the Law" (Edinburgh: Heriot-Watt University, 1977).
31. John Rawls, *A Theory of Justice* (Cambridge: Harvard University Press, 1971), p. 302.
32. This parallels Rawls's point about the distinction between the existence and the "worth" of a liberty: op. cit., p. 204f.

33. *TRS*, pp. 277–78.
34. Ibid., pp. 234–38; also Chapter 11.
35. Ibid.
36. Ibid., p. 201

PART FOUR
Law and Politics

10

Dworkin on Rights and Utilitarianism

Rolf Sartorius

Although they were written independently over the span of roughly a decade, the essays contained in *Taking Rights Seriously*[1] display considerable unity due to the prominence of two major theoretical themes in Dworkin's still developing thought about legal and political theory. First, there is Dworkin's theory of adjudication and its attendant anti-positivist implications concerning the nature of the judicial role and the connection between law and morality. Second, there is Dworkin's theory of political rights and its associated critique of utilitarianism. These two major themes are linked by what is yet a third significant theoretical theme: Dworkin's understanding of the relationship between political rights and those standards—principles, as against policies—that are to provide the basis for the decision of hard legal cases. I have commented at length on Dworkin's theory of adjudication elsewhere,[2] and although I have serious doubts concerning the limited role that he would permit considerations of policy to play in the decision of hard cases, my views on this score differ little from that of some of his other critics.[3] I shall thus confine myself here to a consideration of Dworkin's theory of political rights. There are a number of central questions about that theory which must be answered before we can claim to understand just what Dworkin would require of us if we are, as I now believe we should, to take rights seriously. Of particular significance is the question of precisely what relationship obtains between Dworkin's rights thesis and utilitarianism as a principle of social choice. I shall argue that Dworkin comes too close to adopting a form of utilitarianism to take rights as seriously as they should be taken.

I. THE FORMAL CONCEPTION OF RIGHTS

Dworkin shares with many of his contemporaries the following formal conception of what it is for an individual to have a justified normative claim of right: A claim of right is one the satisfaction of which takes priority over the satisfaction of competing claims that are based on considerations concerning the promotion of the general welfare, except where the consequences of satisfying it would be extremely severe. Just how severe the utilitarian consequences of

From 1981 *Utah Law Review* 263. Reprinted by permission of the author and *Utah Law Review*.

satisfying a claim of right must be before that claim may be justifiably overriden will, Dworkin suggests, reflect the weight of that right. Although it is clear that Dworkin believes that some rights have considerably more weight than others, it is also clear that he believes that no political right has so little weight that it may be justifiably overriden simply because the consequences for the general welfare of doing so will be marginally better than those of observing it.[4]

Understood in this way, claims of right "trump" utilitarian arguments in matters of morality and politics; in law, cast as arguments of principle, they cannot be defeated by arguments of social policy. As John Rawls has put it with respect to the principles of distributive justice which he defends, claims of right are "absolute" with respect to considerations of utility.[5] The satisfaction of claims of right on this view represents an individuated political or moral goal[6] that is sensitive to the relations amongst persons[7] and attentive to *who* gets what.[8] Utilitarianism in any form, which only looks to the aggregate (sum total or average) satisfaction level of a group of individuals, makes the fundamental error of being oblivious to distinctions amongst persons. It makes the mistake of extending what appears to be a plausible model of rational prudential choice, within which distributional features of satisfaction have no more relevance than their role in causing changes in the level of satisfaction, to society at large. In effect, utilitarianism treats a collection of individuals as a superperson some of whose interests can be sacrificed as a means of furthering other interests, i.e., the interests of *other persons.*[9]

Seeing himself, each in his own way, as within the Kantian tradition, Dworkin, Rawls and Nozick argue that it is only a recognition of individual rights that can prevent some from being illegitimately treated as means for furthering the ends of others. Each would agree with Joel Feinberg that respect for persons demands that they be treated as bearers of moral rights.[10] Although there is considerable disagreement among current defenders of rights-based theories as to *which* rights people have in virtue of being persons, there is complete agreement on the above formal conception, and on the claim that people do have rights as so conceived. There are, however, two related questions about this formal conception of rights that remain important for Dworkin to answer.

A. We know of Dworkin's views concerning the priority relationship in which claims of right stand to competing claims based simply upon considerations having to do with the promotion of welfare. But in addition to utilitarian and rights-based theories, Dworkin recognizes the existence of accounts of morality based upon the concept of moral duty.[11] Suppose there is a conflict between claims of right and duty in the sense that the satisfaction of one person's claim of right is possible only if another is denied the opportunity to do that which he has a duty to do. Is there anything *general* that can be said about the order of priorities in such cases, or are conflicts between rights and duties simply to be treated in the same way as conflicts between rights themselves? Such conflicts would have to be treated in this way, of course, if statements about duty can always be translated without loss of meaning into statements about correlative rights.

B. How *are* conflicts between claims of right to be handled on Dworkin's theory? His claim that principles have a dimension of weight which rules do not, conjoined with his view that principles reflect rights, suggests that some rights are weightier than others and that in cases of conflict the weightiest right ought to prevail. Although this analysis may be fine as far as it goes, I am afraid that it does not go very far. It will permit us to handle simple cases such as the following: (a) *A* claims *x* as a matter of right *R'* against *B* who claims *x* as a matter of right *R''*, where *R'* and *R''* are not of equal weight; (b) *A*'s claim to *x* invokes more than one right at least one of which is equal in weight to the single right which is invoked in *B*'s claim to *x*; (c) More than two people are involved, but all of the rights involved in the claims of the members of one group are weightier than any of the rights involved in the counter claims of the members of the other group, and the groups are equally numerous; (d) More than two people are involved, and the rights involved in the claims of one group are as numerous and as weighty as those involved in the counter claims of the other group, but the groups are not of equal size. Beyond these and similar cases, the plausible notion that rights have different weights suggests little about what is to be done when claims of rights conflict. When legal rights are at issue, Dworkin's theory of adjudication requiring judges to make that decision which fits best with "the soundest theory of law"[12] (i.e., the theory which fits best without constitutional structure and values) may provide the basis for an acceptable answer to the two person case. I am not sure that this model provides any guidance at all, however, for resolving conflicting claims of right that may be made against legislative bodies.

The source of the difficulties, of course, is that Dworkin's formal conception of rights at best puts constraints upon, but by no means implies, any particular principle of right action. Although Dworkin is not explicitly concerned with the construction of a general moral theory, he does owe us an explanation of what principles are to guide legislative action as part of his general account of what it means for government to take rights seriously. As Nozick has pointed out, there are a number of genuine options available to the defender of a rights-based theory on this score, of particular importance being the distinction between treating rights as side constraints on action (i.e., as constraints which may not be violated in the pursuit of goals) as against treating them as goals (in the sense of claims which are to be maximally satisfied).[13] Nozick argues convincingly that adopting a maximization principle with respect to rights—e.g., act so as to minimize violations of rights!—will be liable to essentially the same sort of objection as is utilitarianism on the score of sacrificing some person's rights to the benefit of others. Familiar cases involving the punishing of innocents in order to prevent great *harm*, for instance, can easily be redescribed as maximally efficient means for minimizing the violation of peoples' *rights*.[14] A "utilitarianism of rights," in short, may suffer from the same structural flaw as classical utilitarianism: ignoring the distributional features of situations in which claims (of whatever sort) are maximally satisfied in the aggregate.

Should Dworkin wish to follow Nozick in construing rights as side constraints, it would be interesting to know whether or not he accepts Nozick's further argument that this will lead to a libertarian side constraint prohibiting aggression against others, including paternalistic aggression.

> Thus we have a promising sketch of an argument from moral form to moral content: the form of morality includes *F* (moral side constraints); the best explanation of morality's being *F* is *p* (a strong statement of the distinctness of individuals); and from *p* follows a particular moral content, namely, the libertarian constraint.[15]

If Dworkin should follow Nozick *this* far, it may be asked whether the libertarian rights that he would be committed to would be compatible with the kind of redistributive programs called for by his liberal conception of a just society.[16] For although Dworkin surely does not accept anything like Nozick's view of private property rights, I suspect that Nozick and other libertarians would argue that their criticism of the positions of liberals such as Rawls and Dworkin does not require any more foundation than that of taking libertarian rights seriously.

II. WHAT RIGHTS DO WE HAVE?

An abstract right to equal concern and respect is treated as "fundamental and axiomatic"[17] by Dworkin in the sense that more specific political rights are argued to be required by it. Such rights may be rights *to* institutions of a particular sort or rights *against* institutions already in place. Although Dworkin argues that a vast range of political rights follow from the basic right to equal concern and respect, he is careful to qualify his claims concerning the right's axiomatic character in two significant ways. First, the right to equal concern and respect is the basis of political rights and not necessarily all or even most moral rights that individuals have against other individuals.[18] Second, it may not provide the basis for even *all* political rights, and it may not be the *only* basis for the rights that it does support.[19]

What is the content of this basic right to equal concern and respect? Dworkin writes:

> What does it mean for the government to treat its citizens as equals? This is, I think, the same question as the question of what it means for the government to treat all its citizens as free, or as independent, or with equal dignity. In any case, it is a question that has been central to political theory at least since Kant.[20]

Dworkin elsewhere speaks of the basic right as one to an "equal share of respect and resources"[21] and his discussion of Rawls' theory of justice suggests that this right is rooted in the equally shared human "capacity to make plans and give justice."[22] Equal *respect*, as I understand Dworkin, implies the liberal refusal to give higher value to the life prospects, plans, and personal preferences of some as opposed to others. It recognizes each individual not only as an autonomous being with his own life to lead but as entitled to his own conception of how he ought to go about leading it. Thus Dworkin has considerable admiration for the conception of liberty as independence, which he finds in Mill's *On Liberty*.[23] Equal *concern*, as I understand it, reflects the fact that all have an equal call upon a fair share of the social resources required to carry out the particular life plans that they have. I speak of *fair* rather than *equal* shares here because according to Dworkin equal concern need imply neither equal treatment[24] nor equal distributive shares.[25]

On the face of it, the rights to equal respect and concern appear to tug in different directions. The former suggests a Kantian notion of autonomy of the sort emphasized by Nozick in his explanation of why people have any rights at all and of why they have libertarian rights against coercive interference in particular.[26] Equal respect means respect for the choices of others. It is this conception of equality which is reflected in the language used by Dworkin in the passage from *Liberalism* quoted above.[27] The notion of equal concern, on the other hand, suggests the utilitarian preoccupation with general welfare maximization and a willingness to interfere with individual liberty when necessary to achieve that end. The libertarian, opposed to paternalism, will view the redistributive programs of the modern welfare state as showing too much concern and too little respect. On the libertarian view, one cannot maximize for both respect and concern at once; respect must take priority when the two conflict.

It might be replied on Dworkin's behalf that the apparent tension between what respect and concern for persons respectively require is simply the result of perhaps unfortunate choice of language. Political philosophers these days are overly fond of presenting their pet theories as what is *really* called for by respect for persons; knowing how radically different these theories turn out to be, should we not simply view the Kantian jargon as just so much window dressing and rather attend to the principles to which any given theory is committed and the arguments given for them? This I am more than prepared to do, but upon closer examination my worries about the relationship between Dworkin's theory and utilitarianism deepen rather than go away.

III. THE RIGHTS THESIS AND UTILITARIANISM

To those unfamiliar with Dworkin's work, the description of his theory of rights presented above would suggest that his position has a familiar and quite unproblematic general structure. Rights are understood in the by now familiar anti-utilitarian sense of trumps. A fundamental right connected with the notion of human personhood is posited, and the other rights are argued to follow from it. But a look at the way in which Dworkin's rights thesis develops in the essays contained in *Taking Rights Seriously* reveals that talk of rights enters the discussion in a most unconventional manner. For Dworkin explicitly suggests in a number of places that in spite of the trump role played by claims of rights over utilitarian arguments in particular cases, the theory being presented is or could be viewed as a modified form of utilitarianism.[28] The idea of a theoretical reconciliation of the natural rights and utilitarian traditions is surely dramatic. But I believe that the suspicion that this is one *tour de force* that not even Dworkin can bring off is well founded. Here the tension between equal concern and equal respect is much more than a surface phenomenon.

Dworkin distinguishes between the *personal* preferences that an individual may have for certain goods, liberties, etc., and the *external* preferences that the same individual may have about how to respond to the preferences of others.[29] Prejudice against others as well as the desire that others not act in ways for which one feels disapproval are examples of external preferences. Although they reflect sources of satisfaction just as genuine as personal preferences, on Dworkin's view external preferences are ruled out in making utilitarian calculations of desirable social policy. For example, in deciding whether it would maximize satisfaction to prohibit pornographic literature, the policymaker must not take into account some citizens' desires that others not read pornography.

Dworkin's striking and highly problematic suggestion is then that if the utilitarian principle is modified so as to exclude external preferences, it will turn out to be either equivalent to or provide a foundation for the basic right to equal concern and respect!

> I wish now to propose the following general theory of rights. The concept of an individual political right, in the strong anti-utilitarian sense . . . , is a response to the philosophical defects of a utilitarianism that counts external preferences and the practical impossibility of a utilitarianism that does not. It allows us to enjoy the institutions of political democracy, which enforce overall or unrefined utilitarianism, and yet protect the fundamental right of citizens to equal concern and respect by prohibiting decisions that seem, antecedently, likely to have been reached by virtue of the external components of the preferences democracy reveals.[30]

Elsewhere, Dworkin speaks of a utilitarian principle qualified in this way as "the only defensible form of utilitarianism."[31] In other passages, Dworkin suggests that some form of rule ("institutional") utilitarianism—presumably itself qualified so as to exclude consideration of external preferences—might provide the foundation for the fundamental right to equal concern and respect.[32] That is to say, a rule utilitarian theory qualified to exclude consideration of external preferences might account for specific political rights that function as trumps against utilitarian arguments in particular cases and provide a basis for (what would be its social mirror image) a qualified utilitarianism as a rule of social choice (a principle of legislation) in a democracy such as our own.

Dworkin's numerous discussions of utilitarianism suggest that a utilitarian principle will be acceptable if it rules out *only* external preferences. Rights, then, perform the task of ruling out such preferences. The argument in the following passage relies on the further assumption that rights exist *only* as a means of excluding external preferences from utilitarian calculations:

> What can be said, on the general theory of rights I offer, for any particular right of property? What can be said, for example, in favor of the right to liberty of contract sustained by the Supreme Court in the famous *Lochner* case, and later regretted, not only by the court, but by liberals generally? I cannot think of any argument that a political decision to limit such a right, in the way in which the minimum wage laws limited it, is antecedently likely to give effect to external preferences, and in that way offend the right of those whose liberty is curtailed to equal concern and respect. If, as I think, no such argument can be made out, then the alleged right does not exist.[33]

Dworkin has recently disclaimed the view that all political rights reflect the distinction between external and personal preferences and has pointed out that his argument in favor of certain economic rights in his essay *Liberalism* makes use of the notion of a fundamental right to equal concern and respect in a way that does not bring the distinction into play.[34] And in the Introduction to *Taking Rights Seriously* he wrote:

> Chapter 12 suggests . . . that the right to concern and respect is fundamental among rights . . . because it shows how the idea of a collective goal may itself be derived from that fundamental right. If so, then concern and respect is a right so fundamental that it is not captured by the general characterization of rights as trumps over collective goals . . . because it is the source both of the general authority of collective goals and of the special limitations on their authority that justify more particular rights.[35]

Dworkin's disclaimer, however, does not provide a basis for reinterpreting the many passages in *Taking Rights Seriously* that imply a reconciliation between his theory of rights and utilitarianism. And although the discussion of economic rights in *Liberalism* does not *explicitly* make use of the distinction between external and personal preferences, the argument implicitly assumes that the external preferences of some that others have lesser distributional shares are to be ruled out. Also, in *Liberalism* it is explicitly suggested that a utilitarian principle suitably modified so as to exclude the consideration of external preferences "enforces" rather than "invades . . . the right of citizens to be treated as equals."[36] As to the quotation from the conclusion to the Introduction of *Taking Rights Seriously,* I can find nothing in Chapter 12 to support the claim that Dworkin makes for it. I conclude that the position suggested in that passage represents a quite dramatic break from the attempt to reconcile rights and utilitarianism which is present throughout *Taking Rights Seriously* and is to be found in his essay *Liberalism* as well. I believe this is as it should be.

I agree with the claim that the only call that a utilitarian principle of welfare maximization has upon us will reflect its status as derivative from more fundamental principles concerning human rights. I suspect that such a derivative utilitarian principle will not exclude all external preferences, and am very confident that it will exclude many preferences that are not external. On the former score, I am not sure that even the altruistic preferences that Dworkin discusses need be excluded[37] and I am quite uneasy about the idea that all forms of paternalism are objectionable simply because they reflect external preferences.[38] On the latter score, there appear to be numerous examples of kinds of preferences that ought not to count in utilitarian arguments, and that thus reflect moral and political rights, which are not external preferences. Violations of Rawlsian principles of justice that require equal political liberties and equal opportunity to compete for favored social and economic positions, and that countenance only certain kinds of inequalities in social and economic advantage, might all be called for by a utilitarian principle which permitted the well being of some to be sacrificed as a means of enhancing the well being of others. The institution of slavery, for instance, need not reflect anyone's (external) preference that slaves receive a lesser share of goods and opportunities but merely the view that the institution is maximally efficient when the advantages and disadvantages to all are given *equal concern. Equal respect* for slaves as persons, on the other hand, should lead us to agree with Rawls that the institution is unjust because it violates peoples' rights. That considerations of justice are absolute with respect to considerations of utility means, among other things, that the benefits accruing to the beneficiaries of an unjust institution are to be "tossed out," as Rawls puts it, in the course of any appraisal of the overall moral merits of that institution.[39] Indeed, included among those preferences that must be tossed out, because giving them their due would lead to the violation of others' rights, are at least some preferences that are associated with what Dworkin calls "prejudice . . . rationalization . . . and personal aversion" in his discussion of Devlin's views concerning the enforcement of morality.[40] Prejudices, for instance, reflect external preferences; irrationally mistaken conceptions of fact do not. Yet according to Dworkin's own account, either might provide the basis for a moral position that if adopted by the government would violate the rights of homosexuals.[41]

Rawls once suggested that the only major theoretical modification of utilitarianism that is called for by his theory of justice is that satisfactions which violate the principles of justice be given no weight in making utilitarian calculations.[42] Much of what Dworkin has written in *Taking Rights Seriously* can be taken to contain the similar suggestion that all that is wrong with utilitarianism is that it gives weight to external in addition to personal preferences. But any such suggestion, as Rawls himself quickly acknowledged,[43] radically misrepresents the fundamental difficulty which besets any form of utilitarian theory. For although there surely are certain kinds of preferences which ought to be "tossed out" when the maximization of welfare is a legitimate enterprise, taking rights seriously requires us to admit that the very enterprise of welfare maximization is often morally impermissible because engaging in it will violate the right that persons have not to be treated as means for the furtherance of the ends of others.

NOTES

1. R. Dworkin, *Taking Rights Seriously* (1977).
2. See R. Sartorius, *Individual Conduct and Social Norms* (1975), pp. 181–210; R. Sartorius, "Social Policy and Judicial Legislation," *American Philosophical Quarterly* 8 (1971): 151.
3. See, e.g., Kent Greenawalt, "Policy, Rights, and Judicial Decision," *Georgia Law Review* 11 (1977): 991.
4. See *TRS*, p. 92.
5. John Rawls, "Justice as Fairness," *Philosophical Review* 67 (1958): 164, 190.
6. See *TRS*, p. 90.
7. See Rawls, "Justice as Fairness," p. 187.
8. See R. Nozick, *Anarchy, State, and Utopia* (1974), pp. 149–231.
9. Ibid., pp. 32–33.
10. See Joel Feinberg, "The Nature and Value of Rights," *Journal of Value Inquiry* 4 (1970): 243, 252.
11. *TRS*, pp. 170–73.
12. Ibid., p. 66.
13. Nozick, *Anarchy, State, and Utopia*, pp. 28–29.
14. Ibid.
15. Ibid., p. 34.
16. See R. Dworkin, "Liberalism," in S. Hampshire, ed., *Public and Private Morality* (1978), p. 113.
17. *TRS*, p. xv.
18. Dworkin, "Seven Critics," *Georgia Law Review* 11 (1977): 1201, 1260.
19. *TRS*, pp. xiv–xv, 272; "Seven Critics," pp. 1260–61.
20. Dworkin, "Liberalism," p. 127.
21. *TRS*, p. 267.

22. Ibid., p. 182.
23. Ibid., pp. 259–65.
24. Ibid., pp. 223–39.
25. Dworkin, "Liberalism," p. 129, note 5.
26. Nozick, *Anarchy, State, and Utopia,* p. 32.
27. See text accompanying note 20.
28. See notes 29–37 and accompanying text. Two papers that appeared after the first draft of this paper was written in 1978 support my reading of Dworkin as defending a purified form of utilitarianism. See Jules Coleman, "Book Review: *Taking Rights Seriously,*" *California Law Review* 66 (1978): 917, H. L. A. Hart, "Between Utility and Rights," *Columbia Law Review* 79 (1979): 845.
29. See *TRS*, pp. 234–35.
30. Ibid., p. 277.
31. Ibid., p. 276.
32. Ibid., pp. 95–96, 191 note 1, 271. Rule utilitarianism is the view that we should select social institutions (rather than particular actions) on the basis of whether they will maximize satisfaction.
33. Ibid., p. 278.
34. Dworkin, "Seven Critics," p. 1260.
35. *TRS*, p. xv.
36. Dworkin, "Liberalism," p. 134.
37. *TRS*, p. 277.
38. There may, of course, be other arguments against paternalism. See, e.g., Sartorius, "The Enforcement of Morality," *Yale Law Journal* 81 (1972): 891.
39. Rawls, "Justice as Fairness," p. 184.
40. *TRS*, p. 254.
41. Ibid., pp. 249–50.
42. Rawls, "Justice as Fairness," p. 191.
43. Ibid., p. 193.

11
Between Utility and Rights

H. L. A. Hart

I.

I do not think that anyone familiar with what has been published in the last ten years, in England and the United States, on the philosophy of government can doubt that this subject, which is the meeting point of moral, political and legal philosophy, is undergoing a major change. We are currently witnessing, I think, the progress of a transition from a once widely accepted old faith that some form of utilitarianism, if only we could discover the right form, *must* capture the essence of political morality. The new faith is that the truth must lie not with a doctrine that takes the maximisation of aggregate or average general welfare for its goal, but with a doctrine of basic human rights, protecting specific basic liberties and interests of individuals, if only we could find some sufficiently firm foundation for such rights to meet some long familiar objections. Whereas not so long ago great energy and much ingenuity of many philosophers were devoted to making some form of utilitarianism work, latterly such energies and ingenuity have been devoted to the articulation of theories of basic rights.

As often with such changes of faith or redirection of philosophical energies and attention, the new insights which are currently offered us seem to dazzle at least as much as they illuminate. Certainly, as I shall try to show by reference to the work of two now influential contemporary writers, the new faith has been presented in forms which are, in spite of much brilliance, in the end unconvincing. My two examples, both American, are taken respectively from the Conservative Right and the Liberal Left of the political spectrum; and while the former, the Conservative, builds a theory of rights on the moral importance of the *separateness* or *distinctness* of human persons which utilitarianism is said to ignore, the latter, the Liberal Left, seeks to erect such a theory on their moral title to equal concern and respect which, it is said, unreconstructed utilitarianism implicitly denies. So while the first theory is dominated by the duty of governments to respect the separateness of persons, the second is

---

 Reprinted (with omissions) from *Columbia Law Review* 79, no. 5 (June 1979). A shorter version of this essay was delivered as the John Dewey Memorial Lecture at the Law School of Columbia University on November 14, 1978. I am indebted to Derek Parfit for many helpful suggestions and criticisms of both the style and substance of the present version.

dominated by the duty of governments to treat their subjects as equals, with equal concern and respect.

II.

For a just appraisal of the first of these two theories it is necessary to gain a clear conception of what precisely is meant by the criticism, found in different forms in very many different modern writers, that unqualified utilitarianism fails to recognize or abstracts from the separateness of persons when, as a political philosophy, it calls on governments to maximise the total or the average net happiness or welfare of their subjects. Though this accusation of ignoring the separateness of persons can be seen as a version of the Kantian principle that human beings are ends in themselves it is nonetheless the distinctively modern criticism of utilitarianism. In England Bernard Williams[1] and in America John Rawls[2] have been the most eloquent expositors of this form of criticism; and John Rawls's claim that "Utilitarianism does not take seriously the distinction between persons"[3] plays a very important role in his *A Theory of Justice.* Only faint hints of this particular criticism flickered through the many different attacks made in the past on utilitarian doctrine, ever since Jeremy Bentham in 1776 announced to the world that both government and the limits of government were to be justified by reference to the greatest happiness of the greatest number, and not by reference to any doctrine of natural rights: such doctrines he thought so much "bawling upon paper,"[4] and he first announced them in 1776 in a brief rude reply[5] to the American Declaration of Independence.

What then does this distinctively modern criticism of utilitarianism, that it ignores the moral importance of the separateness of individuals, mean? I think its meaning is to be summed up in four main points, though not all the writers who make this criticism would endorse all of them.

The first point is this: In the perspective of classical maximising utilitarianism separate individuals are of no intrinsic importance but only important as the points at which fragments of what *is* important, i.e. the total aggregate of pleasure or happiness, are located. Individual persons for it are therefore merely the channels or locations where what is of value is to be found. It is for this reason that as long as the totals are thereby increased there is nothing, if no independent principles of distribution are introduced, to limit permissible trade-offs between the satisfactions of different persons. Hence one individual's happiness or pleasure, however innocent he may be, may be sacrificed to procure a greater happiness or pleasure located in other persons, and such replacements of one person by another are not only allowed but required by unqualified utilitarianism when unrestrained by distinct distributive principles.

Secondly, utilitarianism is not, as sometimes it is said to be, an individualistic and egalitarian doctrine, although in a sense it treats persons as equals, or of equal worth. For it does this only by in effect treating individual persons as of *no* worth; since not persons for the utilitarian but the experiences of pleasure or satisfaction or happiness which persons have are the sole items of worth or elements of value. It is of course true and very important that, according to the utilitarian maxim, "everybody [is] to count for one, nobody for more than one"[6] in the sense that in any application of the greatest happiness calculus the equal pains or pleasures, satisfactions or dissatisfactions or preferences of different persons are given the same weight whether they be Brahmins or Untouchables, Jews or Christians, black or white. But since utilitarianism has no direct or intrinsic concern but only an instrumental concern with the relative *levels* of total well-being enjoyed by different persons, its form of equal concern and respect for persons embodied in the maxim "everybody to count for one, nobody for more than one" may license the grossest form of inequality in the actual treatment of individuals, if that is required in order to maximise aggregate or average welfare. So long as that condition is satisfied, the situation in which a few enjoy great happiness while many suffer is as good as one in which happiness is more equally distributed.

Of course in comparing the aggregate economic welfare produced by equal and unequal distribution of resources account must be taken of factors such as diminishing marginal utility and also envy. These factors favour an equal distribution of resources but by no means always favour it conclusively. For these are also factors pointing the other way, such as administrative and transaction costs, loss of incentives and failure of the standard assumption that all individuals are equally good pleasure or satisfaction machines, and derive the same utility from the same amount of wealth.

Thirdly, the modern critique of utilitarianism asserts that there is nothing self-evidently valuable or authoritative as a moral goal in the mere increase in totals of pleasure or happiness abstracted from all questions of distribution. The collective sum of different persons' pleasures, or the net balance of total happiness of different persons (supposing it makes sense to talk of adding them), is not in itself a pleasure or happiness which anybody experiences. Society is not an individual experiencing the aggregate collected pleasures or pains of its members; no person experiences such an aggregate.

Fourthly, according to this critique, maximising utilitarianism, if it is not restrained by distinct distributive principles, proceeds on a false analogy between the way in which it is rational for a single prudent individual to order his life and the way in which it is rational for a whole community to order its life through government. The analogy is this: it is rational for one man as a single individual to sacrifice a present satisfaction or pleasure for a greater satisfaction later, even if we discount somewhat the value of the later satisfaction because of its uncertainty. Such sacrifices are amongst the most elementary requirements of prudence and are commonly accepted as a virtue, and indeed a paradigm of practical rationality, and, of course, any form of saving is an example of this form of rationality. In its misleading analogy with an individual's prudence, maximising utilitarianism not merely treats one person's pleasure as replaceable by some greater pleasure of that same person, as prudence requires, but it also treats the pleasure or happiness of one individual as similarly replaceable without limit by the greater pleasure of other individuals. So in these ways it treats the division between persons as of no more moral significance than the division between times which separates one individual's earlier pleasure from his later pleasure, as if individuals were mere parts of a single persisting entity.

III.

My second example of contemporary right-based social philosophy[7] is that put forward with very different political implications as one ground for rights in the original, fascinating, but very complex web of theory spun by Professor Ronald Dworkin in his book *Taking Rights Seriously.*[8] Dworkin's theory at first sight seems to be, like Nozick's, implacably opposed to any form of utilitarianism; so much so that the concept of a right which he is concerned to vindicate is expressly described by him as "an anti-Utilitarian Concept." It is so described because for Dworkin "if someone has a right to something then it is wrong for the government to deny it to him even though it would be in the general interest to do so."[9]

In fact the two writers, in spite of this surface similarity, differ on almost every important issue except over the conviction that it is a morality of individual rights which both imposes moral limits on the coercive powers of governments, and in the last resort justifies the use of that power.

Before I turn to examine in detail Dworkin's main thesis I shall summarise the major differences between these two modern philosophers of Right. For Nozick the supreme value is freedom—the unimpeded individual will; for Dworkin it is equality of concern and respect, which as he warns us does not always entail equality of treatment. That governments must treat all their citizens with equal concern and respect is for Dworkin "a postulate of political morality,"[10] and, he presumes, everyone accepts it. Consequently these two thinkers' lists of basic rights are very different, the chief difference being that for Dworkin there is no general or residual right to liberty as there is for Nozick. Indeed though he recognizes that many, if not most, liberal thinkers have believed in such a right as Jefferson did, Dworkin calls the idea "absurd."[11] There are only rights to specific liberties such as freedom of speech, worship, association, and personal and sexual relationships. Since there is no general right to liberty there is no general conflict between liberty and equality, through the reconciliation of these two values is generally regarded as the main problem of liberalism; nor, since there is no general right to liberty, is there any inconsistency, as conservatives often claim, in the liberal's willingness to accept restriction on economic but not on personal freedom. This is why the political thrust of these two right-based theories is in opposite directions. So far from thinking that the State must be confined to the night-watchman's functions of protecting a few basic negative rights but not otherwise restricting freedom, Dworkin is clear that the State may exercise wide interventionist functions; so if overall social welfare fairly assessed would be thereby advanced, the State may restrict the use of property or freedom of contract; it may enforce desegregation, provide through taxation for public education and culture; it may both prohibit discrimination on grounds of sex or colour where these are taken to be badges of inferiority, and allow schemes of reverse racial discrimination, if required in the general interest, even in the form which the Supreme Court has recently refused to uphold in *Bakke*'s case.[12] But there is no general right to liberty: so the freedom from legal restriction to drive both ways on Lexington Avenue and the freedom, later regretted but upheld in *Lochner*'s case[13] against State legislation, to enter into labour contracts requiring more than ten hours work a day were, as long as they were left unrestricted, legal rights of a sort; but they were not and cannot constitute moral or political rights in Dworkin's strong "anti-Utilitarian" sense, just because restriction or abolition of these liberties might properly be imposed if it advanced general welfare. Finally, notwithstanding the general impression of hostility to utilitarianism suggested by his stress on the "anti-Utilitarian" character of the concept of a right, Dworkin does not reject it wholly as Nozick does, but, as in the Lexington Avenue and labour contract examples, actually endorses a form of utilitarianism. Indeed he says "the vast bulk of the laws which diminish my liberty are justified on Utilitarian grounds."[14] But the utilitarianism which Dworkin endorses is a purified or refined form of it in which a "corrupting"[15] element which he finds in vulgar Benthamite utilitarianism is not allowed to weigh in determining decisions. Where the corrupting element does weigh it destroys, according to Dworkin, the fair egalitarian character, "everybody to count for one, nobody for more than one," which utilitarian arguments otherwise have. This corrupting element causes their use or the use of a majority democratic vote (which he regards as the nearest practical political representation of utilitarianism) to violate, in the case of certain issues, the fundamental right of all to equal concern and respect.

Before we consider what this "corrupting" element is and how it corrupts I wish to stress the following major point. Dworkin interestingly differs from most philosophers of the liberal tradition. He not merely seeks to draw a vital distinction between mere liberties which may be restricted in the general interest like freedom of contract to work more than ten hours a day, and those preferred liberties which are rights which may not be restricted, but he attempts to do this without entering into some familiar controversial matters. He does not make any appeal to the important role played in the conduct of individual life by such things as freedom of speech or of worship or of personal relations, to show that they are too precious to be allowed to be subordinated to general welfare. So he does not appeal to any theory of human nature designed to show that these liberties are, as John Stuart Mill claimed, among "the essentials of human well-being,"[16] "the very ground work of our existence"[17] or to any substantive ideal of the good life or individual welfare. Instead Dworkin temptingly offers something which he believes to be uncontroversial by which to distinguish liberties which are to rank as moral rights like freedom of speech or worship from other freedoms, like freedom of contract or in the use of property, which are not moral rights and may be overridden if they conflict with general welfare. What distinguishes these former liberties is not their greater substantive value but rather a relational or comparative matter, in a sense a procedural matter: the mere consideration that there is an "antecedent likelihood"[18] that if it were left to an unrestricted utilitarian calculation of the general interest or a majority vote to determine whether or not these should be restricted, the balance would be tipped in favour of restriction by that element which, as Dworkin believes, corrupts utilitarian arguments or a majority vote as decision procedures and causes them to fail to treat all as equals with equal concern and respect. So anti-utilitarian rights essentially are a response to a defect—a species of unfairness—likely to corrupt some utilitarian arguments or a majority vote as decision procedures. Hence the preferred liberties are those such as freedom of speech or sexual relations, which are to rank as rights when we know "from our general knowledge of society"[19] that they are in danger of being overridden by the corrupting element in such decision procedures.

What then is this element which may corrupt utilitarian argument or a democratic vote? Dworkin identifies it by a distinction between the personal and external preferences[20] or satisfactions of individuals, both of which vulgar utilitarianism counts in assessments of general welfare and both of which may be represented in a majority vote. An individual's personal preferences (or satisfactions) are for (or arise from) the assignment of goods or advantages, including liberties, to himself; his external preferences are for such assignments to others. A utilitarianism refined or purified in the sense that it counted only personal preferences in assessing the balance of social welfare would for Dworkin be "the only defensible form of Utilitarianism"[21] and indeed it is that which justifies the "vast bulk of our laws diminishing liberty."[22] It would, he thinks, genuinely treat persons as equals, even if the upshot was not their equal treatment. So where the balance of personal self-interested preferences supported some restriction on freedom (as it did according to Dworkin in the labour contract cases) or reverse discrimination (as in *Bakke*'s case), the restriction or discrimination may be justified, and the freedom restricted or the claim not to be discriminated against is not a moral or political right. But the vulgar corrupt form of utilitarianism counts both external and personal preferences and is not an acceptable decision procedure since (so Dworkin argues) by counting in external preferences it fails to treat individuals with equal concern and respect or as equals.[23]

Dworkin's ambitious strategy in this argument is to derive rights to specific liberties from nothing more controversial than the duty of governments to treat their subjects with equal concern and respect. His argument here has a certain Byzantine complexity and it is important in assessing it not to be misled by an ambiguity in the way in which a right may be an "anti-Utilitarian right." There is a natural interpretation of this expression which is not Dworkin's sense; it may naturally be taken merely to mean that there are some liberties so precious for individual human life that they must not be overridden even in order to secure an advance in general welfare, because they are of greater value than any such increase of general welfare to be got by their denial, however fair the *procedure* for assessing the general welfare is and however genuinely as a procedure it treats persons as equals. Dworkin's sense is *not* that; his argument is not that these liberties must be safeguarded as rights because their value has been compared with that of the increase in general welfare and found to be greater than it, but because such liberties are likely to be defeated by an unfair form of utilitarian argument which by counting in external preferences fails to treat men as equals. So on this view the very identification of the liberties which are to rank as rights is dependent on the anticipated result of a majority vote or a utilitarian argument; whereas on the natural interpretation of an "anti-Utilitarian right" the liberties which are to rank as rights and prevail over general welfare are quite independently identified.

Dworkin's actual argument is more complicated[24] than this already complex story, but I do not think what is omitted is needed for its just assessment. I think both the general form of the argument and its detail are vulnerable to many different objections. The most general objection is the following. What moral rights we have will, on this view, depend on what external preferences or prejudices are current and likely at any given time in any given society to dominate in a utilitarian decision procedure or majority vote. So as far as this argument for rights is concerned, with the progressive liberalisation of a society from which prejudices against, say, homosexual behaviour or the expression of heterodox opinions have faded away, rights to these liberties will (like the State in Karl Marx) wither away. So the more tolerant a society is, the fewer rights there will be; there will not merely be fewer occasions for asserting rights. This is surely paradoxical even if we take Dworkin only to be concerned with rights against the State. But this paradox is compounded by another. Since Dworkin's theory is a response specifically to an alleged defect of utilitarian argument it only establishes rights against the outcome of utilitarian arguments concerning general welfare or a majority democratic vote in which external preferences are likely to tip the balance. This theory as it stands cannot provide support for rights against a tyranny or authoritative government which does not base its coercive legislation or considerations of general welfare or a majority vote. So this particular argument for rights helps to establish individual rights at neither extreme: neither in an extremely tolerant democracy nor in an extremely repressive tyranny. This of course narrows the scope of Dworkin's argument in ways which may surprise readers of his essay "What Rights Do We Have?"[25] But of course he is entitled to reply that, narrow though it is, the reach of this particular argument extends to contemporary Western democracies in which the allegedly corrupting "external preferences" hostile to certain liberties are rife as prejudices. He may say that *that* is good enough—for the time being.[26]

However, even if we accept this reply, a close examination of the detail of the argument shows it to be defective even within its limited scope; and the ways in which it is defective show an important general failing. In constructing his anti-utilitarian, right-based theory Dworkin has sought to derive too much from the idea of equal concern and respect for persons, just as Nozick in constructing his theory sought to derive too much from the idea of the separateness of persons. Both of course appear to offer something comfortably firm and uncontroversial as a foundation for a theory of basic rights. But this appearance is deceptive: that it is so becomes clear if we press the question why, as Dworkin argues, does a utilitarian decision procedure or democratic vote which counts both personal and external preferences, *for that reason,* fail to treat persons as equals, so that when as he says it is "antecedently likely" that external preferences may tip the balance against some individual's specific liberty, that liberty becomes clothed with the status of a moral right not to be overridden by such procedures. Dworkin's argument is that counting external preferences corrupts the utilitarian argument of a majority vote as a decision procedure, and this of course must be distinguished from any further independent moral objection there may be to the actual decision resulting from the procedure. An obvious example of such a vice in utilitarian argument or in a majority vote procedure would of course be double counting, e.g., counting one individual's (a Brahmin's or a white man's) vote or preference twice while counting another's (an Untouchable's or a black man's) only once. This is, of course, the very vice excluded by the maxim "everybody [is] to count for one, nobody for more than one" which Mill thought made utilitarianism so splendid. Of course an Untouchable denied some liberty, say liberty to worship, or a black student denied access to higher education as a result of such double counting would not have been treated as an equal, but the right needed to protect him against this is not a right to any specific liberty but simply a right to have his vote or preference count equally with the Brahmin's or the white man's. And of course the decision to deprive him of the liberty in question might also be morally objectionable for reasons quite independent of the unfairness in the procedure by which it was reached: if freedom of religion or access to education is something of which no one should be deprived whatever decision procedure, fair or unfair, is used, then a right to the freedom would be necessary for its protection. But it is vital to distinguish the specific alleged vice of unrefined utilitarianism or a democratic vote in failing, e.g., through double counting, to treat persons as equals, from any independent objection to a particular decision reached through that procedure. It is necessary to bear this in mind in considering Dworkin's argument.

So, finally, why is counting external preferences thought to be, like the double counting of the Brahmin's or white man's preference, a vice of utilitarian argument or a majority vote? Dworkin actually says that the inclusion of external preference *is* a "form of double counting."[27] To understand this we must distinguish cases where the external preference is *favorable* to, and so supports, some personal preference or want for some good or advantage or liberty from cases where the external preference is hostile. Dworkin's simple example of the former is where one person wants the construction of a swimming-pool[28] for his use and others, non-swimmers, support this. But why is this a "form of double counting"? No one's preference is counted twice as the Brahmin's is; it is only the case that the proposal for the allocation of some good to the swimmers is supported by the preferences both of the swimmer and (say) his disinterested non-swimmer neighbor. Each of the two preferences is counted only as one; and surely *not* to count the neighbor's disinterested preference on this issue would be to fail to treat the two as equals. It would be "undercounting" and presumably as bad as double counting. Suppose—to widen the illustration—the issue is freedom for homosexual relationships, and suppose that (as may well have been the case at least in England when the old law was reformed in 1967[29]) it was the disinterested external preferences of liberal heterosexuals that homosexuals should have this freedom that tipped the balance against the external preferences of other heterosexuals who would deny this freedom. How in this situation could the defeated opponents of freedom or any one else complain that the procedure, through counting external preferences (both those supporting the freedom for others and those denying it) as well as the personal preferences of homosexuals wanting it for themselves, had failed to treat persons as equals?

It is clear that where the external preferences are hostile to the assignment of some liberty wanted by others, the phenomenon of one person's preferences being supported by those of another, which, as I think, Dworkin misdescribes as a "form of double counting," is altogether absent. Why then, since the charge of double counting is irrelevant, does counting such hostile external preferences mean that the procedure does not treat persons as equals? Dworkin's answer seems to be that if, as a result of such preferences tipping the balance, persons are denied some liberty, say to form certain sexual relations, those so deprived suffer because by this result their concept of a proper or desirable form of life is despised by others, and this is tantamount to treating them as inferior to or of less worth than others, or not deserving equal concern and respect. So every denial of freedom on the basis of external preferences implies that those denied are not entitled to equal concern and respect, are not to be considered as equals. But even if we allow this most questionable interpretation of denials of freedom, still for Dworkin to argue in this way is altogether to change the argument. The objection is no longer that the utilitarian argument or a majority vote is, like double counting, unfair as a procedure because it counts in "external preference," but that a particular *upshot* of the procedure where the balance is tipped by *a particular kind* of external preference, one which denies liberty and is assumed to express contempt, fails to treat persons as equals. But this is a vice not of the mere externality of the preferences that have tipped the balance but of their content: that is, their liberty-denying and respect-denying content. But this is no longer to assign certain liberties the status of ("anti-Utilitarian") rights simply as a response to the specific defects of utilitarianism as Dworkin claims to do. Yet that is not the main weakness in his ingenious argument. What is fundamentally wrong is the suggested interpretation of denials of freedom as denials of equal concern or respect. This surely is mistaken. It is indeed least credible where the denial of a liberty is the upshot of a utilitarian decision procedure or majority vote in which the defeated minority's preferences or votes for the liberty were weighed equally with others and outweighed by numbers. Then the message need not be, as Dworkin interprets it, "You and your views are inferior, not entitled to equal consideration concern or respect," but "You and your supporters are too few. You, like everyone else, are counted as one but no more than one. Increase your numbers and then your views may win out." Where those who are denied by a majority vote the liberty they seek are able, as they are in a fairly working democracy, to continue to press their views in public argument and to attempt to change their opponents' minds, as they in fact with success did after several defeats when the law relating to homosexuality was changed in England, it seems quite impossible to construe every denial of liberty by a majority vote based on external preferences as a judgment that the minority whom it defeats are of inferior worth, not entitled to be treated as equals or with equal concern and respect. What is true is something different and quite familiar but no support for Dworkin's argument: namely that the procedural fairness of a voting system or utilitarian argument which weighs votes and preferences equally is no guarantee that all the requirements of fairness will be met in the actual working of the system in given social conditions. This is so because majority views may be, though they are not always, ill-informed and impervious to argument: a majority of theoretically independent voters may be consolidated by prejudice into a self-deafened or self-perpetuating bloc which affords no fair opportunities to a despised minority to publicise and argue its case. All that is possible and has sometimes been actual. But the moral unacceptability of the results in such cases is not traceable to the inherent vice of the decision procedure in counting external preferences, as if this was analogous to double counting. That, of course, would mean that every denial of liberty secured by the doubly counted votes or preferences would necessarily not only be a denial of liberty but also an instance of failing to treat those denied as equals.

I do not expect, however, that Professor Dworkin would concede the point that the triumph of the external preference of a majority over a minority is not as such a denial of equal concern and respect for the defeated minority, even if in the face of my criticism he were to abandon the analogy which he uses to support the argument between such a triumph and the procedural vice of double counting, which vice in the plainest and most literal sense of these not very clear phrases certainly does fail to treat all "as equals" or with "equal concern and respect." He would, I think, simply fall back on the idea than any imposition of external preferences is tantamount to a judgment that those on whom they are imposed are of inferior worth, not to be treated as equals or with equal concern and respect. But is this true? Of course that governments should as far as possible be neutral between all schemes of values and impose no external preferences may be an admirable ideal, and it may be the true centre of liberalism, as Dworkin argues, but I cannot see that this ideal is explained or justified or strengthened by its description as a form of, or a derivative from, the duty of governments to show equal concern and respect for their citizens. It is not clear why the rejection of his ideal and allowing a majority's external preferences denying a liberty to prevail is tantamount to an affirmation of the inferior worth of the minority. The majority imposing such external preferences may regard the minority's views as mistaken or sinful; but overriding them, for those reasons (however objectionable on other grounds), seems quite compatible with recognising the equal worth of the holders of such views and may even be inspired by concern for them. In any event both the liberal prescription for governments, "impose no scheme of values on any one," and its opposite, "impose this particular conception of the good life on all," though they are universal prescriptions, seem to have nothing specifically to do with equality or the value of equal concern and respect any more than have the prescriptions "kill no one" and "kill everyone," though of course conformity with such universal prescriptions will involve treating all alike in the relevant respect.[30]

Though the points urged in the last paragraphs destroy the argument that denial of liberty on the basis of external preferences is a denial of equal concern and respect and the attempted derivation of rights from equality, this does not mean that such denials of freedom are unobjectionable or that there is no right to it: it means rather that the freedom must be defended on other grounds than equality. Utilitarian arguments, even purified by the exclusion of external preferences, can produce illiberal and grossly inegalitarian results. Some liberties, because of the role they play in human life, are too precious to be put at the mercy of numbers even if in favourable circumstances they may win out. So to protect such precious liberties we need rights which are indeed "anti-Utilitarian rights" and "anti-" much else, but so far as they are "anti-

Utilitarian" they are so in the common and not the Dworkinian sense of that expression, and they are needed as a shield not only against a preponderance of external preferences but against personal preferences also. Freedom of speech, for example, may need to be defended against those who would abridge and suppress it as dangerous to their prosperity, security, or other personal interests.[31] We cannot escape, as Dworkin's purported derivation of such rights from equality seeks to do, the assertion of the value of such liberties as compared with advances in general welfare, however fairly assessed.

It is in any case surely fantastic to suppose that what, for example, those denied freedom of worship, or homosexuals denied freedom to form sexual relations, have chiefly to complain about is not the restriction of their liberty with all its grave impact on personal life or development and happiness, but that they are not accorded *equal* concern and respect: that others are accorded a concern and respect denied to them. When it is argued that the denial to some of a certain freedom, say to some form of religious worship or to some form of sexual relations, is essentially a denial of equal concern and respect, the word "equal" is playing an empty but misleading role. The vice of the denial of such freedom is not its inequality or unequal impact: if that *were* the vice the prohibition by a tyrant of all forms of religious worship or sexual activity would not increase the scale of the evil as in fact it surely would, and the evil would vanish if all were converted to the banned faith or to the prohibited form of sexual relationship. The evil is the denial of liberty or respect; not *equal* liberty or *equal* respect: and what is deplorable is the ill-treatment of the victims and not the relational matter of the unfairness of their treatment compared with others. This becomes clear if we contrast with this spurious invocation of equality a genuine case of a failure to treat men as equals in the literal sense of these words: namely literal double counting, giving the Brahmin or the white man two votes to the Untouchable's or black man's single vote. Here the single vote given to the latter is indeed bad just because the others are given two: it is, unlike the denial of a religious or sexual freedom, a genuine denial of *equality* of concern and respect, and this evil *would* vanish and *not* increase if the restriction to a single vote were made universal.

IV.

I conclude that neither Nozick's[32] nor Dworkin's attempt to derive rights from the seemingly uncontroversial ideas of the separateness of persons or from their title to equal concern and respect succeeds. So in the rough seas which the philosophy of political morality is presently crossing between the old faith in utilitarianism and the new faith in rights, perhaps these writers' chief and very considerable service is to have shown, by running up against them, some of the rocks and shoals to be avoided, but not where the safe channels lie for a prosperous voyage. That still awaits discovery. Much valuable work has been done, especially by these and other American philosophers, but there is much still to be done to identify the peculiar features of the dimension of morality constituted by the conception of basic moral rights and the way in which that dimension of morality relates to other values pursued through government; but I do not think a satisfactory foundation for a theory of rights will be found as long as the search is conducted in the shadow of utilitarianism, as both Nozick's and the Dworkin's in their different ways are. For it is unlikely that the truth will be in a doctrine mainly defined by its freedom from utilitarianism's chief defect—neglecting the separateness of persons—or in a doctrine resting, like Dworkin's, everything on "equal concern and respect" as a barrier against an allegedly corrupt form of utilitarianism.

NOTES

1. J. Smart and B. Williams, "A Critique of Utilitarianism," *Utilitarianism, For and Against* (1973), pp. 108–18; and B. Williams, "Persons, Character and Morality," in *The Identity of Persons,* edited by A. Rorty, (1977).
2. See J. Rawls, *A Theory of Justice* (1971), pp. 22–24, 27, 181, 183, 187.
3. Ibid., p. 187.
4. J. Bentham, "Anarchical Fallacies," in Bowring, ed., *Works of Jeremy Bentham* 2 (1843), p. 494.
5. For an account of this reply included in "An Answer to the Declaration of the American Congress" (1776) by Bentham's friend John Lind, see my "Bentham and the United States of America," *Journal of Law and Economics* 19 (1976): pp. 547, 555–56.
6. See J. S. Mill, "Utilitarianism," chapter 5 in *Collected Works of John Stuart Mill,* vol. 10 (1969), p. 157; Bowring, ed., J. Bentham, "Plan of Parliamentary Reform," in *Works of Jeremy Bentham,* vol. 3 (1843), p. 459.
7. The original version of this essay included a discussion of Robert Nozick's *Anarchy, State and Utopia,* which is omitted in this reprinting, (Ed.)
8. R. Dworkin, *Taking Rights Seriously* (1977) (hereinafter, *TRS*).
9. Ibid., p. 269.
10. Ibid., p. 272.
11. Ibid., p. 267. Yet "Hercules" (Dworkin's model of a judge) is said not only to believe that the Constitution guarantees an abstract right to liberty but to hold that a right to privacy is a consequence of it. Ibid., p. 117.
12. *Regents of the University of California* v. *Bakke,* 438 U.S. 265 (1978); and *TRS,* pp. 223–39, and *New York Review of Books,* Nov. 10, 1977, pp. 11–15.
13. See *Lochner* v. *New York,* 198 U.S. 45 (1905), and *TRS,* pp. 191, 269–278.
14. Ibid., p. 269. It is clear that this means "adequately justified," not merely "said to be justified."
15. Ibid., p. 235.
16. J. S. Mill, "Utilitarianism," p. 255.
17. Ibid.
18. *TRS,* p. 278.
19. Ibid., p. 277.
20. Ibid., pp. 234–38, 275–78.
21. Ibid., p. 276.
22. Ibid., p. 269.
23. Ibid., pp. 237, 275.
24. The main complications are: (1) Personal and external preferences may be intertwined in two different ways. A personal preference, e.g., for the segregated company of white men, may be parasitic on an external preference or prejudice against black men, and such "parasitic" preferences are to rank as external preferences not to be counted. (Ibid., p. 236). They are, however, to be distinguished from certain personal preferences when, although they too involve a reference to others, do so only in an instrumental way, regarding others as a means to their personal ends. So a white man's preference that black men be excluded from law school because that will increase his own chances of getting in (ibid., p. 234–35) or a black man's preference for reverse discrimination against whites because that will increase the number of black lawyers, is to rank as a personal preference and is to be counted. (2) Though personal and external preferences are in principle distinguishable, in practical politics it will often be impossible to discriminate them and to know how many of each lie behind majority votes. Hence whenever external preferences are

likely to influence a vote against some specific liberty, the liberty will need to be protected as an "anti-Utilitarian right." So the "anti-Utilitarian" concept of a right is "a response to the philosophical defects of a utilitarianism that counts external preferences and the practical impossibility of a utilitarianism that does not." (Ibid., p. 277). Notwithstanding this "practical impossibility," there are cases where according to Dworkin valid arguments may be made to show that external preferences are not likely to have tipped the balance. See his comments on *Lochner*'s case (ibid., p. 278) and *Bakke*'s case (see note 11 and accompanying text) and his view that most of the laws limiting liberties are justified on utilitarian grounds (*TRS*, p. 269).

25. *TRS*, pp. 266–78.

26. This argument from the defect of unreconstructed utilitarianism in counting external preferences is said to be "only one possible ground of rights" (ibid., p. 272, and *TRS*, [2d printing, 1977] p. 356), and is stated to be applicable only in communities where the general collective justifications of political decisions is the general welfare. Though Dworkin indicates that a different argument would be needed where collective justification is not Utilitarian (*TRS*, [2d printing, 1977] p. 365), he does not indicate how in such a case the liberties to be preferred as rights are to be identified.

27. *TRS*, p. 235.

28. Ibid.

29. Sexual Offences Act, 1967, c. 60.

30. My suspicions that the ideas of "equal concern and respect" and treatment "as equals" are either too indeterminate to play the fundamental role which they do in Dworkin's theory or that a vacuous use is being made of the notion of equality are heightened by his latest observations on this subject. (See "Liberalism," in Hampshire, ed., *Public and Private Morality* [1978], pp. 127–28, 136–40). Here he argues that in addition to the liberal conception of equal concern and respect there is another, conservative conception which, far from requiring governments to be as neutral as possible between values or theories of the good life, requires them to treat all men as a "good man would wish to be treated," according to some particular preferred theory of the good life. On this view, denials of certain forms of sexual liberty as well as the maintenance of social and economic inequalities, if required by the preferred moral theory, would be the conservative form of treating all as equals and with equal concern and respect. But a notion of equal concern and respect, hospitable to such violently opposed interpretations (or "conceptions of the concept") does not seem to me to be a single concept at all, and it is far from clear why either of these two conceptions should be thought of as forms of equal concern and respect to all. Though the claim that liberal rights are derived from the duty of governments to treat all their citizens with equal concern and respect has the comforting appearance of resting them on something uncontroversial ("a postulate of political morality" which all are "presumed to accept," (*TRS*, p. 272), this appearance dissolves when it is revealed that there is an alternative interpretation of this fundamental duty from which most liberal rights could not be derived but negations of many liberal rights could.

31. Dworkin certainly seems to endorse utilitarian arguments purified of external preferences, yet he states that his arguments against an unrestricted utilitarianism are not in favor of a restricted one. (*TRS* [2d printing, 1977], p. 357). The contrary impression is given by earlier statements such as that the vast bulk of laws which diminish our liberty are justified on utilitarian grounds, (*TRS*, p. 269) and the following comment on the right of liberty of contract claimed in *Lochner*'s case: "I cannot think of any argument that a political decision to limit such a right . . . is antecedently likely to give effect to external preferences and *in that way* offend the right of those whose liberty is curtailed to equal concern and respect. If as I think no such argument can be made out then the alleged right does not exist." Ibid., p. 278 (emphasis added).

32. See note 7.

12

Liberalism and the Claims of Community: The Case of Affirmative Action

Michael Sandel

INTRODUCTION

Contemporary liberalism defends a strong notion of individual rights, but also demands of its citizens a high measure of mutual engagement. It insists on the "plurality and distinctness of individuals," but also requires that we "share one another's fate," and view our natural talents as common assets.[1]

The liberal's emphasis on sharing would seem to require a strong theory of community—an account, that is, of the way our identity as citizens is shaped by our common aims and endeavors. But it is unclear how a theory of community such as this could fit with liberalism's individualist aspirations. This perplexity appears more sharply when we consider more closely the liberal theory from which it arises.

The liberalism I have in mind, most fully elaborated by Rawls, is defined by the claim that the right is prior to the good, and in two senses.[2] The priority of the right means first, that individual rights cannot be sacrificed for the sake of the general good, and second, that the principles of justice that specify these rights cannot be premised on any particular vision of the good life.

The claim for the priority of the right commits this liberalism to a certain picture of the person, a picture on which the self is seen as prior to and independent of its interests and ends. The priority of the self means that I am never defined by my aims and attachments, but always capable of standing back to survey and assess and possibly to revise them. Only if the self is prior to its ends can the right to be prior to the good; only if my identity is never tied to the aims and interests I may have at any moment can I think of myself as a free and independent agent, capable of choosing my own plan of life.[3]

Of what sort of community could an "independent" self be a member? He is, of course, free to join in voluntary association with others, and so capable of community in the cooperative sense. But he is incapable of membership in any community bound by moral ties antecedent to choice, incapable of belonging to any community engaging the identity as well as the interests of the par-

From *Liberalism and the Limits of Justice* (Cambridge University Press, 1982), 135–47. Reprinted by permission of the author and Cambridge University Press. The Introduction was written especially for this volume and is printed by permission of the author.

ticipants. Such a community—call it "constitutive" as against merely "cooperative"—would implicate its members in a citizenship more thoroughgoing than the liberal self can know.

Now liberalism as an ethic of sharing regards each person as a rightful participant in the combined assets and endowments of his fellow citizens. But on the cooperative vision of community alone, it is unclear what the moral basis for this sharing could be. Short of the constitutive conception, deploying an individual's assets for the common purpose would seem an offense against the "plurality and distinctness of individuals" that this liberalism seeks above all to respect. Ronald Dworkin's argument for affirmative action provides a practical illustration of what is at stake for justice in a theory of community, and what goes wrong with the liberal position when it tries to do without one.

THE CASE OF AFFIRMATIVE ACTION

Dworkin defends affirmative action admissions policies for professional schools such as medicine and law on the grounds that they are an effective, or at least possibly effective means to a desirable social goal, namely, to increase the presence of blacks and other minorities in these socially strategic professions and so eventually "to reduce the degree to which American society is over-all a racially conscious society" (11).[4] His basic argument is an argument of social utility. Affirmative action is justified, not because those who are given preference are entitled to an advantage, whether in compensation for past discrimination or for any other reason, but simply because "helping them is now an effective way of attacking a national problem" (12).

But Dworkin, like Rawls, believes that no social policy can be justified, however well it serves the general welfare, if it violates individual rights. He therefore considers the argument that affirmative action violates the rights of those whites it puts at a disadvantage and in some cases excludes. He concludes in the negative: the idea that preferential treatment "presents a conflict between a desirable social goal and important individual rights is a piece of intellectual confusion" (12).

One version of the argument Dworkin considers is a claim that taking race into account is unfair because it fixes on a quality beyond a person's control. Dworkin answers that this does not distinguish race as a criterion but applies equally to most standards typically used in college and university admissions, including intelligence. While it is true that persons do not choose their race,

> it is also true that those who score low in aptitude or admissions tests do not choose their levels of intelligence. Nor do those denied admission because they are too old, or because they do not come from a part of the country underrepresented in the school, or because they cannot play basketball well, choose not to have the qualities that made the difference. (15).

Race may seem a different factor because exclusions based on race have historically expressed prejudice or contempt for the excluded race as such. But whites excluded as a result of affirmative action are excluded not out of contempt but only on the same sort of instrumental calculation that justifies the more familiar criteria. While it is true that a white with marginal test scores would have been accepted if he were black, "it is also true, and in exactly the same sense, that he would have been accepted if he had been more intelligent, or made a better impression in his interview . . . . Race is not, in *his* case, a different matter from these other factors equally beyond his control" (15).

Another version of the argument Dworkin considers is the claim that by admitting blacks with lower test scores than those achieved by some whites who are excluded, affirmative action violates the right of applicants to be judged on the basis of merit. Dworkin responds that what counts as merit cannot be determined in the abstract but depends on those qualities deemed relevant to the social purpose the institution serves. In the case of medical and law schools, intelligence as measured by standardized tests may well be among the relevant characteristics, but it is by no means the only appropriate consideration, as the long-standing practice of admissions committees attests. Other attributes of person and background are typically weighed in assessing the likely ability of the applicant to perform the needed function, and where being black is relevant to the social purpose at hand, being black must count as merit as well.

> There is no combination of abilities and skills and traits that constitutes "merit" in the abstract; if quick hands count as "merit" in the case of a prospective surgeon, this is because quick hands will enable him to serve the public better and for no other reason. If a black skin will, as a matter of regrettable fact, enable another doctor to do a different medical job better, then that black skin is by the same token "merit" as well (13).

Dworkin acknowledges that some may find dangerous the argument counting race as a form of merit, but "only because they confuse its conclusion—that black skin may be a socially useful trait in particular circumstances—with the very different and despicable idea that one race may be inherently more worthy than another" (12).

Implicit in much of Dworkin's argument is the idea that no one can justly claim his rights are violated by affirmative action programs, because no one, white or black, *deserves* to go to medical school or law school to begin with; no one has an antecedent right to be admitted. To be sure, those who meet to the fullest extent the conditions established for admission are *entitled* to be admitted, and it would be wrong to exclude them. But it cannot be said that they or any others *deserve* to be admitted, for at least two reasons. First, their having the relevant characteristics is in most cases no doing of theirs; their native intelligence, family environment, social and cultural opportunities, and so on are for the most part factors beyond their control, a matter of good fortune. And in any case, no one is entitled that medical schools or law schools undertake to reward any particular kind of qualifications in the first place. What counts as a qualification for any particular task depends on the qualities that task happens to require, nothing more. The benefits associated with the professions are thus not rewards for superior attainment but incentives to attract the relevant qualities. There can therefore be no antecedent right to be judged according to any particular set of criteria.

From this it seems clear that Dworkin's arguments coincide with Rawls's theory in several respects. The notion that traditional criteria of admission, as well as race, are no doing of the applicant recalls Rawls's argument that the advantages of the fortunate are arbitrary from a moral point of view. Dworkin's argument that there is no such thing as "merit" in the abstract, without reference to the purposes institutions may define and pursue, parallels Rawls's argument against meritocracy that the concepts of merit and virtue and moral worth have no antecedent or pre-institutional moral status and so cannot provide an independent standpoint from which otherwise just institutions could be criticized. And the general implication of Dworkin's argument, that no one, black or white, deserves to go to medical or law school, that no one has an antecedent right to be admitted, corresponds to Rawls's distinction between moral desert and legitimate expectations.

Rawls's and Dworkin's positions are similar in a more general sense as well. Both are rights-based theories, defined in explicit opposition to utilitarian conceptions, and seek to defend certain individual claims against the calculus of social interests. But notwithstanding their individualist aspirations, both rely on a theory of the subject that has the paradoxical effect of confirming the ultimate frailty, perhaps even incoherence, of the individual whose rights they seek above all to secure. We have already seen how on Rawls's conception the self threatens at different points in the argument either to dissolve into a radically disembodied subject or to collapse into a radically situated subject. As we shall now see, Dworkin's argument for affirmative action illustrates how these perplexities, identified first in the abstract, find consequence in practice.

Central to any case for affirmative action is the ability to distinguish discrimination against blacks and other minorities, as in historic color bars and anti-Jewish quotas, from discrimination in favor of blacks and other minorities of the kind involved in affirmative action programs. Dworkin argues that justification for the first sort of discrimination typically depends in part on 'the despicable idea that one race may be inherently more worthy than another,' while justification for the second depends instead on the utilitarian notion that society as a whole would gain by having more widely representative medical and legal professions.

With respect to the first justification, Rawls, like Dworkin, would clearly reject the idea that one race may be inherently more worthy than another. What is striking to recall is why, on Rawls's theory of the subject at least, this despicable idea must be wrong. For Rawls, the fallacy with the claim that whites are inherently more worthy than blacks is not that it denies the intrinsic worth of blacks but that it falsely attributes an intrinsic worth to whites, and so attributes to them an unfounded claim of desert. The reason is that for Rawls, the concept of moral worth, like the concept of the good, is "secondary to those of right and justice, and it plays no role in the substantive definition of distributive shares."[5] Persons can no more have an intrinsic worth than they can have intrinsic merit or desert, that is, a worth or merit or desert that is theirs prior to or independent of what just institutions may attribute to them. And as we have seen, no one can strictly speaking be said to deserve anything because no one can be said to *have* anything, at least not in the undistanced, constitutive sense of possession necessary to a desert base. On Rawls's theory of the subject, no person or race can be inherently more worthy or deserving than another, not because all are intrinsically worthy and deserving—and equally so—but because none is intrinsically worthy or deserving, and so all claims must equally await the arrival of just institutions.

Some will object to Dworkin's argument for affirmative action—and to Rawls's theory of justice insofar as it supports it—on the standard meritocratic grounds that the individual possesses his attributes in some unproblematic sense and therefore deserves the benefits that flow from them, and that part of what it means for an institution or distributive scheme to be just is that it rewards individuals antecedently worthy of reward. But Rawls and Dworkin present powerful arguments against these assumptions which defenders of meritocracy would be hard-pressed to meet. The difficulty with Dworkin's argument, it seems to me, lies elsewhere; it concerns the possible alternative visions of the subject that remain once the meritocratic conception of the individual is rejected. And this returns us to the problem of the bounds of the self.

We have already considered the difficulties associated with the notion of a person essentially dispossessed, barren of constituent features, without intrinsic worth or desert, and wholly dependent for his life prospects on the rights and opportunities institutions of justice may dispense. We have remarked as well the irony that a person so morally disempowered should be the product of a liberal ethic designed to establish the rights of the individual as inviolable. But if the denial of individual desert and the insistence on the bounds between the self and its attributes lead in the direction of a radically disembodied subject, the notion of common assets poses a different threat to the integrity of the self in its implication that the bounds between the self and the other must somehow be relaxed. For unless some principle of individuation other than a merely empirical one can be found, the danger here is the drift into a radically situated subject.

On Dworkin's argument for affirmative action, this perplexity takes the following form: Once admission or exclusion cannot plausibly be seen to depend on a notion of "merit" in the abstract or on an antecedent individual claim, the alternative is to assume that the collective ends of the society as a whole should automatically prevail. But the bounds of the relevant society are never established, its status as the appropriate subject of possession never confirmed. Once the self, *qua* individual self, is dispossessed, the claims of the individual fade to betray an underlying utilitarianism which is never justified. And as Rawls implies early on, utilitarianism is in a sense the ethic of the unbounded subject, the ethic that fails to take seriously the distinction between persons.

For Dworkin, however, utilitarian considerations are precisely the ones that distinguish the legitimate discrimination involved in affirmative action from the unjustifiable sort based on prejudice and contempt. If it cannot be said that some are inherently more *worthy* than others, it can at least be said that some are more *valuable* than others with respect to the social purposes at hand, and discrimination on this basis is justifiable. So long as a policy of preferential treatment *uses* people for the sake of worthy ends rather than *judges* people as more or less worthy in themselves, it is permissible. So long as an exclusion based on race is motivated not by prejudice but by an "instrumental calculation," a "rational calculation about the socially most beneficial use of limited resources," or an idea such as the one that "black skin may be a socially useful trait" (12), the exclusion is consistent with utilitarian considerations and may be justifiable. A person's expectations, unless they are founded on rights in Dworkin's special sense of the term, must always give way in the face of a "more general social concern," as when a small businessman must go under so that a new and superior road might be built (15). Although their disappointment is understandable, even worthy of our sympathy, rejected applicants can no more stand in the way of the medical profession society needs than the small businessman can stand in the way of the superhighway.

Although Dworkin's argument assumes that where no individual rights are at stake, social policy is properly decided on utilitarian grounds, he never says why this should be so. Apart from showing why utilitarian arguments cannot defeat individual rights, his theory does not offer an explicit defense of utilitarian ethics as such, and says little about why utilitarianism should prevail when individual rights are not involved. Dworkin may not feel the need to justify his underlying utilitarian assumptions because they seem on the surface to have a certain self-evident appeal. If no individual has an antecedent claim to the benefits of his accidentally given assets and endowments, it might seem natural to suppose that the society as a whole therefore does. But as we saw in the discussion of common assets and the difference principle, this assumption is without warrant. The arbitrariness of an individual's assets argues only against the proposition that the individual owns them or has a privileged claim to their benefits, not in favor of the proposition that some particular society owns them or has a privileged claim with respect to them. And unless this second proposition can be established, there would seem no grounds for favoring a utilitarian dispensation of such assets and endowments rather than just letting them lie where they fall.

Without some conception of a wider subject of possession, such as Rawls's notion of common assets seems also to require, there would seem no obvious reason why these assets should be made to serve general social ends rather than individual ones. To the contrary; in the absence of some wider subject of possession, to regard 'my' abilities and endowments as mere instruments of a wider social purpose is to use me as a means to others' ends, and thus to violate a central Rawlsian and Kantian moral injunction.

The moral oddness of basing university admissions on the assumption Rawls and Dworkin suggest, whether or not affirmative action is involved, might be illustrated by imagining the following letters of rejection and acceptance written to convey the moral basis of the policy they recommend:

Dear (Unsuccessful) Applicant,

We regret to inform you that your application for admission has been rejected. Please understand that we intend no offense by our decision. Your rejection indicates neither that we hold you in contempt nor even that we regard you as less deserving of admission than those who were accepted.

It is not your fault that when you came along society happened not to need the qualities you had to offer. Those admitted instead of you were not themselves deserving of a place, nor worthy of praise for the factors that led to their admission. We are in any case only using them—and you—as instruments of a wider social purpose.

You will likely find this news disappointing in the sense that your hopes of reaping the benefits given those whose qualities do coincide with society's needs at any given moment will not be realized. But this sort of disappointment occurs whenever an individual's preferences must give way to society's preferences, and should not be exaggerated by the thought that your rejection reflects in any way on your intrinsic moral worth; please be assured that those who were admitted are intrinsically as worthless as you.

You have our sympathy in the sense that it is too bad you did not happen to have the qualities society happened to want when you applied. Better luck next time. Sincerely yours . . .

Dear (Successful) Applicant,

We are pleased to inform you that your application for admission has been accepted. Through no doing of your own, it turns out that you happen to have the traits that society needs at the moment, so we propose to exploit your assets for society's advantage by admitting you to the study of medicine/law.

No praise is intended or to be inferred from this decision, as your having the relevant qualities is arbitrary from a moral point of view. You are to be congratulated, not in the sense that you deserve credit for having the qualities that led to your admission—you do not—but only in the sense that the winner of a lottery is to be congratulated. You are lucky to have come along with the right traits at the right moment, and if you choose to accept our offer you will ultimately be entitled to the benefits that attached to being used in this way. For this, you may properly celebrate.

You, or more likely your parents, may be tempted to celebrate in the further sense that you take this admission to reflect favorably, if not on your native endowments, at least on the conscientious effort you have made to cultivate your abilities and overcome the obstacles to your achievements. But the assumption that you deserve even the superior character necessary to your effort is equally problematic, for your character also depends on fortunate circumstances of various kinds for which you can claim no credit. The notion of desert seems not to apply to your case.

We look forward nonetheless to seeing you in the fall. Sincerely yours . . .

As these letters suggest, the policy Rawls and Dworkin defend can be troubling even for those who do not hold the meritocratic assumptions they effectively call into question. One can imagine, for example, a response along the following lines:

I do not claim that I, as an individual, either possess (in any exclusive sense) the assets with which I am endowed, or that I have any special moral claim on the fruits of their exercise. I acknowledge that I am indebted in a complex variety of ways for the constitution of my identify—to parents, family, city, tribe, class, nation, culture, historical epoch, possibly God, Nature, and maybe chance—and I can therefore claim little or no credit (or for that matter, blame) for having turned out the way I have. Sorting out just who or what is accountable for this or that part of me is a difficult if at times indispensible moral activity which after a certain point may become impossible to complete. But I agree in any case that I do not deserve to be admitted to any particular opportunity in any antecedent moral sense, first because I do not possess in my own right the qualities that would make me eligible, and second, because even if I did, I would not be entitled that the rules in force reward any particular set of attributes or qualifications rather than others.

From this it seems reasonable to suppose that what at first glance appear as "my" assets are more properly described as common assets in some sense; since others made me, and in various ways continue to make me, the person I am, it seems appropriate to regard them, insofar as I can identify them, as participants in "my" achievements and common beneficiaries of the rewards they bring. Where this sense of participation in the achievements and endeavors of (certain) others engages the reflective self-understandings of the participants, we may come to regard ourselves, over the range of our various activities, less as individuated subjects with certain things in common, and more as members of a wider (but still determinate) subjectivity, less as "others" and more as participants in a common identity, be it a family or community or class or people or nation.

One consequence of an enlarged self-understanding such as this is that when "my" assets or life prospects are enlisted in the service of a common endeavor, I am likely to experience this less as a case of being used for others' ends and more as a way of contributing to the purposes of a community I regard as my own. The justification of my sacrifice, if it can be called a sacrifice, is not the abstract assurance that unknown others will gain more than I will lose, but the rather more compelling notion that by my efforts I contribute to the realization of a way of life in which I take pride and with which my identity is bound. While it would, of course, remain true that I could not, as an individual, claim credit for possessing the qualities relevant to the common endeavor, I could nonetheless take pride in my fitness to contribute in this way, and this fitness, perhaps even more than the benefits I might glean, would be just cause for celebration.

This is not, of course, to say that a claim on "my" resources from just any quarter can be described in this way. The scope of community ties, however expansive, is not without limit. Even an enlarged self, conceived as a community, has its bounds, however provisional its contours may be. The bounds between the self and (some) others are thus relaxed on the intersubjective account, but not so completely relaxed as to give way to a radically situated subject. The bounds that remain are not given by the physical, bodily differences between individual human beings, but by the capacity of the self through reflection to participate in the constitution of its identity, and where circumstances permit, to arrive at an expansive self-understanding.

A further feature of the intersubjective description of common assets is that it renders the dispossession of the person as it appears from the individualistic point of view less ultimately disempowering. While the argument from arbitrariness systematically deprives the subject, *qua* individual person, of its attributes and possessions, leaving a self so shorn of empirically identifiable features as to dissolve into abstraction—"The person has disappeared; only attributes remain"—the notion of a wider subject of possession goes some way toward reconstituting the person and restoring its powers. If I cannot be the owner, I can at least be the guardian of the assets located "here," and what is more, a guardian for a community of which I count myself a member.

None of this is an argument against affirmative action as such. But it does suggest a further moral issue that Dworkin must address before his argument for affirmative action can be complete, and that is the question of how to establish the relevant subject of possession, or how to identify those among whom the assets I accidentally bear are properly regarded as common. To put the point another way, utilitarianism is an ethic of sharing. (In this respect, it resembles the difference principle.) As such it must presuppose some antecedent bond or tie among those whose satisfactions it would maximize and whose efforts and expectations it would expend in the process. Otherwise it is simply a formula for using some as means to others' ends, a formula deontological liberals are committed to reject.

But Dworkin's position on this question is ambiguous at best. At times he speaks as though no account of a wider subject of possession is required, as though it is enough for a utilitarian argument to succeed that an individual expectation come up against "some more general social concern," where that expectation is not protected as a matter of right. On this interpretation, I must share "my" assets with "society as a whole," not because this particular society has made me what I am and so is responsible for these assets and endowments in a way that I, individually, am not, but rather on the dubious assumption that "society" is the residuary beneficiary of the free-floating assets that remain once the individual is dispossessed. This assumes without argument that "society" in some indeterminate sense (all of humankind?) has a prior claim on whatever assets the individual does not. But simply because I, as an individual, do not have a privileged claim on the assets accidentally residing "here," it does not follow that everyone in the world collectively does. For there is no reason to think in advance that their location in "society's" province (or for that matter, within the province of humankind) is any less arbitrary from a moral point of view. And if their arbitrariness within *me* makes them ineligible to serve *my* ends, there seems no obvious reason why their arbitrariness within a particular society should not make them ineligible to serve that society's ends as well.

Dworkin speaks at other times as though he does have a determinate subject of possession in mind after all, and that it is the nation-state. He writes, for example, that "*American society* is currently a racially conscious society," and that it is the goal of affirmative action " to reduce the degree to which *American society* is over-all a racially conscious society." These programs are said to provide "an effective way of attacking a *national* problem" (11–12, emphasis added). But if Dworkin means to claim that, for the sake of determining university admissions and career prospects, the purposes of the *national* community properly predominate, then he must say a good deal more about why this should be so. And part of this argument would have to include some evidence of the nation's responsibility for having cultivated the qualities and endowments it would now enlist, its capacity to engage the reflective self-understanding of its members as the basis of their common identity, and its ability to claim if not agreement at least allegiance to the purposes that would arise from this identity. It would need to demonstrate, in short, that of the various communities and forms of identity, the nation is the one that is properly entitled to define the common purpose and to deploy the common assets necessary to its pursuit, at least insofar as university education and the choice of certain professional careers are concerned. It may or may not be the case that the American nation today defines a community in the relevant sense;[6] but insofar as Dworkin means to invoke the nation as the relevant subject of possession, it remains for him to show that this is so.

Despite Dworkin's passing references to the nation, both he and Rawls seem generally to assume that once the rights of the individual are dealt with, an unspecified social claim predominates without any account of a determinate community or wider subject of possession being required. Thus Dworkin speaks of the need to serve the "more general social concern," and to provide "what the more general society most needs," (15) and Rawls writes of the need to arrange distributive schemes so as to further "the common interest," and to serve "prior and independent social ends."[7]

We might summarize the difficulties with this assumption as follows: First, there is no such thing as "*the* society as a whole," or "*the* more general society," taken in the abstract, no single "ultimate" community whose preeminence just goes without argument or further description. Each of us moves in an indefinite number of communities, some more inclusive than others, each making different claims on our allegiance, and there is no saying in advance which is *the* society or community whose purposes should govern the disposition of any particular set of our attributes and endowments.

Second, if there is no such thing as "*the* society as a whole," taken in the abstract, then it would seem unlikely that any particular society, arbitrarily identified, could have any greater claim to some particular set of endowments than the individual in whom they accidentally reside, for surely their location within the province of such an arbitrarily identified community could be no less arbitrary from a moral point of view. In particular there would be no obvious reason why "more general social concerns" as such should in all cases defeat more local or particular concerns merely in virtue of their generality. It is interesting to note in this connection that utilitarianism in its earlier, theological versions (as in Tucker and Paley) did offer an explicit account of the ultimate subject of possession—namely God—whose purposes necessarily predominated over more local concerns.[8] But once utilitarianism turns secular, the relevant subject of possession is no longer a settled matter, and the grounds for asserting the precedence of one range of concerns over another must await some further description of the relevant subject or community and the basis of its claims.

Finally, unless it is possible to identify the relevant community across which "my" assets are properly shared and to establish its credentials, Dworkin's argument for affirmative action and Rawls's notion of common assets have the effect either of contradicting the central Kantian and Rawlsian injunction against using some as means to others' ends, or evading this contradiction by relaxing altogether the bounds between the self and the other, thus failing to take seriously the distinction between persons.

NOTES

1. See John Rawls, *A Theory of Justice* (Oxford: Oxford University Press, 1971), pp. 101–2.
2. This paragraph and the two that follow summarize an argument developed more fully in Sandel, *Liberalism and the Limits of Justice* (Cambridge: Cambridge University Press, 1982), pp. 1–65, 147–83.

3. On the priority and independence of the liberal self, see John Rawls, *A Theory of Justice,* p. 560, and Rawls, "Kantian Constructivism in Moral Theory," *The Journal of Philosophy* (September 1980): 544–45.

4. Page numbers indicated in parentheses refer to Dworkin, "Why Bakke Has No Case," *New York Review of Books,* 24, No. 18 (November 10, 1977).

5. Rawls, *A Theory of Justice,* pp. 312–13.

6. An illuminating discussion of the nation as a community can be found in Samuel Beer, "Liberalism and the National Idea," *The Public Interest,* no. 5 (Fall, 1966): 70–82. He distinguishes between the centralization of government and the process of national integration and points out that the two tendencies, however interdependent, are not guaranteed to coincide. In national integration, the nation is "made more of a community," and the sense in which its members share a common life deepens.

7. Rawls, *A Theory of Justice,* pp. 311, 313.

8. See Alasdair MacIntyre, "Egoism and Altruism," *Encyclopedia of Philosophy,* Paul Edwards, ed., vol. II, (New York: Macmillan, 1967), pp. 462–66.

13

Dworkin's Critique of Wealth Maximization

Richard Posner

My views on wealth maximization have been criticized by a number of philosophers and philosophically minded lawyers.[1] One of these critics, Ronald Dworkin, seems to me fairly representative, and I shall address here his most important criticisms.

First Dworkin argues that wealth is not "a component of social value"—not the only component and not even "one component of social value among others."[2] This may seem a bold challenge to conventional wisdom, which holds that wealth is *a* value, if not the only or the most important value. But his argument is actually a play on words, for Dworkin defines a component of social value as "something worth having for its own sake,"[3] and no one values wealth for its own sake. To argue that wealth is not a social value because it is not an end in itself is, however, to adopt an eccentric definition of "social value." If I say, "Loyalty is a social value because it facilitates the organization of productive activity," I am not misusing the English language by attaching the term "social value" to a mediate rather than an ultimate goal.

Dworkin rests his argument on an example that conceals the instrumental character of wealth maximization. The example is the following. Derek has a book that he would sell for $2 and that Amartya would pay $3 to have. An omniscient tyrant shortcircuits the market system and gives the book to Amartya without compensating Derek. As Dworkin argues, it is difficult to see how society is better off as a result. But suppose we change the figures. Let the book be worth $3,000 to Amartya and $2 to Derek. Then the transfer probably will increase the amount of happiness in society, even if Derek is not compensated. This is especially likely if Derek might receive one of these delicious windfalls sometime. Of course, in arguing along these lines I am hitching wealth maximization to utility maximization, but I am willing to do this because, as stressed in the last chapter, happiness is one of the ultimate goods to which wealth maximization is conducive. The relationship between wealth and utility is obscured by the particular numbers Dworkin uses in his example.

Another feature of the Amartya-Derek example requires comment: the absence of a plausible reason for taking the transaction away from the market

---

From *The Economics of Justice* (Harvard University Press, 1981), 107–15. Reprinted by permission of the author and the Harvard University Press.

and putting it into the hands of a "tyrant." Suppose we change the example as follows. Derek owns a home, and Amartya owns an airline. An airport is built near Derek's home, and Amartya's airline produces noise that reduces the value of the home by $2,000. Derek sues the airline, alleging a nuisance. The evidence developed at trial shows that it would cost the airline $3,000 to eliminate the noise and thereby restore Derek's home to its previous value; on these facts the court holds that there is no nuisance. This example is analytically the same as Dworkin's, but it illustrates more realistically than his how a system of wealth maximization would operate in a common law setting, and it makes less plausible his argument that wealth is not a "component of social value" in a reasonable sense of this expression.

Dworkin discerns a problem of circularity in my attempt to derive a system of rights from a goal of maximizing wealth. It is the familiar problem of "wealth effects," to which I referred briefly in the last chapter. In asserting that a rise in the price of some good will lead to a fall in the quantity demanded of the good, the economist normally ignores the effect of the price change on incomes even though the income effect may feed back into price. The rise in price will reduce the incomes of consumers, and a consumer's demands may change with a change in his income. Since the demand for some goods may actually rise as incomes fall (potatoes in Ireland is the conventional example), an increase in the price of a good could, as a result of the feedback effect mentioned above, result in an increase in the demand for the good, rather than, as normally assumed, a decrease. Empirical study has failed to discover a good that behaves in this way, but it is theoretically possible that there is one. Similarly, it is theoretically possible that the initial assignment of a good might determine its ultimate assignment, even if transaction costs were zero, especially where the good was a very large part of the individual's wealth—like a glass of water in the desert.[4] This has long been known, but again no one has come up with a realistic example.

Dworkin offers an example.[5] Agatha is assumed to have a talent for writing brilliant detective stories but a preference for some less remunerative activity (call it gardening). If Sir George, a publisher, owns her labor, he will compel her to write detective stories, and she will be able to buy her freedom only by promising to continue writing detective stories, because that is the only activity in which she could hope to earn a sum large enough to induce Sir George to free her. If he is initially assigned the right to her labor, therefore, she will remain a slave—whether to him or to whomever she borrows money from to buy her freedom. If she is initially assigned the right to her labor, however, she will not write detective stories, or not so many, and Sir George will not be able to buy the right to her labor. Thus it seems that economic analysis does not yield a determinate initial assignment of rights.

But this ignores the fact that if Agatha were free she almost certainly *could*—not would—write more detective stories than she would write if she were a slave. People have an incentive to work harder when they work for themselves than when they work for other people. As a slave, Agatha has no incentive to work hard, because the fruits of her labor inure to Sir George rather than to her. He will try to prevent her from shirking, but this will be difficult to do; it is especially difficult to establish and enforce output norms for such a nonroutine activity as writing stories. Suppose the value of her output to Sir George is $1 million, but if she were free she could produce detective stories worth $1.2 million in the same amount of time. Then presumably she could produce detective stories worth $1 million in less time and have time left over for gardening. If so, she could and would buy her freedom. Having done so, she will be worse off than if she had been free from the outset (she owes $1 million, plus interest, to whoever financed the purchase of her freedom). But that is not the point. The point is that wealth maximization leads to a determinate solution in the Agatha-Sir George case once it is assumed that she could produce more if she were free than if she were a slave. Since she would retain her freedom if given it from the first and would purchase it if she began as Sir George's slave, the initial assignment does not determine the final assignment. Transaction costs are therefore minimized by making her free in the first place.[6]

A problem of indeterminancy may arise, however, if rights are being assigned when a society first comes into existence. In the Agatha-Sir George example it was easy to obtain a determinate rights assignment, because only one good in society was unowned—Agatha's labor. With every other good having a market or shadow price, one could compute, in principle at least, the effects on aggregate wealth of assigning Agatha's labor to herself or to Sir George. But suppose no goods are yet owned: land, labor, sexual access—everything is up for grabs. How can each good be assigned to its most valuable use when no values—no market or shadow prices—exist? This is the problem of wealth effects with a vengeance. All rights have yet to be assigned; assignment of rights on so massive a scale is bound to affect prices; and prices in turn will affect the question of whom the rights should be assigned to.

The problem is exaggerated in two respects. First, we need not be troubled in any case where the particular issue of policy that we are concerned with is marginal to the society as a whole. Even moving from negligence to strict liability for automobile accidents would not have so large an effect on prices as to prevent a comparison of the total wealth of society before and after the change. Second, the assignment of rights at the outset of social development is unlikely to determine the allocation of resources many generations later. Suppose at the beginning one man owned all the wealth in a society. To exploit that wealth, he would have to share it with other people—he would have to pay them to work for him. His remaining wealth would be divided among his children or other heirs at his death. Thus, over time, the goods and services produced and consumed in the society would be determined not by his preferences but by those of his employees and heirs. Probably after several generations most prices in this society, both market and shadow prices, would be similar to those in societies in which the initial distribution of wealth was more equal. If so, it means the initial distribution of wealth will eventually cease to have an important effect on the society's aggregate wealth. In that event we can ask the question: what initial assignments of rights would most quickly move the society to its eventual wealth level? The answer suggested in the last chapter is that assigning labor rights to their "natural" owners and splitting up land into the smallest parcels in which the available economies of scale can be exploited will minimize transaction costs and thus move the society more rapidly to the level it would eventually reach anyway, even if all rights were initially assigned to one man.[7]

Dworkin makes the separate argument that wealth maximization is unlikely to "produce more total welfare-for-others activity than other, more compromising, economic and political structures."[8] Granted, that if the social objective is to maximize the transfer of wealth from the more to the less productive, setting a proximate goal of wealth maximization may be the wrong approach (although the amount of wealth transferred is in general positively related to the wealth of a society). But I do not argue that wealth maximization would *maximize* transfers (or protection of rights, or happiness), only that it would give us some of all of these things. Dworkin thinks we could get more of all three by aiming directly at each. But because there is no common currency in whch to compare happiness, sharing, and protection of rights, it is unclear how to make the necessary trade-offs among these things in the design of a social system. Wealth maximization makes the trade-offs automatically. If there is a better approach, it is not obvious and Dworkin has not described it.

Dworkin states that production for others "has no inherent moral value if [the producer] acts with the intention of benefiting only himself."[9] He reaches this conclusion as a matter of definition: moral value consists solely "in the will or intentions of the actor."[10] That is a narrow definition. If the effect of encouraging wealth maximization is to yoke selfish desires—which in most people are their strongest desires—to the service of other people, and to do so without coercion, these features of wealth maximization should commend it to the altruistic designer of a social system.

Dworkin argues that judges could promote utility more effectively by aiming directly at its maximization than by trying to maximize wealth as a proxy for it. He therefore invites the (utilitarian) judge to consider, for example, that although "the community will pay more for candy than for medical care lost through the noise of a candy machine, . . . the candy will be bad for its health and therefore its long-term utility."[11] He thinks a utility-maximizing judge faced with a decision to either "protect the workers of an ailing and possibly noncompetitive industry or hasten their unemployment by structuring rights in favor of a developing new industry" might choose the former.[12] Logically, Dworkin's utilitarian judge should also consider, in deciding a criminal case, whether the criminal derived more pleasure from the criminal act than the victim suffered pain. But even an extreme utilitarian would hesitate to turn judges loose from all moorings in ascertainable fact by inviting them to consider happiness in the manner suggested by Dworkin. Wealth maximization is, to be sure, imperfectly correlated with utility maximization, but the costs—in uncertainty, in protracted litigation, and in error—of using utility as a legal standard support using wealth as a proxy for it. The case for wealth maximization in common law adjudication is even stronger when the objections to utilitarianism discussed in the last chapter, besides the difficulty of measurement, are brought into play. A rule utilitarian might use wealth maximization as his rule; this is the practice of many economists.

Turning to positive analysis, Dworkin argues for rejection of the finding that common law rules are best explained as if judges sought to maximize wealth, no matter how well that explanation conforms to the facts, unless and until there emerges a generally accepted theory of why this should be so. He illustrates with an example that can be simplified as follows. Imagine that in the last ten cases decided by the Illinois Supreme Court, the sequence of affirmances and reversals (affirmance = 1 and reversal =0) was 1101100111. Would we say that this sequence explained the pattern of affirmances and reversals? No, it simply describes it. Now let a group of people make up their own sequences—0011001100, 0001110101, and so on. Suppose one of these sequences accurately described the next ten decisions of the Illinois Supreme Court. Would we say that the person who suggested that sequence had succeeded in explaining the pattern of decisions? Again the answer is no. It would be odd to suggest, however, that the reason the sequence fails as an explanation is that it has not been related to the motivations or biology of judges; it fails because it does not tell us anything interesting about the world. Suppose instead we found that the pattern of affirmances and reversals in all appellate courts in the United States over the last hundred years conformed perfectly to the formula $R_t = \sqrt{A_{t-1}}$; that is, the number of reversals (R) in any period (t) is the square root of the number of affirmances (A) in the previous period. If this "law" were found to be highly significant in repeated testing on different bodies of data, we would feel that we had made an exciting, if puzzling, discovery. We would say that we had "explained," in a meaningful sense of the term, the pattern of affirmances and reversals by appellate courts, although we would be troubled if we could suggest no reason why the pattern should take such a form.

If the common law can best be explained as if the judges were trying to maximize social wealth, this is a less mysterious fact than my hypothetical "law" of affirmances and reversals. The common law assumed its modern shape in the nineteenth century, a period when economic values were an imporant part of the prevailing ideology. Also, as mentioned earlier in this chapter, the common law tends to regulate behavior in areas where redistribution is difficult to accomplish and where, therefore, the only way for a group to increase its wealth is to support policies that lead to an increase in the wealth of society as a whole, in which the group will share. There are also the evolutionary models of the common law that Dworkin mentions.[13] No doubt it is an embarrassment to the supporters of the economic theory of the common law that there are so many explanations of why the common law is efficient. But the empirical regularity found by the economic theorists is not so arbitrary and improbable that it should be disregarded until we have a generally accepted theory tying this regularity to the motivations or the biology of judges, litigants, or legislators.

NOTES

1. See e.g., Jules Coleman, "Efficiency, Utility and Wealth Maximization," *Hofstra Law Review* 8 (1980); Ronald Dworkin, "Is Wealth a Value?" *Journal of Legal Studies* 9 (1980): 191; Anthony T. Kronman, "Wealth Maximization as a Normative Principle," *Journal of Legal Studies* 9 (1980): 227; Ernest J. Weinrib, "Utilitarianism, Economics, and Legal Theory," *University of Toronto Law Journal* 30 (1980): 307; Joseph M. Steiner, "Economics, Morality, and the Law of Torts," *University of Toronto Law Journal* 26 (1976): 235–39.

I should like to comment briefly on what I take to be the central, or at least the most powerful, criticisms of Professors Weinrib and Steiner. Weinrib argues that the concept of the hypothetical market, which plays such a large role in the theory of wealth maximization, is critically different from that of an actual market in that in an actual market both parties to a transaction are made better off by the transaction, and this element of compensation is absent in a hypothetical market transaction (e.g., *A* runs down *B* and injures him, and is absolved from liability because the cost of precautions to *A* exceeded the expected accident costs of his conduct). Weinrib's objection is obviated if my argument from ex ante compensation is accepted. Moreover, he fails to note that even actual market transactions frequently have a noncompensatory element, in that adverse effects of such transactions on nonparties are not compensated. Professor Steiner objects that the hypothetical-market approach violates the economist's strictures against interpersonal comparisons of utility, but this point is answered in the last chapter, where I point out that interpersonal comparisons of wealth do not pose the acute measurement problems that have led economists to forswear interpersonal comparisons of utility.

2. Dworkin, "Is Wealth a Value?" p. 195.

3. Ibid.

4. In the desert setting as usually described, the glass of water is the only thing of value; someone who lacks it has zero wealth and therefore cannot buy it from someone who has it. This is an extreme example of how the distribution of wealth can affect resource use, but it is parallel to the example of a price increase that affects resource use via its effect on incomes and, through that effect, on consumer demands.

5. Dworkin states that the example was offered for another purpose; see Dworkin, "Is Wealth a Value?" p. 224, but see ibid., pp. 208–9.

6. Dworkin states "that a theory that makes the moral value of slavery depend on transaction costs is grotesque." Ibid., p. 211. He does not elaborate.

7. An implication of this analysis is that it is possible to speak of efficient rights assignments in premodern, premonetary societies, an issue considered further in chapter 6 of *The Economics of Justice*.

8. Dworkin, "Is Wealth a Value?" p. 211.

9. Ibid., pp. 211–12.

10. Ibid., p. 211.

11. Ibid., p. 218.

12. Ibid.

13. See ibid., p. 220; these theories are discussed in William M. Landes and Richard A. Posner, "Adjudication as a Private Good," *Journal of Legal Studies* 8 (1979): 259–384.

PART FIVE
A Reply by Ronald Dworkin

A Reply by Ronald Dworkin

I am very grateful for all the articles collected in this volume, and have learned from each of them. I cannot hope to reply to—or even acknowledge—all the important points they raise. I have selected issues that seem most relevent to current jurisprudential and political argument.

SOPER

Professor Soper suggests a form of positivism that might simply incorporate all of my claims about legal practice, if they are sound, as refinements. Positivism, on this view, insists that propositions of law, if true, are true in virtue of some social practice specifying their truth conditions. But it does not insist that the truth conditions thus specified cannot include moral conditions. Suppose I am right, for example, that judges characteristically decide hard cases by appealing to principles that are themselves justified as figuring in the best justification of settled law, and that this process of justification includes a moral dimension as I claim. The entire scheme of decision I describe is then itself a social practice, which identifies as true propositions of law supported by the principles that provide the best justification. Suppose two lawyers or judges disagree about some proposition of law because they disagree about some proposition of political morality. They might both be positivists, on this account of positivism, even though each thinks some proposition of law is true which cannot be proved true by appeal to pedigree, and even though each argues that the truth of his proposition depends upon the truth of some principle of morality. They are both positivists because each acknowledges that morality is made relevant by social practice, namely the social practice that I describe.

I do not, of course, wish to debate with Soper about names. I had taken positivism to make two important and related claims that his version of positivism does not make, however, and my quarrel is with these claims, not with a label. The first argues that it is characteristic of a legal system that some more-or-less mechanical test provides necessary and sufficient conditions for the truth of propositions about what the law is, as distinct from propositions about what the law should be. In Chapter 2 of *Taking Rights Seriously* I described this as a test of pedigree distinguished from content; I meant that positivism insists that the tests for law should be matters of social history rather than matters of policy or morality that might be inherently controversial. Hart, for example, describes his rule of recognition, not simply as just another obligation-imposing rule, but as a secondary rule stipulating public features whose presence or absence will be decisive in identifying other rules as legal rules. He says that the acceptance of this sort of secondary rule marks the transition from a pre-legal society to a society with law, because the public features made decisive by the secondary rule will cure the defect of uncertainty latent in pre-legal practice. It is, no doubt, compatible with this picture that the secondary rule may itself contain vague terms, or in some other way include some mild degree of indeterminacy. But a secondary rule that simply referred all issues of obligation directly back to standing social practices of obligation would (as Hart makes plain in his discussion of international law) make no change at all in the *status quo*. Such a secondary rule would introduce no further determinacy and could not mark a transition to anything. These objections would apply *a fortiori,* I would have thought, to a secondary rule of the sort Soper contemplates when he imagines a sovereign who commands only: Do what justice requires.

The important question is not, however, whether Hart or any other particular legal philosopher is committed to the thesis that the test for law must make law reasonably demonstrable. That thesis is connected to a more general theory of law—in particular to a picture of law's function. This is the theory that law provides a settled, public and dependable set of standards for private and official conduct, standards whose force cannot be called into question by some individual official's perception of policy or morality. This theory of law's function acknowledges, as it must, that no set of public rules can be complete or completely precise. But it therefore insists on a distinction between occasions on which the law, so conceived, does dictate a decision and occasions on which, in the language of positivists, the judge must exercise his discretion to make new law just because the law is silent. The distinction is vital, on this view of the law's function, because it is important to acknowledge that when reasonable men can disagree about what the law requires, a judicial decision cannot be a neutral decision of the sort promised in the idea of law. It is more honest to concede that the decision is not, in this case, a decision of law at all.

So the thesis that some more or less mechanical test of pedigree identifies law is in this way connected with a political theory about the point or function of law, and with the theory of judicial discretion that is a necessary part of that theory. The theory I defend, on the contrary, supposes the different and more ambitious function for law I have in various places described. If positivism is relaxed in the way Soper suggests it might be, so as to accommodate the description of legal practices I provide, then the case for orthodox theory about the point of law is correspondingly weakened, and the case for the view I endorse advanced.

The second claim I took positivism to make is also connected with a more general theoretical position that would have to be modified if this claim were abandoned. This second claim is most clearly put in the following way. We may suppose propositions of law to be true or false, accurate or inaccurate, without thereby accepting any ontology beyond an empiricist's ontology. The truth of a proposition of law, when it is true, consists in ordinary historical facts about individual or social behaviour including, perhaps, facts about beliefs and attitudes, but in nothing metaphysically more suspicious. Oliver Wendell Holmes made that claim when he said that law is not a brooding omnipresence in the sky. Positivists need not be reductionist in the *semantic* sense: they need not argue that propositions of law mean the same thing as historical propositions about behavior or beliefs or attitudes. But it is part of their programme (or so I thought) to be reductionist in the weaker sense captured in the claim that the truth conditions of propositions of law do not include anything but such historical conditions.

This claim is, of course, consistent with the causal thesis, plainly true, that beliefs about justice are often causally responsible for the behaviour that constitutes law. Legislators, for example, often enact law because it seems to them just. The claim is also consistent with the different thesis that *beliefs* about justice may be part of the truth conditions of propositions of law. A positivist may hold a theory of statutory interpretation such that, if a statute provides that a contract is invalid when it is unconscionable, and the vast majority of people thinks that a particular sort of contract is unjust, then that sort of contract is, as a matter of law, invalid. This theory makes beliefs about moral facts, not moral facts themselves, decisive for propositions of law. But for a Soper positivist the legal validity of a contract might depend, not on whether a contract is believed to be unjust, but whether it is unjust. That theory *is* inconsistent with the reductionist's claim, because it makes a moral fact itself part of the truth conditions of a proposition of law.

The weak programme of reductionism is not satisfied by showing that propositions of law are sometimes true in virtue of historical facts alone. It must be shown that all the propositions the theory takes to be true are true in virtue of such facts. Soper's positivism cannot claim this. If a social practice makes morality systematically relevant to legal issues (and Soper concedes, *arguendo,* that our own legal system may well do so), then the truth of propositions of law will systematically depend upon the truth of propositions of morality. The truth of the former will consist, at least partially, in the truth of the latter. So the promised ontological separation of law from morals fails. In order to suppose that there are legal facts within such a system, one must suppose that there are moral facts as well.

This explains why Hart's point, that positive law sometimes uses explicit moral language, is not a pocket into which a general theory of law that makes morality systematically relevant, even in the absence of any explicit incorporation, can be dropped. Hart presumably would extend his discussion of the "open texture" of legal languages (which he applies to words like "reasonable") to moral terms that figure in positive law (like the "cruel and unusual" clause of the American Constitution) as well. He would then say that the word "cruel" has a settled core of application in the United States (it applies to the bastinado) but a penumbra of uncertainty (reasonable men and women differ whether capital punishment is in itself cruel). When a case (like *Furman* v. *Georgia*) falls within the penumbra, then a judge must exercise his own discretion to decide, though his decision thereafter extends the core of the concept for legal purposes.

This analysis of the role of moral language in legal provisions is entirely consistent with the weak reductionist programme I described. It makes the truth of the proposition of law, that the bastinado is unconstitutional, consist in beliefs that it is cruel. But it could not be extended to cover the theory of adjudication I describe. Suppose, however, that my understanding is wrong, and that Hart would reject this analysis of moral language in law. Suppose he would say that whether capital punishment is unconstitutional depends entirely on whether it is, as a matter of moral fact, cruel, and not just on whether it is sufficiently widely believed to be so, or on whether some judge, in the exercise of his discretion, so decides. (We should then wonder why he did not offer a parallel analysis of all "open texture" language and shrink the role of judicial discretion accordingly.) But if this is a sensible distinction, and if propositions about the constitutionality of punishment can be true, then there must be (to put the point in an old-fashioned way) an objective realm of moral facts. I had thought it was part of Hart's ambition (and of the ambition of positivists generally) to make the objective standing of propositions of law independent of any controversial theory either of meta-ethics or of moral ontology.

Hart would not need to accept an objective realm of facts about cruelty, of course, if he did not insist that propositions about capital punishment can be true in the way in which propositions that do not depend upon the correct understanding of moral language can be true. He might say that, once the Constitution has made the constitutionality of punishment depend upon its cruelty, then all such claims, taken literally, are either false or neither true nor false.[1] But that is a plausible extension of Hart's general theory (if at all) only on the assumption that the use of moral language is an occasional, rather than a systematic, feature of familiar legal systems. If my account of our own legal practice is right, and Hart sought to embrace that account within his own system in this way, he would end by saying that, for us, hardly any propositions at all are true. In any case the marriage of the two theories, which Soper contemplates, would be dissolved by that last radical claim.

Conceptual or descriptive?

Soper raises another interesting issue at the beginning of his essay. He distinguishes conceptual theories of law from descriptive theories. He says that the positivist's theory is conceptual and my theory descriptive, for the following reason. Positivists make a claim that holds good (if they are right) for all legal systems, not simply as a matter of generalization, but as a matter of necessity. I make claims, on the other hand, about a particular legal system only. I argue that the characteristic practice of judges in our own legal system does not fit the positivist's account of what all legal systems must be like. If I am right, then the positivist's claim, which is universal, must be wrong. But it does not follow that my description is therefore true of any legal system but our own. So my position must be descriptive while theirs is conceptual.

I am glad that Soper raised this issue, because I am often asked whether I mean my theory to be conceptual like positivism, or descriptive only. Do I mean to offer a general theory of what law must be like, or only a better account of one particular version of law? I do not, I am afraid, understand the force of the distinction in this context. The positivist's theory of law is surely conceptual in some sense. But in what sense? Does Soper think that the positivist's theory (that propositions of law cannot be true in virtue of morality) is a linguistic theory about the "standard" or "ordinary language" use of the word "legal" or "law." On that interpretation, the positivist claims that it follows from the way "legal" is used that a legal right simply cannot depend on moral facts in the way I argue it can, just as someone else might say that it follows from the way "sister" is used that a sister cannot be a man. But if I produce an alleged counterexample—if I produce an instance of a legal right that I say is a legal right in virtue of a moral right—then my claim must *also* be a linguistic one. I must claim that the word "legal" is properly used in such a way as to include this case. My claim is as much linguistic as his, though it may be more guarded. It cannot be "merely" descriptive—or merely about the facts of the one case cited as a counterexample—the way that a counterexample to an empirical generalization can be. Suppose I claimed to have found a male sister, and thus to have produced a counterexample to the claim that, as a matter of linguistic usage, sisters cannot be men. I do not simply claim to have discovered a new non-linguistic fact which refutes a linguistic theory. Unless I show the linguistic theory to be *linguistically* incorrect, I cannot have found the fact I say I have found. Suppose I found a man whom the speech-community was in the habit (knowing him to be a man) of calling a sister. If I cite him as a counterexample, I do so because I take this linguistic practice to be part of the practice that provides the correct use of "sister." That is a point about the correct use of a word, not simply about the facts of an isolated case. If positivism is conceptual because it is linguistic, and if my theory provides even one counterexample, then my theory must be conceptual because linguistic as well.

I put the matter hypothetically, because I do not accept that positivism is a theory about linguistic practice. (There is no standard use of the words "legal" or "law" to which the positivist can appeal. In any case, he does not rely on dictionary definitions nor statistics of linguistic usage in his arguments.) But in what other sense shall we understand the positivist to be making a conceptual claim rather than simply a descriptive generalization? If the positivist merely said that, in every country or political subdivision he has studied, legal rights are not taken to be established by moral arguments, and that he therefore believes that they are never taken to be established in that way, then his claim would not seem to be conceptual at all. Someone may suggest that positivism is conceptual because it *proposes* that legal concepts should be used in a certain way, for clarity or convenience or for some political motive. But if positivism is simply hortatory in that way, and if my theory does produce a "counterexample" in our own legal system, then this must be because I have shown that competing and better motives recommend contrary usage of these concepts. If so, then I must be relying on some theory about desirable conceptual divisions of the same sort as the theory on which he relies, though my theory may not be as articulate as his. Once again, if his theory is properly called conceptual because hortatory, so is mine.

I speak hypothetically, again, because I think it misunderstands positivism just as much to say that it is hortatory as to say that it is linguistic. Theories of law are conceptual, but not in either of these ways. The concepts of law and legal right are contested concepts. Positivism defends a particular conception, and I have tried to defend a competing conception of these concepts. We disagree about what legal rights are in much the same way as philosophers who argue about justice disagree about what justice is. I concentrate on the details of a particular legal system with which I am especially familiar, not simply to show that positivism provides a poor account of that system, but to show that positivism provides a poor conception of the concept of a legal right. My argument is not that positivism is wrong as an account of our legal system though it might be right in its account of other legal systems as, for example, some historian might argue that a particular theory about the causes of war is wrong in its explanation of the War of the Austrian Succession though it might be right about several other wars.

The analogy to arguments about the concept of justice is useful. Suppose someone argues against utilitarian theories of justice by showing that these theories fail to explain why slavery is unjust in some actual or imaginary situation in which slavery in fact maximises utility. He might concede that in other actual or imaginary situations slavery is counter-utilitarian, but his argument is meant to show that even then slavery is not unjust *because* it is counter-utilitarian. He intends to show that utilitarianism is not a satisfactory conception of justice; if that is right, *nothing* is unjust simply in virtue of being counter-utilitarian. My argument has the same ambition. I appeal to complex, modern legal systems to show that since, in these systems, the truth of a proposition about legal rights may consist in some moral fact, the positivist conception of legal rights must be a poor one. I conclude that we must abandon the positivist conception in favor of a different conception of the sort I describe. This conception makes the institutional practice and history of each jurisdiction relevant to the truth of propositions about legal rights, though not necessarily decisive. It follows that in some jurisdictions legal rights are sharply at variance with any defensible background political morality. They hold, in spite of this variance, by institutional fiat. This is not, however, because positivism provides a good conception of legal rights for these jurisdictions, but rather because the right conception yields that conclusion there.

COLEMAN

I agree with Professor Coleman that what he calls negative positivism—the theory that legal systems can be imagined whose members do not think that moral claims figure among the truth conditions for propositions of law—is a trivial theory, and that what he calls the hard facts version of positivism is a false theory. He describes a form of positivism different from both which he calls law-as-convention. This holds that the authority of law everywhere depends on a fundamental convention of some sort, even though it may be controversial, in some legal systems, exactly what the fundamental convention requires in particular cases. The convention might be very abstract. It might stipulate that law is whatever justice requires, in which case judges will have to rely on moral principle to decide particular cases. But their warrant for doing so will then be the convention that law depends on justice.

This is, I think, much the same suggestion that Professor Soper made in his essay. But Coleman supplies a rather different form of argument. He says there is a difference between controversy about what the reigning convention, properly understood, really is, and controversy about what follows from the reigning convention, and he seems to think that controversy of the former sort poses a greater problem for law-as-convention. This is a doubtful distinction. If American judges disagree about whether they have the power to overrule congressional statutes they deem offensive to the Constitution, then we might report this disagreement in either of two ways. We might say either that they disagree about whether there is a convention that they have that power, or that they agree on a more abstract convention to the effect that judges have all but only the powers given to them by the best interpretation of the constitution, but disagree about whether it follows from that more abstract convention that they have the particular power in question. Neither their judicial nor their linguistic behavior would force us to choose one rather than the other of these descriptions.

If I am right, then this reveals the sovereign weakness in the idea of law-as-convention, at least as Coleman pictures it. That thesis can answer any apparent counterexample, which shows judges disagreeing at some fundamental level about what counts as law, by supposing some more abstract convention of the sort I just described. Hart, Raz, and other contemporary positivists rightly reject this strategy. It leaves legal positivism too close to the trivial theory that in every legal system officials accept the requirement that they must make their decisions about the law in the way such decisions ought to be made. Law-as-convention therefore seems caught in the following difficulty. It must stipulate some interesting level of concreteness that any convention must have if it is to count as the fundamental legal convention of a community. But if it then offers the universal claim, that every legal system displays a convention at that level of concreteness, this claim is false, as Coleman seems to recognize. And if it offers only the existential claim, that some legal systems provide conventions of that sort, it is only negative positivism back again.

Coleman confirms this second danger by the examples he offers of the kind of convention he has in mind. A community might develop the convention that no principle is to be used in legal reasoning unless it has been mentioned in the preamble or statutes or in committee reports, and that each principle is to be assigned a weight which depends on the number of times it has been mentioned there. Or that judges must decide hard cases by flipping a coin. The claim that such systems are conceivable is no more than the thesis of negative positivism. It says only that "there exists at least one conceivable rule of recognition (and therefore one possible legal system) that does not specify truth as a moral principle among the truth conditions for any proposition of law." And since I agree with Coleman that this is uninteresting, I have no reason to argue whether we should call the particular systems he imagines "legal systems." I shall make briefer comments on a number of other points raised by Coleman's essay.

1. I agree that the failure of the social rule theory to account for all cases of rights and duties does not entail that it cannot account for legal rights and obligations. I said only that the failure of the social rule theory to account for all rights removes one argument that it accounts for legal rights.

2. Positivism is not self-defeating if it offers a general political theory as an argument why we should adopt a conception of law that makes the truth value of *particular* propositions of law independent of moral or political theory. On the contrary, since theories of law cannot sensibly be understood as linguistic analyses, or neutral accounts of social practice, I can think of no way to defend positivism or any other theory of law except by appeal to political morality.

3. Coleman's discussion of my arguments in "Hard Cases," from which he draws the conclusion that I am myself more of a conventionalist than I recognize, fails to notice the difference between the following two questions: (1) What is the best political theory and the ideal legal system?; and (2) What is the best justification that can be provided for the actual legal system we have? The question I put to Hercules is the latter. I ask him to compose the best justification that can be provided for the community's actual legal history. Though this question is different from the former question, it also engages the moral convictions of any judge who tries to answer it, because two judges, with different background moralities, will offer different sets of principles as the best possible justification of their own legal history. Of course each might be forced to recognize, in the justification he provides, principles for which he himself has little enthusiasm, and he might be forced to assign more or less weight to principles he does accept than the weight his ideal theory would assign. But since different sets of principles will be consistent with legal history, the question of which of these provides the best justification of that history will be a matter of moral judgment.

LYONS

In my view any theory of law, including positivism, is based in the end on some particular normative political theory. Professor Lyons is skeptical about this claim. He agrees that some positivists provide political arguments for their positivism: Bentham, for example, and Raz. But he thinks that other positivists believe that law is a matter of social fact, not because this is in some way desirable but just because that is how things happen to be. He cites Hart as an example, and says that "Hart does not embrace the wider concept of law [according to which immoral laws are nevertheless law] on the ground that law would better serve its purpose if it were that way."

But in fact Hart says (in just the pages Lyons cites):

> Plainly we cannot grapple adequately with this issue if we see it as one concerning the proprieties of linguistic usage. For what really is at stake is the comparative merit of a wider and a narrower concept or way of classifying rules generally effective in social life. If we are to make a reasoned choice between these concepts it must be because one is superior to the other in the way in which it will assist our theoretical inquiries, or advance and clarify our moral deliberations, or both.

Hart's main argument for the "wider" concept is that it facilitates thinking and acting correctly in cases of moral conflict, because it "offers no disguise for the choice between evils which, in extreme circumstances, may have to be made." This is not the language of someone who thinks that the concept of law just happens to be either a wide or a narrow concept.

This passage argues against Lyons's claim that Hart takes "the essential nature of law" to be "given." But Hart seems to be relying, here, not on any particular political theory, about how law ought to function, but only on some hypothesis about how to think clearly about the issues he mentions. So this is no evidence for my thesis either, that even positivists must rely, in the end, on a normative political theory. I would point, instead, to Hart's discussion, much earlier in the same book, of the inadequacies of any system of political organization that uses only what Hart calls primary rules.[2] Such a system, he says, would suffer from certain specific defects: the rules would be uncertain, static, and inefficient. He develops his own account of the main elements of law by showing how the device of a secondary rule of recognition responds to these particular defects by making possible a new set of rules that are flexible, efficient, and certain. This, I believe, does support my suggestion about the political basis of positivism. If Hart had identified a different set of defects in the primitive system—if he had pointed to the fact that a regime of primary social rules would provide no forum for testing whether these rules reflected any coherent set of principles about the rights and obligations the state should enforce—he would, I think, have been led to a rather different account of developed legal systems.

But I certainly do not mean to claim that all the leading positivists understood that their arguments were based in some political theory about the proper functioning of legal institutions. Many of them would have rejected my suggestion, perhaps indignantly. In spite of his later disavowal, which I just quoted, Hart begins his book suggesting that he intends it to be a certain kind, at least, of linguistic study, though he is quick to add, in the spirit of J. L. Austin, that this does not mean that it is not also an essay in descriptive sociology. I believe that many positivists did not understand their own arguments, or at least that we must understand these arguments differently if we are to make sense and use of them.

For how could the social fact theory of law "just happen" to be right, as things in fact are, in the way Lyons has in mind? It is very implausible to suppose that this theory is true "analytically" just in virtue of the meaning of the word "law." For the long jurisprudential debate establishes, if nothing else, that someone who takes up a controversial view about which criminal procedures are invalid under the Constitution, before the Supreme Court has decided the issue, is not guilty of self-contradiction even though he may be wrong. And in what other way might the social fact theory "just happen" to be true, other than in virtue of linguistic rules?

Much of what I said in my reply to Soper is pertinent here as well. The concept of law functions within our legal culture as a contested concept. It is, in that respect at least, like the concept of justice. We do not think of two theories of justice—a contract theory and a utilitarian theory—as each trying to discover the correct linguistic rules, established in linguistic conventions of some sort, about when political claims are true analytically or by definition. Rawls and Hare do not disagree about the correct way to talk, but about what should or should not be done. Justice is a contested concept because it provides a focus for disagreement about a certain range of issues, not a repository for what has already been agreed.

The concept of law must be understood on the same model. So none but the most trivial theory of law could possibly be understood as an account of the linguistic conventions governing that concept's use. Theories of law—positivism and its competitors—are conceptions of that concept in the way that theories of justice are conceptions of justice. Of course it does not follow, just from the bare fact that the concept of law is a contested concept, that it is a political concept. Beauty, after all, is a contested concept, but not necessarily a political one. Law is a political concept not just because it is contested but because of the way it is contested. It takes its sense from its use: from the contexts of debates about what the law is, and from what turns on which view is accepted. And all this is deeply, densely political. So until someone suggests a different point to our legal practices—a point that makes such practice innocent of political theory—we would do well to look for the deep sources of important theories of law in some assumptions of political morality, about how judges should in general or in principle decide cases, for example, or about what social functions we should call upon our legal institutions to perform. I have tried, in the places Lyons cites, to do this for positivism, and my success does not depend on whether positivists consciously embraced the political basis I attribute to them. It would be wiser to ask how far this basis, if we accepted it, would justify the conception of law they set out.

Lyons also questions another suggestion I have made. I believe there are reasons of fairness why the principles presupposed by past legal decisions should be applied in future decisions of the same community as well. He agrees that fairness argues in this direction in communities whose past decisions are in the main reasonably fair. But he is doubtful that any argument of fairness holds if the past decisions have been largely wicked or grossly unfair. Lyons does not develop his views in this essay, but Hart makes a related point in a recent expansion of an earlier essay about legal and moral obligation,[3] and I shall discuss Hart's arguments in the context of Lyons's doubts.

I argue that legal rights are genuine rights: they supply what might be called a moral kind of reason for a judicial decision. I use the awkward construction "a moral kind of reason" rather than "a moral reason" to avoid confusion. We sometimes use the word "moral" to contrast what we call moral rights with legal rights: we say (for example) that though someone has a moral right to the aid of his neighbors in certain circumstances, he has no legal right to it. I have tried, on various occasions, to explain the force of this contrast; in particular I have tried to show that it is a distinction between rights of different kinds, from different sources, both of which are nevertheless genuine rights because they both provide reasons for action that rest, in the end, on moral considerations. Legal rights are different from the rights we call moral, when we have that distinction in mind, because legal rights are rights based in the political history and decisions of the community and have special institutional force against judges in litigation. But legal and "moral" rights are nevertheless species of a common genus: they are both, in the broader sense I described, creatures of morality.

The distinction between legal and moral rights nevertheless accounts for a familiar phenomenon. A judge's duty to enforce a legal right might under certain circumstances conflict with a moral duty not to enforce it; this is a conflict between two kinds of rights, both based in considerations of morality, and under some extreme circumstances it would be proper for a judge to resolve the conflict by allowing the legal right to be overridden by the moral right, even though, for practical reasons, this might require him actually to lie by denying that any legal right exists.

Hart, following Bentham, disagrees with this account of the connection between moral and political rights. He insists that legal rights are more profoundly different from moral rights. He denies that both are species of a common genus and that legal rights in themselves offer reasons of a moral kind for a judicial or any other kind of decision. He says that someone may have a legal right when there is *no* reason, not even a weak and easily overridden reason, why judges should enforce or officials should respect that reason, and he gives the familiar example of a wicked legal system like Nazi Germany, in which he believes that people had legal rights that were in no sense rights based in considerations of political morality.

He argues against my view with uncharacteristic vehemence. He says my view is incoherent, based on last resort arguments, and hopeless. But these attacks, I think, can be attributed to his wholly mistaken view of my reasons for thinking that legal rights are grounded in political morality. Let me explain, through an imaginary case, what he thinks my main argument is. Imagine that the Reichstag in Nazi Germany has enacted a variety of statutes discriminating against Jews including, for example, a confiscatory law purporting to award the property of certain Jews to certain aryans. Hart thinks I am committed to recognizing that the best justification of Nazi law must then contain the principle that Jews are less worthy than aryans. Suppose I do accept that,[4] and also that the aryans named in the confiscatory law have a legal right to the property of Jews assigned to them. How can I say that these legal rights are in any way grounded in moral considerations, or that there can be a moral kind of reason for enforcing them, even a weak one that is overridden by competing moral considerations?

My main argument, Hart thinks, is this: since the bad principle that Jews are less worthy than aryans figures in the best justification available for the Nazi legal system, it becomes a good principle or at least a sufficiently good principle to supply some moral reason for enforcing the legal rights of aryans under the confiscatory statute. Hart, properly, has nothing but contempt for that argument. How can a bad principle become a reason for action, even a weak reason, simply because it is the best that can be said, by way of justification, for wicked deeds? But I am mystified why he should think that this *is* my argument.

He has, I think, confused my account of how legal rights are identified, in hard cases, with my reasons for thinking that legal rights, once identified, have some claim to be enforced in court. He thinks that whatever principles I say figure in the process that identifies legal rights must be the very principles I believe provide the moral argument for respecting those rights. Of course that would be a great confusion, as we can see by considering not legal rights but rights in virtue of a promise. Suppose *A* promises *B* that *A* will fire *C*, who has had a quarrel with *B*, and a dispute later arises about the correct interpretation of *A*'s promise. (Was it a tacit assumption that *A* would inflict the injury only if he discovered, after investigation, that *B* was in the right in his quarrel with *C*, or did *A* in effect promise to injure *C* without regard to the merits of that quarrel?) If we are asked to arbitrate we might decide that the promise was made out of a particular conception of the duties of friendship, which requires support in a quarrel right or wrong, and that it should be interpreted in that light. But if we thought that *A* had any reason to keep the promise so interpreted, even a weak one, we would be relying on the morality of promise-keeping, not on this conception of friendship that we might ourselves find unattractive and unworthy.

I do not make that mistake, and I am puzzled why Hart should think I have. Nothing in any argument I make suggests it. But what then are my reasons for thinking that bad laws can create genuine rights? What are the analogues, in law, to the reasons that might make us think that bad promises should be kept? Suppose some aryan named in the confiscatory statute brings an action in trespass against the particular Jew from whom "his" property was taken. The judge must decide whether to enforce this bad statute. If he is morally sensitive, he will see moral reasons for ignoring it, and for lying if a lie would be successful. But what arguments might he have, to set against these moral arguments, for enforcing it?

He might reason in this way. "The officials of this community on the whole accept and enforce the rights and duties the Reichstag announces, and the people are therefore publicly encouraged to make their plans and decisions on that basis. In fact the people themselves accept the Reichstag's decisions and the executive orders made by other officials about who must go to the front, who may have ration tickets, and so forth. For that reason my decision is more complex, more a matter of choosing between conflicting principle, than if the confiscatory statute had never been passed. If the people accept the burdens of a particular process, they have some claim to the benefits of decisions reached under that process as well. Of course it does not follow that this or any other statute enacted by the Nazi regime should actually be enforced. In this case there are very strong, perhaps compelling, moral reasons of a different sort for refusing to enforce the statute if I can manage this."

A judge might find, that is, just in the fact that the Nazi regime is an operating political system which enjoys the respect and compliance of officials and citizens alike, enough to force him to acknowledge that the aryan plaintiff has at least some weak case in political morality for what he asks. This is not the argument Hart describes as my "last resort" argument. He thinks I mean to argue that if the confiscatory statute has been enforced before, in favor of some other aryan, the plaintiff in later cases can appeal to the moral principle that like cases should be treated alike, and he replies that this argument would be unavailable on the occasion of the first enforcement of the statute. But the argument I am now considering does not depend on the fact that the particular statute in question has been enforced before, but on the very different and more general political situation I described, that the central power of the community has been administered through an articulate constitutional structure the citizens have been encouraged to obey and treat as a source of rights and duties, and that the citizens as a whole have in fact done so.

Hart is in a very bad position to object to this more general argument. He argues, remember, that what he calls the "wider" concept of law should be chosen, and so "immoral" laws nevertheless counted as law, precisely because "to withhold legal recognition from iniquitous rules may grossly oversimplify the variety of moral issues to which they give rise." We cannot capture the moral complexity of the challenge Nazi law presented to judges, Hart says, if we do not acknowledge that the bad law was nevertheless a law. But this can be so—a bad law can make a situation morally more complex—only if the bad law *affects* the moral situation, and the confiscatory statute cannot have affected the situation morally unless the right it gave the aryan was some kind of moral right. Hart is therefore in a kind of dilemma here. If he agrees that the confiscatory statute gave the plaintiff some weak claim of a moral kind, based just in the fact that the plaintiff's community and officials accept the decisions of the Reichstag as reasons for action, then he undercuts his complaint against me. But if he denies that the statute gave the plaintiff any claim at all of that sort, then he undercuts his argument why we should say that it gave the plaintiff a legal right.

I have been describing an argument a judge might accept why his decision must be a choice between conflicting principles of morality. I do not mean that a judge must accept an argument of that kind whenever the bulk of the people regard some atrocious political regime as legitimate or accept its commands as rights and duties. For the question whether a particular history gives rise to even a minimal moral right that the dictates of those in power be enforced is, obviously, a moral question, and different officials might answer it differently. My point is rather that the question of whether a statute gives rise to legal rights is just that moral question, so that a judge who denies that the confiscatory statute provides even a weak reason for deciding for the aryan plaintiff has no reason to say that the statute creates any legal rights at all. We need the idea of a legal right, which someone might have in virtue of a bad law, in order to express the conflict between two grounds of political rights that might sometimes conflict: in order to express the idea that the community's political history often provides an independent ground for a moral argument that may compete with, though it may fall before, other moral arguments that are disconnected from that history. But the concept of legal right can serve that useful purpose only if we do not use it when we mean to *deny* that this independent ground is in fact available, when we mean to assert that the case presents no moral conflict at all.

If we want to define the terms of our jurisprudence so as to illuminate the structure of complex political decisions, we must be careful not to break the connection between legal and moral rights entirely. But suppose Hart were to turn his back on his own counsel, and now insist that the aryan plaintiff just *does* have a legal right, in the nature of the case, even though that right presents no moral reason at all for deciding in his favor. We are suddenly in the peculiar world of legal essentialism. Why does the plaintiff just, in the nature of the case, have a legal right? It cannot be in virtue of the linguistic rules governing the phrase "legal right." The concept of a legal right is a contested concept, and therefore is not governed by necessary and sufficient conditions laid down in linguistic rules. What other reason might legal philosophy provide? I can think of none. A theory of legal right makes sense only as a theory of when there is at least some minimal ground, in political history, for a political decision honoring the supposed right.

I should like to take this occasion to make a more general point about the role of immoral laws and wicked legal systems in contemporary jurisprudence. It is a mistake to turn, as legal philosophers so often do, to Nazi Germany and other tyrannies as a crucial test of any theory about the connection between moral and legal rights. For this assumes that it is (in Lyons's phrase) somehow given, pre-analytically, whether people in Nazi Germany had legal rights and obligations or not, so that we can reject out of hand any theory that gives an answer contrary to what we "know" about that situation. But this is not given; on the contrary we need a theory of legal rights in order to decide whether there were legal rights there. Wicked legal systems should be treated, that is, like hard cases that turn on which conception of law is best rather than easy cases whose proper resolution we already know and can therefore use to test any particular conception for adequacy. (They are not very important hard cases, from the practical point of view, because the judgments we make about foreign wicked legal systems are rarely hinged to decisions we have to take.)

If Hart were able to convince me that it follows, from my opinions about law and legal rights generally, that no one in Germany had any legal rights at all, I would change my opinion on the latter issue, not give up some important feature of those opinions, like the crucial idea that legal rights must be understood as species of moral rights. (Of course I could do that while still maintaining that some unjust laws are still laws.) I do not mean that I am dogmatic about the connection between moral and legal rights, or that I hold the positions I do as an article of faith, but only that I accept them for broader reasons that would not be shaken by the discovery that it commits me to changing my mind about what to say about certain historical events.

RAZ

Dr. Raz's new postscript makes two main points.[5] First, that the arguments I have made against various forms of legal positivism, since "the Model of Rules" was first published in 1969, do not rely on the distinction I made in that article between rules and principles, or on the argument I constructed using that distinction. Second, that my new arguments are more ambitious because they try to show that legal positivism misdescribes the character of legal argument even in "easy" cases, when lawyers and judges agree what the outcome must be because the case falls under some established and unchallenged rule of law. I accept both these comments, but I do not think they entail the break or change in my views Raz supposes.

I introduced the distinction between rules and principles in the following way.[6] Rules bind in an all-or-nothing fashion, while principles argue in favor of a decision, but not necessarily conclusively, so that someone does not abandon a principle in recognizing that it is not absolute. I used this distinction in my original argument. I said that one thesis characteristic of positivism—that all the legal standards of a community can be identified by some master rule or test accepted by at least the bulk of officials in that community—might seem plausible so long as we fix our attention only on legal rules. Rules depend so heavily on canonical language that they are almost invariably produced by a discrete and self-conscious act of legislation by some institution whose power depends on general acceptance of its legitimacy. The master rules that different positivists have suggested are typically rules bestowing law-making authority on institutions of that sort, so that if we set out to test the thesis that law is only what a master test identifies as law, and look only to standards that act as rules, we may think that experience confirms the thesis. But once we see that judges appeal to other kinds of standards, of the sort I called principles, then the thesis will fall unless it can be defended in one of two ways. Either those principles that are not rules must be shown to be not legal standards at all, but only extra-legal standards to which judges turn in the exercise of some discretion, or they must be shown to be captured by some master test or rule after all, in spite of first appearances. My article suggested that neither of these defenses could succeed.

It would be, I said, arbitrary to refuse to consider the kinds of principles I described as legal standards. This exclusion could be justified only on the circular ground that these principles are not captured in a master rule accepted by the vast bulk of officials. Nor can we find any single master rule, accepted by the great majority of legal officials, that identifies all and only those principles to which judges have appealed in argument. If we try to compose such a master rule, we will end with the vacuous rule that judges must enforce, as principles of law, those principles of justice which are appropriate in legal argument. That vacuous rule, I said, concedes the failure of the master rule thesis.

The distinction between rules and principles plays an important part in this argument, but only to direct attention to the existence of the standards that are different from what we ordinarily think of as legal rules. So the argument is unaffected by any quarrel about the exact character of the distinction, or whether principles can be said to be a kind of rule or rules a kind of principle. If judges characteristically use standards like those I offered as examples of principles, then my argument remains to be answered even by a positivist who rejects my account of the logical differences between these and more familiar kinds of rules.

The discussion, happily, has moved on. Dr. Raz, so far as I know, is the only defender of positivism who has taken up the first defense of the master rule thesis I had suggested. He refuses to call any standard "law" unless it meets what he calls the "sources" test. He does not deny that judges often appeal to principles which have not been established in any prior act of legislation, and that judges treat these principles as grounded, not in any social fact about the history of the community, but in political morality. But exactly for that reason he denies these principles the title of law, and insists that judges who appeal to them are appealing to extra-legal sources, whose existence in no way threatens the master rule test, which is a test for legal not extra-legal sources. Raz offers no argument *why* these principles are not part of "the law," except the circular argument that they do not meet the sources test and therefore fail the test of a master rule.

The other lawyers who have defended the master rule test against my argument have tried the second line of defense I suggested. They argue that we can construct a suitably sophisticated master rule, which almost every official in our own legal community does accept, and which captures just those principles on which our judges do rely in legal argument. Or at least that we can construct such a rule if we allow moral criteria to figure in its content. (They argue, in fact, that I have myself supplied such a master rule in my description of the process a mythical judge, Hercules, would use in deciding hard cases.) I consider this argument in my reply to Soper and Coleman, in this volume, and suggest that this strategy withdraws rather than defends the master rule thesis.

So I resist Raz's suggestion that I have altered the "weaponry" of my earlier argument. The distinction between logical types of standards plays the role it did, but that role is merely to identify troublesome standards which can be described in other ways by those who reject my distinction. I accept Raz's second suggestion, that my criticism of positivism is now broader in scope than it was earlier, because I have added other arguments. But he joins an important criticism to this suggestion. He says it is now apparent that a further claim I make—that judges do not have discretion to decide cases either way whenever settled rules of law have run out—is the premise rather than the result of my arguments.

He makes clear, in the new postscript, what he thinks the "discretion" argument is about. He says that judges have discretion whenever they are required, by the law, to appeal to extra-legal standards, so that the issue of discretion is just the issue whether the word "law" should be used to describe all the standards judges have a duty to enforce or only the smaller set of such standards which meet the "sources" test. This threatens to make the question of discretion entirely verbal because we can use the word "law" the way Raz would like, in which case judges by definition would have discretion when established rules do not decide a case, but we can also use the word in a wider sense, in which case they would not necessarily have discretion in such cases. I think Raz's use is arbitrary because it does not represent ordinary usage and is pointless as a stipulative recommendation. But he is entitled to use the word as he wishes, and I would have no interest in the question of discretion if this were merely a question which stipulative definition we should accept of the word "law."

I am interested in a more important issue; whether litigants can ever be said to be entitled to a particular decision in their favor, in virtue of the history of legal practice, when established legal rules have run out. Judges have discretion, in the strong sense I distinguished, when neither party has a right to win in virtue of this history, and the judge is therefore free to decide in whatever way he believes would be best or most fair for the future, all things considered. It is an important question, for both the theory and practice of adjudication, whether judges have discretion in this strong sense whenever their decision is not dictated by rules. I mean my arguments in favor of the "rights thesis" to be arguments that they do not, and I do not simply assume, as Raz suggests, that I am right.

Raz says that someone who accepts the "sources" thesis may also accept the "rights" thesis, and may in fact think that in every case one or another party is entitled to a decision in his or its favor. If that is so, and the "sources" thesis allows that these rights may include rights grounded in past legal practice, then that thesis is less interesting than might first appear. It is not the substantive thesis that litigants only have rights of this sort when particular institutions have decided they do or there is some explicit custom to that effect. It is only the linguistic thesis that for some reason their rights should not be called "legal" rights unless they have been established in this particular way. I do not think that the classical texts of legal positivism should be read to make only that tepid point. I think they are, in fact, best understood as making the important substantive claim this disavows, and which I have been arguing against.

I should mention, finally, Raz's comment, in his postscript, that in "Hard Cases" I seem to have endorsed the idea I elsewhere challenge, that there is such a thing as "the law," meaning a discrete set of principles and other standards that alone is relevant in determining the decisions people are entitled to have from courts. I do not think that "Hard Cases" endorses that idea. Hercules will have a set of opinions about the rights any litigant will have before him, which he will work out in the way I described. But he will do this, as Raz says, by applying his general background morality to the interpretation of legal history, to find the best justification of that history, and this means that he will not have a distinct set of principles, which he identifies for himself as legal principles, separate from the rest of his background morality, which alone is involved in those calculations.

GREENAWALT

Professor Greenawalt rejects my suggestion that judges characteristically decide hard civil law cases on grounds of principle rather than policy. He also rejects my claim that they should do so. I replied at great length in *Taking Rights Seriously*[7] and I will not repeat here what I said there. I will, however, try to report some of the more important arguments in what I now think is a simpler and more direct way. I do not mean to abandon any of the arguments I made in *Taking Rights Seriously,* and those interested in Greenawalt's article should therefore look at the longer reply there.

A judge might ask himself two different questions in an ordinary civil action. "Does the plaintiff, all things considered, have a right to what he asks?" This is the question of principle. "Will it make the community better off as a whole if I decide for the plaintiff?" That is the question of policy. Either question will engage the political convictions of any judge who tries to answer it, but the convictions they engage will be different. The question of principle appeals to the judge's theory of legal rights, which in turn draws on his theory about the personal or "moral" rights members of the community have against one another and the political rights they have against the various officials of the community, including him. The question of policy draws on his convictions about the ideal society and the best strategy for reaching that ideal.

Could these two questions be the same question for some particular judge? Yes, if he thinks that the only "moral" rights and duties people have are exactly the legal rights and duties the wisest and fairest legislator would choose to lay down for the future. This "policy" theory of moral rights and duties is not actually incoherent. But it is very implausible. Consider what it would require of people in day-to-day life. Suppose some recondite economic argument, drawing on the very latest empirical data and technical analysis, suggests that the best solution to the pollution problem lies in a zoning scheme splitting a city in two roughly equal parts, each of which now contains neighborhoods and areas very like the other. Within one zone no one will be allowed to emit any smoke or other pollutant whatsoever; within the other anyone may pollute to his heart's (or balance sheet's) content. According to the policy theory of morality, everyone who happened to live in the zone that would be pollution-free under the ideal scheme, for whatever complex economic and meteorological reasons, would already have a moral duty not to burn leaves, and every person in the other zone a moral right to build a sulphuric acid factory in his garden. This is implausible, among other reasons, because it proposes a scheme of moral rights and duties that not even the most conscientious agents could employ in their individual decisions about what to do to or demand from others.

Still, if a judge did hold the policy theory of moral rights, however implausible it seems to us, there might be no practical difference, for him, between the question of principle and the question of policy. He would ask the second question (we might say) in order to answer the first. His decisions would not contradict but on the contrary tend to confirm my suggestion that judges decide hard cases on grounds of principle. But of course most judges, like most people, would reject the policy theory of rights, which is why my suggestion has practical importance. If a judge who *rejects* that theory nevertheless decides cases by constructing and then retrospectively applying the rule he thinks best for the future, this counts as a counterexample, and if such judges very often decide cases this way, then I am wrong.

We must now notice a different moral theory, however, which is much more plausible than the policy theory of rights, but looks rather like it. When no clear rule of law or established custom has settled the question whether or how much some one may pollute the community's air, people all have a duty to pollute no more than is fair and reasonable, and what is fair and reasonable depends on a comparison of the benefits someone would forego (for himself or others) if he did not pollute with the harm he would cause to others if he did, as these contrasting benefits and harms would be judged by a reasonably conscientious and informed person in his position. The "comparative harm" theory of moral rights and duties (from which this maxim about pollution is drawn) has a much more limited range than the policy theory, and is not open to the most obvious objections against it. It is, in fact, a theory that has very wide appeal and substantial basis in the popular morality of modern communities.

If we assume that many judges accept some version of the comparative harm theory, then the cases Greenawalt calls to our attention (and those I had myself mentioned in the articles he criticises) no longer seem likely counterexamples. Of course judges who accept that theory of moral rights would have to consider harms and benefits in order to decide nuisance cases on grounds of principle. They would nevertheless recognize a difference between the following two questions: (1) What concrete rights did this defendant and this plaintiff have in virtue of the comparative harm theory, given all the facts and the knowledge and opinion available to them? and (2) Which legal rules about pollution would, in fact, be in the best interests of the community as a whole in the long run?

We have already noticed one difference: the second question invites information and analysis of a sort and level ruled out by the first. But there are other differences, brought to light when we realize that no remotely plausible answer to the first could depend on the zoning arrangement we had decided might be the best answer to the second. For even if everyone, acting privately, had reason to think that some zoning system would be desirable from the standpoint of overall collective welfare, no one could have any adequate basis for deciding that the ideal pollution-free zone would either exclude or embrace him. Too much would depend here on exactly the kind of information about all the costs of drawing the line one place or another that is ruled out by the question of principle; in any case the exact line drawn would be to some extent arbitrary anyway. The latter point is irrelevant to the question of policy. The best solution for the future requires drawing some line, and drawing a somewhat arbitrary line is better than drawing none. But just the fact that any line would be arbitrary blocks the argument that anyone has, before the actual line is drawn, a moral duty to behave as if that line had, in fact, been drawn already.

This is only the beginning of any serious attempt to analyze the conceptual differences between arguments of principle and arguments of policy. But we have learned something, even in this brief discussion, about how to look for counterexamples to my suggestion that a judicial decision is normally a decision about principle. What would count as a clear counterexample? Only a case in whch a judge finds for a plaintiff in circumstances that make it very unlikely that he thinks that the defendant had a duty not to act as he did. If, in private nuisance suits, judges began to define zones in the way we have been imagining, by drawing lines across a map, we would have some good candidates. In the long reply I mentioned earlier, in *Taking Rights Seriously,* I examined each of Greenawalt's suggested candidates and tried to explain why each fails. The zoning example invites the question, however, whether judges do decide on grounds of policy in those very different kinds of cases when they partly take over the administration of some department of government—a school board, for example—and therefore make decisions that are very much matters of drawing lines across maps. I will not explore those cases, though they are different from ordinary civil cases in ways that might allow the conclusion that even they are decided on principle.

We should turn to the second of the two major issues Greenawalt discusses now, however, because the motive behind the distinction between policy and principle must in the end govern the way we apply that distinction in particular cases. Why should we object to a judicial decision based only on an argument of policy? Suppose it is conceded that the plaintiff had no moral or legal right that the defendant not pollute, and the defendant no moral or legal duty not to pollute. But a judge nevertheless thinks it would be better for the community, all things considered, if factories lying in some class or group or area to which the defendant belongs, not cause the kind of pollution the defendant did cause, and accordingly holds the defendant liable in damages for some loss the plaintiff suffered. His opinion defines the class or group or area as he thinks best, stipulates the desirable rule for the future, and then applies that rule to the case at hand so that the defendant is required to pay funds over to the plaintiff. What has gone wrong here? Why do we have any reason for disquiet?

Once again my original reply to Greenawalt considers this issue at some length. The central point, however, now seems to me to lie in some fundamental assumptions about the quality of a decent social organization, which I can only state, in this space, somewhat abstractly. How can we live together, in political society, and yet be independent? Some children between two domains of individual decision is necessary. There must be a domain of individual moral sovereignty: we must each be morally free to make some decisions answerable only to our own particular conceptions of the best lives for us to lead, to our own aims and projects, our own developed attachments and concerns. If there were no such decisions, no domain in that sense private, then we would not be independent people but only something for others. But there must also be decisions that fall outside that domain, when we are answerable to claims of others that we not injure them or take up resources that are properly theirs. Otherwise the domain of our own sovereignty would be pointless: we could make no plans, have no projects, because these would constantly be defeated by the unregulated acts of others.

The connected concepts of moral rights and duties provide our main instruments for stating and enforcing this distinction in day-to-day life. My convictions about peoples' rights and duties are my beliefs about the proper way to draw this line. Of course we disagree, among ourselves, about exactly what rights and duties we and others do have. This is not (in any case not necessarily) a defect in the institution of rights and duties, because a society that agreed wholly about this crucial matter would have lost any sense of the gravity of the issues involved. But it does mean that the following standard is of crucial importance. Each person must act consistently with his own convictions about what rights others have, rather than in disregard of these convictions, because we would otherwise have abandoned any shared sense that we make up a community governed by the requirement of justice.

This states what we might call the subjective principle of rights: no one should act toward another in ways inconsistent with his own reasonably reflective theory of the moral rights he and they have in common. General acceptance of this principle is not enough, of course, to insure a decent community. People may disagree too much about rights, or may agree on a wholly inadequate theory of rights. But we may fairly say that general acceptance of the subjective principle is a necessary condition for decent social organization.

It is doubly necessary that the subjective principle be respected on those special occasions when the collective police power of the state, with all its coercive apparatus, is deployed against some individual citizen. Any decent political order will accept the political version of the subjective principle: that the state must not exercise coercive force against anyone unless the officials directing that coercion believe that the person coerced has a duty to behave as he is made to do. Of course his duties may be changed by appropriate acts of legislation, though we may disagree about the details of how legislation may do this. A legislature may impose on someone a duty he did not previously have—a duty not to pollute at all if he falls within a pollution-free zone drawn up and published in advance of any attempt to punish him for polluting. But the subjective principle requires that the officials believe that some duty, grounded somehow, does exist in order that coercive force be justified.

We might, in the end, wish to accept an even stronger though more complex principle: that each official must believe that his use of force against individual citizens is justified, not only by his own opinions of their rights, but by some more general theory which can be said to be the theory that underlies the law of the community as a whole. That further idea will lead us, in the case of judges, to something like the theory of adjudication I described in Chapter 4 of *Taking Rights Seriously,* because that is the obligation Hercules takes up. But we do not need this further idea to justify the thesis which is our present concern, that judges ought to decide ordinary civil cases on grounds of principle rather than policy, because that is only a restatement and application of the simpler idea I said was plainly necessary. It is only the subjective principle of right taken to be a requirement of any minimally decent political order.

If a judge holds some general theory about moral rights and duties according to which a defendant, in the particular circumstances in which he acted, had no duty to behave other than as he did, then the judge commits a very grave injustice in treating him as if he did, in fact, have such a duty. Does it make a difference if the judge believes that the community will go better, for some reason, if he does violate that principle in this case? How could it? For if the judge believes the defendant had no duty, he believes that in these circumstances the defendant was genuinely, properly free to act for himself, free from the demands of others. The judge must make up his mind. If he honestly, after suitable reflection, is convinced that people do generally have some duty the defendant violated, in the circumstances in which the defendant acted, then the argument he offers to show this must be an argument of principle. It must be the kind of argument that might show this, which means that it is subject to the kinds of constraints we identified earlier. But if the judge has no such argument and nevertheless forces the defendant to compensate the plaintiff, then he excludes the defendant from the community of those whose autonomy matters. It would be a terrible mistake to say that if rights are anyway controversial it matters less whether judges feel bound to respect the subjective principle of rights. The value in that principle is deep; or, rather, the disvalue in offending it is deep and goes far beyond surprising some defendant who did not expect to be held liable. For what is at stake is not merely surprise but the respect we show each other in insisting that justice is important even when we disagree what it is.

One question remains. If all this is as simple and straightforward as I am now suggesting, why has my proposal, that judges do and should decide on arguments of principle, been so much resisted, not only by Greenawalt but also by others? I think they have taken too narrow a view of what an argument of principle can be, because they have not been careful to distinguish between an argument of policy and a consequentialist argument. This has led them to think that certain familiar consequentialist arguments, like the arguments necessary to apply the comparative harm theory of moral rights and duties to particular cases, must be arguments of policy. This confusion has worsened not only jurisprudence but legal scholarship more generally, because academic lawyers ought to consider, more carefully than they have, whether people really do have the moral duties the comparative harm principle states. And if so, in what circumstances? If we simply call all arguments of this sort "policy" arguments, we relieve ourselves from the burden of any such study, and then we are checked only by our raw intuitions about what would be unfair.

REGAN

Professor Regan's subtle article canvasses a number of topics, some of which are treated in my replies to other essays in this volume. His major point is original and important. I say that political rights, in the strong sense with which I have been concerned, are trumps over some background justification like utility, and I argue that judges in ordinary common law cases try to decide which party has a right to win rather than which decision would be best for the community on the whole. Regan points out a difficulty in combining these two claims. He says that no one can have a right to win an ordinary civil law suit in that strong sense of right. Consider the *Carroll* case he discusses. Suppose the legislature has to decide whether to make barge owners liable for damages if they do not provide a bargee when the barge is moored. It would seem reasonable for the legislature to make them liable if it thought this would serve the general welfare, or to deny liability if it thought that would serve the general welfare better. But then (Regan says) no one has a political right, in the strong sense, to either decision, so no one could have a right to win in *Carroll*.

This is an interesting argument, because it reminds us of the importance of distinguishing between legislative rights, which are rights to or against certain legislation, and legal rights, which are, among other things, rights to win in court. Both kinds of institutional rights are rights in the strong sense, but they hold against different institutions and, for that reason, have different content. People have an abstract legal right to the benefit of the consistent application of the principles that figure in the best justification of legal history as a whole. They have no such right, even in the abstract, against the legislature. In this distinction lies our answer to Regan's puzzle: no one has a legislative right to a statute either denying or imposing liability for barge damage, but in the absence of such a statute someone may or may not have a legal right to compensation for such damage.

The distinction certainly needs more attention than I have given it, however, and Regan's argument provides an occasion. It goes too far to say that nothing like the abstract legal right I just described—the right to the benefit of the best justification of the past—holds against the legislature. The Constitution provides a limited right of that sort. But no one has a right, beyond what the Constitution requires, that the legislature not break with the past. On the contrary, people have a right that it do just that when the past has been defective in a certain way. Suppose the legal history of some community has in no way recognized a right to a decent level of medical care. No such right figures in the best justification of the record of past statutes and judicial decisions. No one has, in virtue of his abstract legal right that courts enforce the best justification of the past, a concrete legal right that a court order the government to provide medical care if he cannot provide it for himself. But everyone may nevertheless have a right that the legislature provide such medical care. The fact that even the best interpretation of the community's legal history recognizes no such right provides no answer to the argument that, as a matter of sound political morality, it would be wrong for the legislature to refuse medical care now even though providing it is against the interests of the community as a whole.

So people have two distinct kinds of political rights, both of which are trump rights. They have rights against the legislature whose source lies in moral and political theory that is independent of the community's legal history. They have rights against courts whose source lies in the best interpretation of the established public order of the community, and therefore in calculations of moral and political theory that are densely entwined with that history. This is the crux of the distinction between legislative and legal rights or (as some would put it) between morality and law. The latter distinction is misleading because, as I just said, morality is involved in the derivation of both concrete legal and concrete legislative rights. We draw on the same background morality in deciding whether someone has a legal right to medical care as we do in deciding whether he has a legislative right to it. If a judge recognizes a legislative right to medical care, he is for that reason more likely to recognize a legal right as well, because if two accounts of past practice both fit that practice reasonably well, he will properly consider that one account provides a better justification if it more closely approximates people's legislative rights. But this does not make legal rights and legislative rights identical, even in "hard" cases when this influence of legislative on legal rights is greatest.

We have so far noticed one reason why legal and legislative rights may not match, yet both be full trump rights. The legal record may be defective in not recognizing rights that people, in fact, as a matter of the soundest political morality, really have—the right to decent medical care, for example. But legal and legislative rights may differ for other, more complex reasons, and the example Regan discusses illustrates one of these. Perhaps the best justification of the standing rules of negligence law supposes that people have the moral rights and duties recommended by the comparative harm theory described in my reply to Greenawalt. By hypothesis, these are rights and duties in the absence of legislation or some other form of social decision to the contrary. Many of our moral rights against one another, after all, are conditional on the absence of any contrary political decision to the contrary. If no such decision regulates some aspect of our behavior toward one another—the way we drive on roads others use, for example—then our rights with respect to that behavior will depend critically on general moral principle stipulating what it is reasonable to expect in such circumstances. If there are posted speed limits, however, then we may have a right only to expect that these limits will be obeyed, even if previous practice had stipulated slower driving.

The moral rights and duties people have in the absence of legislation are genuine rights and figure in the best justification of legal practice and hence in determining what rights people have to win law suits. But, of course, this kind of right cannot hold against a legislature, so the legislature does nothing wrong—violates no rights—in instituting a traffic code or a regulatory system for barges whose effect is to alter the concrete personal rights people had before, even if it does so for no better reason than that the community is marginally better off with the code than without. Of course the legislature *may* violate political rights when it legislates private law. Perhaps (contrary to what Regan supposes) people who are injured by an untended barge do have a legislative right to compensation, in which case the legislature would do wrong to deny liability when its only ground for doing so is some marginal gain to the public as a whole. But we need some argument for these legislative rights, if we think they exist, beyond the fact that people have legal rights to compensation before such legislation is adopted. So Regan's argument does not, after all, justify his conclusion that the legal rights at issue in a case like *Carroll* cannot be rights in the strong sense, that is, rights as trumps.

I shall comment briefly on a different though related topic Regan explores. He discusses my suggestion, that the fact that courts deal in rights rather than policies helps to explain why we demand much more by way of consistency from courts than we do from legislatures. In fact (as Regan's discussion brings out) we demand more consistency of courts in what we might think are two distinct ways. We demand a certain kind of consistency over time from courts, which we do not expect from legislatures even when legislatures justify their decisions on grounds of rights, except insofar as legislatures are limited by the Constitution. This difference is instinct in the distinction we have been studying just now, between legal and legislative rights. Since the most abstract legal right is the right to the consistent enforcement of the principles provided by the best justification of the past, judges seeking to honor legal rights must believe that the principles they apply are in that sense embedded in the community's past legal practice. Of course judges, like other lawyers, will disagree about what principles best justify the legal record as a whole, and so some judicial decisions will seem radical departures from past practice. But judges must nevertheless accept a responsibility of consistency according to their own best judgment of what consistency requires. Legislatures have no such responsibility. On the contrary they have a duty to reject even the best interpretation of the past if they believe that the principles provided in that interpretation fall short of what people's actual rights require. So they must, as I said, honor the right to medical care, if they believe people have such a right, in spite of the fact that our legal history, even seen in its best light, rejects rather than embraces that right.

This difference is quite independent of the further difference, which applies to judges and legislatures alike, between the kinds of consistency required by arguments of principle and arguments of policy. This is not a matter of consistency over time; it is not a matter of whether or how far officials have a right to correct what they take to be past error. It is rather a matter of how far they must extend the range of a particular standard in order to be justified in subscribing to that standard at all, in order to regard it as justifying anything they do. Here I agree with most of what Regan says. He is in general correct in his summary of my views about what rights are and about the kind of consistency they require. The legislature is free to say that history is wrong in rejecting a right to medical care. It is free to say that people have such a right, and to justify a general program of subsidized medical care for those who cannot afford it. But it is not free to say that though all people have that right it will provide medical care for only some of those who cannot afford it.

The position is quite different if it justifies subsidized medical care on grounds of policy. Suppose it says that it will provide medical care in order to reduce economic loss through lost days at work, but will concentrate this care in certain urban centers where it can be delivered relatively cheaply. Or that it will limit such care to certain sections of the country in order to test its impact more precisely, before committing too many resources to it. Or that it will limit such care to certain states because this will reduce lost days enough to provide a useful boost to overall prosperity, and it has other uses for the money that would be required for a more general program. All this might be bad politics. It might be injustice as well, if these grounds of distinction were a disguise for racial or sectional discrimination. But there is no injustice just in the fact that a program designed to achieve a particular social goal is not extended to everyone, or even to everyone whose benefit would, in fact, advance that goal.

This is the difference between the requirements of consistency in arguments of principle and in arguments of policy. In one respect Regan's account is too limited, however. He finds the root of this distinction in the fact that many policies are, using his term, "satiable." But consistency, of the sort required for principle, is not required even for policies that are not satiable. It is always better to have more efficiency rather than less if this is gained without cost to other goals. But it cannot always be gained without such cost, and government may properly decide to curtail efficiency in order to promote, for example, a cultural tradition. It need observe no requirement of even-handedness in making this compromise. It need not insure that the immediate or even long-term benefits of the culture it creates will be as easily available to the farm as the metropolis. It would be otherwise if government had argued that efficiency must be compromised for culture because people have a right to the life of the mind.

MACKIE

John Mackie's main comments about my theory of adjudication are political, but before he states his political reservations he notices what seem to him to be at least problems for my views. Some of these have been raised by others, and have already been taken up in this reply, but one problem is raised by Mackie alone. In Chapter 13 of *Taking Rights Seriously,* I allow that in certain cases (which I suppose must be very rare in complex legal systems) the argument for one side may be equally as good as the argument for the other. I call such cases "ties." Mackie argues that my claim that ties must be rare is based on what he calls too simple a "metric." It assumes an ordinary balance between two weights exactly counterpoised, so that if the slightest additional weight were added to either side the balance would be destroyed and the scales would tip. But, Mackie argues, cases that have no right answer may be cases in which one cannot choose between two sides, not because they are in this sense exactly in balance, but because the cases are incommensurate. In print he offers an example of facial likeness, but the point can be put more forcefully, as Mackie has done in conversation, directly about hard cases. Let us imagine a case that seems to provide a tie in the sense I described. We believe that two theories of law, which yield contrary decisions, offer exactly as good a justification of the preceding statutes and precedents. But now suppose we find one old, unimportant, and dim precedent that is justified on one theory but not the other. If the two theories were in exact equipoise, the newly discovered precedent, however dim, must be decisive. But in fact the newly discovered precedent may not affect our conviction that there is nothing to chose between the theories. We may well be reluctant to say that the discovery of such a case could make all that difference. If so, Mackie argues, then the original stalemate was not a tie of exact equipoise, but a case of incommensurability, and my arguments that exact ties must be rare do not show that incommensurabilities must be rare.

Mackie's argument assumes, however, an account of the way in which theories justify institutional history that is in two ways different from the account I recommend. First, he assumes that a justification of a body of material automatically becomes better, as a justification, when it justifies a greater percentage—even a very marginally greater percentage—of that material. I see no reason why that should be so. When two theories compete along what I have called the dimension of fit, the contest is not to see how many distinct bits of institutional history each explains. (Indeed, we have no principle of individualization of bits of history of the sort such a contest would require. How many bits of history are there in a complex statute? Does a complex case, with many parties, or a group action, count as more bits than a simpler case?) The contest along that dimension supposes a metric that is less precise and more a matter of characterization. Each of two theories may fit "reasonably" but not very well the "great bulk" of precedents, and yet one be preferred to the other because it can more plausibly be seen as explaining the "trend" of recent decisions. In that case, the justification for neither is improved simply by the discovery of one or two older cases explained by one but not the other. Secondly, the conception of justification I described does not provide that any improvement along the dimension of fit is automatically an improvement in overall justification. It provides for a threshold of fit that must be met by any theory that is ultimately to qualify, but argues that if two theories each pass that threshold, the choice between the two will be governed by political morality. But I concede that my thesis, that ties will be rare, presupposes a conception of morality other than some conception according to which different moral theories are frequently incommensurate.

Mackie's main objection is, as I say, a political objection. He notices that in a short book-review of *No Right Answer*?[8] I said that in certain of the pre-Civil War slavery cases (I had in mind principally the due process cases) the better legal argument justified a decision against the slave catchers and in favor of the alleged slaves, though the judges reached the opposite decision. Mackie constructs a legal argument, meant to follow the form of argument I recommend, that would justify the decision the judges reached, and remarks that reasonable judges of good will might just as easily have accepted his argument as mine. He does not mean (I think) that each of the two arguments is in fact of equal weight. No doubt he thinks that his argument is, in fact, better than mine, on the particular cases in question. But his point is simply that it is not certain that the judges who had to decide these questions would have found my argument better, so that readers should not think that the method of adjudication I recommend would necessarily provide more attractive decisions even in the United States or Britain.

I am reluctant to agree even to this more limited claim. The judges who decided these cases were, as citizens, politically committed: they were anti-slavery on grounds of principle. They therefore had views about the rights of individuals, and in particular about the rights of blacks as people, that I think would have made my argument preferable to them, as a legal argument, had they recognized the proper role of such principles in legal argument. My historical claim assumes a legal position that I share with Professor Cover (the author of the book I reviewed) but which Mackie contests: it assumes that the due process slavery cases were hard cases, not decided in advance by the plain meaning of constitutional provisions and statutes. But of course if the judges thought that the matter was foreclosed by such positive law, then they would not have entertained the arguments Mackie constructed for them either.

This is simply quibbling about particular historical cases, however, and does not touch Mackie's more general point. That is that my theory of adjudication gives judges more political power than positivism does, and that we should recommend my theory only if (or when) we are satisfied that we want judges rather than legislators or other officials to have that power. Is this correct? Mackie anticipates that I will make the following reply: "Positivism gives judges as much political power as my theory does. Positivism also recognizes the distinction between easy cases, in which the law is settled and the judge is duty bound to decide as the law dictates, and hard cases in which the judge is free to exercise a legislative discretion. My theory only recommends that judges make political decisions in hard cases, and positivism also recommends this, because the exercise of a legislative discretion is the exercise of political power." Mackie responds, in advance, that my reply fails because my theory designates more cases as hard cases—allows more room to challenge what is taken to be settled law—than positivism does. His argument here consists only in citing my view that the due process slavery cases were not governed by settled law. But that is a bad argument. Mackie himself says, on this point, only that "it is far from clear that (the pertinent) provisions offend against due process." That is not to say that it is clear that they do not. But suppose that he is in this case a better American constitutional lawyer than Cover is or I am, and that he is right. It follows only that we have made a mistake in our analysis of the law, not that my theory of adjudication in some way legitimizes that mistake. Nor does legal history suggest that lawyers who call themselves positivists—like, for example, Holmes—are especially reluctant to find unsettled what others thought clearly established.

It is, in fact, a difficult question whether my theory allows more "settled" law to be challenged. Much depends upon details of doctrine and practice in particular jurisdictions—for example whether these allow overruling of undesirable precedents. But Mackie might have made a stronger argument than he did. He might have said that positivism allows a judge to be more deferential to other institutions when he makes "new law" in hard cases, and perhaps even encourages him to do so. Since positivism argues that no party has a right to any particular decision in a hard case, a positivist judge may accept a general responsibility to reach the decision that he thinks the legislature would have reached, either in deference to some theory of democracy or in the interests of smooth government. (I suggested, in the book review, that the pre-Civil War judges may have been influenced by a sense of that responsibility.) My theory of adjudication, on the other hand, insists that parties have legal rights in hard cases, and a judge who accepts a duty to try to identify these rights cannot be moved, against his theory of what these rights are, by any competing consideration of democracy or efficient government. So Mackie may be right, for this reason, in supposing that the political convictions of judges matter more under my theory.

But there are two countervailing considerations. First, it is a notorious complaint against both British and American judges that they smuggle political convictions into decisions under cover of pretending to discover what the legislature "really" intended or "would have done if aware of the problem."[9] Some critics charge that this is deliberate; others that it is unconscious. Indeed, in many cases in which apparently deferential judges appeal to legislative intention or to counterfactuals about what the legislature would have done, it is silly to suppose that they succeed in finding the right answer to these questions because there are no right answers to find.

These charges of hypocrisy or self-deception provide a useful check to Mackie's own charge that my theory plays fast and loose with the law. (I am indebted to him for explaining to me what the latter charge really means. I had thought the allusion was to women who were, perfectly consistently, both fast and loose at the same time.) He thinks that my theory will increase deception, because judges will pretend that they are finding determinate solutions to legal issues when they are really legislating their personal convictions. This accusation, of course, begs the question of whether the theoretical background to my recommendations is sound. If it is, then judges *are* doing their best to find the rights of the parties, and there is no deception. But even if my theoretical claims are indefensible, the fraud, if there is any, seems to be in the other court. Hercules makes plain, in his opinions, the influence of political morality on his decisions. Positivists who appeal to legislative intention or counterfactuals often hide the influence of their convictions behind a screen decorated by nonsense.

The second countervailing fact is more complex in its implications. Positivism argues that judges, in the exercise of their discretion to make new law in hard cases, are free to make new law in the name of policy as well as principle. My theory includes the rights thesis, which argues that since the duty of judges, even in hard cases, is to identify the rights of the parties, judges in such cases should appeal to arguments of principle and not arguments of policy. My reply to Greenawalt in this volume, discusses the issue of whether the rights thesis makes much difference in practice. I argue that it will always make some difference, and that the degree of the difference will depend upon the area of the law in question—in particular whether the judge holds a consequentialist theory of the right that make up that area. This issue is relevant now, because the risks to individual freedom are far greater, I think, when judges are invited to make new law on judgments of policy (like the judgment that a certain sort of conduct is damaging to the public welfare, or that penalities should be increased so as to provide greater deterrence) than when judges are asked to protect the moral and political rights citizens of their community have. The risk, in the former case, is that judges will erode individual liberty to a degree greater than that which the ordinary political process, with its checks and inertias, could do unaided. The risk, in the latter case, is largely negative: that judges will be conservative and will make less use of their power than they might by refusing to recognize individual rights that the political process has not already established in positive law. These are generalizations, and neither holds true inevitably or absolutely. It is not difficult to imagine cases in which judges can do great harm, even in civil cases, by enforcing a false conception of the rights of property. But the rights thesis poses a practical question that Mackie should at least add to his list of political questions made relevant by my theory. Suppose it is true that judges applying the rights thesis are unlikely substantially to limit individual freedom, beyond what the legislature has done, when their political convictions are conservative, but will increase personal freedom when their convictions are liberal. Then liberals, at least, will find that thesis a better bet than Mackie's ancient con game.

WOOZLEY

Professor Woozley believes that I am confused about the concept of truth, and I believe he is. Consider the following extraordinary passage from his essay:

> I can have grounds for asserting *p*, even if *p* has no truth value, and even indeed if I *know* that *p* has no truth value . . . . Reasonable, hard-headed lawyers can properly discuss the question (and disagree with each other in their answers to it) what the right answer to a question of law is, even though they agree there is not a right answer—yet. So having grounds for asserting *p* does not imply that *p* has a truth value—unless to say that *p* is true (false) just means the same as saying that we have better (worse) grounds for asserting *p* than for asserting $\sim p$. But it quite obviously does not.

This is, I think, a buzzing hive of confusions.

Start at the end. Woozley says, in effect, that having grounds for asserting some proposition does not presuppose that the proposition can be true because it does not presuppose that it *is* true. This is a mistake in logic, for the simple reason that "can be true" is different from "is true." We often say, in retrospect, that though we had good grounds for saying something, it turned out that what we said was false. This shows only what is anyway obvious, that having good grounds for some belief is different from knowing that it is true. It does not show how we can have grounds for believing something when we know it is not true—when we know, indeed, that it cannot be true. What could "grounds" possibly mean, in this context, except good reasons for thinking something true? What could asserting mean except claiming something to be true?

Most of what Woozley says in this passage is therefore incoherent. Of course his hard-headed lawyers, who say that there is a right answer even while denying that there can be a right answer, might have in mind the right answer to two different questions. They might mean that there is a right answer to what the law should be though no right answer to what it is. But they cannot think there both is and is not a right answer to the same question unless they are a touch harder in the head than they should be.

Now consider Woozley's discussion of my literary exercise example. He says he understands the exercise I describe, in which an answer is the right answer to some question of character or interpretation about a novel, even if the author has said nothing about the matter, if that answer is more consistent with what the author did say than its negation. He accepts the idea that one answer might really, in fact, be more consistent—indeed he suggests that only an idiot would deny this. But he promptly forgets all this when he offers his own account of *Emma*. He says there could not be a right answer to the question whether Emma marries Mr. Knightley, if Jane Austen had died before writing the chapter in which Emma does marry him, even if the proposition that Emma married him fits the uncompleted narrative much better than the proposition that she did not. "What all this shows," he says, "is that the question whether *p* is true is *not* the question whether *p* gives the best narrative fit with the hard facts. The question whether *p* is true is still left on our hands, even after the question of its narrative fit is settled."

The only argument he offers for this is plainly inadequate. He says that the proposition that Emma marries Knightley would still provide the best narrative fit if Jane Austen, unaccountably, had married him off to Harriet Smith at the end, though it would then be false. But of course it would *not* then provide the best fit, at least according to the enterprise I described, because it is a requirement of best fit, within that enterprise, that the proposition in question not contradict anything the author has explicitly said.

Woozley is not really relying on this bad argument. He thinks he is relying on what we might call an external notion of truth, a notion that is not defined by the practices of the enterprise but is brought to that enterprise from outside. This is why he says that no amount of narrative consistency can establish the truth of any proposition about Emma, that the question of truth is simply a further question, still left on our hands when we have finished making whatever case for the proposition is warranted by the ground rules of the enterprise in question. But if we follow Woozley in this, and employ a concept of truth external to the literary exercise, then everything he himself says about Emma is not only wrong but crazy. For the only external idea of truth we have available is historical truth, according to which the proposition that Emma married Knightley is true only if "Emma" and "Knightley" refer to actual historical characters who, as a matter of historical fact, once married one another. But these are fictional not historical characters, so the proposition that Emma married Knightley is, as a matter of historical truth, not true. (It is either, according to which answer we give to a classical question in the philosophy of language, false or neither true nor false.) It certainly is not made true, as Woozley says it is, by the fact that Jane Austen said it. If historical truth is in question, Jane Austen told a great fib.

When Woozley makes the truth of propositions about Emma turn on what

Jane Austen said, he is not using an external notion of truth after all. He is simply insisting on one set of ground rules defining truth within the literary exercise (what the author said) rather than the set I described (what the author said together with narrative consistency with what the author said). Truth is left over, for him, when narrative consistency is settled only because he has stipulated a notion of truth in which narrative consistency does not figure in the conditions of truth. If he insists that his enterprise is the only possible literary enterprise, then he contradicts what he has already said, which is that some people (those he calls the "Holmes nuts") actually use the one I described. He makes parallel, positivistic assumptions about the only notion of truth the legal enterprise could use. But here he is contradicted not by any "nuts" but by the "hard-headed lawyers" whose arguments he describes.

Woozley's arguments are a mess. Why does he find himself in this position? He has been misled by the mirage of a concept of truth that somehow escapes the fact that all our concepts, including our philosophical concepts, take the only meaning they have from the function they play in our reasoning, argument, and conviction. Much of the automatic, familiar skepticism of law students and academic lawyers is the upshot of exactly that mirage. They believe in a mysterious and highly blurred idea of "real" truth, which they express only in metaphors, and which I doubt can be expressed in any other way. They can say that a proposition is "really" true only if it accurately describes facts that are "out there," or part of "the fabric of the universe," or "locked into" an "independent reality" or something of that sort. Then they announce that since moral claims, for example, or claims about what the law is in hard cases, describe nothing that is "out there," such claims cannot be "really" true. But this is no argument at all unless these metaphors can be unpacked in the following way. We must be able to assign some nonmetaphorical sense to the claim that the injustice of slavery, for example, is "out there," such that people who say "slavery is really unjust" mean that the injustice of slavery is "out there" in just that sense. When we try to do this the argument collapses. Does someone who thinks that the injustice of slavery is "out there" think that our beliefs about slavery are forced upon us by physical properties of objects, as our belief that fire engines are red might be said to be forced on us by such properties? If so, almost no one who says that slavery is really unjust means that the injustice is "out there." Does it mean that everyone, in fact, has a reason for opposing slavery? If so, then people who say slavery is really unjust do mean that the injustice is "out there." But why are they then wrong?

The concept of truth, and the concept of an answer being the right answer, are like our other concepts; their meaning lies in their complex function. Skepticism is possible, either about part of some enterprise, or globally, about the enterprise as a whole, but skepticism of either form needs to be defended by arguments that employ our actual concept of truth and don't suppose some transcendent kind of truth that can be expressed only metaphorically and mockingly. So skeptical arguments about morality must be moral arguments, skeptical arguments about literary characters must be literary arguments, and skeptical arguments about right answers in law must be legal arguments.[10]

Woozley thinks that what constitutes truth in some practice or enterprise cannot be affected by the structure and practices of that enterprise, though he makes no effort at all to say what truth can then be. That is why he says, so confidently, that truth about characters in a novel can have nothing to do with narrative consistency. But he also recognizes that people think there are right answers, and that they have better grounds for some claims than others, when truth in his sense is, as he thinks, out of the question. So he invents a new concept, the concept of having grounds for asserting a proposition, and tries to marry his common sense to his skepticism by saying that someone may have good grounds for asserting a proposition even when he knows that it cannot possibly be true.

This is, as I said, a kind of nonsense, but it is also a step in the right direction. Woozley (and others who are disposed to follow him in this strange progress) can simply retire the concept of truth and replace it with permutations of the concept of having good grounds for assertion. He says that I can talk about truth or about what it is reasonable to assert, but I should not confuse the two. I do not think they can be entirely separated in the way he thinks they can, but put that point aside. Will he allow me to say that in hard cases at law one answer might be the most reasonable of all, even though competent lawyers will disagree about which answer is the most reasonable? If so I can say everything I want to say, or have said, about this issue, though in language that will allow Woozley to hold on to his odd ideas about what truth is.

MacCORMICK

Professor MacCormick provides an elegant statement of my recommendations about adjudication, but he declares that the program I describe will not work because there can be no such thing as the single best justification of the legal record. There is only the best justification relative to a particular judge's (or other lawyer's) set of convictions, and it is a mistake to think that one set of convictions can be right and others wrong from an independent or neutral standpoint. He says that I concede as much when I say that John Rawls's use of the technique of reflective equilibrium supposes a constructive rather than a natural model of ethical reasoning. We should take this in stages.

MacCormick thinks that the constructive model, as I described it, rejects what is often called the subjective nature of moral judgments in favor of some form of relativism. I took some care to deny this: I said that the constructive model is compatible with the theory that moral judgments can be objectively true or false but does not depend upon that theory as the natural model does.[11] I would now go further. The two models differ about an important point of political morality, but since each is a positive theory about what political officials should do, they are equally committed to the idea that claims of political morality may be true or false or, if one prefers, more or less accurate.[12] The two models disagree about the following issue. The natural model allows an agent to follow moral intuitions even though he cannot bring all his intuitions under some general scheme of abstract principle. But the constructive model forbids this. If we apply the constructive model to political officials, for example, that model insists that it is unfair for such officials to act except on the basis of a general and coherent set of principles and policies.

There are several positive arguments—of political morality not of metaphysics—in favor of the constructive model of political responsibility, some of which I suggested in the essay MacCormick discusses, and that is why, as I also suggested, the constructive model is especially appropriate for reasoning about justice and other aspects of political theory. It does not follow that there are no occasions when the natural model is more appropriate. Perhaps there are reasons why people should follow the natural model in their personal lives, but use the constructive model when they hold political office and are charged with developing a theory of justice for a community and not simply for themselves. I do believe that judges must follow the constructive model in developing the theories of past law necessary for adjudication. It is not their job to show which principles are best independently of history, but to show which principles provide the best justification of a particular legal record, and the kind of consistency the constructive model demands is instinct in that responsibility.

So I cannot accept MacCormick's suggestion that I have myself conceded the kind of moral skepticism or relativism that denies that one justification of the legal record may be better than another, and one may be the best that can be constructed. Nor do I think that he himself has provided any grounds for that kind of relativism. I do accept his account of what we might call the phenomenology of the judicial decision. Hercules can proceed in the way MacCormick describes, constructing general theories of law that he believes are the best that can be constructed. Other, less powerful judges can imitate Hercules in the way MacCormick also describes. These judges will disagree with one another. But how can this show that all of them are wrong? MacCormick says that there is no independent or neutral standard—no "Archimedian point"—from which it can be decided who is right. Of course there is not. A neutral point of view is the point of view of someone with no moral convictions, and nothing about morality could possibly be decided from such a point of view. But that includes the negative thesis of morality, that no moral claim is "really" right or accurate or sound or true, because that is also a moral claim, if it is a sensible claim at all.

MacCormick also says that a judge faced with his case of *X* v. *Y* could discover principles with roots in the law to support each side. No doubt, but that is no more an argument that there is not right answer than the argument that there are considerations for and against the right to subsidized medicine is an argument that there can be no right answer to the question whether people are entitled to it. In fact MacCormick at several points in this essay reports his own opinions about the political rights people have, opinions that are just as controversial as the legal issues that arise in a hard case. He sometimes seems to suggest the following account of his political and legal views. He, for his part, thinks that the case for one side or the other on some disputed issue of law or politics is, in fact, stronger, but this is only his opinion, from the standpoint of his own deepest convictions, and therefore is not "really" right. But this seems to me a deep confusion. It depends on assigning some sense to "The case for *Y* is *really* stronger" that is different from "The case for *Y* is stronger," and these two propositions differ, so far as I can see, in emphasis or confidence only. Curiously, MacCormick has no hesitancy in ascribing objective truth to his *skeptical* convictions. He says, at the end of his essay, that there is no right answer to some of the questions he raises, but he exempts *that* question. Reasonable people disagree about whether moral judgments can be "really" true. If MacCormick does not allow truth when reasonable people can disagree, and there is no canonical proof, why does he think there is a right answer to the question of moral "objectivity"?

I might perhaps say, once again, that my interest in the question whether there can be one right answer to a hard case at law is a negative interest. Various critics have argued, as MacCormick does, that certain claims I make about adjudication cannot be accepted because there can be no right answer in a hard case. So I am anxious to show that they have offered no grounds for the latter claim, as I try to do, for example, in my reply to Woozley above. But I do not think that it is either useful or possible to develop any general argument that there can be right answers in hard cases. For there can be no better argument for that thesis than the ordinary kind of legal argument someone might make to show that *X* in MacCormick's case has, all things considered, a legal right to recover his damages. Or to show that he does not. There can be no different or better kind of argument designed to prove that there can be a right answer in such a case than an argument that tries to show what the right answer is. And no way to show that there cannot be a right answer except to show why all such arguments would be inadequate as legal arguments.

I shall make much briefer comments about some of MacCormick's other points. (1) His suggestion, that retroactivity is no problem in cases when opposing rights conflict, neglects the important distinction between abstract and concrete rights. It does not follow, from the fact that people in principle have a right to compensation when they are injured by careless conduct, that a particular plaintiff has a right to be compensated for, for example, emotional injury. Courts try to determine whether the plaintiff, in fact, has the concrete right he claims, and this is a matter of deciding upon the best theory of law, with the best assignment of relative weight to competing abstract rights. It is not, if this means something different, a matter of establishing a "preference" between them.

(2) My account of the force of a right, which supposes that someone has a right if it is wrong for the state to treat him in a certain way even for the general benefit, does not commit me to the view that duties are substantively prior to rights. For that formal account leaves open the question whether the state has some duty because the injury it commits when it violates that duty is in some way special, or whether the injury is special only because the state has the duty.[13]

(3) MacCormick's discussion of my "Lexington Avenue" argument offers a new defense of the so-called right to liberty. I argue that on many occasions liberty is properly limited for no better reason than marginal improvements in the general welfare, and that there is therefore no general right to liberty, but only rights to particular liberties that must be established by showing that some particular limit on liberty, like censorship, is wrong for some reason other than the general importance of liberty. MacCormick makes a direct attack on this argument by proposing that, in fact, no constraint on liberty is justified unless it falls within one of three exceptions to the rule that liberty must not be limited: incapacity, special privilege attached to office, or competing rights such as rights to economic well-being. But this thesis seems to fail

in the very example I used and he discusses: traffic regulation. What competing rights justify making Lexington Avenue one way? Suppose New York names Lexington Avenue one way and then finds that the gains in traffic flow do not justify the expense of maintaining the signs. Does it violate competing rights if it rescinds its earlier decision?

SARTORIUS

Many of Professor Sartorius's points are also made in Hart's essay in this volume, and call for no further reply. But it might be useful for me to respond to one specific claim Sartorius makes: that in spite of my rejection of utilitarianism, as a general political theory, much of what I have written endorses a version of utilitarianism, namely utilitarianism which is "restricted" because it does not allow "external" preferences to figure in the calculation of when the community is better off on the whole. His misunderstanding begins in his account of my account of rights. He refers to what he calls the "now familiar" idea that rights are trumps over utility. But I meant this idea, that rights are trumps, to apply more generally.

Rights cannot be understood as things people have, come what may, no matter what general justification for political decisions is in play. We construct political theories as a package, and the rights that package assigns individuals must vary with what else is in the package. The idea of rights as trumps is a *formal* idea: it fixes the general function of rights within any particular theory that uses the idea at all. We can therefore think about the content of rights at two different levels of analysis. When we are engaged in constructing a general political theory, we must consider what package—what general justification for political decisions together with what rights—is most suitable. This is the characteristic exercise of moral and political philosophers who must, so far as this is possible, think of political theory as a whole. But on other occasions we must take the general scheme of some political theory as fixed and consider what rights are necessary as trumps over the general background justification that theory proposes. This is more often the position of lawyers, particularly lawyers attempting to construct the best justification of our constitutional system. Since utilitarianism, whatever its defects, has had great appeal, and since it is arguable, at least, that the best justification of our own legal practice shows utilitarianism as the general background theory supporting most legislation, it is an important practical question which rights would be required by a political theory having that general character. It does not follow from any answer to that question that the package of utilitarianism, together with those qualifying rights, is better than an entirely different package, but only that it is better than utilitarianism without those rights.

I urged the distinction between external and personal preferences and the exclusion of external preferences from any utilitarian calculation in that spirit, though I now think that the distinction has much wider use. I said that the resulting package, restricted utilitarianism, was the only defensible form of utilitarianism, and I offered it as a more plausible interpretation of our own constitutional structure than could be provided by unrestricted utilitarianism. My particular purpose, in the essay Sartorius discusses, was to show that liberalism, conceived as equality, sharply limits the use of utilitarian arguments and justifies rights to the distinct liberties provided in our Constitution as a trump over such arguments. So that rights to these liberties can be defended, in a society otherwise committed to utilitarianism, without appeal to any general right to liberty. Many readers, besides Hart and Sartorius, understood me in some way to be embracing restricted utilitarianism as the best general political theory, and though I took pains to deny this in the introduction to *Taking Rights Seriously,* where the essay first appeared, my language obviously encouraged that misunderstanding. I have corrected it elsewhere, as Sartorius acknowledges, and am happy to repeat the correction now.[14]

I find one further aspect of Sartorius's article troublesome. He says that he is unsure about my suggestion that, insofar as social decisions are to be justified by appeal to the preferences of the community, altruistic preferences should not count. And he adds that he is uneasy about the idea that paternalistic regulations are objectionable because they reflect external preferences. I discuss these objections more fully in my reply to Hart. But since the central point is of great importance I shall summarize it here as well. Excluding external preferences from any calculation of what the community wants does not rule out either aid to orphans or seat-belt legislation. It means only that these programs must find some justification other than in the play of external preferences. Aid to orphans might be justified on grounds of equality or other grounds of justice, which is, of course, a very different justification from the fact that people think it justified on these grounds. If aid to orphans can be justified in this way, then the case for orphans need not rely on external preferences. It is as strong in a community that does not want to help orphans as in a community that does. If it is not justified on grounds of justice—or some other ground that does not count external preferences—then the fact that people think it is or want to help orphans for some other reason, cannot cure this defect. The same holds for seat-belts. Perhaps compulsory seat-belts are justified by a utilitarian calculation that counts only personal preferences. Perhaps they are justified as a matter of equal concern towards drivers or passengers who would not otherwise wear them. But if they cannot be justified in some such way, then they are not justified simply on the ground that the majority wants the freedom of a minority limited in this way.

HART

Professor Hart's objections show what I think is a comprehensive misunderstanding of my arguments about external preferences, which my earliest statement of these arguments, as I now see, encouraged, and it might therefore be helpful for me to restate the argument and then consider his objections in that light. Suppose a community of many people including Sarah. If the constitution sets out a version of utilitarianism which provides in terms that Sarah's preferences are to count for twice as much as those of others, then this would be an unacceptable, nonegalitarian version of utilitarianism. But now suppose that the constitution enacts only the standard form of utilitarianism, that is, that it is neutral toward all people and preferences, but that a surprising number of people love Sarah very much, and therefore strongly prefer that her preferences count for twice as much in the day-to-day political decisions made in the utilitarian calculus. When Sarah does not receive what she would have if her preferences counted for twice as much as those of others, then these people are unhappy, because their special Sarah-loving preferences are unfulfilled. If these special preferences are themselves allowed to count, therefore, Sarah will receive much more in the distribution of goods and opportunities than she otherwise would. I argue that this defeats the egalitarian cast of the apparently neutral utilitarian constitution as much as if the neutral provision were replaced by the rejected version. Indeed, the apparently neutral provision is then self-undermining because it gives a critical weight, in deciding which distribution best promotes utility, to the views of those who hold the profoundly unneutral (some would say anti-utilitarian) theory that the preferences of some should count for more than those of others.

The reply that a utilitarian would give to this argument is obvious: utilitarianism does not give weight to the truth of that theory, but just to the fact that many people (wrongly) hold that theory and so are disappointed when the distribution the government achieves is not the distribution they believe is right. It is the fact of their disappointment, not the truth of their views, that counts, and there is no inconsistency, logical or pragmatic, in that. But this reply is too quick. For there is, in fact, a particularly deep kind of contradiction here. Utilitarianism must claim truth for itself, and therefore must claim the falsity of any theory that contradicts it. It must itself occupy, that is, all the logical space that its content requires. But neutral utilitarianism claims (or in any case presupposes) that no one is, in principle, any more entitled to have any of his preferences fulfilled than any one else is. It argues that the only reason for denying the fulfillment of one person's desires, whatever these are, is that a greater number or more intense desires must be satisfied instead. It insists that justice and political morality can supply no other reason. That is, we might say, the neutral utilitarian's *case* for trying to achieve a political structure in which the average fulfillment of preferences is as high as possible. The question is not whether a government can achieve that political structure if it counts political preferences like the preferences of the Sarah lovers or whether the government will, in fact, then have counted any particular preference twice and so contradicted utilitarianism in that direct way. It is rather whether the government can achieve all this without implicitly contradicting that case.

Suppose the community contains a Nazi, for example, whose set of preferences includes the preference that aryans have more and Jews less of their preferences fulfilled because of who they are. A neutral utilitarian cannot say that there is no reason in political morality for rejecting or dishonoring that preference, for not dismissing it as simply wrong, for not striving to fulfill it with all the dedication that officials devote to fulfilling any other sort of preferences. For utilitarianism itself supplies such a reason: its most fundamental tenet is that peoples' preferences should be weighed on an equal basis in the same scales, that the Nazi theory of justice is profoundly wrong, and that officials should oppose the Nazi theory and strive to defeat rather than fulfill it. A neutral utilitarian is, in fact, barred, for reasons of consistency, from taking the same politically neutral attitude to the Nazi's political preference that he takes to other sorts of preferences. But then he cannot make the case just described in favor of highest average utility computed taking that preference into account.

I do not mean to suggest, of course, that endorsing someone's right to have his preference satisfied automatically endorses his preference as good or noble. The good utilitarian, who says that the push-pin player is equally entitled to satisfaction of that taste as the poet is entitled to the satisfaction of his, is not for that reason committed to the proposition that a life of push-pin is as good as a life of poetry. Only vulgar critics of utilitarianism would insist on that inference. The utilitarian says only that nothing in the theory of justice provides any reason why the political and economic arrangements and decisions of society should be any closer to those the poet would prefer than those the push-pin player would like. It is just a matter, from the standpoint of political justice, of how many people prefer the one to the other and how strongly. But he cannot say that about the conflict between the Nazi and the neutral utilitarian opponent of Naziism, because the correct political theory, his political theory, the very political theory to which he appeals in attending to the fact of the Nazi's claim, does speak to the conflict. It says that what the neutral utilitarian prefers is just and accurately describes what people are, as a matter of political morality, entitled to have, but that what the Nazi prefers is deeply unjust and describes what no one is entitled, as a matter of political morality, to have. But then it is contradictory to say, again as a matter of political morality, that the Nazi is as much entitled to the political system he prefers as is the utilitarian.

The point might be put this way. Political preferences, like the Nazi's preference, are on the same level—purport to occupy the same space—as the utilitarian theory itself. Therefore, though the utilitarian theory must be neutral between personal preferences like the preferences for push-pin and poetry, as a matter of the theory of justice, it cannot, without contradiction, be neutral between itself and Naziism. It cannot accept at once a duty to defeat the false theory that some peoples' preferences should count for more than other peoples' and a duty to strive as to fulfill the political preferences of those who passionately accept that false theory, as energetically as it strives for any other preferences. The distinction on which the reply to my argument rests, the distinction between the truth and the fact of the Nazi's political preferences, collapses, because if utilitarianism counts the fact of these preferences it has denied what it cannot deny, which is that justice requires it to oppose them.

We could escape this point, of course, by distinguishing two different forms or levels of utilitarianism. The first would be presented simply as a thin theory about how a political constitution should be selected in a community whose members prefer different kinds of political theories. The second would be a candidate for the constitution to be so chosen; it might argue for a distribution that maximized aggregate satisfaction of personal preferences in the actual distribution of goods and opportunities, for example. In that case the first theory would argue only that the preferences of the Nazi should be given equal weight with the preferences of the second sort of utilitarian in the choice of a constitution, because each is equally entitled to the constitution he prefers, and there would be no contradiction in that proposition. But, of course, the neutral utilitarian theory we are now considering is not simply a thin theory of that sort. It proposes a theory of justice as a full political constitution, not simply a theory about how to choose one, and so it cannot escape contradiction through modesty.

Now the same argument holds (though perhaps less evidently) when the political preferences are not familiar and despicable, like the Nazi theory, but more informal and cheerful, like the preferences of the Sarah lovers who think that her preferences should be counted twice. The latter might, indeed, be Sarahocrats who believe that she is entitled to the treatment they recommend by virtue of birth or other characteristics unique to her. But even if their preferences rise from special affection rather than from political theory, these preferences nevertheless invade the space claimed by neutral utilitarianism and so cannot be counted without defeating the case utilitarianism provides. My argument, therefore, comes to this: If utilitarianism is to figure as part of an attractive working political theory, then it must be qualified so as to restrict the preferences that count by excluding political preferences of both the formal and informal sort. One very practical way to achieve this restriction is provided by the idea of rights as trumps over unrestricted utilitarianism. A society committed to unrestricted utilitarianism as a general background justification might achieve that disqualification by adopting a right to political independence: the right that no one suffer disadvantage in the distribution of goods or opportunities in consequence of the fact that others think he should have less or care less for him than they do for other people. The right of political independence would have the effect of insulating Jews from the preferences of Nazis, and those who are not Sarah lovers from the preferences of those who adore her.

A parallel right of moral independence can be defended in a similar way. Neutral utilitarianism rejects the idea that some ambitions that people might have for their own lives should have less command over social resources and opportunities than others, except as this is the consequence of weighing all preferences on an equal basis in the same scales. It rejects the argument, for example, that some peoples' conception of what sexual experience should be like, and of what part fantasy should play in that experience, and of what the character of that fantasy should be, are inherently degrading or unwholesome. But then it cannot (for the reasons just canvassed) count the moral preferences of those who do hold such opinions in the calculation whether individuals who form some sexual minority, like homosexuals, should be prohibited from the sexual experiences they want to have. The right of moral independence is part of the same collection of rights as the right of political independence. It is necessary to provide a trump over an unrestricted utilitarian defense of laws prohibiting homosexual practices in a community of those who find offense just in the idea that their neighbors are gay, in much the same way as the latter right is necessary as a trump over a utilitarian argument for giving Jews less or Sarah more in a society of Nazis or Sarah lovers.

I suggested, in my original formulation of the present argument, that if a utilitarian counts preferences like the preferences of the Sarah lovers, then this is a "form" of double-counting because, in effect, Sarah's preferences are counted twice, once on her own account, and once through the second-order preferences of others that incorporate her preferences by reference. Hart says that this is a mistake, because, in fact, no one's preferences are counted twice, and it would *under*count the Sarah lovers' preferences, and so fail to treat them as equals, if their preferences in her favor were discarded. There would be something in this last point if votes rather than preferences were in issue, because if someone wished to vote for Sarah's success rather than his own, his role in the calculation would be exhausted by this gift, and if his vote was then discarded he might well complain that he had been cheated of his equal power over political decision. But preferences (as these figure in utilitarian calculations) are not like votes in that way. Someone who reports more preferences to the utilitarian computer does not (except trivially) diminish the impact of other preferences he also reports; he rather increases the role of his preferences overall, compared with the role of other peoples' preferences, in the giant calculation. So someone who prefers Sarah's success to the success of people generally, and through the contribution of that preference to an unrestricted utilitarian calculation secures more for her, does not have any less for himself—for the fulfillment of his more personal preferences—than someone else who is indifferent to Sarah's fortunes.

I do not think that my description, that counting his preferences in favor of Sarah is a form of double counting, is misleading or unfair. But this description was meant to summarize the argument, not to make it, and I will not press that particular characterization. (Indeed, as Hart notices, I made it only about some of the examples I gave in which unrestricted utilitarianism produced obviously inegalitarian results.) Hart makes more substantial points about a different example I used, which raised the question of whether homosexuals have the right to practice their sexual tastes in private. He thinks I want to say "that if, as a result of [preferences that express moral disapproval of homosexuals] tipping the balance, persons are denied some liberty, say to form some sexual relations, those so deprived suffer because by this result their concept of a proper or desirable form of life is despised by others, and this is tantamount to treating them as inferior to or of less worth than others, or not deserving of equal concern and respect."

But this misstates my point. It is not the result (or as Hart later describes it the "upshot") of the utilitarian calculation that causes or achieves the fact that homosexuals are despised by others. It is rather the other way round: if someone is denied liberty of sexual practice in virtue of a utilitarian justification that depends critically on other peoples' moralistic preferences, then he suffers disadvantage in virtue of the fact that his concept of a proper life is already despised by others. Hart says that the "main weakness" in my argument—the feature that makes it "fundamentally wrong"—is that I assume that if someone's liberty is restricted this must be interpreted as a denial of his treatment as an equal. But my argument is that this is not inevitably or even usually so, but only when the constraint is justified in some way that depends on the fact that others condemn his convictions or values. Hart says that the interpretation of denial of liberty as a denial of equal concern is "least credible" in exactly the case I discuss, that is, when the denial is justified through a utilitarian argument, because (he says) the message of that justification is not that the defeated minority or their moral convictions are inferior, but only that they are too few to outweigh the preferences of the majority, which can only be achieved if the minority is in fact denied the liberty it wishes. But once again this ignores the distinction I want to make. If the utilitarian justification for denying liberty of sexual practice to homosexuals can succeed without counting the moralistic preferences of the majority in the balance (as it might if there was good reason to believe what is, in fact, incredible, that the spread of homosexuality fosters violent crime) then the message of prohibition would, indeed, be only the message Hart finds, which might be put this way: "It is impossible that everyone be protected in all his interests, and the interests of the minority must yield, regrettably, to the concern of the majority for its safety." There is (at least in my present argument) no denial of treatment as an equal in that message. But if the utilitarian justification cannot succeed without relying on the majority's moralistic preferences about how the minority should live, and the government nevertheless urges that justification, then the message is very different and, in my view, nastier. It is exactly that the minority must suffer because others find the lives they propose to lead disgusting, which seems no more justifiable, in a society committed to treating people as equals, than the proposition we earlier considered and rejected as incompatible with equality that some people must suffer disadvantage under the law because others do not like them.

Hart makes further points. He suggests, for example, that it was the "disinterested" political preferences of liberals that tipped the balance in favor of repealing laws against homosexual relationships in 1967 in England, and asks how anyone could object that counting *those* preferences at that time offended anyone's rights to be treated as an equal. But this question misunderstands my point in a fundamental way. I do not argue—how could anyone argue?—that citizens in a democracy should not campaign and vote for what they think is just. The question is not whether people should work for justice, but rather what test we and they should apply to determine what is just. Utilitarianism holds that we should apply this test: we should work to achieve the maximum possible satisfaction of the preferences we find distributed in our community. If we accepted this test in an unrestricted way, then we would count the attractive political convictions of the 60s liberals simply as data, to be balanced against the less attractive convictions of others, to see which carried the day in the contest of number and intensity. Conceivably the liberal position would have won this contest. Probably it would not have.

But I have been arguing that this is a false test, which in fact undermines the case for utilitarianism, if political preferences of either the liberals or their opponents are counted and balanced to determine what justice requires. That is why I recommend, as part of any overall political theory in which utilitarianism figures as a background justification, rights to political and moral independence. But the liberals who campaigned in the interests of homosexuals in England in the 60s most certainly did not embrace the test I reject. They, of course, *expressed* their own political preferences in their votes and arguments, but they did not *appeal to* the popularity of these preferences as providing an argument in itself for what they wanted, as the unrestricted utilitarian argument I oppose would have encouraged them to do. Perhaps they appealed instead to something like the right of moral independence. Nor is it necessary for us to rely on any such argument inconsistent with that right. Nor is it necessary for us to rely on any such argument to say that what they did was right, and treated people as equals. The proof is this: the case for reform would have been just as strong in political theory even if there had been very few or no heterosexuals who wanted reform, though, of course, reform would not then have been practically possible. If so, then we cannot condemn the procedure that, in fact, produced reform on the ground that the procedure offended anyone's right to independence.

Hart's misunderstanding here was no doubt encouraged by my own description of how rights like the right to moral independence function in a constitutional system, like that of the United States, that uses rights as a test of the legality of legislation. I said that a constitutional system of this sort is valuable when the community as a whole harbors prejudices against some minority or convictions that the way of life of that minority is offensive to people of good character. In that situation, the ordinary political process is antecedently likely to reach decisions that would fail the test we have constructed, because these decisions would limit the freedom of the minority and yet could not be justified, in political theory, except by assuming that some ways of living are inherently wrong or degrading, or by counting the fact that the majority thinks them so as itself part of the justification. Since these *repressive* decisions would then be wrong, for the reasons I offer, the constitutional right forbids them in advance.

Of course the decision for reform that Hart describes would not—could not—be a decision justified only on these offending grounds. Even if the benign liberal preferences figured as data rather than argument, as I think they should not, no one would be in a position to claim the right to moral or political independence as a shield against the decision that was, in fact, reached. But someone might have been led to suppose, by my discussion, that what I condemn is any political process that would allow any decision to be taken if peoples' reasons for supporting one decision rather than another are likely to lie beyond their own personal interests. I hope it is now plain why this is wrong. *That* position would not allow a democracy to vote for social welfare programs, or foreign aid, or conservation for later generations. Indeed, in the absence of an adequate constitutional system, the only hope for justice is precisely that people will vote with a disinterested sense of fairness. I condemn a political process that assumes that the fact that people have such reasons is itself part of the case in political morality for what they favor. Hart's heterosexual liberals may have been making the following argument to their fellow citizens. "We know that many of you find the idea of homosexual relationships troubling and even offensive. Some of us do as well. But you must recognize that it would deny equality, in the form of moral independence, to count the fact that we have these feelings as a justification for penal legislation. Since that is so, we in fact have no justification for the present law, and we ought, in all justice, to reform it." Nothing in this argument counts the fact that either the liberals or those they address happen to have any particular political preferences or convictions as itself an argument: the argument is made by appeal to justice, not to the fact that many people want justice. There is nothing in that argument that fails to treat homosexuals as equals. Quite the contrary. But this is just my point.

I shall consider certain of the remaining objections Hart makes together. He notices my claim, that the rights people have depend on the background justification and political institutions that are also in play, because the argument for any particular right must recognize that right as part of a complex package of other assumptions and practices that it trumps. But he finds this odd. It may make sense to say, he remarks, that people *need* rights less under some forms of government than others. But does it make sense to say that they *have* less rights in one situation rather than another? He also objects to my suggestion (which is, of course, at the center of the argument I made in the last section) that rights that have long been thought to be rights to liberty, like the right of homosexuals to freedom of sexual practice or the right of pornography users to look at what they like in private, are in fact (at least in the circumstances of modern democracies) rights to treatment as an equal. That proposition, which Hart calls "fantastic," would have the consequence, he says, that a tyrant who had forbidden one form of sexual activity or the practice of one religion would actually eliminate the evil rather than increase it if he broadened his ban to include all sex and all religions, and in this way removed the inequality of treatment. The vice in prohibitions of sexual or religious activity, he says, is in fact that these diminish liberty, not equal liberty; adding a violation of equality to the charge makes equality an empty and idle idea with no work to do.

These different objections are plainly connected, because they suppose that whatever rights people have are at least in large part timeless rights necessary to protect enduring and important interests fixed by human nature and fundamental to human development, like interests in the choice of sexual partners and acts and choice of religious conviction. This is a familiar theory of what rights are and what they are for, and I said that I would not give my reasons, in this essay, for thinking that it is in the end an inadequate theory of rights. I did say that this theory is unlikely to produce a defense of the right I have been considering, which is the right of moral independence as applied to the use of pornography, because it seems implausible that any important human interests are damaged by the prohibition of dirty books or films. But that is not much of an argument against the general fundamental-interest theory of rights, because those who accept that theory might be ready to concede (or perhaps even to insist) that the appeal to rights in favor of pornography users is an error that cheapens the idea of rights, and that there is nothing in political morality that condemns the prohibition of pornography altogether if that is what will best fulfill the preferences of the community as a whole.

My aim is to develop a theory of rights that is relative to the other elements of a political theory, and to explore how far that theory might be constructed from the exceedingly abstract (but far from empty) idea that government must treat people as equals. Of course that theory makes rights relative in only one way. I am anxious to show how rights fit into different packages, so that I want to see, for example, which rights should be accepted as trumps over utility if utility is accepted, as many people think it should be accepted, as the proper background justification. That is an important question because, as I said, at least an informal kind of utilitarianism has for some time been accepted in practical politics. It has supplied, for example, the working justification of most of the constraints on our liberty through law that we accept as proper. But it does not follow from this investigation that I must endorse (as I am sometimes said to endorse) the package of utilitarianism together with the rights that utilitarianism requires as the best package that can be constructed. In fact I do not. Though rights are relative to packages, one package might still be chosen over others as better, and I doubt that in the end any package based on any familiar form of utilitarianism will turn out to be best. Nor does it follow from my argument that there are no rights that any defensible package must contain—no rights that are in this sense natural rights—though the argument that there are such rights, and the explanation of what these are, must obviously proceed in a rather different way from the route I followed in arguing for the right to moral independence as a trump over utilitarian justifications.

But if rights figure in complex packages of political theory, it is both unnecessary and too crude to look to rights for the only defense against either stupid or wicked political decisions. No doubt Hitler and Nero violated whatever rights any plausible political theory would provide; but it is also true that the evil these monsters caused could find no support even in the background justification of any such theory. Suppose some tyrant (an Angelo gone even more mad) did forbid sex altogether on penalty of death, or banned all religious practice in a community whose members were all devout. We should say that what he did (or tried to do) was insane or wicked or that he was wholly lacking in the concern for his subjects, which is the most basic requirement that political morality imposes on those who govern. Perhaps we do not need the idea of equality to explain that last requirement. (I am deliberately cautious here.) But neither do we need the idea of rights.

We need rights, as a distinct element in political theory, only when some decision that injures some people nevertheless finds *prima facie* support in the claim that it will make the community as a whole better off on some plausible account of where the community's general welfare lies. But the most natural source of any objection we might have to such a decision is that, in its concern with the welfare or prosperity or flourishing of people on the whole, or in the fulfillment of some interest widespread within the community, the decision pays insufficient attention to its impact on the minority; some appeal to equality seems a natural expression of an objection from that source. We want to say that the decision is wrong, in spite of its apparent merit, because it does not take the damage it causes to some into account in the right way and therefore does not treat these people as equals entitled to the same concern as others.

Of course, that charge is never self-validating. It must be developed through some theory about what equal concern requires, or, as in the case of the argument I offered, about what the background justification itself supposes that equal concern requires. Others will inevitably reject any such theory. Someone may claim, for example, that equal concern requires only that people be given what they are entitled to have when their preferences are weighed in the scales with the preferences, including the political and moral preferences, of others. In that case (if I am correct that the right to sexual freedom is based in equality) he would no longer support that right. But how could he? Suppose the decision to ban homosexuality even in private is the decision that is reached by the balance of preferences that he thinks respects equality. He could not say that, though the decision treats homosexuals as equals, by giving them all that equal concern for their situation requires, the decision is nevertheless wrong because it invades their liberty. If some constraints on liberty can be justified by the balance of preferences, why not this one?[15] Suppose he falls back to the idea that sexual freedom is a fundamental interest. But does it treat people as equals to invade their fundamental interests for the sake of minor gains to a very large number of other citizens? Perhaps he will say that it does, because the fundamental character of the interests invaded have been taken into account in the balancing process, so that if these are outweighed the gains to others, at least in the aggregate, were shown to be too large in all fairness to be ignored. But if this is so, then deferring to the interests of the outweighed minority would be giving the minority more attention than equality allows, which is favoritism. How can he then object to the decision the balancing process reached? So if anyone really does think that banning homosexual relationships treats homosexuals as equals, when this is the decision reached by an unrestricted utiltarian balance, he seems to have no very persuasive grounds left to say that that decision nevertheless invades their rights. My hypothesis, that the rights which have traditionally been described as consequences of a general right to liberty are, in fact, the consequences of equality instead, may in the end prove to be wrong. But it is not, as Hart says it is, "fantastic."

SANDEL

I agree with a good deal in Professor Sandel's remarks about my discussion of affirmative action programs. We might dispose of one issue (which in this context I believe to be largely verbal) at the outset. Sandel says that my argument for affirmative action is a utilitarian argument. This is, in context, true enough, because I suggest that particular members of minority races have no right to preference, either in reparation for past injustice to others of their race, or for any other reason. The proper justification of affirmative action programs—if these can be justified at all—lies instead in the benefits such programs might provide for the community as a whole. But "utilitarianism" is often used, not as synonymous with all forms of consequentialism, but to describe a special form that makes a political decision correct only if the decision maximizes utility across some community, and this is generally taken to mean maximizing average happiness or the degree to which people's preferences are satisfied. I do not suppose that all the arguments for affirmative action must be utilitarian arguments in that sense. On the contrary we might well think that a community with less racial consciousness is a better community, on the whole, for reasons that go beyond the happiness this brings to the average citizen, and that affirmative action is justified because it will reduce racial consciousness in the long run. But I believe that Sandel's doubts about my arguments do not depend on characterizing them as utilitarian in the ordinary sense, but rather on the fact that they appeal to benefits for the community as a whole, which they do.

Sandel's major objection depends on a much more important and I think mistaken charge, which is that my arguments suppose that society in some way "owns" or "possesses" the talents of its members and is "entitled" to use these talents for its own good. He arrives at this conclusion in the following way. I do not believe that individuals are entitled to any particular rewards or places just in virtue of the talents they happen to have. I therefore do not believe that individuals "own" their own talents. But I must therefore assume that society does own these talents, that society is the "wider subject of possession" of the abilities of its members. This, Sandel thinks, is a fallacy. "The arbitrariness of an individual's assets argues only against the proposition that the individual owns them or has a privileged claim to their benefits, not in favor of the proposition that some particular society owns them or has a privileged claim with respect to them. And unless this second proposition can be established, there would seem no grounds for favoring a utilitarian dispensation of such assets and endowments rather than just letting them lie where they fall." He himself, he says, prefers the idea that talents are the property of neither society nor the atomic individual, but of a wider subjectivity in which individuals and society are in some way merged.

I agree that it does not follow, from the fact that individuals do not own their talents, that society does. But I do not use any such argument. It seems to me, in fact, a great mistake to bring ownership or possession of talents into the discussion at all, and I certainly do not rely on these concepts in the arguments I make. Do individuals "possess" their own talents? Only, I think, in a bizarre sense of possession; but if we want to say that Smith possesses Smith's talent for mathematics, this is not so contingently, as if someone else might have possessed these same talents, but as a kind of truism. Do individuals own their own talents? What can that mean to ask? We can give this question no sense except to treat it as asking whether individuals are entitled to particular rewards in virtue of "possessing" particular talents. But then the proposition that Smith either does or does not own his talents for mathematics cannot be produced as an *argument* why he is or is not entitled to a particular job. For the proposition about ownership, if it means anything at all, just states the conclusion it would then be meant to support. Indeed, the idea of ownership, either of talents or of material goods, has, I think, no useful role to play in the abstract levels of political theory, because it is parasitic on rather than generative of basic principles of political and personal morality. Once we see this, Sandel's particular criticism of my position, and his own ambitious Hegelian account of some "wider subjectivity" as the owner of talents, seem equally misjudged.

The important principle, that individual people are not entitled to any particular job or income just because of their abilities, does not depend on any assumption about whether people "own" these abilities, and therefore does not depend on any theory or picture of the "self" as either including or excluding these properties. It depends on questions of political morality that do not intersect these (in my opinion, obscure) metaphysical issues. Someone who holds the meritocratic theory, that people are entitled to jobs in virtue of their talents, must provide an argument which brings their claim under some appealing and more general argument for rights. They cannot do this, as I just said, by urging that people own their talents, because this proposition, assigning it the only sense it can have, simply begs the question. In my articles on affirmative action I considered and rejected various other arguments for the meritocratic theory; but of course it does not follow, from the failure of the arguments I considered, that no better argument will ever be found.

Sandel is correct to insist, however, that a decent argument in favor of affirmative action, which appeals to some promised benefit for the community as a whole, cannot consist only in reasons why such programs violate no rights. It must provide some definition of the relevant community, and of community benefit, and show why that benefit to that community justifies some particular program. But once again the assumption that the community "owns" or "possesses" the talents of its members, even if it made sense, could not provide the needed argument. Nor do I ever suggest that it could.

Utilitarians have provided a variety of arguments for their general claim, that a decision is just if it maximizes the utility of society defined in some way, but none of these relies on the idea that society owns its members' talents, or indeed, on the more general idea, on which this depends, that society is an entity even capable of owning or possessing. Some utilitarians seem to think that pleasure or happiness or the satisfaction of desire is a good in itself, so that any program that maximizes these commodities is justified because it produces a desirable state of affairs. Others make the very different (and in my own view more plausible argument) that maximizing the satisfaction of desire is justified because this treats each individual as equally entitled to concern and respect. In two recent articles I have begun a rather different argument about what equal concern and respect requires.[16] Justice requires, on this view, that each individual have an equal share of the resources that can be distributed by political action, but on the condition that the calculation of equal shares must be sensitive to the choices an individual makes about work and consumption. It follows that what one person should receive, by way of goods and opportunities, depends on the cost to others in the community of his having what he has, and this means that the calculation of equal shares will in many circumstances resemble a utilitarian calculation.

I offer these different theories of justice only as examples of how "benefit to the community" might be defined and then justified without relying on any assumption that personifies society or supposes that societies "own" anything. Nor does someone who embraces one or another of these theories need to make it his exclusive standard of social benefit. He might well think, as I said, that a community in which people treat one another with respect unsullied by racial prejudice is valuable for reasons other than the value of happiness or of any conception of equal shares, and this appealing idea does not depend on personifying society either. Sandel's preoccupation with personification, ownership, and possession is a false step.

Still, any argument that uses the idea of benefit to the community as a whole—utilitarianism, equality of resources, or the concept of a social virtue like the virtue of mutual respect—must propose some means of deciding what the relevant community is. Sandel is perfectly correct in his observation that such theories, and particularly utilitarianism, have neglected that issue, mainly, I think, because it is so difficult. If United States economic policy is to be dictated by utilitarianism, should the effects on the citizens of Mexico be counted or not? If government must treat all members of the community with equal concern and respect, does the relevant community, for the United States government, embrace Mali? Sandel's idea of wider "subjectivity" will not prove useful here, however, because anyone using that idea will have to decide upon an appropriate community in order to decide how far the subjectivity extends, rather than vice versa.

But he is right to insist that some notion of community be chosen that gives putative members some reason to regard the community as theirs. We can, that is, distinguish what I have elsewhere called an active notion of community from a passive one.[17] Totalitarianism uses a passive notion; the community extends to the reach of the state's policy and military power. Liberalism uses an active notion: no one should be asked to sacrifice in the name of the community unless he can see his own efforts reflected in the virtues of that community and so take pride in these virtues. How does all this bear on the problem of affirmative action?

Sandel says that my arguments at once deny the moral worth of citizens by denying that they own the talents and virtues that can give them this worth, and then require some citizens to make sacrifices for the good of the community as a whole while supplying no reason why they should see their interests linked with the interests of that community. There are, I think, two distinct mistakes here. I do not deny that individuals have talents, or that they can take pride in these, or that they can find in these, if they hold the necessary beliefs about value, evidence of their own moral worth. I say only that these talents do not entitle them to any particular status or job or reward, and that is surely something quite different. The confusion rises, once again, from Sandel's assumption that I mean to deny that individuals "own" their talents. I deny this only if it means that their talents entitle them to specific rewards; otherwise I do not deny it because I cannot understand it. I cannot see how my position entails anything whatsoever about moral worth.

Do I suppose that citizens must be made to make sacrifices in favor of a community which has not been shown to be, in the active sense, their community? On the contrary I insist that this would be injustice.[18] But "sacrifice" means giving up, or being made to give up, something to which one is otherwise entitled. So this kind of argument requires two steps. Sandel must show how it follows from the proper, active sense of community that people who achieve high scores on admission tests are *prima facie* entitled to a university place in preference to someone else who scores lower but has other qualities useful for the profession. If he can do this, then he can justly say that my proposal, that the latter should nevertheless sometimes be preferred, involves a sacrifice that must be justified by showing how the community that gains can be said to be their community in the necessary active sense. This could, I think, easily be shown. But it is not necessary because no one has yet shown that any sacrifice is involved. No notion of community, no matter how rich or Hegelian, can collapse the two steps of the argument that is required.

POSNER

Judge Posner believes that judges should decide cases, whenever possible, so as to maximize the aggregate wealth of society. He has ransacked a great variety of ethical theories in search of normative support for this position. But his arguments have a characterisitc weakness. He attacks complex issues of economic and moral theory with a sledgehammer, deploying one-sentence arguments which begin in observations about what is probable and end in the kind of certitude one might earn only after volumes of analysis. His project is nevertheless important, because the fashionable use of economic theory in legal analysis still lacks any philosophical support.

In two essays I argued that this support cannot be found in the idea that wealth is valuable in itself, which is silly.[19] Nor is it likely to be found in the more plausible idea that wealth is valuable instrumentally. I suggested a very different account of why it often seems right that judges should reach the decisions that the wealth maximization test would predict, which is that sound and familiar moral principles recommend these decisions in some, though not in all, relevant cases. This account relies on moral principles like the principle of comparative harm I described in my reply to Greenawalt. Posner's remarks included in this volume represent his answer to these various arguments. He begins by calling my statement, that wealth cannot be considered itself a component of value, misleading, because I mean that it cannot be valuable for its own sake and no one thinks that it can. I said myself that almost no one would think that wealth was a component of value. The possible exception I had in mind was in fact Posner, and I set out, in a footnote, various comments and arguments he has made which assume that wealth is valuable in itself, and which must be abandoned once it is conceded, as he now seems to concede, that this is preposterous. I spent the bulk of my essay considering and rejecting various arguments that wealth ought to be maximized for its instrumental value. Posner neither acknowledges nor confronts most of what I said on that score.

Instead he dwells on my argument, involving the example of Derek and Amartya, that was designed only to show, if it needed showing, that wealth could not be supposed to be valuable for its own sake. He answers the argument by changing the facts of my example so that it is no longer even relevant. He asks us to assume, directly contrary to the assumption I made, that overall utility would be improved by stealing the book from Derek and giving it to Amartya. But my purpose was to show that wealth maximization could only be thought useful if it happens to improve utility or produces some other gain it makes sense to value for its own sake. So Posner has changed the subject as well as the example.

My Agatha-Sir George story was offered, not to illustrate the problem of circularity Posner mentions, but to show that the wealth maximization account of rights fails even if we break out of that circle by assuming that some rights are already in place when we try to justify others on wealth-maximization grounds. It fails because it cannot show why we attach the great importance we do to certain rights, like the right not to be enslaved. Of course Posner might have said that if that right is not supported on wealth-maximization grounds, it is not right at all, and our enthusiasm for it is only sentimentality. But he takes the more cautious route of trying to show that wealth maximization does support this and other rights we regard as fundamental.

I used the example I did in order to show that we cannot be confident that the wealth-maximization test would guarantee a right to control one's own labor. Posner's response makes everything depend on his flat statement "that if Agatha were free she almost certainly *could*—not would—write more detective stories than she would write if she were a slave. People have an incentive to work harder when they work for themselves than when they work for other people," he says, and so "she could and would buy her freedom." But as I pointed out in my original article, these various assumptions depend on contingent facts that might very well not hold. Posner has a weakness for *a priori* psychology—it is a weakness in the school of economics he would like to represent. He has no right to assume that any particular person could produce more wealth in the same time, at any particular activity, if he worked for himself than if he worked as the slave of an intelligent master. This depends, among other things, on features of conscious and unconscious motivation and patterns of dependence that few psychologists would claim wholly to understand. (The "incentive" that people who work for themselves normally have is the incentive to work longer hours, which would be irrelevant in this case.) Nor should Posner assume that any particular person would make the particular trade for the particular brand of freedom that Agatha would have available, even if he would then be able to produce more in the same time. Would Agatha,in fact, trade the benign administration of Sir George for the uncertainties of self-employment when her gain from the trade, at best, would be so marginal? Of course we cannot be confident that she would not, but we cannot be confident that she would. And in any case it is, as I said, a grotesque idea that slavery is morally wrong only if the person enslaved would, in fact, have been able and willing to purchase freedom if born in chains. Posner complains that I have not elaborated this last suggestion. Does it need elaboration?

The circle I described, which remains however we dispose of examples like the Agatha-Sir George case, is this: wealth maximization, as an ethical standard, insists that rights should be assigned so as to reach the position that would be reached anyway, through economic activity, even if rights were initially assigned in some different way. But we cannot even speculate about what situation economic activity would produce unless we make assumptions about the wealth and other rights of individuals. Posner's new attempt to escape this circle is spectacularly unsuccessful. He now asks us to assume that in the long run any given society would generate much the same distribution of rights and wealth no matter what its initial distribution of these, so that we do not, in fact, have to make any particular assumptions to calculate the long-term results. But the argument he makes to show this fails, not only because it rests on wholly arbitrary assumptions about what would "probably" happen, but because it assumes exactly the right under discussion, which is the right to control one's own labor. Posner says that even if one person initially controlled all social wealth he would have to pay others to work for him, and that this would in the long-run distribute wealth so that prices would come to depend on general preferences and not just his. But he would not have to transfer funds by paying others if all others were his slaves, so this argument simply confirms what is evident anyway, that economic analysis must assume something about what rights people have in order to demonstrate what rights they should be given.

Posner replies to various other objections I made, to his account of the moral value of wealth maximization, by embracing a pluralism of values rather than only one. Wealth maximization is good not because it produces more happiness than a standard aimed entirely at happiness, or more "sharing" or more protection of rights than standards aimed entirely at one or the other of these values, but because it gives us a mixture of all three goals. It is odd that he gives overall happiness any place at all in this trilogy, because he elsewhere says in the strongest possible terms that the idea of overall happiness makes no sense. "The 'interpersonal comparison of utilities' is anathema to the modern economist, and rightly so, because there is no metric for making such a comparison."[20] Each of the other goals he names is odd in its own way as well. Posner uses "sharing" in a Pickwickean sense: someone who single-mindedly aims for personal gain displays the moral virtue of beneficence if, in spite of his best efforts to keep all the consumer surplus from some transaction for himself, some part of it nevertheless accrues to others. I objected to this: I said that wealth maximization can get no further than independent credit for producing noble character, beyond whatever other benefits it might or might not bestow upon society, in virtue of this peculiar kind of "altruism." Posner now replies only by calling attention to these other benefits. So he has now abandoned the idea that "sharing" is an independent goal in his trilogy after all. The appearance of "the protection of rights" in the trilogy is even more curious. Posner insists that people only have the rights that the best strategy for maximizing wealth would assign them; but if this is so then wealth maximization cannot intelligibly claim to be of instrumental value because it protects people's rights.

So Posner cannot coherently embrace any of the three goals he lists. But more trouble breaks out in his idea that wealth maximization is a superior standard for adjudication because it gives us some of all three rather than simply maximizing one. Many different standards might give us some of each of these goals. If wealth maximization is superior this must be because it gives us a better mix. But Posner seems to deny that it makes sense to speak of a better mix. He says that "because there is no common currency in which to compare happiness, sharing, and the protection of rights, it is unclear how to make the necessary trade-offs among these things in the design of a social system," and then praises wealth-maximization because it "makes the trade-offs automatically." This will not do. He must choose between one of the two following positions. (1) Though it is "unclear" what the best mix is, we can nevertheless make crude but intelligent speculations about this, through moral philosophy, and when we do we shall discover that wealth maximization brings us closer to our approximations of the best mix than other theories of adjudication can. In that case his argument for wealth-maximization has not even begun, because he has not even begun to indicate how we should decide, independently of wealth-maximization, even approximately what mix is best.

(2) There is no best mix, even approximately, and wealth-maximization is valuable because it allows us to pretend that there is. We can point to the social design achieved by wealth-maximization "automatically" and then declare that the levels of happiness, the kinds of "sharing," and the particular rights established in that design are "just about" the best, or at least better than those any other system would produce. This is, I think, the actual upshot of Posner's present defense of wealth-maximization, but it is too shabby to credit.

In fact he relies much more on utilitarianism, in spite of his earlier denounciation of that thesis, than on the other members of his trilogy, but he has no answer to my question why judges should take wealth maximization as a conclusive proxy for utility instead of reserving the option of correcting the wealth maximization test by the direct pursuit of utility on those occasions when this seems wise. His rule-utilitarian response is misplaced. Of course rules that tell judges not to look to very specific issues of utility in particular cases—not to consider, for example, how much pain a particular criminal will suffer if punished—might maximize utility in the long run. The question is whether utility is maximized by a rigid practice that tells judges never to look beyond wealth maximization, never to examine probable utility effects even in cases like those I describe when the utility costs of wealth maximization are likely to be large. Posner thinks there are only two possibilities: unrelenting use of wealth-maximization as a proxy for utility, or full act-utilitarianism. But this is simply too crude.

My comments about the power of wealth-maximization as an explanation of past patterns of judicial decision were not, as I emphasized, intended to justify ignoring whatever correlations legal scholars are able to produce. I meant only to emphasize that these correlations provide no explanation, but only clues about where an explanation might be found, until they are connected to a plausible motivational story, and I offered two projects that might be pursued. I said that an explanation might be found in the supposed link between wealth maximization and utility, but I also indicated certain *prima facie* problems in that project. I said that a better explanation might be found in the idea I mentioned above. We might try to identify theories of political morality, not that justify wealth-maximization, but that provide independent justification, at least within the appropriate range, for just the decisions that wealth-maximization would also predict. Posner's present suggestion, that "economic values were part of the prevailing ideology" in the nineteenth century, is too quick and too ambiguous to be of much help. Does he mean that the nineteenth-century judges did think that social wealth was of value for its own sake? Or that they were all utilitarians who thought that wealth-maximization was a good false target for utility? Or that they held moral theories that independently justified the decisions that wealth-maximization would predict?

NOTES

1. See J. L. Mackie, *Ethics: Inventing Right and Wrong* (1978), chapter 1.
2. Hart, *The Concept of Law* (Oxford, 1961), p. 89 ff.
3. Hart, *Essays on Bentham* (Oxford, 1982), p. 147 ff.

4. In fact, I do not accept it, though the issue is not relevant to the present dispute. Two somewhat independent points should be noticed. (1) An explanation does not provide a justification of a series of political decisions if it presents, as justificatory principles, propositions that offend our ideas of what even a bad moral principle must be like. This explains why the explanation of a series of statutes, that they were enacted in order to win the next election, does not provide a justification of those statutes. In *Taking Rights Seriously* (p. 343), however, I said that, "I should not want to put much reliance on the screening power of the concept of a moral principle. There is no persuasive analysis of that concept that *insures* that the principle that blacks are less worthy of concern than whites can be rejected as not a principle at all." (Emphasis now added.) I am less confident now that the best conception of that concept would not rule out blatantly discriminatory propositions. If it would, then we should reject, on this ground alone, the idea that a discriminatory principle might figure in the best justification of Nazi law.

(2) In any case the question whether a particular proposition counts as a justification of a group of political decisions—even a relatively poor justification—depends on whether it shows those decisions in a better light to suppose they were taken out of respect for that proposition than to suppose that they are taken haphazardly or for no particular reason at all. Principles we think wrong, even unacceptable, would meet that test. Perhaps the best justification of tort rules, at some point in our own history, would be provided by the principle that people are responsible for protecting themselves against the negligence of others. That principle seems wrong to us, and we would vote against legislation that carried it out. But we can see how it fits into a general picture of human responsibility that has a certain appeal because it assigns weight—though in our view very excessive weight—to virtues we ourselves recognize as virtues in other contexts. We can treat the principle the way Hercules, as I supposed in Chapter 2 of *Taking Rights Seriously,* might treat the concept of dignity. We can agree that the legal record is seen in a better light if it is understood as enforcing this principle of individual responsibility than if it is seen only as random or whimsical.

We would take quite the contrary view of the alleged principle that Jews are less worthy than aryans. This "justification" would, in our eyes, make the legal record worse just in the degree of its success in explaining what was done. It would make the legal record not as good but as bad as it could possibly be (see my "Law as Interpretation," *Critical Inquiry* 1982). Though, as I said, this point is not important in the present discussion of the connection between legal and moral rights, it would be of great importance in certain other contexts. Imagine some hard case arising in Nazi Germany involving a Jew, but not a case arising directly under one or another of the discriminatory statutes. Suppose an aryan sues a Jew in tort, for example, and the case is a hard one because lawyers are divided whether the pertinent standard is one of negligence or strict liability. The aryan plaintiff might argue that, since the best justification of German law as a whole includes the principle that Jews are less worthy than aryans, the correct conclusion of law, in the instant case, is that Jews are strictly liable to aryans even when one aryan would only be liable to another for negligence. A German judge, even if he accepts the point that he must decide hard cases by extending the best justification of the past, need not accept this particular argument, because he need not recognize the discriminatory principle as playing any part in that justification. Plainly this raises interesting questions about the adjudication of hard cases in wicked places that I must not pursue here.

5. I replied at length, in Chapter 3 of *Taking Rights Seriously,* to the arguments Dr. Raz makes in the essay reprinted here and I will not undertake to summarize my reply here. Though he says that his arguments "refuted" the positions they attacked, he has not commented on my reply, and does not do so in his new Postscript.

6. I much prefer my own statement of the distinction between principles and policies to Raz's reformulation which makes the distinction turn on the difference between absolute and prima facie standards. Nor did I mean myself to reformulate the original distinction when, in a later essay, I used the word "principle" more precisely to describe a sub-class of the larger set of standards I first used "principle" to describe. For I made this distinction in the first essay, and there said that, for purposes of that essay, I would use "principle" to include policies as well as principles in the narrower sense. See Chapter 2 of *Taking Rights Seriously.*

7. Harvard University Press and Duckworth, paperback, p. 294.

8. *New York University Law Review* 53 (1978): 1–32.

9. See, e.g., J. Griffith, *The Politics of the Judiciary* (1977).

10. See my article, "Please Don't Talk about Objectivity Any More," *Critical Inquiry,* 9, no. 1 (September 1982): 179–200, to be published by the Pheonix Press under the title *The Politics of Interpretation.* An earlier version appears in *Texas Law Review,* 60, no. 3 (March 1982).

11. *Taking Rights Seriously,* p. 162.

12. Phrases like "independent moral reality," which I used in describing the natural model, I now believe to be distinctly unhelpful. What can it mean to say that the proposition, that poor people ought to have subsidized medical care, describes an objective moral reality? If it means something obviously silly—that everyone agrees about that proposition, for example—then the natural model is not committed to that idea. If it means simply that anyone who denies that poor people ought to have subsidized medical care has made a mistake, then anyone who accepts that poor people ought to have medical care believes in "an independent moral reality," whichever of the two models of official responsibility he accepts.

13. *Taking Rights Seriously,* p. 171.

14. Sartorius finds my statements about the *Lochner* case specially damning. These statements should be read in context. I had proposed restricted utilitarianism as the best form of utilitarianism, and then asked, "What can be said, on the basis of the general theory of rights I offer, for . . . the right to liberty of contract . . . in the famous *Lochner* case?" I meant in this way to consider whether any argument could be made, along the lines I had explored, that the right recognized in that case is necessary to protect employers against the effects of external preferences, and I said, misleadingly, that if no such argument can be found the right does not exist. I should have made plain that I meant that the right does not exist within the general theory of restricted utilitarianism I was exploring.

15. *Taking Rights Seriously,* pp. 266–72.

16. "What Is Equality?", Parts I and II, *Philosophy and Public Affairs* 10, nos. 3 and 4 (Summer and Fall 1981).

17. See "Why Liberals Should Believe in Equality", *New York Review of Books* 30, no. 1 (February 3, 1983): 33–34.

18. See article cited in note 17.

19. "Is Wealth a Value?" *Journal of Legal Studies* 9 (1980): 191; "Why Efficiency?" *Hofstra Law Review* 8 (1980): 563.

20. R. Posner, *The Economics of Justice* (Harvard University Press, 1981) p. 79. Compare Posner's statement, in the essay in this volume, that "many" economists use wealth-maximization as a proxy for utility. If these statements are consistent, it can only be because the sense of "utility" in question is not the sense we need in order to make the goal of maximizing happiness coherent.

Selected Bibliography on Ronald Dworkin

Alexander, Lawrence and Bayles, Michael. "Hercules or Proteus? The Many Theses of Ronald Dworkin." *Social Theory and Practice* 5 (1980): 267-304.

Anon. Note. "Dworkin's 'Rights Thesis.'" *Michigan Law Review* 74 (1976): 1167-99.

Bell, Richard S. Note. "Understanding the Model of Rules: Toward a Reconciliation of Dworkin and Positivism." *The Yale Law Journal* 81 (1972): 912-48.

Benditt, Theodore M. *Law as Rule and Principle: problems of legal philosophy.* Stanford, Cal.: Stanford University Press, 1978.

———. *Rights.* Totowa, N.J.: Rowman and Littlefield, 1982. Chapter 6.

Bodenheimer, Edgar. "Hart, Dworkin, and the Problem of Judicial Lawmaking Discretion." *Georgia Law Review* 11 (1977): 1143-72.

Brilmayer, R. Lea. "The Institutional and Empirical Basis of the Rights Thesis." *Georgia Law Review* 11 (1977): 1173-200.

Carrió, G. *Legal Principles and Legal Positivism.* Buenos Aires: Abeledo-Perrot, 1971.

Churchill, Robert P. "Dworkin's Theory of Constitutional Law." *Hastings Constitutional Law Quarterly* 8 (1980): 47-91.

Christie, George. "The Model of Principles." *The Duke Law Journal* (1968): 649-69.

Cohen, Marshall. "He'd Rather Have Rights." *The New York Review of Books* 24 (May 26, 1977): 37-39.

Coleman, Jules. "Book Review: *Taking Rights Seriously.*" *California Law Review* 66 (1978): 885-919.

———. "Legal Duty and Moral Argument." *Social Theory and Practice* 5 (1980): 377-407.

Coval, S. C., and Smith, J. C. "Some Structural Properties of Legal Decisions." *The Cambridge Law Journal* 32 (1973): 81-103.

Denvir, John. "Professor Dworkin and an Activist Theory of Constitutional Adjudication." *Albany Law Review* 45 (1980): 13-56.

Greenawalt, Kent. "Discretion and Judicial Decision: The Elusive Quest for the Fetters That Bind Judges." *Columbia Law Review* 75 (1975): 359-99.

Griffiths, John. "Legal Reasoning from the External and the Internal Perspectives." *New York University Law Review* 53 (1978): 1124-49.

Hart, H. L. A. "American Jurisprudence Through English Eyes: The Nightmare and the Noble Dream." *Georgia Law Review* 11 (1977): 969-89.

Haslett, D. W. "The General Theory of Rights." *Social Theory and Practice* 5 (1980): 427-59.

Johnson, Conrad. "Legal and Moral Change: Deriving Rights and Duties from the Preexisting." *Social Theory and Practice* 5 (1980): 305-30.

Levenbook, Barbara. "D-theories, Discretion, and the Justification of Adjudication." *Social Theory and Practice* 5 (1980): 331-45.

Levinson, Sanford. "Taking Law Seriously: Reflections on 'Thinking Like a Lawyer.'" *Stanford Law Review* 30 (1978): 1071-109.

Lyons, David. "Principles, Positivism and Legal Theory." *The Yale Law Journal* 87 (1977): 415-35.

MacCallum, Gerald C., Jr. "Dworkin on Judicial Discretion." *The Journal of Philosophy* 60 (1963): 638-41.

Munzer, Stephen R. "Right Answers, Preexisting Rights, and Fairness." *Georgia Law Review* 11 (1977): 1055–68.
Nickel, James W. "Dworkin on the Nature and Consequences of Rights." *Georgia Law Review* 11 (1977): 1115–42.
Perry, Thomas D. "Contested Concepts and Hard Cases." *Ethics* 88 (1977): 20–35.
Postema, Gerald J. "Bentham and Dworkin on Positivism and Adjudication." *Social Theory and Practice* 5 (1980): 347–76.
Sager, Lawrence G. "Rights Scepticism and Process-Based Responses." *New York University Law Review* 56 (1981): 417–45.
Sandalow, Terrance. "Judicial Protection of Minorities." *Michigan Law Review* 75 (1977): 1162–95.
Smith, J. C. *Legal Obligation.* Toronto and Buffalo: University of Toronto Press, 1976. Chapter 9.
Raz, Joseph. "Professor Dworkin's Theory of Rights." *Political Studies* 26 (1978): 123–37.
Richards, David A. J. "Rules, Policies, and Neutral Principles: The Search for Legitimacy in Common Law and Constitutional Adjudication." *Georgia Law Review* 11 (1977): 1069–114.
Sartorius, Rolf. "The Justification of Judicial Decision," *Ethics* 78 (1968): 171–87.
———. "Social Policy and Judicial Legislation." *American Philosophical Quarterly* 8 (1971): 151–60.
———. "The Enforcement of Morals." *The Yale Law Journal* 81 (1972): 891–910.
———. *Individual Conduct and Social Norms.* Encino, Cal.: Dickenson, 1975: 181–210.
———. "Bayes' Theorem, Hard Cases, and Judicial Decision." *Georgia Law Review* 11 (1977): 1269–2175.
Smith, M. B. E. "Rights, Right Answers, and the Constructive Model of Morality." *Social Theory and Practice* 5 (1980): 409–26.
Tapper, Colin. "A Note on Principles." *Modern Law Review* 34 (1971): 628–34.
Ten, C. L. "The Soundest Theory of Law." *Mind* 88 (1979): 522–37.
Weinreb, Lloyd L. "Law as Order." *Harvard Law Review* 91 (1978): 909–59.

Contributors

E. PHILIP SOPER holds undergraduate and graduate degrees, including a Ph.D. in philosophy, from Washington University in St. Louis. He graduated from Harvard Law School in 1969 and served the following year as clerk to Justice White of the Supreme Court of the United States. After completing work in philosophy at Oxford, he spent two years at the Council on Environmental Quality in Washington, D.C. He began his academic career at the University of Michigan in 1973.

JULES L. COLEMAN, currently Professor of Philosophy at the University of Arizona, has published numerous articles in analytic jurisprudence, tort theory, and the foundations of welfare economics. He is writing a book on the foundations of torts and preparing a book of readings on the economic analysis of law.

DAVID LYONS has taught at Cornell University since 1964, where he is now Chairman of the Sage School of Philosophy and Professor of Philosophy and Law. His writings include *Forms and Limits of Utilitarianism* and *In the Interest of the Governed.*

JOSEPH RAZ is Fellow of Balliol College, Oxford. His publications include *The Concept of a Legal System; Practical Reason and Norms;* and *The Authority of Law.*

KENT GREENAWALT is Cardozo Professor of Jurisprudence at Columbia University School of Law. He has taught and written in the areas of legal philosophy, constitutional law, and criminal law. Having recently completed an essay and set of teaching materials on Discrimination and Reverse Discrimination, he is now working on moral claims to disobey the law and the responses of legal institutions to such claims.

DONALD H. REGAN is Professor of Law in the University of Michigan Law School. He teaches constitutional law and writes on moral and political philosophy. He is the author of *Utilitarianism and Co-operation.*

JOHN MACKIE, who died in 1981, was Fellow of University College, Oxford and Reader in Philosophy in the University of Oxford. His publications include *The Cement of the Universe: A Study in Causation; Problems from Locke; Ethics: Inventing Right and Wrong;* and *Hume's Moral Theory.*

A. D. WOOZLEY is University Professor Emeritus of Philosophy and Law at the University of Virginia.

NEIL MACCORMICK has been Regius Professor of Public Law and the Law of Nature and Nations at the University of Edinburgh since 1972, and was Dean of the Faculty there from 1973 until 1976. Previously he was a Fellow of Balliol College, Oxford (1967–72) and a Lecturer at St. Andrew's University (1965–67). His principal publications are *Legal Reasoning and Legal Theory; H. L. A. Hart;* and *Legal Right and Social Democracy.*

ROLF SARTORIUS is Professor of Philosophy at the University of Minnesota. He is the author of *Individual Conduct and Social Norms: A Utilitarian Account of Social Union and the Rule of Law* and of many articles in the philosophy of law, political philosophy, and ethics. He has also edited a volume of essays on *Paternalism.*

H. L. A. HART, formerly Professor of Jurisprudence in Oxford University and President of Brasenose College, Oxford is the author of *Causation in the Law* (with A. M. Honoré), *The Concept of Law; Law, Liberty and Morality;* and *Punishment and Responsibility: Essays in the Philosophy of Law.*

MICHAEL SANDEL is Assistant Professor of Government at Harvard University where he teaches political philosophy. He is the author of *Liberalism and the Limits of Justice.*

RICHARD POSNER is a Judge of the United States Court of Appeals for the Seventh Circuit and is a Senior Lecturer at the University of Chicago Law School. In his academic work he has specialized in the application of economics to law.

Von Canon Library
214466
REMOTE K 246 .R66 1984 / Ronald Dworkin and contemporary j